The Development
and Treatment
of Girlhood Aggressio

The Development
and Treatment
of Girlhood Aggression

Edited by

Debra J. Pepler
York University and The Hospital for Sick Children

Kirsten C. Madsen
The Hospital for Sick Children

Christopher Webster
Earlscourt Child and Family Centre
and *St. Joseph's Health Care Centre*

Kathryn S. Levene
Earlscourt Child and Family Centre

LAWRENCE ERLBAUM ASSOCIATES PUBLISHERS
2005   Mahwah, New Jersey   London

Lawrence Erlbaum Associates, Inc., Publishers
10 Industrial Avenue
Mahwah, New Jersey 07430

Cover design by Kathryn Houghtaling Lacey

Library of Congress Cataloging-in-Publication Data

Copyright information can be obtained by contacting the Library
of Congress.
p. cm.
Includes bibliographical references and index.
ISBN 0-8058-4039-7 (cloth : alk. paper)

Printed in the United States of America
10   9   8   7   6   5   4   3   2   1

This book is dedicated to the memory of Robert B. Cairns, who has provided innovation, inspiration, and integration for research on the development of aggression.

Together with Beverley Cairns, Bob was one of the first researchers to raise concerns about girls' aggression, how girls' aggression develops, and implications for the next generation.

Contents

Foreword
                                                   xi
Kenneth Goldberg

Introduction
Girlhood Aggression: Building Bridges Between   xv
    Research and Treatment
Debra J. Pepler and Kirsten Madsen

Part I: Girls' Aggression: Developmental Issues

1 Aggressive Girls on Troubled Trajectories: 3
    A Developmental Perspective
Debra J. Pepler and Wendy Craig

2 Developmental Approaches to Studying Conduct   29
    Problems in Girls
Kate Keenan, Magda Stouthamer-Loeber, and Rolf Loeber

Commentary
A Relationship Focus on Girls' Aggressiveness   47
    and Conduct Disorder
Kate McKnight and Martha Putallaz

Part II: Girls' Physical Aggression

3 Gender Differences in the Prevalence of Physically   55
      Aggressive Behaviors in the Canadian Population
      of 2- and 3-Year-Old Children
      Raymond H. Baillargeon, Richard E. Tremblay,
      and J. Douglas Willms

4 African-American Girls and Physical Aggression: 75
      Does Stability of Childhood Aggression Predict
      Later Negative Outcomes?
      Shari Miller-Johnson, Bertrina L. Moore,
      Marion K. Underwood, and John D. Coie

Commentary
      New Research Approaches to the Study of Aggression   97
      Lea Pulkkinen

Part III: The Social Nature of Girls' Aggression

5 The Development of Aggressive Behaviors Among   105
      Girls: Measurement Issues, Social Functions,
      and Differential Trajectories
      Hongling Xie, Beverley D. Cairns, and Robert B. Cairns

6 To Die For: Violent Adolescent Girls' Search   137
      for Male Attention
      Sibylle Artz

Commentary
      The Importance of Social Context and Relationships   161
      in Female Aggression
      Pierrette Verlaan

Part IV: Aggressive Girls in Treatment

7 Girls Growing Up Angry: A Qualitative Study   169
      Kathryn S. Levene, Kirsten C. Madsen, and Debra J. Pepler

8 Girls in the Juvenile Justice System: Risk Factors   191
        and Clinical Implications
   Leslie D. Leve and Patricia Chamberlain

Commentary
     The Treatment of Aggressive Girls: 217
        Same But Different?
   Wendy M. Craig

Part V: Aggressive Girls Grow Up

9 Maternal Conduct Disorder and the Risk   225
        for the Next Generation
   Mark Zoccolillo, Daniel Paquette, and Richard Tremblay

10 Girls' Aggression Across the Life Course: Long-Term   253
        Outcomes and Intergenerational Risk
   *Dale M. Stack, Lisa A. Serbin, Alex E. Schwartzman,
   and Jane Ledingham*

Commentary
     Aggression Among Females   285
   Joan McCord

Author Index   289

Subject Index   303

Foreword

In early 1999, Earlscourt Child and Family Centre and the La Marsh Centre for Research on Violence and Conflict Resolution at York University agreed to work together to host an international symposium in Toronto on aggression among girls. Both organizations deal with such aggression from various perspectives, and we felt the field might be advanced by bringing together professionals who could share their most recent findings.

We were encouraged by the enthusiastic response to the symposium from both presenters and participants. There was a sense of importance and urgency during the proceedings. Finally, social scientists, clinicians, teachers, and policy analysts were all gathered together to reflect specifically on the development and treatment of girlhood aggression. Because this focus would have been inconceivable a decade ago, a sense of history making was also evident.

Indeed at the 1988 Earlscourt Symposium on Childhood Aggression in Toronto, girls were hardly mentioned. In the 1991 publication of that symposium's proceedings, *The Development and Treatment of Childhood Aggression*, the word *girls* was not listed in the subject index. Studies on childhood aggression largely excluded girls; treatment interventions for young girls with aggression were unknown. However, two presenters at the 1988 symposium did, lament this state of affairs and called for studies focusing on the development of girlhood aggression.

Historically, in community-based settings dealing with children exhibiting aggressive behavior, such as Earlscourt Child and Family Centre, interventions have not been gender specific. Boys referred to treatment outnumbered girls by a factor of four or five, and the girls who did come for help did not receive gender-specific treatment. Girls, for example, attended anger-management treatment groups alongside boys and were mixed with boys in small treatment classrooms. Yet data collected at

Earlscourt started to show that girls lagged behind boys in treatment success, alerting us to the need to reconsider our approach.

The importance of forging an effective treatment intervention specifically for aggressive girls was also brought home through longitudinal studies. These showed that, although the sequelae of childhood aggression were often similar between boys and girls, they differed in one significant way: Both aggressive boys and aggressive girls were at risk of early sexual promiscuity, yet girls had the further risk of becoming pregnant and raising a new generation of children exhibiting aggressive behavior.

In the past decade, enormous steps have been taken for young girls with behavior problems, but much remains to be learned, and new interventions are still to be tested. At Earlscourt, for example, we initiated the Earlscourt Girls Connection in 1996 to offer these girls a gender-specific intervention tailored to their unique needs; girls are coming in more than double the number we anticipated. Now scientific studies of girlhood aggression abound across North America. Treatment outcomes need to be carefully examined because there are many questions to be considered. Why have girls historically been underreferred to mental health services? What is it about gender-specific interventions that may make them more effective for girls? Are the trajectories of boys and girls with aggressive behavior different in ways that should shape gender-specific interventions?

Even the most fundamental questions about girlhood aggression remain unanswered. Do girls aggress like boys? Are the ways in which they aggress changing? Can antisocial, aggressive girls be as easily identified as their male equivalents? Are more gender-specific measures necessary? Are aggressive girls more likely than aggressive boys to be rejected by their parents and peers? This book touches on all of these questions and more.

Here at Earlscourt Child and Family Centre, the development of early risk lists for boys and girls—the EARL-20B and EARL-21G—has provided our line clinicians with up-to-date findings on risk and protective factors in the onset and maintenance of boyhood and girlhood aggression. Further use of these lists in longitudinal and clinical studies can help us come up with more effective treatment interventions.

With this compilation of presentations from the 1999 symposium, an even larger audience may consider various perspectives, longitudinal findings, and treatment explorations focused entirely on girlhood aggression. We hope this volume is a springboard for research and clinical efforts in the field for many years to come. It signifies a resolve to apply new, more appropriate approaches to easing the plight of girls with aggressive behaviors and interrupt intergenerational cycles of violence.

I wish to acknowledge the invaluable assistance of Debra Pepler, whose expertise, thoughtfulness, and care were instrumental in shepherding our planning for the symposium, and in the development of the Earlscourt Girls Connection; and Kathy Levene, Earlscourt's clinical director, whose advocacy for gender-specific interventions for troubled young girls has been unwavering.

—Kenneth Goldberg, MSW.
Executive Director
Earlscourt Child and Family Centre
Toronto, Ontario

Introduction
Girlhood Aggression: Building Bridges Between Research and Treatment

Debra J. Pepler
York University and The Hospital for Sick Children

Kirsten Madsen
The Hospital for Sick Children

After decades of neglect, the light has begun to shine on the issue of girlhood aggression. In recent years, there has been a burgeoning of research focused on the development and outcomes of girls' aggression (cf. Björkqvist & Niemëla, 1992; Cairns & Cairns, 1994; Moffitt et al., 2001; Pulkinnen, 1992). This research interest has been paralleled by questions about what interventions are appropriate and effective in supporting the optimal development of girls who show aggressive behavior problems and associated difficulties. This volume provides some of the pioneering research in the field of girlhood aggression.

Although this book's focus is on the development and treatment of girls' aggression, many chapters include complementary data on boys' aggression, providing a benchmark for this emerging area of research. It is difficult to consider girls' aggression independent of what we know about aggressive boys because boys have been in the spotlight since the early concern with delinquency during the child guidance movement (Horn, 1989; Spaulding & Balch, 1983). There is no denying that aggressive boys present a major concern to society. From early childhood on, aggressive behavior problems are more prevalent among boys than girls; boys are more likely than girls to engage in delinquency and other criminal activities (Moffitt et al., 2001; Tremblay, 2000). As boys move into adulthood, their aggressive patterns of behavior may persist as wife assault, child abuse, and other violent behaviors, which are more characteristic of men than women (Huesmann, Eron, Lefkowitz, & Walder, 1984). Why worry about aggressive girls if there are fewer of them and their behavior problems do not pervade throughout the community as do those of aggressive boys? The contributors to this volume provide convincing answers to this question. They help us understand that, although the problems of aggressive girls are not as immediately obvious and salient as those of aggressive boys, the outcomes for these high-risk girls may in fact be as troubling and costly as those of boys. In particular, the contributors challenge us to look in different contexts and at different outcomes to assess the importance of understanding and intervening in girls', compared with boys' aggression. From a developmental perspective, they challenge us to focus on the nature of girls' aggression, the relationship contexts in which it unfolds, and the complexity of psychosocial difficulties as aggressive girls grow into the mothers of tomorrow.

AIMS OF THE PRESENT VOLUME

The three central aims of the present volume are to (a) highlight current understanding of the development of girls' aggression, (b) identify key components for preventing and treating the constellation of problems experienced by aggressive girls, and (c) raise new questions for future research. We began our collective work with a symposium that brought together researchers from different disciplines across North America to present their current work, encourage discussions, and raise the kinds of questions that might help guide and stimulate future scientific exploration. Developmental and social considerations permeated the conference. The researchers described a continuum of severity in girls' aggressive behaviors from normative behaviors among 2- to 3-year-olds (Baillargeon, Tremblay, & Wilms, chap. 3, this volume) to adaptive aggression (Miller-Johnson, Moore, Underwood, & Coie, chap. 4, this volume; Xie, Cairns, & Cairns, chap. 5, this volume), conduct disorders (CD), serious delinquent behaviors (Keenan, Stouthamer-Loeber, & Loeber, chap. 2, this volume; Leve & Chamberlain, chap. 8, this volume; Zoccolillo, Paquette, & Tremblay, chap. 9, this volume), and the extreme cases of violence in teenage girls (Artz, chap. 6, this volume). Each presentation had its own perspective, and each speaker was able to contribute a slightly different outlook on the nature and development of girls' aggression. To further enhance the scope of this volume, we invited five prominent researchers to provide a commentary on chapter sections. In doing so, we were able to include colleagues from North America and Scandinavia, where much of the early work on girls' aggression began. The commentators draw on their own knowledge and research experience to provide valuable opinions concerning the contributors' results and recommendations relating to the development and treatment of girls' aggression.

DEVELOPMENT OF GIRLHOOD AGGRESSION

The perspectives provided by the authors in this volume highlight the diverse constellation of factors that moderate the development of girls' aggression. There are individual factors (e.g., motor restlessness, temperaments, academic difficulties), family factors (e.g., abuse, parenting problems), peer factors (e.g., social isolation, conflictual peer relations), and relationship factors (e.g., aggressiveness by romantic partners). The chapters also draw attention to the many forms of aggression that girls exhibit as they face each stage of their unfolding lives.

The problem of girls' aggression is presented as a continuum from normative forms of behavior to extreme and serious attacks. Baillargeon and his colleagues (chap. 3) help us understand the normal forms of aggression that girls express in the early years of life. Their research shows that, according to ratings by persons knowledgeable about the children (usually mothers), girls are not as physically aggressive as boys even at ages 2 and 3. However, girls are rated to be just as physically aggressive as boys when they are provoked in these early childhood years. Therefore, from a normative perspective, the nature and form of girls' aggression seem to depend on the circumstances in which girls find themselves. The vast majority of girls grow out of a reliance on physical aggression in early childhood. However, some of them shift to other forms of social aggression within the peer context. We learn from the chapters by Xie and her colleagues (chap. 5), and Miller-Johnson and her colleagues (chap. 4) that those girls who continue to use physical aggression in middle childhood are at particularly high risk for adjustment problems in adolescence. Artz (chap. 6) highlights how social aggression such as rumor spreading can escalate to serious forms of aggression and assault by troubled girls.

The importance of relationships in girls' lives is a theme that permeates this volume. The family seems to be of particular importance. The results from the pilot study conducted by Keenan, Stouthamer-Loeber, and Loeber (chap. 2) indicate that parents' marital conflict has a greater association with conduct disorder (CD) symptoms in girls than boys. The strain in family relationships, particularly in the relationship between an aggressive girl and her mother, are brought to light through the qualitative research by Levene, Madsen, and Pepler (chap. 7). Peer relationships are also critical in girls' development. From a longitudinal perspective, Stack, Serbin, Schwartzman, and Ledingham (chap. 10) illustrate that girls who are aggressive and socially withdrawn in a peer context have the most negative outcomes in adulthood. Even when aggressive girls have friends, these relationships become alliances of power, rather than consistently positive sources of support. According to Artz (chap. 6), aggressive girls' friendships are often ambivalent and serve as channels of access to potential male partners. The concern with aggressive girls' relationships with male partners is also raised by Leve and Chamberlain (chap. 8). In the course of their interventions, they found that troubled girls placed too much emphasis and reliance on boyfriends. Consequently, these girls had few positive experiences with female friends. Xie and her colleagues (chap. 5) raise the theme of connectedness with friends. They artfully demonstrate how adaptive it can be for girls who are well connected within the peer group to use social aggression to manipulate relationships. In contrast to physically aggressive girls, socially aggressive girls seem to be at no greater risk for arrest later in life than girls who exhibited low levels of aggression.

In our efforts to understand the course, changing nature, and long-term outcomes of girls' aggression, we are challenged to maintain a sharp developmental focus. What is normative at one stage is atypical in a subsequent stage. For example, physical aggression is normative in early childhood, but becomes atypical in middle childhood and adolescence, when most girls' levels of physical aggression have markedly decreased. The transformation and diversification of girls' aggression reflects the emerging developmental challenges, events, and changing social relationships in their lives. At this point, many questions remain regarding the developmental course of girls' aggression compared with that of boys.

Girls' aggressive behavior problems have many similarities to those of boys, as Pepler and Craig (chap. 1) make clear. However, there are gender differences in the manifestation and timing of aggression. Xie and her colleagues (chap. 5) provide a careful analysis of the social forms of aggression that are more typical of girls than boys. In some respects, the developmental course of girls' aggressive behavior problems lags behind that of aggressive boys. Miller-Johnson and her colleagues echo the results of others, such as Moffitt et al. (2001), in noting the later onset of criminal activity and arrest for girls compared with boys. This developmental lag should be interpreted cautiously, however, because it does not imply that troubled girls are free of aggressive behavior problems prior to adolescence. The clinically referred girls described in the research by Levene and her colleagues were experiencing a wide range of problems at home and at school. The challenge for researchers and clinicians alike is to acquire a gender-specific lens to identify girls who are exhibiting aggressive behavior problems early in their lives and to provide the appropriate supports across multiple domains to promote healthy development.

THE TREATMENT OF GIRLS' AGGRESSION

The field of girls' aggression is emerging from the shadows. The research in this book draws attention to many important factors related to the development of girls' aggression, and it provides insight into how to target aggression at various developmental stages. Pepler and Craig (chap. 1), in particular, lay out the developmental course of aggression, pointing to relationships and areas in girls' lives that should be dealt with during intervention efforts. Stack et al. (chap. 10) further stress the importance of protective factors, such as academic strength in programming for aggressive girls. With the qualitative studies by Levene et al. (chap. 7) and Artz (chap. 6), we are able to gain an appreciation of the complexity of aggressive girls' lives from a clinical perspective. The girls' stories focus attention on the troubles that aggressive girls experience in their families, with their peers, and within romantic relationships. These personal stories illustrate the importance of supporting the development of healthy relationships in prevention and intervention initiatives. At this point we are at an early stage in the quest to develop effective interventions for aggressive girls. The qualitative research by Levene and her colleagues (chap. 7) has formed the basis for developing the Earlscourt Girls Connection Program—a comprehensive treatment approach to working with aggressive girls and their families. Leve and Chamberlain (chap. 8) provide an approach to interventions with aggressive adolescent girls. Their recommendations for programming for aggressive girls offer essential guidelines for the design of gender-specific treatments. There is an urgent need to develop and evaluate programs for aggressive girls across the developmental spectrum. With early identification and effective intervention, we can help aggressive girls avoid their troubling behaviors, integrate themselves into healthy peer contexts, and avoid pathways into deviant and criminal activities.

FUTURE RESEARCH

Given that the topic of girls' aggression is still in its early phases of investigation, the potential for future research is extensive. Research themes repeatedly surface in the chapters of this book, and questions seem to jump off the pages. At times a question is posed, such as Pepler and Craig's (chap. 1) question about how parenting affects girls' behavior. Reading on, we learn how other authors' research can begin to address that very question, such as in the chapter by Stack and her colleagues (chap. 10). In the later part of this chapter, early outcome data are presented on the parenting of women who had aggressive histories as girls and how their background in turn affected their offspring. The confluence of the themes within the chapters begins to form a collective framework for approaching research on girls' aggression. Each chapter, however, provides particular perspectives and questions about the development and treatment of girls' aggression. Many of the authors, such as Baillargeon et al. (chap. 3), Xie et al. (chap. 5), and Zoccolillo et al. (chap. 9) have grappled with the substantial definitional and methodological challenges in studying girls' aggression.

The family emerges as an important theme in the developmental course of aggressive girls and an area that requires considerably more research. Keenan and her colleagues found that marital conflict relates more strongly to girls' aggressive behavior than it does to boys' aggression. Levene and her colleagues (chap. 7) found the family to be a dominant theme in interviews conducted with the girls in treatment and their parents. They found that many of the clinically referred girls had repeatedly experienced the loss of a family member and often discussed the effect of an absent or neglectful father. At the same time that the clinically referred girls spoke of the loss of their fathers, the interviews with both the parents and girls revealed an emerging theme of conflict between mothers and their aggressive daughters. Although mother–daughter conflict is normative and part of the natural development of individual identity and autonomy (Graber & Brooks-Gunn, 1999), research is needed to identify how the conflict discussed by the aggressive girls and their parents differs from the normal patterns of conflict experienced by nonaggressive girls. How do the life struggles and conflicts described by these mothers differ from those of other mothers and perhaps contribute to their daughters' aggression? Several chapters raise the issue of abuse and girls' exposure to violence and conflict within their families (Keenan et al., chap. 2, this volume; Levene et al., chap. 7, this volume; Pepler & Craig, chap. 1, this volume). At this point there is a pressing need for prospective analyses of the family processes associated with the development of girls' aggressive behavior problems. Similar questions can be raised about the processes within peer and romantic relationships that may function to constrain an aggressive girl on a troubled trajectory or, conversely, enable her to move onto a healthier pathway.

Many methodological and definitional issues related to girls' aggression remain unresolved. Keenan and her colleagues (chap. 2) point out that even the prevalence of CD in girls and the criteria with which to measure it are under debate (Zahn-Waxler, 1993; Zoccolillo, 1993). As they note, if the prevalence of CD is indeed lower in girls than boys, then by investigating the protective factors for being female, we may be able to develop more effective treatments for boys with CD. Keenan and her colleagues identify empathy as a potential factor that differentiates the development of aggressive problems in girls compared with boys. Coinciding with issues about the protective factors related to the development of CD in girls, however, are questions about whether the lower prevalence of CD translates into a higher prevalence of other disorders for girls.

The conference brought researchers in the field together to share knowledge that would lay a foundation for understanding, preventing, and treating aggression in girls. Although, as Zoccolillo and his colleagues (chap. 9) point out, the field of study is fairly new and the questions are numerous, the development and evaluations of treatment are essential. It is encouraging that researchers and practitioners, such as the groups at the Oregon Social Learning Center and Earlscourt Child and Family Centre, have begun to develop gender-specific programs for girls, but these programs are in the earliest phases of development. Evaluation and refinement of such programs is key. The knowledge provided by the authors in this volume, as well as many others around the world, has tremendous potential to inform practice with troubled girls. The challenge that stands before us is to transfer our knowledge to those on the front lines so they can implement and evaluate programs tailored to the challenges faced by aggressive girls, their families, and support systems.

POLICY IMPLICATIONS

This volume presents ongoing work in the area of girlhood aggression. There is now a growing body of research indicating that girls' aggression is a predictor of long-term psychological, social, academic, health, and intergenerational problems (Cairns & Cairns, 1994; Moffit et al., 2001; Robins, 1986; Stack et al., chap. 10, this volume; Xie et al., chap. 5, this volume; Zocolillo et al., chap. 9, this volume). Given that girls at risk can be detected early (Stack et al., chap. 10, this volume; Zocolillo et al., chap. 9, this volume), prevention should be a policy priority. Prevention efforts may take many forms depending on the girls' strengths and weaknesses and their family circumstances. They may include skills training, academic assistance, mental health and medical services, as well as early and persistent parenting support. Although early prevention initiatives during infancy and early childhood are currently being championed, development continues through the lifespan. Therefore, prevention and intervention efforts must be transformed to accommodate the changing needs and challenges of troubled school-age children as well as adolescents. The education system is vital in prevention efforts. Because staying in school is a protective factor, girls should be provided with incentives and encouragements for staying in school to prevent early parenthood (Stack et al., chap. 10, this volume). Effective interventions for aggressive girls can only be accomplished through a coordination of the many systems that circumscribe girls' lives. It is essential to build collaborations between teachers and clinicians, among educational and community institutions, and among those who are integral to girls' everyday lives. Finally, as we come to recognize the individual and social costs of girls' aggression, we need government support for the development and evaluation of evidence-based prevention and intervention programs.

SUMMARY

The authors who have contributed to this book provide much of the essential groundwork for future research. They lay out promising developmental contextual models of girls' aggression. Girlhood aggression is an exciting new area of study. We hope this volume provokes thought and discussion about the issues of girlhood aggression and stimulates new directions for future research into the problems that aggressive girls experience. In the coming years, we need to turn our attention to developing empirically based, gender-sensitive interventions for aggressive girls. As the blueprints for the future of this research area are slowly drafted, we can already recognize that the dynamic processes in the development of girls' aggression are complex and interrelated. We are just beginning to understand the similarities and differences in the nature and courses of aggressive girls' and boys' development. Important questions related to ethnic and social variations in girls' and boys' development remain to be answered. We also need to assess how contextual variables interact with individual variables, such as the timing of puberty, to shape different developmental trajectories. In all of these considerations, we need to step back from an intense focus on the problem to ask more general questions about the changing nature of girls' aggression, the adaptive functions of their aggression, and the processes that relate to the continuity and discontinuity in girls' development across the lifespan.

REFERENCES

Björkqvist, K., & Niemëla, P. (Eds.). (1992). *Of mice and women: Aspects of female aggression* . San Diego: Academic Press.

Cairns, R. B., & Cairns, B. D. (1994). *Lifelines and risks: Pathways of youth in our time.* Cambridge, England: Cambridge University Press.

Graber, J. A., & Brooks-Gunn, J. (1999). "Sometimes I think you don't like me": How mothers and daughters negotiate the transition into adolescence. In M. Cox, & J. Brooks-Gunn (Eds.), *Conflict and cohesion in families: Causes and consequences. The advances in family research series* (pp. 207–242). Mahwah, NJ: Lawrence Erlbaum Associates.

Horn, M. (1989). *Before it's too late: The child guidance movement in the United States, 1922–1945*. Philadelphia: Temple University Press.

Huesmann, L. R., Eron, L. D., Lefkowitz, M. M., & Walder, L. O. (1984). Stability of aggression over time and generations. *Developmental Psychology, 20,* 1120–1134.

Moffitt, T. E., Caspi, A., Rutter, M., & Silva, P. A. (2001). *Sex differences in antisocial behaviour: Conduct disorder, delinquency, and violence in the Dunedin Longitudinal Study.* Cambridge, England: Cambridge University Press.

Pulkinnen, L. (1992). The path to adulthood for aggressively inclined girls. In K. Björkqvist & P. Niemëla (Eds.), *Of mice and women: Aspects of female aggression* (pp. 113–121). San Diego: Academic Press.

Robins, L. N. (1986). The consequences of conduct disorder in girls. In D. Olweus, J. Block, & M. Radke-Yarrow (Eds.), *Development of antisocial and prosocial behavior: Research, theories, and issues* (pp.385–414). Orlando, FL: Academic Press.

Spaulding, J., & Balch, P. (1983). A brief history of primary prevention in the twentieth century: 1908 to 1980. *American Journal of Community Psychology, 11*(1), 59–80.

Tremblay, R. E. (2000). The development of aggressive behavior during childhood: What have we learned the past century. *International Journal of Behavioral Development, 24*(2), 129–141.

Zahn-Waxler, C. (1993). Warriors and worriers: Gender and psychopathology. *Development and Psychopathology, 5,* 79–89.

Zoccolillo, M. (1993). Gender and the development of conduct disorder. *Development and Psychopathology, 5,* 65–78.

Part I

GIRLS' AGGRESSION: DEVELOPMENTAL ISSUES

1

Aggressive Girls on Troubled Trajectories: A Developmental Perspective

Debra J. Pepler
*LaMarsh Research Centre for Violence
and Conflict Resolution, York University*

Wendy M. Craig
Department of Psychology, Queen's University

Why worry about aggressive girls? Until recently researchers have largely focused their studies of aggression on the risks and developmental trajectories for aggressive boys. Generally, girls' aggressive behavior problems are thought to be less prevalent and serious than those of boys (Offord, Boyle, & Racine, 1991; Statistics Canada, 1998). Therefore, it is not surprising that the theoretical models and empirical foundation for understanding the development of aggression have been based on research on aggressive boys. The purpose of the present chapter is neither to debate gender differences in aggression nor deflect concerns for male aggression, but to highlight the developmental risks, processes, and outcomes in the development of girls' aggression. Accordingly, we have focused on the interactions of aggressive girls within their primary social environments to begin to understand the development of their problem behaviors.

THEORETICAL PERSPECTIVES ON THE DEVELOPMENT OF GIRLS' AGGRESSION

A developmental model of risk informs an understanding of developmental processes over time by highlighting the importance of person–environment interactions (Rutter, 1990). According to this model, development is shaped by an interaction of risk and protective factors, which reside both within individuals and their environments. Although we recognize the importance of individual characteristics, we believe that the trajectories of aggressive children can best be understood within a social interactional framework. Accordingly, interactions within the family, peer, and broader contexts are considered key determinants for socialization (Cairns & Cairns, 1994; Cicchetti & Aber, 1998; Patterson, Reid, & Dishion, 1992). In addition, we conceptualize risk as a dynamic construct. As such an outcome of risk processes in one stage (e.g., an aversive behavioral style in early childhood arising from dysfunctional family interaction) may lay the foundation for risk processes in a subsequent stage (e.g., for strained peer interactions in school). There is a cumulative effect of risk both within and across time. Children are at greatly increased risk for adjustment difficulties if they experience more than one risk factor (Garmezy & Rutter, 1983). There is also a progressive accumulation of the consequences of individual factors (cumulative continuity) and the responses they elicit during social interaction (interactional continuity; Caspi, Elder, & Bem, 1987). Therefore, the development of aggression in children is determined by individual characteristics of children interacting with social contexts.

In this chapter, we provide a developmental perspective on the problems and potential risks faced by aggressive girls in various social contexts. Drawing from our research and that of others, we have focused on individual characteristics of aggressive girls and the risks they face in relationships including: parent–child relationships, sibling relationships, peer relationships, and romantic relationships. Close relationships such as these have been identified as central to girls' development (Brown & Gilligan, 1992; Gilligan, 1982; Maccoby, 1998). Therefore, by examining the problems associated with girls' aggression in emerging social relationships, we consider the roles of individual and social context processes in contributing to the development and continuity in girls' aggression.

DEVELOPMENTAL PROFILE OF GIRLS' AGGRESSION

The nature and form of aggression changes with development. These changes emerge as a result of maturation within the child together with changing social interactions and expectations. For both boys and girls, aggression is most prevalent during the toddler years (Tremblay et al., 1995). As most children develop, they learn that aggressive strategies are not adaptive, and they acquire the language and social skills necessary to sustain positive interactions. For children being propelled along a maladaptive trajectory, their aversive behavioral style is often reinforced by ineffective parenting and negative peer interactions. As they age, there are increasing constraints on girls' and boys' development, with increasingly limited opportunities for positive adaptation (Cairns & Cairns, 1994). Compared with others in their age and gender cohort, extremely aggressive children may also be creating and choosing interactional contexts that maintain their aggressive behaviors and place them at continued risk for problems in the next developmental stages. Once established, girls' aggression predicts later aggressive tendencies over several developmental transitions, similar to the predictions for boys (Cairns, Cairns, Neckerman, Ferguson, & Gariepy, 1989; Campbell, Pierce, March, & Ewing, 1994; Pulkkinen, 1987; Sanson, Oberklaid, Prior, Amos, & Smart, 1996).

During infancy and toddlerhood, there are few differences between girls and boys in the rates of aggression (Keenan & Shaw, 1994). Around the age of 4, however, girls' aggressive behavior problems decrease at a faster rate than those of boys (Prior, Smart, Sanson, & Oberklaid 1993; Rose, Rose, & Feldman, 1989). By the time of school entry, there are stable gender differences in aggressive behavior problems that persist throughout childhood and adolescence. Girls are two to four times less likely than boys to exhibit aggressive behavior problems and conduct disorders (CDs) in childhood and adolescence (Offord et al., 1991; Prior et al., 1993).

The developmental sequence of aggression starts with physical aggression, which declines starting in the preschool years and is replaced by verbal and social aggression as children acquire advanced verbal and social skills, as well as increased social intelligence (Björkqvist, Osterman, & Kaukiainen, 1992). These differing forms of aggression are highlighted not only in this chapter, but throughout the volume. Physical aggression, as the label suggests, comprises physically assaultive behaviors such as hitting, kicking, pushing, tripping, and scratching. Gender differences are most pronounced in physical aggression (Eagly & Steffen, 1986; Hyde, 1984; Maccoby & Jacklin, 1980). Verbal aggression refers to face-to-face verbal confrontations such as insults, threats, name calling, and hurtful teasing. Girls and boys are relatively equal in their use of verbal aggression (Björkqvist et al., 1992). There is a more subtle form of aggression that is often indirect and thereby covert. It has been labeled *indirect aggression* (Björkqvist et al., 1992), *relational aggression* (Crick & Grotpeter, 1993), and *social aggression* (Cairns et al., 1989; Galen & Underwood, 1997; Xie, Cairns, & Cairns, chap. 5, this volume). This type of aggression is characterized by collusion, exclusion, alienation, ostracism, and character defamation (Cairns et al., 1989; Crick & Grotpeter, 1993). Data suggest that girls exhibit this form of behavior more frequently than boys; however, gender differences vary according to the method and respondent. Xie and her colleagues (chap. 5, this volume) note that this form of aggression is advantageous for girls because it can be effected covertly and without detection. Lagerspetz, Björkqvist, and Peltonen (1988) argued that indirect social aggression may be more effective within girls' social contexts of small intimate peer groups than in boys' more extensive and less defined peer groups.

In general, girls are more advanced than boys in making the developmental transition from physical to verbal and social forms of aggression (Björkqvist et al., 1992). The aggression of school-age girls and boys differs not only in frequency, but also in form. Observations on the school playground indicate that girls exhibit physical aggression only half as frequently as boys (Serbin, Marchessault, McAffer, Peters, & Schwartzman, 1993). In this study, much of boys' physical aggression on the playground was mild and expressed within the context of rough-and-tumble play. The controversy regarding the extent of gender differences in aggression may, in part, be a function of samples and methodologies. When extreme samples of aggressive girls and boys are compared, there are few differences in the manifestations of aggression. In school-based observations, Cairns and Cairns (1994) found that highly aggressive boys and girls did not differ in the frequency or severity of hostile exchanges. Our observations of aggression and bullying on the school playground also revealed no gender differences in the rates of verbal and physical aggression among children in Grades 1 to 6 (Craig & Pepler, 1995, 1997; Pepler, Craig, & Roberts, 1998). We should be particularly concerned about girls who engage in physical aggression, which is non-normative for their gender, because they are at risk for a range of adjustment difficulties in adolescence and adulthood (Pulkkinen, 1992).

The controversy about girls' use of physical aggression may be informed by adolescents' self-reports, which indicate that girls' physical aggression is not as rare as crime statistics and adult ratings might lead one to expect. In the Ontario Child Health Study (OCHS), 7% of adolescent girls acknowledged physically attacking people compared with 12% of boys; 21% of girls and 30% of boys admitted to getting into many fights (Offord et al., 1991). In interviews about their conflicts, 25% of Grade 7 girls and 12% of Grade 11 girls admitted physically fighting with other girls (Cairns et al., 1989). Perhaps we need not worry about all girls, but we do need to be concerned for girls who are at the extreme end of the aggression continuum. Cairns and Cairns (1994) noted that the most aggressive girls in their longitudinal study engaged in serious antisocial behaviors such as stabbing of sisters, brothers, or fathers and violent fights with other females. Therefore, the focus of concern for girls' aggression may fall on a small group of girls who engage in physical and other forms of aggression that are similar to their male peers (Pulkkinen, 1992). At this point we turn to girls' individual characteristics that place them at risk for developing aggressive behavior problems.

Child Characteristics Relating to Girls' Aggression

In considering girls' aggression from a developmental psychopathology perspective, we consider both the factors residing within the child and the interactional processes in her developmental context that converge to initiate and maintain a maladaptive trajectory (Sroufe, 1997). The individual child factors provide the setting conditions within which interactions unfold along the life course. We consider three risk factors with the child—hyperactivity/inattention, early pubertal development, and social cognitions—that may be liabilities for girls who are unable to achieve the normative trajectory of positive social interactions and relationships (Sroufe, 1997).

Hyperactivity/Inattention. Hyperactivity is an individual characteristic apparent early in life and related to the later development of boys' aggressive behavior problems (Moffitt, 1993). There is a high degree of overlap between CD and hyperactivity (Offord et al., 1991). As with CD, the prevalence rates for attention deficit hyperactivity disorder (ADHD) are substantially lower for girls compared with boys. There is some evidence that girls' and boys' symptoms differ. Girls tend to show symptoms related to Attention Deficit Disorder (ADD), such as inattentiveness and other cognitive impairments, whereas boys show symptoms related to hyperactivity, such as disruptive behavior and high activity levels (Szatmari, Boyle, & Offord, 1989). In a review of CD and its comorbid symptoms, Loeber and Keenan (1994) concluded that the influence of ADD on the persistence and seriousness of problems was less for girls than for boys, although a higher proportion of girls with ADD are likely to experience CD compared with boys with ADD. Bates and his colleagues (1991) found that girls' hyperactivity at age 3 predicted externalizing behavior problems at 8 years of age, whereas hyperactivity was not a significant predictor for boys' externalizing problems.

In an examination of the problems associated with girls' aggression, we analyzed data from the National Longitudinal Survey of Children and Youth (NLSCY; Pepler & Sedigdeilami, 1998). Using the sample of 10- and 11-year-old children for whom there were both self-report and parent-report data, we identified a group of highly aggressive girls and compared them to nonaggressive girls and highly aggressive boys. As Fig. 1.1 indicates, aggressive girls were rated by both themselves and their parents as having more inattention and hyperactivity problems than nonaggressive girls. Therefore, these aggressive girls are exhibiting another form of non-normative behavior, which may set them apart from mainstream groups of girls and compound their adaptational problems.

Although parents rated aggressive girls as less hyperactive and inattentive than aggressive boys, the aggressive girls' and boys' self-ratings did not

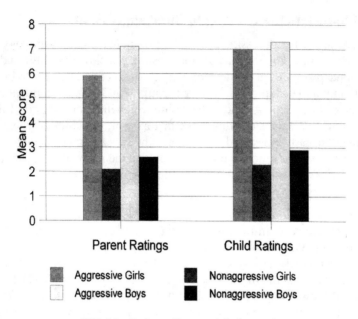

FIG. 1.1   Ratings of hyperactivity/inattention.

differ. The difference in the girls' perceptions and those of their parents may
be noteworthy. If girls' problems are manifested in attentional difficulties
rather than overt high activity levels, parents may not be aware of the nature
or extent of the problems that aggressive girls experience in school. These
data suggest that, although less prevalent in the general population of girls
than boys, hyperactivity/inattention problems may pose a comparatively
high risk for girls' development of aggressive problems as they do for boys.

From the perspective of developmental psychopathology, the question
we need to consider is: In what ways would hyperactivity/inattention place
a girl at risk for an aggressive rather than a positive developmental trajectory? It has been suggested that girls' hyperactivity is a marker for developmental immaturity because motor impulsivity together with low vocabulary
scores predict conduct problems among girls at school entry (Olson &
Hoza, 1993). If a girl experiences difficulties regulating her behaviors and
attention, she may be challenged to achieve social and academic tasks (cumulative continuity) and elicit negative interactional processes involving
peers and adults (interactional continuity). From a social interactional perspective, girls' attentional and behavioral difficulties may make it difficult
for parents to establish the limits and supports required for the development
of positive social skills. Siblings may also find it difficult to interact with
sisters whose behaviors are generally underregulated. Similar social

interactional problems are likely to unfold in the school where girls' hyperactive/inattentive behaviors drain teachers' attention and energy and strain peer relationships. From an academic perspective, these attentional problems may contribute to learning difficulties. Over the long term, academic difficulties may lead to school alienation and dropout, thereby restricting employment opportunities for troubled girls.

Puberty. The timing of puberty is another child characteristic that may place aggressive girls at risk of developing or consolidating antisocial behavior patterns. Aggressive girls are more likely to enter the pubertal transition earlier than their nonaggressive agemates (Connolly, Pepler, Craig, & Taradash, 2000; Japel et al., 1999). Therefore, aggressive girls are more likely than others to face the challenges of early pubertal timing. Girls who mature early may not be fully prepared to meet the social tasks of enterng romantic relationships, moving into older mixed-sex peer groups, and increasing independence. Aggressive girls who mature early are less likely than nonaggressive girls to have developed the positive social interactional skills to successfully negotiate these new challenges (cumulative continuity). Furthermore, early maturing aggressive girls may experience risk processes in interactions with others. Older boys may be attracted to their advanced sexual development. At the same time, vulnerable girls may be attracted to older delinquent males who "are able to obtain possessions (e.g., cars, clothes, or drugs) by theft or vice that are otherwise inaccessible to teens ... delinquency appears to offer an effective means of knifing off childhood apron strings" (Caspi, Lynam, Moffitt, & Silva, 1993, p. 28). Therefore, associations with older peers may introduce aggressive girls to more norm violations, sexual precocity, contact with the law, and truancy (Caspi & Moffitt, 1991; Stattin & Magnusson, 1990). These social context variables can further constrain aggressive girls' development along a troubled trajectory (interactional continuity).

Aggressive girls enter adolescence already vulnerable for maladaptive psychological outcomes. Evidence suggests that early pubertal maturation may amplify the antisocial tendencies of aggressive girls and also increase the likelihood of their victimization. In mixed-sex school settings, aggressive girls who experience early pubertal development tend to know and associate with older, deviant peers (Caspi et al., 1993). These processes are consistent with the theoretical model in which biological and social risk factors are presumed to exert both reciprocal and cumulative effects on adjustment. Accordingly, adolescent girls most vulnerable to negative outcomes are those who experience the simultaneous occurrence of early pubertal maturation, extensive involvement in deviant peer groups, and increased conflict within family interactions to be discussed later.

Social-Cognitive Factors.   At an individual level, social-cognitive processes may underlie the divergence in aggressive behavior patterns for girls and boys. Once girls can identify themselves and others as females, their aggression in playgroups declines and becomes less normative (Fagot, Leinbach, & Hagan, 1986). The majority of girls learn that aggression is not consistent with the female sex stereotype and adjust their behaviors accordingly (Heimer & De Coster, 1999). By the end of early childhood, children are not only aware of sex roles, but are somewhat rigid in their perceptions of behaviors appropriate for females and males (Fagot, Leinbach, & Hort, 1994). Both girls and boys are aware of the strong aggressive component in the male stereotype. Therefore, girls are likely to experience dissonance between behaving aggressively and cognitions of appropriate female behavior. Girls may also consider aggression as an inappropriate social problem-solving strategy for their gender. In a study of children's anticipated consequences, Perry, Perry, and Weiss (1989) found that girls expected more guilt and parental disapproval for aggression than boys. These social cognitions about sex-role expectations and anticipated consequences may play a key role in the observed sex differences in children's aggression.

What operates to maintain aggressive girls' behavioral patterns against the normative tide of reduced aggression? The answer lies in both individual and interactional processes. Aggressive girls' behaviors may be undercontrolled due to individual factors such as hyperactivity and interactional factors such as ineffective parenting. In fact these girls may find their coercive behaviors effective in controlling others (Patterson, 1982). Within their social contexts, however, these behaviors elicit strained interactions. Girls who continue to be aggressive are perceived as somewhat deviant by their peers and adults. According to social-cognitive theory (e.g., Dodge, 1993), these perceptions shape the responses of adults and peers to aggressive girls who, in turn, may perceive others as hostile and respond accordingly. In this way, reciprocal negative social cognitions create an interactional context that may mitigate or exacerbate the girls' aggressive behavior.

In summary, the child factors of hyperactivity and puberty, together with social-cognitive processes, may underlie the emergence of dysfunctional social interactions of aggressive girls within their family and peer contexts. At this point, we turn to an examination of family interactional processes that may relate to the development of girls' aggression.

Family Context

As the primary socialization context in children's early years, interactions within the family lay the foundations for subsequent relationships. There is evidence from attachment research that children who are insecurely attached are at elevated risk for externalizing behavior problems (Greenberg, Speltz, & DeKlyen, 1993). There is some evidence that parent–child attachments may be more strongly related to aggression for girls than for boys (Brooks, Whiteman, & Finch, 1993). Given their greater propensity to play at home (Maccoby, 1986), girls' development may be more contingent on family circumstances than that of boys, who tend to play in larger groups and roam in the broader community. In addition to proximity, the intimacy and longevity of relations within the family may present opportunities for the expression of aggression by girls, which are not present in the larger social contexts of school and community (Pepler & Moore, 1993). In the following sections, we examine the potential effect of family interactions from the bidirectional perspectives of parents' behaviors with their daughters and girls' behaviors toward their parents.

Parenting Practices.   There is a controversy among researchers as to whether early socialization experiences within the family differ for girls and boys and, consequently, underlie differences in aggressive behavior problems (Maccoby, 1998). Eron (1992) postulated that girls would be less aggressive than boys given that parents use less harsh punishment in response to girls' than boys' aggression. In contrast, Lytton and Romney (1991) concluded that gender differences in aggression were likely not due to differential parenting practices. Their meta-analysis indicated that parents discourage aggressive or antisocial behavior only slightly and nonsignificantly more in girls than in boys. Maughan, Pickles, and Quinton (1995) also found equivalent exposure to harsh punishment, which was similarly related to conduct problems for girls and boys. There is considerable evidence that for both girls and boys, harsh physical punishment relates directly to the development of aggressive behavior problems (Dodge, Bates, & Pettit, 1990). Therefore, it is likely that the basic risk processes underlying the association between hostile parenting and the development of aggression are similar for girls and boys.

We were able to examine the relation of parenting to girls' aggressive behavior problems within the NLSCY. The construct of *ineffective parenting* comprised seven questions pertaining to problems managing the child and punishment of child related to parent's mood. As indicated in Fig. 1.2, the parents of both aggressive girls and boys indicated more ineffective parenting strategies than the parents of nonaggressive girls and boys. These data suggest that the long-established relation between ineffective parenting and boys' problem behaviors also applies to girls (Loeber & Stouthamer-Loeber, 1986). Aggressive girls do not seem to be protected within the family as Eron (1992) postulated—parents' behaviors with aggressive girls were equally ineffective as those with aggressive boys. Inef-

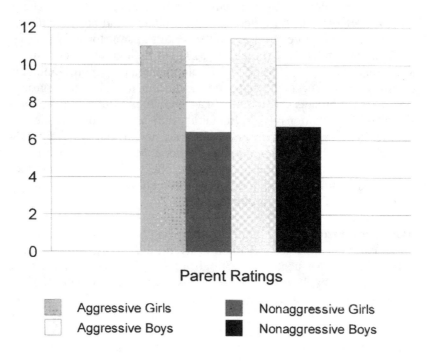

FIG 1.2   Ratings of ineffective parenting.

fective parenting may have a more deleterious long-term effect on girls than boys given that family relationships are salient for girls and parents provide models for girls' future parenting skills. However, this conclusion is tentative because further research is required to elucidate the interactional processes between parents and their daughters that support the development of aggressive behaviors.

Girls' Aggression With Parents.   Girls are often as aggressive as boys in interactions with their parents. These conflictual interactions likely represent bidirectional processes that may comprise a risk for aggressive girls. In observations of family problem-solving interactions, Kavanagh and Hops (1994) observed adolescent girls to be more aggressive with their parents than boys, although parents' ratings of boys' and girls' aggressive problems did not differ. The parent–child interactions were marked by reciprocity: If the problem solving was conflictual, both parents and their children contributed to the negative process.

As indicated in Fig. 1.3, our analyses of the NLSCY data reveal that aggressive girls reported significantly higher levels of conflict with their parents than nonaggressive girls. The parents' ratings of conflicts with their aggressive daughters and sons were similarly elevated compared with those of parents of nonaggressive children. These data suggest that family relationships involving aggressive children are characterized by considerable conflict and difficulties negotiating the day-to-day issues that naturally arise in the lives of early adolescents and their parents.

Although the NLSCY questionnaires did not separate interactions with mothers and fathers, there is some research that draws attention to specific difficulties in the relationship between aggressive girls and their mothers (Pakaslahti, Spoof, Asplund-Peltola, & Keltikangas-Jarvinen, 1998). In Kavanagh and Hops' (1994) observations, mothers interacting with daughters tended to be less positive and more aggressive than mothers with sons. In a study of young offenders, Dowler (1995) found that female young offenders reported receiving more violent treatment from their mothers than their nonoffending counterparts. Furthermore, 92% of the female young offenders had committed at least one violent act against their mothers compared with 38% of the female nonoffenders. Contrary to expectations, the

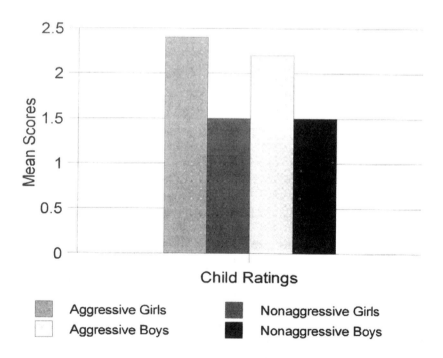

FIG. 1.3   Ratings of parent–child conflict.

young offender girls were also more likely than young offender boys to have been violent with their mothers. Within the mother–daughter relationship, hostile interactions may give rise to negative social cognitions for both the girl and her mother, leading to further troubles in their relationship. In future research, we need to examine whether a conflictual mother–daughter relationship is particularly problematic for aggressive girls.

From the perspective of developmental psychopathology, we might ask in what way family interactions would influence an aggressive girl's pattern of adaptation or maladaptation within different developmental stages? This question requires appreciably more research that examines the interactional processes between girls and their parents. In the early stages of development, we need to consider the ways in which parents stimulate, control, and regulate their daughters' behaviors. Parents who are faced with a dysregulated girl may have trouble achieving the rhythms and cadence that characterize positive interactions. The affect associated with parenting behaviors is also critical. Children who are faced with harsh and hostile parents are likely to reflect these emotional states in their behaviors toward parents. As children mature, these hostile behaviors and accompanying hostile social cognitions become increasingly hard for parents to deal with; they also limit the opportunity to engage in open, problem-solving styles that promote autonomy in the child.

As girls enter adolescence, particularly if they have matured early, they strain their parents' capacities to provide developmentally appropriate limitations and monitoring. The risk of this strain is greater for girls who have matured early, moved into older mixed-sex peer groups, and are establishing romantic relationships with older deviant boys. By this time, as the NLSCY data suggest, aggressive girls' relationships are characterized by considerably more conflict than those of nonaggressive girls. With high conflict, the opportunities to achieve appropriate and supportive responses to the developmental challenges of adolescence are jeopardized. Paradoxically, girls who need the most support to keep them on a healthy, adaptive trajectory are those who have the most strained and least supportive relationships with their parents (Pakaslahti et al., 1998).

Family interactions are a key area for future research on girls' aggression. The intimacy and tension of girls' interactions with their parents may give rise to frequent conflicts and consolidate girls' aggressive interactional patterns within close relationships. If girls express their anger and aggression primarily within the family context, their behavior problems may be less visible and less troublesome within the broader contexts of school and community compared with those of boys. Nevertheless, girls' difficulties in developing positive interactional styles within the family may place them at high risk for aggression and victimization in subsequent relationships. A hostile interactional pattern established between an aggressive girl and her parents may lay the foundation for continuing strained relationships and potential elder abuse in later years.

Sexual Abuse. A consideration of family risk factors for the development of aggression in girls would be incomplete without a consideration of sexual abuse. Girls who have been sexually abused display an array of both internalizing and externalizing behavior problems (Kendall-Tackett, Williams, & Finkelhor, 1993). In a meta-analysis, Kendall-Tackett and her colleagues found that the highest effect sizes for sexual abuse were for externalizing behaviors, such as sexualized behaviors and aggression. Almost half the victims of child sexual abuse exhibited aggressive/antisocial symptoms. The aggressive tendencies of sexually abused girls are often displayed in interaction with siblings (Gomes-Schwartz, Horowitz, Cardarelli, & Sauzier, 1990). The sibling relationship—the social context considered in the next section—may reflect interparental aggression and provide a training ground for aggressive problem-solving styles in the home. Girls' experiences of abuse within the family may limit their capacity to form trusting relationships and may provide models of ineffective parenting, which they carry forward to their own motherhood.

Girls' Aggression With Siblings. We believe that sibling interactions provide an important context in which to consider risks for aggressive girls. Patterson (1986) articulated how aggressive children regularly engage in fighting with their siblings and how siblings contribute directly to the coercive processes that train aggressive children in aversive strategies. Although Patterson's observations were conducted in families with aggressive boys, there is no reason to believe that the processes would be different for aggressive girls. Observations of sibling interaction reveal that female siblings were just as aggressive as their male counterparts during the preschool and early school years (Abramovitch, Corter, Pepler, & Stanhope, 1986; Pepler, Abramovitch, & Corter, 1981). In a study of siblings in late childhood, brothers and sisters did not differ in rivalry and negative behavior (Dunn, Slomkowski, & Beardsall, 1994). Among high school students, there are also few differences between sisters and brothers in aggressive behavior directed to siblings (Goodwin & Roscoe, 1990).

For aggressive girls, the sibling relationship may be a flashpoint for their aggressive behavior as Patterson (1986) postulated. Troubled sibling relationships may be a particular problem within families experiencing marital disharmony or strained stepparent relationships (Jenkins, 1992). In our study of children of battered women, extreme forms of aggression toward the sibling was a key variable differentiating well-adjusted girls from those who were rated as having high levels of behavior problems (Pepler & Moore, 1993).

Several unique characteristics of the sibling relationship may account for girls' tendencies to express aggression in this context. Siblings live in the same household, are involved in continual interactions with each other and the same set of parents, and typically share space, toys, clothes, and their parents' love and attention (Pepler, Corter, & Abramovitch, 1982). As a result of time spent together and the frequency of interactions, siblings become very intimate. The sibling relationship is also enduring and cannot usually be permanently ruptured by a serious altercation. When a girl is aggressive toward her sibling, there is no risk of her sibling turning on her and declaring that he or she will never be her sibling again. Hence, within the intimacy of a sibling relationship, girls may be more inclined to express aggression and less likely to suffer for their transgressions of sex-role norms. Tolerance for aggression within sibling interactions may lay the foundations for the use of aggression as a conflict strategy within other intimate relationships with peers and partners.

Peer Context

The peer group asserts its influence concurrently with the family and school during childhood and adolescence. Peer relations function in many ways. On one hand, they are important for a sense of belonging and connections (Rubin, Bukowski, & Parker, 1998). On the other hand, they are a potential source of conflict, alienation, and victimization (Craig & Peters, 1998). Recent evidence has emerged that peers also provide deviancy training to enhance and promote antisocial behavior (Dishion, McCord, & Poulin, 1999). In this section, we consider the converging peer processes in aggressive girls' lives that potentially promote their problem behaviors and maintain their troubled developmental trajectory.

In general, the contexts for girls' and boys' peer interactions are markedly different and likely underlie gender differences in the expression of aggression. Sex segregation in play activities and play partners begins during the preschool period (Maccoby, 1998). Boys tend to engage in more physical and rough play than girls (Hart, DeWolf, Wozniak, & Burts, 1992; Humphreys & Smith, 1987), with opportunities for physical aggression often triggered in the context of rough-and-tumble play (Smith & Boulton, 1990). In contrast, girls tend to play in dyads more often than boys (Pepler, Craig, & Roberts, 1995), providing opportunities for verbal and social aggression such as exclusion, gossip, and collusion directed at the relational bonds between friends (Crick & Grotpeter, 1993). Although boys and girls may not differ in overall rates of prosocial or antisocial behaviors on the playground (Hart et al., 1992; Pepler, Craig, & Roberts, 1995), the risks for boys to accelerate to physical aggression may be greater because of the social context of their play with other boys. However, aggressive girls may be at risk for isolation and rejection if their aggressive behavior interferes with the social task of developing close friendships during middle childhood.

Social-interactional processes within the peer group reflect the differential approval of aggression by girls and boys. Serbin and her colleagues (1993) found that boys rated as aggressive by peers were highly involved with peers on the playground despite behaving aggressively. Girls identified as aggressive by peers were disliked by their classmates and more isolated than aggressive boys on the playground. Serbin and her colleagues (1993) concluded that boys' peer groups may perceive aggression as normative and an extension of rough-and-tumble play. Girls' peer groups, in contrast, may perceive girls' aggression as atypical and react accordingly to isolate aggressive girls. Lack of acceptance within the peer group may, in turn, exacerbate aggressive girls' problems. Coie, Lochman, Terry, and Hyman (1992) found that girls who were not liked by their peers in middle childhood were significantly more likely to have adjustment problems in adolescence than those who were liked.

There is emerging evidence that peer group dynamics may be more alienating for aggressive girls than boys. First, at the social-cognitive level, girls' aggression may be less accepted by peers than boys' aggression. Huesmann, Guerra, Zelli, and Miller (1992) found that boys were more likely to condone aggression than girls. Similarly, Perry and his colleagues (1989) found that children expected male peer groups to be less disapproving of aggression than female peer groups. Consequently, an aggressive girl may be more isolated, rejected, and victimized by her peer group than a similarly aggressive boy whose behavior deviates less from gender norms. As indicated earlier, not only does this peer disapproval manifest itself behaviorally, but it also has an effect on the reciprocal social cognitions of the aggressive girl and her peers. An aggressive girl who is out of step with her peer group may come to see its members as hostile and rejecting. The peer group, in turn, attributes hostile intent to the aggressive girl's awkward and unskilled interactions.

Aggressive girls' difficulties within the peer group were reflected in our analyses of the NLSCY data. According to parent and self-reports, aggressive girls experienced significantly more peer conflicts, fewer peer contacts, less positive peer relations, more victimization, and more associations with deviant peers than nonaggresssive girls and were similar to aggressive boys on these variables (Pepler & Sedighdeilami, 1998). Consistent with research on aggressive boys (Patterson et al., 1992), it appears as if girls' aggressive behavior interferes with the development of positive friendships.

When they are not liked by peers, both aggressive girls and boys are at risk for being bullied, having other children say nasty and unpleasant things, and feeling unsafe and like an outsider at school. The aggressive children are then caught in reciprocally hostile interactions, which may maintain or exacerbate their aggressive tendencies and lead to victimization.

As a result of rejection within the peer group context, aggressive girls may seek other opportunities for peer interaction. There is evidence that aggressive girls tend to gravitate to boys' groups for associations and activities (Barrett, 1979; Serbin et al., 1993). The direction of the effect is not clear. The aggressive girls may seek out male peers because they are ostracized by other girls. Conversely, girls in mixed-sex groups may exhibit more aggression than girls in same-sex groups because of the social context of their interactions. Both girls and boys are more likely to have physical conflicts with boys than with girls (Cairns et al., 1989; Serbin et al., 1993). Within boys' groups, fighting is a general characteristic of the group interaction, rather than being solely a characteristic of an individual male child within the group (Maccoby, 1998). If aggressive girls migrate from same-sex to mixed-sex peer groups, they may experience greater opportunities to learn aggression and establish an aggressive style of problem solving.

In early adolescence, girls may find aggressive strategies somewhat effective. Longitudinal research by Schwartzman and his colleagues indicates that in Grade 7 (age 12), there is a positive correlation between girls' and boys' ratings of opposite-sex likeability and aggression. Our observations also reflect the potential convergence of likeability and aggression at least for a subset of children. On the school playground, girls were equally likely to bully boys and girls, whereas boys almost exclusively bullied other boys (Pepler, Craig, Atlas, & O'Connell, 1998). Some episodes involving girls bullying boys appear to be attention-seeking in intent and a form of precourtship behavior, with positive intent embedded in negative behavior. Thorne (1993) also noted this pattern of interaction between girls and boys in her playground observations: "The ambiguities of borderwork [separation into same-sex peer groups] allow the signalling of sexual or romantic, as well as aggressive, meanings, and the two often mix together" (p. 81). The challenge for aggressive girls seems to be that they lack the social skills to obtain boys' attention through positive means; therefore, they resort to aversive strategies. It follows that girls who use aversive strategies to attract boys' attention are at risk for establishing a dangerous precedent for subsequent dating relations. We are seeing evidence of this in our early adolescent study—girls who bully are more likely to report being aggressive and victimized in early adolescent romantic relationships (Connolly, Pepler, Craig, & Taradash, 2000).

In summary, social cognitions and interactions within the peer group may exacerbate the risks for aggressive girls. Given assortative processes, aggressive and nonaggressive girls may gravitate into different peer groups and, consequently, have different socialization experiences within the peer context. These peer group experiences in childhood and adolescence may have long-lasting effects. In their longitudinal research on at-risk girls, Quinton and his colleagues (1993) concluded that, "a poor choice of peers, once made, appeared to make an important and additional contribution that promoted the risk of poor teenage outcomes" (p. 777). Further research is required to elucidate gender differences in aggression with peers and understand the processes by which the peer group influences the manifestation of aggression.

Why Worry About Aggressive Girls?

Thus far, we have considered the difficulties experienced by aggressive girls in their social relationships within the family and peer group. The data suggest that aggressive girls' relationship difficulties are similar to, but sometimes more strained than, those of aggressive boys. In this section, we turn our attention to other domains of an aggressive girl's development, in which their difficulties may also be similar to those of aggressive boys in the academic and emotional domains.

Academic Difficulties.   The link between aggressive behavior problems and increasingly poor school performance has been well documented for boys (e.g., Patterson, 1986; Patterson, DeBaryshe, & Ramsey, 1989). The risks of school problems appear to be present for aggressive girls as well. Robins (1986) found that four school problems (discipline, expulsion, truancy, and underachievement) clustered similarly and significantly in factor analyses of conduct problems for girls and boys. Recently, Wangby, Bergman, and Magnusson (1999) reported that girls' conduct problems (motor restlessness, aggression) and academic problems (lack of concentration, low school motivation) co-occur in a cluster that is stable from ages 10 to 13. In our analysis of the NLSCY, we found some evidence of academic difficulties for aggressive girls (Pepler & Sedighdeilami, 1998). As with hyperactivity/inattention problems, parents of aggressive girls did not rate their daughters as having academic problems at as high a level as parents of aggressive boys. When the girls were rating their own academic problems, however, the picture was notably different. Aggressive girls rated their academic problems to be as great as those of aggressive boys and significantly greater than those of nonaggressive children.

Evidence of a developmental progression from aggressive behavior problems to academic difficulties can be found in longitudinal studies. Bates and his colleagues (1991) found that girls' difficult behavior in early childhood was associated with poor school competence in middle childhood. Girls' tendency to provide aggressive problem-solving strategies was also linked to poor school performance. In her longitudinal research, Pulkkinen (1992) identified physical aggressiveness in girls as a critical factor related to school achievement. Compared with girls who were verbally or facially aggressive, those who were physically aggressive were less motivated to attend school, had poorer school performance, and received a shorter education. The education of physically aggressive girls was often interrupted by low school motivation, early heterosexual activity, and young motherhood (Pulkkinen, 1992). Truancy and school dropout may be a particular problem for aggressive girls. In their longitudinal study, Cairns and his colleagues found that 47% of girls who had low academic success and high aggressiveness in Grade 7 had dropped out of school prior to completing Grade 11 (Schlossman & Cairns, 1993). An assessment of school achievement for aggressive girls over childhood and adolescence is clearly an area for future research. For school achievement, as for other domains of aggressive girls' lives, there appears to be a cumulative effect of risk with development.

Patterson and his colleagues identified a potential mechanism linking aggressive behavior and academic difficulties by suggesting that aggressive boys' inattentive and disruptive behavior interferes with their academic performance to produce a cumulative deficit (Patterson et al., 1989). A similar process is suggested for aggressive girls by the motor restlessness and concentration problems in the high-risk group identified by Wangby, Bergman, and Magnusson (1999) and the hyperactivity and inattention problems discussed earlier in the chapter. Taken together this constellation of problems raises concerns that girls' neuropsychological problems may place them at risk for conduct problems through similar processes as hypothesized for boys (Moffitt, 1993). Neuropsychological difficulties are presumed to interact with social-interactional processes to exacerbate conduct problems risk within the school context (Moffitt, 1993). Therefore, girls' behavioral and cognitive difficulties may inhibit their ability to learn and place them at risk for strained interactions with their teachers and peers in the school setting. Aggressive girls may be increasingly rejected within an educational setting for their poor performance and behavior, and they may become increasingly alienated as they encounter repeated academic and social failures.

Data from the NLSCY (Pepler & Sedighdeilami, 1998) and Ontario Child Health Study (OCHS; Offord et al., 1991) raise a question about the extent to which aggressive girls' academic difficulties are being identified and addressed. In the OCHS, conduct-disordered girls in the 4- to 11-year-old range were somewhat more likely to receive special education services than conduct-disordered boys (33% and 21%, respectively). By adolescence, however, the proportion of conduct-disordered girls receiving special education was considerably lower than that of boys (7% and 32%, respectively). The 26% difference in girls' rates of utilization across developmental periods cannot be explained by a lower incidence of disorder: Adolescent girls were twice as likely to have CD than school-age girls—4% and 2%, respectively. The cross-sectional design of this community survey cannot reveal the underlying processes. Perhaps in adolescence conduct-disordered girls experience fewer learning problems than younger girls. Alternatively, traditional sex-role expectations may be operating, whereby conduct-disordered girls are channeled to less challenging programs where they require less academic support.

Emotional Problems. A final concern for aggressive girls is the potential for comorbid emotional problems. In her longitudinal analyses of the prognosis for conduct-disordered girls and boys, Robins (1966, 1986) found different adulthood outcomes. Although girls were somewhat less likely than boys to be diagnosed with antisocial personality as adults, they were more likely to experience internalizing disorders such as anxiety and depression. In a review of research on CD and adult outcomes, Zoccolillo (1992) provided evidence of the high co-occurrence of girls' CD with subsequent emotional problems, particularly depression. He argued that conduct-disordered girls may not have a single disorder, but rather a multiple disorder that includes internalizing problems such as depression.

The co-occurrence of aggressive and emotional problems was also evident in our analysis of the NLSCY (Pepler & Sedighdeilami, 1998). According to both parents' and children's own reports, aggressive girls and boys experienced significantly more emotional difficulties (depression, anxiety) than nonaggressive children. The children were also asked questions related to self-concept. Consistent with other difficulties that aggressive children experience, both aggressive girls and boys rated their self-esteem as significantly lower than that of nonaggressive children.

In summary, although aggressive girls may not manifest aggressive behavior problems to the same overt extent as aggressive boys, they appear to experience a range of associated problems similar to aggressive boys, which should not be overlooked. The academic and emotional problems of aggressive girls suggest equal psychosocial impairment, which merits intervention. If support is not provided, these girls are not likely to possess the psychological resources to meet the tasks and relationships of everyday life with a resilient and positive orientation. In this way, the constellation of behavioral, academic, and psychological problems that they experience accumulate to place these girls at risk for increasingly troubled trajectories into adulthood.

Why Worry About Aggressive Girls? A Long Look

The problems that aggressive girls experience in childhood and adolescence lay the foundation for continuing mental health and relationship difficulties. The continuity of aggression into adulthood is similar for girls and boys (Huesmann, Eron, Lefkowitz, & Walder, 1984). Although early aggressiveness of both girls and boys predicts later problems, longitudinal research indicates that the manifestations of aggression may differ for women and men. Robins (1966, 1986) found different adulthood outcomes for conduct-disordered girls and boys. The outcomes differed in form: Girls were somewhat less likely than boys to be diagnosed with antisocial personality as adults, but more likely to experience internalizing disorders such as anxiety and depression. Robins (1986) questioned whether researchers have erred in expecting the same long-term outcomes for girls and boys.

In searching for the sequelae of aggressive behavior problems for girls and boys, researchers should expand their perspectives to include indicators and contexts appropriate for girls, with a particular focus on the quality of their relationships. Early aggressiveness may place girls at risk for being both perpetrators and victims within close relationships. As perpetrators, women may express their aggressive tendencies within such close relationships: Most women convicted of homicide killed members of their own families or friends and acquaintances, rather than strangers (Daly & Wilson, 1988). In a prospective study, Lewis et al. (1991) found that delinquent girls were less likely than a matched sample of boys to be arrested for violent offenses. Other aspects of these women's lives, however, revealed significant dysfunction, violence, and victimization. More than half of the women had been involved in "extraordinarily violent relationships with men" (Lewis et al., 1991, p. 200). Over two thirds of the women had children, and their childrearing was described to include a litany of problems, leading Lewis and her colleagues (1991) to conclude that they had "negligible abilities to provide even minimal support for the next generation" (p. 201).

Further evidence of the long-term relationship difficulties of aggressive girls comes from Robins' longitudinal research. When comparing conduct-disordered girls and boys diagnosed with antisocial personality disorder, Robins (1986) found that the women experienced more marital difficulties and were more neglectful of their children than the men. Women were also more likely to transmit behavior problems to their children than men. Robins (1986) concluded that women's outcomes from childhood CD were not necessarily better than men's, but were different. Other longitudinal research confirms that adulthood outcomes for aggressive girls continue to reflect difficulties in relationships—marital, parent–child, and employment (Huesmann et al., 1984; Serbin, Moskowitz, Schwartzman, &

Ledingham, 1991; Serbin et al., 1998). We must keep in mind that the trajectories to troubled relationships are by no means constrained for aggressive girls. Rutter (1990) found that if an at-risk girl married a prosocial man, she was able to make the transition to positive parenting. To understand the complexity of the developmental trajectories toward troubled or healthy relationships for at-risk girls, there are many questions still to be answered. The understanding that emerges from continuing research on aggressive girls can provide direction for the types of supports they require throughout their childhood, adolescence, and into adulthood.

In summary, there is a need to worry about aggressive girls and to study the challenges facing them throughout development. Although girls and boys begin life with similar behavioral profiles, their trajectories diverge within a few years, with a higher proportion of boys exhibiting aggressive behavior problems. A small subset of girls, however, fall onto and follow an aggressive trajectory. The personal relationships of these girls and women tend to reflect the violence of their youth and present risks for both themselves and their offspring.

AUTHOR NOTE

The research described in this paper was funded by several grants from the Ontario Mental Health Foundation and a grant from Human Resources Development Canada. We are indebted to the students, parents, and teachers who have participated in our research over the years. Requests for reprints can be sent to Debra Pepler, LaMarsh Research Centre, York University, 4700 Keele Street, Toronto, Ontario Canada M3J 1P3, pepler@yorku.ca

REFERENCES

Abramovitch, R., Corter, C., Pepler, D., & Stanhope, L. (1986). Sibling and peer interaction: A final longitudinal follow-up and comparison. *Child Development, 57*, 217–229.

Barrett, D. E. (1979). A naturalistic study of sex differences in children's aggression. *Merrill-Palmer Quarterly, 25*, 193–203.

Bates, J. E., Bayles, K., Bennett, D. S., Ridge, B., & Brown, M. M. (1991). Origins of externalizing behavior: Problems at eight years of age. In D. J. Pepler & K. H. Rubin (Eds.), *The development and treatment of childhood aggression* (pp. 93–120). Hillsdale, NJ: Lawrence Erlbaum Associates.

Björkqvist, K., Osterman, K., & Kaukiainen, A. (1992). The development of direct and indirect aggressive strategies in males and females. In K. Björkqvist & P. Niemëla (Eds.), *Of mice and women: Aspects of female aggression* (pp. 51–64). San Diego, CA: Academic Press.

Brooks, J., Whiteman, M., & Finch, S. (1993). Role of mutual attachment in drug use: A longitudinal study. *Journal of the American Academy of Child and Adolescent Psychiatry, 32*, 982–989.

Brown, L. M., & Gilligan, C. (1992). *Meeting at the crossroads: Women's psychology and girls' development*. Cambridge, MA: Harvard University Press.

Cairns, R. B., & Cairns, B. D. (1994). *Lifelines and risks: Pathways of youth in our time*. Cambridge, England: Cambridge University Press.

Cairns, R. B., Cairns, B. D., Neckerman, H. J., Ferguson, L. L., & Gariepy, J.-L. (1989). Growth and aggression: I. Childhood to early adolescence. *Developmental Psychology, 25*, 320–330.

Campbell, S. B., Pierce, E. W., March, C. L., Ewing, L. J. (1994). Hard to manage preschool boys: Symptomatic behavior across contexts and time. *Child Development, 65*, 836–851.

Caspi, A., Elder, G. H., & Bem, D. J. (1987). Moving against the world: Life course patterns of explosive children. *Developmental Psychology, 23*, 308–313.

Caspi, A., Lynam, D., Moffitt, T., & Silva, P. (1993). Unraveling girls' delinquency: Biological, dispositional, and contextual contributions to adolescent misbehavior. *Developmental Psychology, 29*, 19–30.

Caspi, A., & Moffitt, T. (1991). Individual differences are accentuated during periods of social change: The sample case of girls at puberty. *Journal of Personality and Social Psychology, 61*, 157–168.

Cicchetti, D., & Aber, J. L. (1998). Contextualism and developmental psychopathology. *Development and Psychopathology, 10*, 137–141.

Coie, J. D., Lochman, J. E., Terry, R., & Hyman, C. (1992). Predicting early adolescent disorder from childhood aggression and peer rejection. *Journal of Consulting and Clinical Psychology, 60*, 783–792.

Connolly, J., Pepler, D. J., Craig, W. M., & Taradash, A. (2000). Dating experiences of bullies in early adolescence. *Child Maltreatment, 5*, 299–310.

Craig, W., & Pepler, D. J. (1995). Peer processes in bullying and victimization: An observational study. *Exceptionality Education Canada, 5*, 81–95.

Craig, W., & Pepler, D. (1997). Observations of bullying and victimization on the playground. *Canadian Journal of School Psychology, 2*, 41–60.

Craig, W. M. & Peters, R. (1998). Bullying in Canada. *The Progress of Canada's Children* (3rd ed.). Ottawa: Canadian Council on Social Development.

Crick, N., & Grotpeter, J. (1993). Relational aggression, gender, and social-psychological adjustment. *Child Development, 66*, 710–722.

Daly, M., & Wilson, M. (1998). *Homicide*. New York: Aldine De Gruyter.

Dishion, T., McCord, J., & Poulin, F. (1999). When interventions harm: Peer groups and problem behavior. *American Psychologist, 54*, 755–764.

Dodge, K. A. (1993). Social-cognitive mechanisms in the development of conduct disorder and depression. *Annual Review of Psychology, 44*, 559–584.

Dodge, K. A., Bates, J. E., & Pettit, G. S. (1990). Mechanisms in the cycle of violence. *Science, 250*, 1678–1683.

Dowler, S. (1995). *Youths' perceptions of pornography and their relation to sexual aggression*. Unpublished doctoral dissertation, York University, Toronto, Canada.

Dunn, J., Slomkowski, C., & Beardsall, L. (1994). Sibling relationships from the preschool period through middle childhood and early adolescence. *Developmental Psychology, 30*, 315–324.

Eagly, A. H., & Steffen, V. J. (1986). Gender and aggressive behavior: A meta-analytic review of the social psychological literature. *Psychological Bulletin, 100*, 309–330.

Eron, L. D. (1992). Gender differences in violence: Biology and/or socialization? In K. Björkqvist & P. Niemëla (Eds.), *Of mice and women: Aspects of female aggression* (pp. 89–98). San Diego, CA: Academic Press.

Fagot, B., Leinbach, M. D., & Hagan, R. (1986). Gender labelling and adoption of gender role behaviors. *Developmental Psychology, 22*, 440–443.

Fagot, B., Leinbach, M., & Hort, B. (1994, July). *Gender and aggression.* Paper presented at the meetings of the International Society for the Study of Behavioral Development, Amsterdam.

Galen, B. R., & Underwood, M. K. (1997). A developmental investigation of social aggression among children. *Developmental Psychology, 33,* 589–600.

Garmezy, N. & Rutter, M. (Eds.). (1983). *Stress, Coping, and Development in Children.* New York: McGraw-Hill.

Gilligan, C. (1982). *In a different voice: Psychological theory and women's development.* Cambridge, MA: Harvard University Press.

Gomes-Schwartz, B., Horowitz, J. M., Cardarelli, A. P., & Sauzier, M. (1990). The aftermath of child sexual abuse: 18 months later. In B. Gomes-Schwartz, J. M. Horowitz, & A. P. Cardarelli (Eds.), *Child sexual abuse: The initial effects* (pp. 132–152). Newbury Park, CA: Sage.

Goodwin, M. P., & Roscoe, B. (1990). Sibling violence and agonistic interactions among middle adolescents. *Adolescence, 25,* 451–467.

Greenberg, M. T., Speltz, M. L., & DeKlyen, M. (1993). The role of attachment in the early development of disruptive behavior problems. *Development and Psychopathology, 5,* 191–213.

Hart, C. H., DeWolf, D. M., & Buits, D. C. (1992). Linkages among preschoolers' playground behavior, outcome expectations and parental disciplinary strategies. *Early Education and Development, 3,* 265–382.

Heimer, D., & De Coster, S. (1999). The gendering of violent delinquency. *Criminology, 37,* 277–317.

Huesmann, L. R., Eron, L. D., Lefkowitz, M. M., & Walder, L. O. (1984). Stability of aggression over time and generations. *Developmental Psychology, 20,* 1120–1134.

Huesmann, L. R., Guerra, N. G., Zelli, A., & Miller, L. (1992). Differing normative beliefs about aggression for boys and girls. In K. Björkqvist & P. Niëmela (Eds.), *Of mice and women: Aspects of female aggression* (pp. 77–87). San Diego, CA: Academic Press.

Humphreys, A. P., & Smith, P. K. (1987). Rough and tumble friendship and dominance in school children: Evidence for continuity and change with age in middle childhood. *Child Development, 58,* 201–212.

Hyde, J. S. (1984). How large are gender differences in aggression? A developmental meta-analysis. *Developmental Psychology, 20,* 722–736.

Japel, C., Tremblay, R. E., Vitaro, F., & Boulerice, B. (1999). Early parental separation and the psychosocial development of daughters 6–9 years old. *American Journal of Orthopsychiatry, 69,* 49–60.

Jenkins, J. (1992). Sibling relationships in disharmonious homes: Potential difficulties and protective effects. In F. Boer & J. Dunn (Eds.), *Sibling relationships: Developmental and clinical issues* (pp. 125–138). Hillsdale NJ: Lawrence Erlbaum Associates.

Kavanagh, K., & Hops, H. (1994). Good girls? Bad boys?: Gender and development as contexts for diagnosis and treatment. In T. H. Ollendick & R. J. Prinz (Eds.), *Advances in clinical child psychology* (Vol., 16, pp. 46–79). New York: Plenum.

Keenan, K., & Shaw, D. (1994). The development of aggression in toddlers: A study of low-income families. *Journal of Abnormal Child Psychology, 22,* 53–77.

Kendall-Tackett, K. A., Williams, L. M., & Finkelhor, D. (1993). Impact of sexual abuse on children: A review and synthesis of recent empirical studies. *Psychological Bulletin, 113,* 164–180.

Lagerspetz, K., Björkqvist, K., & Peltonen, T. (1988). Is indirect aggression typical of females? Gender differences in aggressiveness in 11- to 12-year old children. *Aggressive Behavior, 14,* 403–404.

Lewis, D. O., Yeager, C. A., Cobham-Portorreal, C. S., Klein, N., Showater, C., & Anthony, A. (1991). A follow-up of female delinquents: Maternal contributions to the perpetuation of deviance. *Journal of the American Academy of Child and Adolescent Psychiatry, 30*, 197–201.

Loeber, R., & Keenan, K. (1994). The interaction between conduct disorder and its comorbid conditions: Effects of age and gender. *Clinical Psychology Review, 14*, 497–523.

Loeber, R., & Stouthamer-Loeber, M. (1986). Family factors as correlates and predictors of juvenile conduct problems and delinquency. In M. Tonry & N. Morris (Eds.), *Crime and justice: An annual review of research* (Vol. 7, pp. 20–149). Chicago: University of Chicago Press.

Lytton, H., & Romney, D. M. (1991). Parents' differential socialization of boys and girls: A meta analysis. *Psychological Bulletin, 109*, 267–296.

Maccoby, E. E. (1986). Social groupings in childhood: Their relationship to prosocial and antisocial behavior in boys and girls. In D. Olweus, J. Block, & M. Radke-Yarrow (Eds.), *Development of antisocial and prosocial behavior: Research, theories, and issues* (pp. 263–284). Orlando, FL: Academic Press.

Maccoby, E. E. (1998). *The two sexes: Growing up apart, coming together.* Cambridge, MA: Harvard University Press.

Maccoby, E. E., & Jacklin, C. N. (1980). Sex differences in aggression: A rejoinder and reprise. *Child Development, 51*, 964–980.

Maughan, B., Pickles, A., & Quinton, D. (1995). Parental hostility, childhood behavior, and adult social functioning. In J. McCord (Ed.), *Coercion and punishment in long-term perspectives* (pp. 34–58). New York: Cambridge University Press.

Moffitt, T. E. (1993). The neuropsychology of conduct disorder. *Development and Psychopathology, 5*, 135–151.

Offord, D. R., Boyle, M. C., & Racine, Y. (1991). The epidemiology of antisocial behavior in childhood and adolescence. In D. J. Pepler & K. H. Rubin (Eds.), *The development and treatment of childhood aggression* (pp. 31–54). Hillsdale, NJ: Lawrence Erlbaum Associates.

Olson, S. L., & Hoza, B. (1993). Preschool developmental antecedents of conduct problems in children beginning school. *Journal of Clinical and Child Psychology, 22*, 60–67.

Pakaslahti, L., Spoof, I., Asplund-Peltola, R. L., & Keltikangas-Jarvinen, L. (1998). Parents' social problem-solving strategies in families with aggressive and non-aggressive girls. *Aggressive Behavior, 24*, 37–51.

Patterson, G. R. (1982). *Coercive family process.* Eugene OR: Castalia.

Patterson, G. R. (1986). The contribution of siblings to training for fighting: A microsocial analysis. In D. Olweus, J. Block, & M. Radke-Yarrow (Eds.), *Development of antisocial and prosocial behavior: Research, theories, and issues* (pp. 235–261). Orlando, FL: Academic Press.

Patterson, G. R., DeBaryshe, B. D., & Ramsey, E. (1989). A developmental perspective on antisocial behavior. *American Psychologist, 44*, 329–335.

Patterson, G. R., Reid, J. B., & Dishion, T. J. (1992). *Antisocial boys.* Eugene OR: Castilia.

Pepler, D. J., Abramovitch, R., & Corter, C. (1981). Sibling interaction in the home: A longitudinal study. *Child Development, 52*, 1344–1347.

Pepler, D. J., Corter, C., & Abramovitch, R. (1982). Social relations among children: Siblings and peers. In K. Rubin & H. Ross (Eds.), *Peer relationships and social skills in childhood* (pp.)New York: Springer-Verlag.

Pepler, D. J., Craig, W. M., Atlas, R., & O'Connell, P. (1998, July). *Observations of bullying on the school playground.* Presented at the XVth biennial meeting of International Society for the Study of Behavioral Development, Berne, Switzerland.

Pepler, D. J., Craig, W. M., & Roberts, W. R. (1995). Social skills training and aggression in the peer group. In J. McCord (Ed.), *Coercion and punishment in long-term perspectives* (pp. 213–228). New York: Cambridge University Press.

Pepler, D. J., Craig, W. M., & Roberts, W. L. (1998). Observations of aggressive and nonaggressive children on the school playground. *Merrill-Palmer Quarterly, 44,* 55–76.

Pepler, D., & Moore, T. (1993, August). *Daughters of abused women: At risk?* Paper presented at the American Psychological Association Convention, Toronto.

Pepler, D., & Sedighdeilami, F. (1998). *Aggressive girls in Canada.* Working paper W-98-30E, Applied Research Branch, Human Resources Development Canada.

Perry, D. G., Perry, L. C., & Weiss, R. J. (1989). Sex Differences in the consequences that children anticipate for aggression. *Developmental Psychology, 25,* 312–319.

Prior, M., Smart, D., Sanson, A., & Oberklaid, F. (1993). Sex differences in psychological adjustment from infancy. *Journal of the American Academy of Child and Adolescent Psychiatry, 32,* 291–304.

Pulkkinen, L. (1987). Offensive and defensive aggression in humans: A longitudinal perspective. *Aggressive Behavior, 13,* 197–212.

Pulkkinen, L. (1992). The path to adulthood for aggressively inclined girls. In K. Björkqvist & P. Niemëla (Eds.), *Of mice and women: Aspects of female aggression* (pp. 113–121). San Diego, CA: Academic Press.

Quinton, D., Pickles, A., Maughan, B., & Rutter, M. (1993). Partners, peers, and pathways. *Development and Psychopathology, 5,* 763–783.

Robins, L. N. (1966). *Deviant children grow up.* Baltimore: Williams & Wilkins.

Robins, L. N. (1986). The consequences of conduct disorder in girls. In D. Olweus, J. Block, & M. Radke-Yarrow (Eds.), *Development of antisocial and prosocial behavior: Research, theories, and issues* (pp. 385–414). Orlando, FL: Academic Press.

Rose, S. L., Rose, S. A., & Feldman, J. F. (1989). Stability of behavior problems in very young children. *Development and Psychopathology, 1,* 5–19.

Rubin, K. H., Bukowski, W., & Parker, J. G. (1998). Peer interactions, relationships, and groups. In (pp. 619–700). In W. Damon (Ed.). *Handbook of Child Psychology* (5th ed.). N. Eisenberg (Volume Ed.) *Social, emotional, and personality development*, Volume 3. New York: Wiley.

Rutter, M. (1990). Psychosocial resilience and protective mechanisms. In J. Rolf, A. S. Masten, D. Cicchetti, K. H. Nuechterlein, & S. Weintraub (Eds.), *Risk and protective factors in the development of psychopathology* (pp. 181–214). Cambridge: Cambridge University Press.

Sanson, A., Oberklaid, F., Prior, M., Amos, D., & Smart, D. (1996, January). *Infancy, toddler and early childhood predictors of externalizing problems at 11–12 years.* Paper presented at the meetings of the International Society for Research on Child and Adolescent Psychopathology, Santa Monica, CA.

Schlossman, S., & Cairns, R. B. (1993). Problem girls: Observations on past and present. In G. H. Elder, J. Modell, & R. D. Parke (Eds.), *Children in time and place: Developmental and historical insights* (pp. 110–130). Cambridge: Cambridge University Press.

Serbin, L. A., Cooperman, J. M., Peters, P. L., Lehoux, P. M., Stack, D. M., & Schwartzman, A. E. (1998). Inter-generational transfer of psychosocial risk in women with childhood histories of aggression, withdrawal or aggression and withdrawal. *Developmental Psychology, 34,* 1246–1262.

Serbin, L. A., Marchessault, K., McAffer, V., Peters, P., & Schwartzman, A. E. (1993). Patterns of social behavior on the playground in 9–11-year-old girls and boys: Relation to

28PEPLER AND CRAIG

teacher perceptions and to peer ratings of aggression, withdrawal and likability. In C. Hart (Ed.), *Children on the playground* (pp. 162–183). New York: SUNY Press.

Serbin, L. A., Moskowitz, K. S., Schwartzman, A. E., & Ledingham, J. E. (1991). Aggressive, withdrawn, and aggressive/withdrawn children in adolescence: Into the next generation. In D. J. Pepler & K. H. Rubin (Eds.), *The development and treatment of childhood aggression* (pp. 55–70). Hillsdale, NJ: Lawrence Erlbaum Associates.

Smith, P. K., & Boulton, M. (1990). Rough and tumble play, aggression and dominance: Perception and behavior in children's encounters. *Human Development, 33,* 271–282.

Sroufe, L. A. (1997). Psychopathology as an outcome of development. *Development and Psychopathology, 9,* 251–268.

Statistics Canada. (1998). *Canadian Crime Statistics, 1997.* No. 85-002-XPE, Vol 18 (11).

Stattin, H., & Magnusson, D. (1990). *Pubertal maturation in female development.* Hillsdale, NJ: Lawrence Erlbaum Associates.

Szatmari, P., Boyle, M., & Offord, D. R. (1989). ADHD and CD: Degree of diagnostic overlap and difference among correlates. *Journal of the American Academy of Child and Adolescent Psychiatry, 28,* 865–872.

Thorne, B. (1993). *Gender play: Girls and boys in school.* New Brunswick, NJ: Rutgers University Press.

Tremblay, R. E., Boulerice, B., Haren, P. W., McDuff, P., Perusse, D., Pihl, R. O., & Zoccolillo, M. (1995). Do children in Canada become more aggressive as they approach adolescence? In *Growing up in Canada: National longitudinal survey of children and youth.* Ottawa: Statistics Canada.

Wangby, M., Bergman, L. R., & Magnusson, D. (1999). Development of adjustment problems in girls: What syndromes emerge? *Child Development, 70,* 678–699.

Zoccolillo, M. (1992). Co-occurrence of conduct disorder and its adult outcomes with depressive and anxiety disorders: A review. *Journal of the American Academic of Child and Adolescent Psychiatry, 31,* 547–556.

2

Developmental Approaches to Studying Conduct Problems in Girls

Kate Keenan
Department of Psychiatry, University of Chicago

Magda Stouthamer-Loeber
Rolf Loeber
Western Psychiatric Institute and Clinic, University of Pittsburgh

The goal of the present chapter is to provide a developmental model of conduct disorder (CD) that is specific to girls. This is a challenging task given the relative lack of large prospective studies on the age of onset, continuity, and course of CD in girls. Moreover, some scientists argue that the diagnosis of CD does not adequately capture the manifestation of antisocial behavior in girls (e.g., Zoccolillo, Tremblay, & Vitaro, 1996). Such an argument is well grounded, and studies using alternative approaches to conceptualizing problem behavior in girls have generated interesting data. However, we believe that diagnostic constructs are useful scientific and clinical tools and warrant further exploration regarding their utility. In the case of CD for girls, it would be premature to draw conclusions about the utility or need for modification. There is a growing body of literature that addresses these issues both directly and indirectly. This literature is reviewed in the present chapter, along with the current theoretical debates on defining conduct problems in girls. In addition, we present pilot data in an effort to preliminarily test a few existing hypotheses about the prevalence and correlates of conduct problems in girls. Finally, we introduce an existing program of study that aims to: (a) test models that include a combination of behavioral, cognitive, and emotional factors as developmental precursors to conduct disorder in girls; (b) elucidate risk and protective factors that influence the development of CD by affecting the precursors, continuity, and severity of CD; and (c) identify other comorbid conditions that affect the course of CD and the development of comorbid CD and internalizing disorders.

OVERVIEW OF CONDUCT DISORDER

Conduct disorder (CD) is characterized by a persistent pattern of behavior that violates societal rules and/or the welfare of others (American Psychiatric Association, 1994). To meet criteria for a diagnosis of CD according to the *Diagnostic and Statistical Manual of Mental Disorders–Fourth Edition* (*DSM–IV*; American Psychiatric Association, 1994), three symptoms are required to occur within a 12-month period. The symptoms include violations of rules, destruction of property, and physical aggression. Age of onset of the first symptom of CD is used to distinguish between child onset (before age 10) and adolescent onset (age 10 or later).

Thus far, research indicates that there are several important differences and similarities between boys and girls in CD and its symptoms. The prevalence of CD appears to be lower in girls than in boys (Costello et al., 1996; Lahey et al., 2000). On average, the level of severity of conduct symptoms with regard to physical harm to others is lower in girls than in boys (Lahey et al., 1998). The risk of developing antisocial personality disorder (APD) among CD boys and girls seems to be about the same (Zoccolillo, Pickles, Quinton, & Rutter, 1992).

However, even these empirically based conclusions have been questioned because of the possibility that sex biases exist in the definition of CD (Hartung & Widiger, 1998). Moreover, the prevalence, correlates, and prognosis of CD in girls has not been adequately assessed in a population-based, representative study. To date the Methods for Epidemiology Child and Adolescent Disorders Area (MECA) study (Lahey et al., 2000) is the only nationally representative study of *DSM* CD in children and adolescents. Thus, the true prevalence of CD in girls is not known.

There appear to be two contrasting approaches toward defining CD for girls. One approach argues for revising the conceptualization of conduct problems so that girls who demonstrate impairing, antisocial behavior can be appropriately identified as having CD. Such a revision may include adding to existing symptoms or changing the number of symptoms required to meet criteria. For example, in one community-based study of over 2,000 school-age girls (Zoccolillo, Tremblay, & Vitaro, 1996), lowering the symptom threshold of *DSM–III–R* CD from three to two symptoms increased sensitivity without sacrificing specificity.

There is also a body of research in which the phenotype of CD in girls is examined. Crick (1995) posited that there are sex-specific forms of aggression, with *relational aggression* being more commonly manifested than physical aggression in girls. Although it is unclear how behaviors indicative of relational aggression (e.g., excluding a child from playing) fit into the diagnostic rubric of CD, the argument that psychiatric nosology may be negatively influenced by gender stereotypes is well founded (Hartung & Widiger, 1998). Thus, studies of the developmental course of CD in girls need to cast a broader net with regard to the assessment of precursors, symptom manifestation, and impairment.

In contrast, Zahn-Waxler (1993) argued that the apparent sex difference in rates of CD reflects true differences in the sociocultural experiences and biogenetic development of boys and girls. Therefore, efforts aimed at creating a variant of CD that is equal in terms of prevalence may not be constructive. If the true prevalence of CD in girls is lower than that for boys, examining sex differences in potential risk factors may yield important information with regard to etiology.

With these nosology issues in mind, we first summarize the existing literature on the developmental course of CD in girls including age of onset, precursors, continuity, and comorbidity.

DEVELOPMENTAL COURSE

Developmental Precursors

Temperamental Problems.   Cole and Zahn-Waxler (1992) posited that dysregulated temperament facilitates the progression from early disruptive problems to CD through the difficulty with managing negative emotions such as anger. Typically, a construct identified as *difficult temperament* has been used as a possible precursor to later antisocial behavior. Results have been fairly consistent in showing stability of temperamental difficultness in the preschool period to behavior problems in the school-age period for both girls and boys. For example, Caspi and colleagues (1995) included elements of emotional lability, restlessness, negativism, and a short attention span in their definition of *lack of control*. This construct, measured at age 3, was significantly associated with CD in girls and boys at age 15. Guerin, Gottfried, and Thomas (1997) reported significant associations between difficult temperament as defined by the Infant Characteristics Questionnaire at 18 months and parent report of aggressive and oppositional behavior at age 12 for girls and boys. Data from the Australian Temperament Project (Prior, Smart, Sanson, & Oberklaid, 1993) revealed that difficult temperament at age 3 to 4 was the best predictor of behavior problems at school age for both sexes.

Attention-Deficit/Hyperactivity Disorder (ADHD). Recent well-controlled studies have provided some support for ADHD as a risk factor for the early onset of CD in boys (Loeber, Green, Keenan, & Lahey, 1995). Little is known, however, about ADHD as a predictor of CD in girls (Lahey et al., 1998). Several community and clinical studies comparing observed and expected comorbidities show that girls with a diagnosis of ADHD have a higher likelihood compared with boys to qualify for a diagnosis of CD (e.g., Bird, Gould, & Staghezza, 1993). However, other studies have not reported a high rate of co-occurrence between ADHD and CD in girls (Breen & Barkley, 1988; Faraone, Biederman, Keenan, & Tsuang, 1991). There may be factors associated with ADHD that mediate the association between it and CD. For example, children with ADHD often demonstrate learning problems (Seidman et al., 1996). Because expectations for early academic skills are often higher for girls than boys (Keenan & Shaw, 1997), these types of deficits in girls may elicit more negative responses from caregivers and teachers, which in turn may place girls at risk for the development of persistent disruptive behavior problems and later CD.

Another hypothesis is that impulsivity may be one of the more important dimensions in the relation between ADHD and CD. Hence, among girls with ADHD, only those who have symptoms of impulsivity would have an increased risk for developing CD, thereby explaining some of the discrepant findings. Some data indicate a role for impulsivity in the etiology of conduct problems in boys (Caspi et al., 1995). However, Seidman and colleagues (1996) reported that, although ADHD girls have higher rates of learning disabilities and perform worse on tasks of attention and academic achievement than non-ADHD girls, they do not demonstrate deficits in executive functioning, which is sometimes defined in terms of impulsivity and poor judgment, as do boys.

Oppositional Defiant Disorder (ODD). ODD also has been identified as an important stepping stone to CD for boys in clinic-based samples (Loeber, Green, Keenan, & Lahey, 1995). In the general population, however, ODD may not serve as an important developmental precursor to CD for girls or boys. For example, in the MECA sample, a cross-sectional, population-based study, only 25% of girls and 33% of boys with CD had ODD (Lahey, McBurnett, & Loeber, 2000). Although the co-occurrence of ODD and CD was statistically significant, the majority of 6 to 17-year-old girls with CD did not have a diagnosis of ODD.

Part of the difficulty in determining the relative risk of ADHD and ODD for CD is the relatively high rate of co-occurrence. In a community-based study of gender differences in ADHD, ODD, and co-occurring ADHD and ODD, Carlson, Tamm, and Gaub (1997) reported that the rate of co-occurrence of ADHD and ODD was equal for girls and boys. Approximately 70% of children with ADHD met criteria for ODD, and approximately 30% of children with ODD met criteria for ADHD. Girls with symptoms of both ADHD and ODD, were rated as having poorer social functioning than boys with symptoms of both ADHD and ODD, including higher scores on a peer dislike scale and higher rating on the Social Problems scale of the Teacher Report Form (TRF). The fact that these girls were at higher social risk than boys may indicate a pathway by which ADHD and ODD are more likely to lead to the development of CD behaviors in girls than in boys (Carlson et al., 1997).

Empathy and Guilt. One possible emotional precursor to CD is a deficit in the development of empathy, emotional responsiveness to others, and internalization of guilt. In general, girls score higher on measures of empathy than boys (Keenan & Shaw, 1997). Girls tend to ruminate more over things they have done wrong, and they report more guilt about inconsiderate behavior than boys (Bybee, 1998). However, evidence suggests that guilt about aggressive incidents declines with age for girls and boys, although the decline is steeper for boys than girls. Between both sexes, children with conduct problems score lower on measures of empathy than nonconduct-disordered children (Cohen & Strayer, 1996).

Not all samples of conduct-disordered or delinquent girls, however, demonstrate a clear deficit in empathy. For example, work by Ogle and colleagues (1995) suggested that a subgroup of antisocial women responds with excessive guilt when exposed to stress. The experience of guilt and empathic concern in girls who have behavior problems may be related to the development of comorbid internalizing problems. Zahn-Waxler and colleagues (1991) suggested that the socialization of empathy in girls who live in chronically stressed environments may place those girls at higher risk for the development of internalizing problems. The combination of disruptive behavior and a concern for how this behavior affects others could lead to comorbid CD and depression.

In summary, there are a number of behavioral and emotional aspects of development that may directly affect the development of CD in girls. To some extent, we would expect that similar areas of deficits would increase the risk of CD in girls and boys, such as early problems with behavioral and emotional regulation. However, given that parents, teachers, and peers respond to the same behaviors in girls and boys differently (Keenan & Shaw, 1997), there will likely be a need for sex-specific transactional models of CD.

Age of Onset of CD

Age of onset is an important dimension in terms of both identifying etiologic factors and developing effective treatment or prevention programs. For example, many researchers and clinicians purport that an early age of onset is prognostic of chronic deviance, whereas a late onset of disruptive behavior tends to be transitory and less serious (e.g., Moffitt, 1993). However, this conclusion is based primarily on research with boys, and there are few data to determine whether age of onset of CD is a salient variable or whether girls are more likely to have an earlier onset of CD.

Silverthorn and Frick (1999) proposed that most antisocial girls follow a delayed-onset pathway, in which putative factors that contribute to antisocial behavior are present in childhood, but the manifestation of antisocial behavior does not occur until adolescence. This theory is based on the assumption that the majority of girls with conduct problems have an onset of conduct problems in adolescence rather than in childhood. However, there is some discrepancy in the literature on the average age of onset of CD for both girls and boys. The inconsistency of results appears to be in large part due to different methodologies and sample characteristics and the reliance on retrospective reporting. For example, in one community-based, cross-sectional sample, the modal age of onset of CD in girls was in early adolescence, whereas for boys it was in late childhood (Cohen et al., 1993). In another community-based sample, there was no sex difference in the age of onset of the first CD symptom, with the average age of onset falling between 5 and 8 (Lahey, Schwab-Stone, et al., 2000). In a study of clinic-referred 4- to 7-year-olds (Webster-Stratton, 1996) with ODD and/or CD, there was no sex difference in the age of onset of problem behaviors. Similarly, findings from the *DSM–IV* field trials indicate that the majority of clinic-referred, school-age girls had an age of onset of CD in early childhood (Lahey et al., 1998).

Prospective studies that have examined the onset of disruptive behavior in females are rare, but the few retrospective studies indicate the presence of sizable early onset and adolescent onset groups (Robins, 1986; Tolan & Thomas, 1995; Zoccolillo, 1993). Whether the early–late onset distinction is important for CD girls in terms of severity and persistence of CD symptoms remains to be tested. It is plausible that girls who develop CD symptoms in childhood differ from those who develop symptoms in adolescence (e.g., more covert and less overt disruptive behavior). However, there is no evidence that age of onset before and after 10 years (as now indicated in the *DSM–IV*) is what best distinguishes them. Girls and boys have different rates of physical maturation, and it is possible that what best distinguishes the two groups is their pubertal status especially in the presence of other risk factors.

Continuity of CD

Most studies show that the stability for disruptive behaviors tends to be as high or higher for females than males. For example, Tremblay and colleagues (1992) showed that aggression exhibited in early elementary school and later delinquency were equally highly correlated in both boys and girls (.76 and .79, respectively). Zoccolillo and colleagues (1992) found that the risk of CD females qualifying for later APD was the same as that for CD males. In a longitudinal study conducted by Robins (1986), referral to a clinic predicted later arrest better in girls than in boys (RIOC = 82.9 vs. 64.2, respectively; cited in Loeber & Stouthamer-Loeber, 1986). Stability of aggression on the Teacher Report Form in a community study conducted by Verhulst and Van Der Ende (1991) showed consistently higher stability coefficients for females than males (.51 vs. 25, respectively). Elliott (1994) reported that, despite a significant sex difference in the prevalence of serious violent offenders, the proportion of offenders continuing their careers into their 20s was the same for females and males. In contrast, Cairns and Cairns (1984) reported that prediction of boys' aggression was higher than for girls in unselected samples. Similarly, in early childhood, Fagot (1984) reported significant correlations between observed aggressive behavior in boys at 1- and 2-year follow-up, whereas stability of aggression in preschool girls was only found at the 1-year follow-up. In the majority of studies of school-age children, however, it appears that disruptive behavior in girls is at least as stable as that of boys.

Comorbidity

Robins (1986) concluded from her research that, "an increased rate of almost every disorder was found in women with a history of conduct problems" (p. 399), including ADHD, anxiety disorders, mood disorders, and substance use (see also Petersen et al., 1993; Zoccolillo, 1993). There are two reasons that it is important to investigate comorbid conditions. First, the emergence of comorbid conditions may indicate different levels of seriousness of disorder, with some comorbid conditions resulting in higher degrees of impairment than single conditions (e.g., Paternite, Loney, & Roberts, 1995). Second, by examining the pattern of development of symptoms of both internalizing and externalizing problems, information on etiology may be revealed.

In a previous review on the comorbidity of CD (Loeber & Keenan, 1994), two themes emerged. First, comorbid conditions in CD girls are relatively predictable. For example, given that adolescent girls, compared with boys, are more at risk for anxiety and depression, a high amount of overlap among such disorders and CD is expected. These results are consistent with Robins (1986), who reported that internalizing disorders were common in women who had CD (64%–73%) and occurred twice as frequently as they did in women without CD (see also review by Zoccolillo, 1992). Second, there appears to be a gender paradox for comorbid conditions, in that the gender with the lowest prevalence of a disorder appears more at risk to develop another relatively rare comorbid condition than the gender with the higher prevalence of a disorder. For example, a Finnish study of adults convicted of homicide (Eronen, Hakola, & Tiihonen, 1996) found that the risk for alcoholism and antisocial personality was three times higher for females than males (Odds Ratios = 37.7 vs. 10.7 and 53.8 vs. 11.7, respectively). Thus, gender and age may be critical parameters in the development of comorbid conditions with CD.

Summary From Literature Review

In terms of age of onset, CD in girls typically begins to emerge in the elementary school period. Based on the existing data, adolescent-onset CD does not appear to be more common in girls than boys. Once CD emerges, it seems quite stable in girls, especially aggressive behaviors. It remains unclear how comorbid conditions affect the development of CD in girls. The triad of CD, depression, and substance use may be more common in girls. There appears to be a gender paradox for comorbid conditions, in that the gender with the lowest prevalence of a disorder appears more at risk to develop another, relatively rare comorbid condition than the gender with the higher prevalence of a disorder.

There are a number of significant questions that remain, each of which may greatly impact research on etiology and prevention. First, what is the prevalence of CD in girls and does it differ from what we know about CD in boys? If girls are indeed at lower risk for CD than boys, we need to explore the apparent protective effect of female gender against CD and how that may be related to the increased risk for depression among girls.

Second, what is the developmental course of CD for girls? Are there specific developmental periods during which girls are at higher risk for manifesting conduct problems; if so, do these developmental periods differ for boys? We propose that each developmental period confers different levels of risk for developing CD for girls and boys. With continued research, a risk profile for each sex at different developmental periods (e.g., toddlerhood, school entry, transition to high school) could be generated with the goal of generating developmentally salient prevention programs for girls and boys. Finally, how do comorbid conditions affect the trajectory of CD in girls? Does the presence of depression or anxiety exacerbate or ameliorate CD? The following section presents preliminary data that begin to address some of these questions.

FEMALE SIBLINGS IN THE PITTSBURGH YOUTH STUDY

There are few studies on the development of CD in girls. Most population-based studies have relatively low rates of CD symptoms in girls, and thus afford little opportunity to examine correlates and sex differences. The goal of this pilot study was to examine the frequency and severity of conduct problems in a sample of girls growing up in high-risk environments in a sample of convenience: The Pittsburgh Youth Study (PYS). The PYS is a longitudinal study of the development of antisocial behavior in a community-based sample of boys. There are three samples of school-age boys in the PYS. In the present study, female siblings from the youngest cohort of boys were included. Information about these female siblings was gathered at Wave L (about 7 years into the longitudinal study). The environments were considered high risk based on two criteria: Half of the brothers of the girls in the sample had been selected because they had engaged in more than one antisocial act, and the majority of families resided in low-income, inner-city neighborhoods. Thus, the sample provides an opportunity to examine rates of conduct problems and test hypotheses about correlates of problem behavior in a community of at-risk sample of school-age girls.

Methods

Of the 503 boys in the youngest cohort of the PYS, 152 (30%) had sisters living in the home. One sister was randomly selected from families with more than one sister. Approximately half of the sisters were younger than the boys, who were on average 13 years of age, with ages ranging from 10 to 17 years (mean = 13 years). Most sisters (84%) were identified as biologically related siblings. Mothers were interviewed about their daughters' current (i.e., in the past 6 months) and lifetime conduct behaviors. In addition, mothers were asked about their daughters' histories of school suspensions, arrests, and pregnancies. As part of the regular assessment of the PYS, a number of postulated risk factors were assessed across three domains:

sociodemographic (socioeconomic status [SES], neighborhood problems, and maternal education); family environment (parental stress and parental conflict); and family psychopathology (parental anxiety/depression and parental substance use).

Results

Rates of CD Symptoms.   Lifetime and current rates of CD symptoms are presented in Table 2.1. These rates are based on the initial oversampling of boys with problem behaviors, a majority of whom live in low-income environments, thus they do not reflect population rates. The most commonly reported behaviors were lying, fighting, truancy, and cruelty to others. Stealing and setting fires were relatively rare behaviors, and vandalizing did not occur.

To compare rates of girls' problem behaviors in the PYS samples to population estimates, maternal reports on girls' conduct problems from the MECA study (Lahey et al., 2000) were generated. Girls in the MECA study ranged in age from 9 to 17 years. The sampling strategy in the MECA study was designed to generate population estimates of behavior problems. Thus, it is a useful comparison to the girls in the PYS who, although nonreferred, are indirectly at risk given the higher rate of problem behaviors in their brothers.

The percentage of girls with zero, one to two, and three symptoms of the seven CD symptoms assessed in both studies were generated and compared

TABLE 2.1

Rate of Conduct Disorder Symptoms in Female Siblings ($N = 152$)

	Lifetime		Current	
Symptom	N	%	N	%
Lying	40	26.3	31	20.4
Fighting	36	23.7	30	19.7
Truancy	24	15.8	14	9.2
Cruelty to others	16	10.5	13	8.6
Stealing	8	5.3	2	1.3
Vandalism	0	0.0	0	0.0
Setting fires	6	3.9	4	2.6

across the two samples (MECA and PYS girls). The results, presented in
Fig. 2.1, demonstrate that slightly more than half of the PYS girls sample
had zero conduct symptoms, compared with almost 90% of the MECA
girls. Thirty-five percent of the PYS girls were reported to have one to two
symptoms, compared with 9.8% of the MECA girls. Finally, 11.8% of the
PYS girls had a lifetime report of three or more symptoms, compared with
less than 1% of the MECA girls.

Impairment. In the current study, impairment was measured via maternal report on three different behaviors: school suspension, arrests, and
pregnancy. Thirty-three percent of the girls in this sample ($n = 51$) had a history of school suspension, 7.2% had had at least one arrest, and 9.2% had
had at least one pregnancy. The total number of lifetime CD symptoms was
significantly associated with school suspension ($r = .39$, $p < .001$) and history of arrest ($r = .29$, $p < .001$), but not pregnancy ($r = .10$).

We also examined the relation between the number of CD symptoms and
the three measures of impairment (Fig. 2.2). With regard to suspension from
school, 19% of the girls with zero conduct symptoms had been suspended at
least once, compared with 37% of the girls with one symptom, 82% of the
girls with two symptoms, and 71% of the girls with three or more symptoms
(overall $\chi^2 = 29.7$, df = 3, $p < .0001$). In contrast, the largest increase in num-

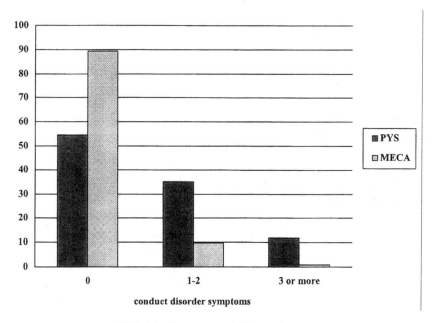

FIG. 2.1   Parent-reported CD symptoms.

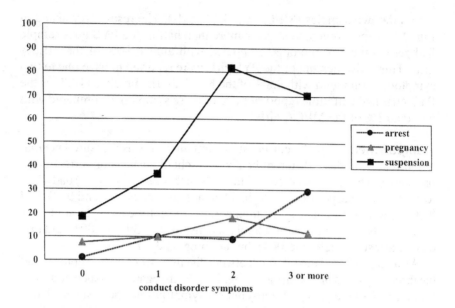

FIG. 2.2   Relation between CD symptoms and impairment.

ber of girls with a history of arrest was between two symptoms (9%) and three or more symptoms (29%) (overall $\chi^2 = 16.8$, df = 3, $p < .001$). There was a non-significant increase in rates of pregnancy among girls with one (10%) versus two (18%) symptoms of CD, but the rate of pregnancy in girls with zero (7.6%) and three (11.8%) symptoms was generally the same (overall $\chi^2 = 1.4$, df = 3, p = n.s.). The analysis on the association between CD symptoms and pregnancy was repeated using the 15- to 17-year-old sisters. The results remained nonsignificant.

Correlates of CD Symptoms.   Pearson correlation coefficients were computed between each hypothesized correlate and the continuous number of CD symptoms in girls. To compare correlates of CD problems in girls and boys, the 152 boys from the youngest sample who had sisters were included in this set of analyses. The boys' average age was 13.

Significant associations with girls' CD symptoms were found within each of the three domains. Low SES, low maternal education, high parental stress, high marital conflict, and parental anxiety/depression and substance use were all associated with conduct symptoms in girls (Table 2.2). To a large degree, similar correlates were identified for boys with a few noted exceptions. Neighborhood problems were significantly associated with CD symptoms in boys, but not in girls. Marital conflict was not a significant correlate of CD symptoms in boys. Fisher's r to z transformations were computed for each correlation that appeared to differ between girls and boys. Only the correlation between marital conflict and CD symptoms was significantly different for girls versus boys.

Discussion

In this sample of nonreferred girls whose brothers were oversampled for problem behaviors, caregivers reported high rates of CD symptoms. In fact, female siblings in the PYS study were 3 times more likely to have one to two symptoms of CD than girls in a community-based study, and they were 10 times more likely to have three or more symptoms of CD. The most common symptoms of CD in this sample were fighting, lying, and truancy—a pattern similar to boys. In addition to high rates of CD symptoms, care-

TABLE 2.2

**Correlates of Conduct Disorder Symptoms
in Girls and Boys (N = 152)**

Correlate	Girls' CD Symptoms	Boys' CD Symptoms
	(r)	(r)
Sociodemographic		
SES	−.21**	−.13
Neighborhood problems	.05	.18*
Maternal education	−.16†	−.08
Family environment		
Parental stress	.31***	.24**
Marital conflicta	.23*	−.13
Family psychopathology		
Parental anxiety or depression	.26**	.21**
Parental substance abuse	.19*	.29***

Note. By Pearson correlation or ANOVA: $\dagger p < .10$; $*p < .05$; $**p < .01$; $*** p < .001$.
aCorrelations are significantly different following Fisher's r to z transformation.

givers reported that girls with CD symptoms were significantly impaired. The total number of CD symptoms was significantly related to school suspensions and arrests. In contrast to other studies, early pregnancy was not associated with CD, suggesting that sexual behavior in this inner-city sample is not necessarily indicative of antisocial behavior. The data on impairment indicate that further exploration of the appropriate symptom threshold for the diagnosis of CD is warranted. In the present study of girls growing up in high-risk environments, school suspension—a measure of impairment with a relatively high base rate—differed from arrest with regard to association with differing numbers of CD symptoms.

Among the correlates measured, sociodemographic, family environment, and history of family psychopathology were all associated with CD symptoms in girls. All three domains also appear to be significant correlates for boys. There may be some important sex differences, however, in the mechanisms by which these domains affect the development of CD in girls and boys. For example, the results suggest that girls may be more affected by problems centering on family relations such as marital conflict. This is consistent with other data suggesting that girls are more sensitive to disruptions in their caregiving environment (Lee, Burkam, Zimiles, & Ladewski, 1994). Boys, in contrast, appear vulnerable to risk factors in the neighborhood environment. The results from this pilot study suggest that sex-specific models are needed and should not be constrained by stereotypical assumptions about the differential factors influencing girls' and boys' development. There was considerable overlap in the profiles of risk: Girls' behaviors were also associated with sociodemographic factors, and boys' behaviors were also associated with family environment factors. Future research requires prospective delineation of the biological, psychological, and social experiences of individual girls and boys, and assessments of how these experiences serve to increase or decrease their vulnerability to specific risk factors.

CURRENT PROGRAM OF RESEARCH

To advance the field and narrow the search for answers to the questions raised in this chapter, we formulated an integrated set of heuristic theoretical models of CD development in girls. From a theoretical point of view, we see the need for a model to be broader than most current theories. We conceptualize that some individual differences (particularly temperament and intelligence) emerge early in life—that temperament and behavior are modified by social interactions first with parents and siblings in the home and then later with peers in the school and community. Social interactions influence inter- and intrapersonal cognitions and self-regulation. To account for these diverse processes, our conceptualization expands on earlier theoretical formulations, including the development of temperament (Buss & Plomin, 1984; Thomas & Chess, 1977), social learning theory (Patterson, 1982), social control theory (Hirschi, 1969), and social cognition theory (Dodge, 1980; Garber, 1992), in the context of the development of risk and protective factors (Garmezy, 1991; Rutter, 1987)

This model is currently being applied in a major study aimed at identifying the developmental precursors, risk factors, and comorbid conditions of CD in girls. The aims of the study are to: (a) test models that include a combination of behavioral, cognitive, and emotional factors as developmental precursors to CD in girls; (b) elucidate risk and protective factors that influence both the development of CD by affecting the precursors and the continuity and severity of CD; and (c) identify other comorbid conditions that affect the course of CD and the development of comorbid CD and internalizing disorders.

Approximately 2,500 six- to eight-year-old girls living in inner-city Pittsburgh are interviewed on a yearly basis. In addition to the girls, their parents and teachers are interviewed. Although the study focuses on CD as a dependent measure, a wide range of conduct problems are assessed, including social and indirect aggression, status offenses, other covert behaviors (e.g., prank phone calls, mail fraud), and sociopathic characteristics (e.g., callousness). In addition to the precursors and risk factors typically studied in relation to CD in boys (e.g., oppositionality, exposure to violence), several potentially important factors are assessed that may have particular relevance for the development of CD in girls. These factors include conflict with mothers and siblings, perceptions of stressful family events, experiences of empathy and guilt, deficits in verbal skills, and early emotional dysregulation.

Another emphasis of the current study is to assess the possibility that comorbid CD and depression may be more common than the occurrence of CD alone. Thus, developmental precursors and risk factors for internalizing problems are also included so that pathways to CD and comorbid internalizing problems can be identified. Finally, because many of the girls in this study have been exposed to significant risk factors, there is an invaluable opportunity to identify individual and environmental factors that lead to resilience in young girls at risk for CD.

The study described previously can expand the knowledge base on CD in girls. Yet its utility can be dramatically increased if it occurs in the context of other investigations on the behavioral and emotional development of girls. The present chapter is designed to stimulate such investigations by highlighting the numerous gaps in our understanding of girls' development and the factors that influence it.

REFERENCES

American Psychiatric Association. (1994). Diagnostic and Statistical Manual of Mental Disorders (Vol. 4th edition). Washington, DC.

Bird, H. R., Gould, M. S., & Staghezza, B. (1993). Patterns of diagnostic comorbidity in a community sample of children aged 9 through 16 years. *Journal of the American Academy of Child and Adolescent Psychiatry, 32*, 361–368.

Breen, M. J., & Barkley, R. A. (1988). Child psychopathology and parenting stress in girls and boys having attention deficit disorder with hyperactivity. *Journal of Pediatric Psychology, 13*, 265–280.

Buss, A. H., & Plomin, R. (1984). *Temperament: Early developing personality traits.* Hillsdale, NJ: Lawrence Erlbaum Associates.

Bybee, J. (1998). The emergence of gender differences in guilt during adolescence. In J. Bybee (Ed.), *Guilt and children* (pp. 113–123). San Diego: Academic Press.

Cairns, R. B., & Cairns, B. D. (1984). Predicting aggressive patterns in girls and boys: A developmental study. *Aggressive Behavior, 10*, 227–242

Carlson, C. L., Tamm, L., & Gaub, M. (1997). Gender differences in children with ADHD, ODD, and co-occurring ADHD/ODD identified in a school population. *Journal of the American Academy of Child and Adolescent Psychiatry, 36*, 1706–1714.

Caspi, A., Henry, B., McGee, R. O., Moffitt, T. E., & Silva, P. A. (1995). Temperamental origins of child and adolescent behavior problems: From age three to age fifteen. *Child Development, 66*, 55–58.

Cohen, D., & Strayer, J. (1996). Empathy in conduct-disordered and comparison youth. *Developmental Psychology, 32*, 988–998.

Cohen, P., Cohen, J., Kasen, S., Velez, C. N., Hartmark, C., Johnson, J., Rojas, M., Brook, J., & Streuning, E. L. (1993). An epidemiological study of disorders in late childhood and adolescence: I. Age- and gender-specific prevalence. *Journal of Child Psychology and Psychiatry, 34*, 851–867.

Cole, P. M., & Zahn-Waxler, C. (1992). Emotional dysregulation in disruptive behavior disorders. In D. Cicchetti & S. L. Toth (Eds.), *Development perspectives on depression* (pp. 173–209). Rochester, NY: University of Rochester Press.

Costello, E. J., Angold, A., Burns, B. J., Stangl, D. K., Tweed, D. L., Erkanli, A., & Worthman, C. M. (1996). The Great Smoky Mountains Study of Youth: Goals, design, methods, and the prevalence of DSM–III–R disorders. *Archives of General Psychiatry, 53*, 1129–1136.

Crick, N. R. (1995). Relational aggression: The role of intent attributions, feelings of distress, and provocation type. *Development and Psychopathology, 7*, 313–322.

Dodge, K. A. (1980). Social cognition and children's aggressive behavior. *Child Development, 51*, 162–170.

Elliott, D. S. (1994). Serious violent offenders: Onset, developmental course, and termination. *Criminology, 32*, 1–21.

Eronen, M., Hakola, P., & Tiihonen, J. (1996). Mental disorder and homicidal behavior in Finland. *Archives of General Psychiatry, 53*, 497–501.

Fagot, B. I. (1984). The consequences of problem behavior in toddler children. *Journal of Abnormal Child Psychology, 12*, 383–396.

Faraone, S. V., Biederman, J., Keenan, K., & Tsuang, M. T. (1991). A family-genetic study of girls with DSM–III Attention Deficit Disorder. *American Journal of Psychiatry, 148*, 112–117.

Garber, J. (1992). Cognitive models of depression: A developmental perspective. *Psychological Inquiry, 3*, 325–340.

Garmezy, N. (1991). Resilience and vulnerability to address developmental outcomes associated with poverty. *American Behavioral Scientist, 34*, 416–430.

Guerin, D. W., Gottfried, A. W., & Thomas, C. W. (1997). Difficult temperament and behaviour problems: A longitudinal study from 1.5 to 12 years. *International Journal of Behavioral Development, 21*, 71–90.

Hartung, C., & Widiger, T. (1998). Gender differences in the diagnosis of mental disorders: Conclusions and controversies of the DSM–IV. *Psychological Bulletin, 123*, 260–278.

Hirschi, T. (1969). *Causes of delinquency*. Berkeley: University of California Press.

Keenan, K., & Shaw, D. S. (1997). Developmental and social influences on young girls' early problem behavior. *Psychological Bulletin, 121*, 95–113.

Lahey, B. B., Goodman, S. H., Canino, G., Bird, H., Schwab-Stone, M., Waldman, I. D., Rathouz, P. J., Miller, T. L., Dennis, K. D., & Jensen, P. S. (2000). Age and gender differences in oppositional behavior and conduct problems: A cross-sectional household study of middle childhood and adolescence. *Journal of Abnormal Psychology, 109*(3), 488–503.

Lahey, B. B., Loeber, R., Quay, H. C., Appelgate, B., Shaffer, D., Waldman, I., Hart, E. L., McBurnett, K., Frick, P. J., Jensen, P. S., Dulcan, M. K., Canino, G., & Bird, H. R. (1998). Validity of DSM–IV subtypes of conduct disorder based on age of onset. *Journal of the American Academy of Child and Adolescent Psychiatry, 37*(4), 435–442.

Lahey, B. B., McBurnett, K., & Loeber, R. (2000). Are attention-deficit/hyperactivity disorder and oppositional defiant disorder developmental precursors to conduct disorder? In M. Lewis & A. Sameroff (Eds.), *Handbook of developmental psychopathology* (2nd ed., pp. 431–445). New York: Plenum.

Lahey, B. B., Schwab-Stone, M., Goodman, S., Rathouz, P., Miller, T.L., Canino, G., Bird, H., & Jensen, P. (2000). Age and gender differences in oppositional behavior and conduct problems: A cross-sectional household study of middle childhood and adolescence. *Journal of Abnormal Psychology, 109*, 488–503.

Lee, V. E., Burkam, D. T., Zimiles, H., & Ladewski, B. (1994). Family-structure and its effect on behavioral and emotional problems in young adolescents. *Journal of Research on Adolescents, 4*, 405–437.

Loeber, R., Green, S. M., Keenan, K., & Lahey, B. B. (1995). Which boys will fare worse? Early predictors of the onset of conduct disorder in a six-year longitudinal study. *Journal of the American Academy of Child and Adolescent Psychiatry, 34*, 499–509.

Loeber, R., & Keenan, K. (1994). Interaction between conduct disorder and its comorbid conditions: Effects of age and gender. *Clinical Psychology Review, 14*, 497–523.

Loeber, R., & Stouthamer-Loeber, M. (1986). Family factors as correlates and predictors of juvenile conduct problems and delinquency. In M. Tonry & N. Morris (Eds.), *Crime and justice* (Vol. 7, pp. 29–149). Chicago: University of Chicago Press.

Moffitt, T. E. (1993). Adolescence-limited and life-cycle-persistent antisocial behavior: A developmental taxonomy. *Psychology Review, 100*, 674–701.

Ogle, R. S., Maier-Katkin, D., & Bernard, T. J. (1995). A theory of homicidal behavior among women. *Criminology, 33*, 173–193.

Paternite, C. E., Loney, J., & Roberts, M. A. (1995). External validation of oppositional defiant disorder and attention deficit disorder with hyperactivity. *Journal of Abnormal Child Psychology, 25*, 453–471.

Patterson, G. R. (1982). *A social learning approach: Vol. 3. Coercive family process*. Eugene, OR: Castalia.

Petersen, A. C., Compas, B. E., Brooks-Gunn, J., Stemmler, M., Ey, E., & Grant, K. E. (1993). Depression in adolescence. *American Psychologist, 48*, 155–168.

Prior, M., Smart, D., Sanson, A., & Oberklaid, F. (1993). Sex differences in psychological adjustment from infancy to 8 years. *Journal of the American Academy of Child and Adolescent Psychiatry, 32*, 291–304.

Robins, L. N. (1986). The consequences of Conduct Disorder in girls. In D. Olweus, J. Black, & M. Radke-Yarrow (Eds.), *Development of antisocial and prosocial behavior: Research, theories, and issues* (pp. 385–414). New York: Academic Press.

Rutter, M. (1987). Psychosocial resilience and protective mechanisms. *American Journal of Orthopsychiatry, 57*, 316–331.

Seidman, L. J., Biederman, J., Faraone, S. V., Weber, W., Mennin, D., & Jones, J. (1996). A pilot study of neuropsychological function in girls with ADHD. *Journal of the American Academy of Child and Adolescent Psychiatry, 36*, 366–373.

Silverthorn, P., & Frick, P. J. (1999). Developmental pathways to antisocial behavior: The delayed-onset pathway in girls. *Development and Psychopathology, 11*, 101–126.

Thomas, A., & Chess, S. (1977). *Temperament and development.* New York: Brunner/Mazel.

Tolan, P. H., & Thomas, P. (1995). The implications of age of onset for delinquency risk: II. Longitudinal data. *Journal of Abnormal Child Psychology, 23*, 157–181.

Tremblay, R. E., Masse, B., Perron, D., Le Blanc, M., Schwartzman, A. E., & Ledingham, J. E. (1992). Early disruptive behavior, poor school achievement, delinquent behavior. *Journal of Consulting and Clinical Psychology, 60*, 64–72.

Verhulst, F. C., & Van Der Ende, J. (1991). Four-year follow-up of teacher-reported problem behaviours. *Psychological Medicine, 21*, 965–977.

Webster-Stratton, C. (1996). Early-onset conduct problems: Does gender make a difference? *Journal of Consulting and Clinical Psychology, 64*, 540–551.

Zahn-Waxler, C. (1993). Warriors and worriers: Gender and psychopathology. *Development and Psychopathology, 5*, 79–89.

Zahn-Waxler, C., Cole, P. M., & Barrett, K. C. (1991). Guilt and empathy: Sex differences and implications for the development of depression. In J. Garber & K. A. Dodge (Eds.), *The development of emotion regulation and dysregulation* (pp. 243–272). New York: Cambridge University Press.

Zoccolillo, M. (1992). Co-occurrence of Conduct Disorder and its adult outcomes with depressive and anxiety disorders—A review. *Journal of the American Academy of Child and Adolescent Psychiatry, 31*, 547–556.

Zoccolillo, M. (1993). Gender and the development of conduct disorder. *Development and Psychopathology, 5*, 65–78.

Zoccolillo, M., Pickles, A., Quinton, D., & Rutter, M. (1992). The outcome of Conduct Disorder: Implications for defining adult personality disorder and Conduct Disorder. *Psychological Medicine, 22*, 1–16.

Zoccolillo, M., Tremblay, R., & Vitaro, F. (1996). DSM–III–R and DSM–III criteria for conduct disorder in preadolescent girls: Specific but insensitive. *Journal of the American Academy of Child and Adolescent Psychiatry, 35*, 461–470.

ACKNOWLEDGMENTS

Support for the work presented in this chapter comes from grants number 1 K01 MH01484-01A1 to Dr. Keenan and 5 R01 MH56630-01A1 to Dr. Loeber from the National Institute of Mental Health, and grant number 1 R01 DA12237-01A1 from the National Institute of Drug Abuse to Dr. Loeber.

Commentary:
A Relationship Focus
on Girls' Aggressiveness
and Conduct Disorder

Kate McKnight
Duke University

Martha Putallaz
Duke University

Tremblay (1991) charged scientists and clinicians with a novel task. Noting the potential for conduct-disordered girls to socialize a new generation of deviance, he urged researchers to explore the development and maintenance of CD exclusively in females. The authors of the preceding two chapters heeded this call. In an attempt to provide insight into and thus prevent the perpetuation of social maladjustment, they created a thoughtful framework of aggression and CD that addresses the experiences, pressures, and concerns specific to development in girls. In different, but complementary, ways their models use both theoretical and contextual cues to explain the emergence and maintenance of externalizing behaviors in young females.

Without completely abandoning the framework used to understand CD in boys, both sets of authors have augmented our understanding of girls' externalizing behaviors by integrating socialization experiences that may be unique to females. Noting the significance of intimacy and relationships in girls' lives, both chapters attend extensively to the social context in which conduct behaviors are learned and reinforced—a necessity for understanding the behavior of girls according to Maccoby (1998).

For example, Pepler and Craig (chap. 1) argued that siblings may serve as a covert forum from which to prepare and practice deviant strategies. Within this context, girls run little risk of being chastised for aggressive techniques that are atypical for their gender. Keenan, Stouthamer-Loeber, and Loeber (chap. 2) provided empirical evidence to support this claim. Specifically, sisters commonly model fighting, lying, and truant behaviors from their brothers. Keenan et al. claimed that strained maternal relationships and marital conflict are particularly salient for young females. Girls may not only model their parents' maladaptive interaction styles, but may also show increased inclinations to internalize negative interpersonal factors within the familial context.

In contrast, some relationship experiences may provide a remedial function. Pepler and Craig claimed that prosocial husbands may negate the risk of early aggressive tendencies, potentially breaking the cycle of dysfunctional parenting and social maladjustment in future generations. These data suggest that the maintenance of CD is interactive, susceptible to both positive and negative social influences. As such, intervention efforts may be targeted at a variety of interpersonal scenarios and developmental stages.

The conclusions from both chapters are summarized in Fig. 2.3. The top segment of the figure illustrates the risk factors contributing to aggressiveness and CD in girls throughout the life span. The bottom segment illustrates the protective factors that likely mitigate or reduce the likelihood of aggressiveness and CD in girls. In keeping with the prior discussion, a striking feature of this figure is the prominent role relationship variables play among the risk and protective factors. Type of parenting experienced, aggressive siblings, parental discord, rejection by peers, association with aggressive peers, close friendships, and choice of marital partner all illustrate the importance of relationships for both the continuity and discontinuity of girls' aggressiveness and CD. Even apparent nonrelationship variables hold important relationship implications. Pepler and Craig pointed out that timing of pubertal development carries risk: Early maturing girls are more likely to interact and develop relationships with older aggressive boys and thus develop similar behavior patterns. Similarly, Keenan et al. suggested that girls with ADHD are more likely to develop learning problems, thus eliciting negative responses from caregivers and teachers who hold higher academic expectations for girls than boys. Given that the socialization of girls involves a strong relationship focus (Maccoby, 1998), it should come as no surprise that girls' relationships figure prominently in the theoretical conceptualization regarding the prediction and prevention of their aggressive and conduct-disordered behavior.

Although both chapters attest to the importance of relationships in girls' lives, the broader social context should be considered as well. When devel-

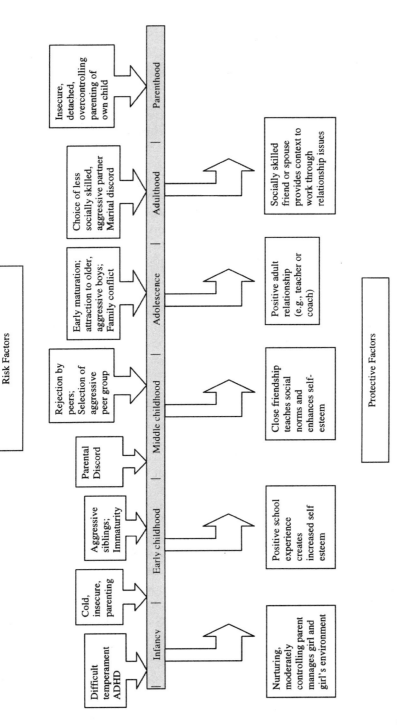

Risk Factors

| Infancy | Early childhood | Middle childhood | Adolescence | Adulthood | Parenthood |

Difficult temperament ADHD

Cold, insecure, parenting

Aggressive siblings; Immaturity

Parental Discord

Rejection by peers; Selection of aggressive peer group

Early maturation; attraction to older, aggressive boys; Family conflict

Choice of less socially skilled, aggressive partner Marital discord

Insecure, detached, overcontrolling parenting of own child

Nurturing, moderately controlling parent manages girl and girl's environment

Positive school experience creates increased self esteem

Close friendship teaches social norms and enhances self-esteem

Positive adult relationship (e.g., teacher or coach)

Socially skilled friend or spouse provides context to work through relationship issues

Protective Factors

FIG. 2.3.   Continuity of Aggressiveness in Girls

49

oping a model of aggressiveness and CD, it is beneficial to consider the motivation children may have for exhibiting certain externalizing behaviors. Envision the child who is continuously bombarded with messages of discrimination, hollow promises, and vague expectations. She witnesses daily violence, yet sees little opportunity for change within her high-risk community. It is quite possible that the functional role of deviant behavior varies according to socioeconomic and ethnic backgrounds. Indeed it appears that aggression may be more normative among African-American girls whose families are less likely to engage in sex-specific socialization practices with their children than are Euro-American families (e.g., Peters, 1988).

Clinicians may gain new perspectives into the etiology of CD by considering how such behaviors may be adaptive for children of specific social environments. Perhaps externalizing behaviors establish dominance and social status, increase self-esteem, or generate positive attention and regard from peers for some girls under certain circumstances. Certainly as gang membership and violence among female youth increases, it is necessary to decipher the motivation behind such loyalty. Perhaps her dedication extends no further than fear of her own personal safety. In contrast, motivation for deviant behavior may not exist as a tangible commodity. Certain children may respond to larger messages from society, deeming them an unimportant component of the world in which they live. Aggressive behavior may help establish a feeling of worth within a society in which they would otherwise be ignored. Once we find out the function of a child's deviance, preventive efforts may be directed at those needs.

To answer questions of motivation, researchers might consider the benefits of self-report measures with open-ended interviews. Children and adolescents from all different socioeconomic and ethnic backgrounds deserve an attentive ear. It may be naive to assume that what we know about the importance of intimacy and relationships extends to all females in diverse populations. The framework and models that we use to explain behavior should be guided, in part, by the girls' own words.

Keeping in mind the themes of context and function, it is notable that both chapters draw attention to relational aggression (also referred to as indirect aggression, social aggression, and social manipulation) within the context of CD in females. For girls, middle childhood marks a developmental period in which the social network tends to grow. Both chapters argue that the widening social sphere provides the context for greater social risks. More specifically, the group dynamic provides a forum for social manipulation that may lead to increased isolation and rejection for some girls. Although there is little doubt that such behaviors hurt children, it is not clear how such behaviors fit into the rubric of CD (Paquette & Underwood, 1999).

Perhaps the most relevant question is one of function. How is relational aggression related to psychopathology? Should we conceptualize social manipulation as entirely pathological or does this behavior serve some normative purpose in girls' development? Gottman and Mettetal (1986) argued that negative evaluation gossip serves necessary developmental functions during middle childhood. Through negative gossip, girls learn the social norms governing their peer group and solidify their acceptance within the group. By critiquing a peer's behavior without open protest from the group, the aggressor may experience feelings of inclusion and trust. Vulnerability is reduced, and a window for self-disclosure is opened. Indeed Gottman and Mettetal reported that one avenue for self-disclosure for girls during this middle childhood period involved engagement in negative evaluation gossip. Hence, negative evaluation gossip could be constructed as a bid for emotional intimacy.

Relational aggression may be derived from a developmentally normative function, but at a certain point it may turn more harmful than exploratory. Should extreme social manipulation exist at the mild end of a deviant continuum? Perhaps high levels of relational aggression in middle childhood should be considered a risk factor for extreme externalizing behaviors in adolescence and young adulthood.

A contrasting conceptualization is that relational aggression may serve a normative and socially adaptive function. Relational and physical aggression may evolve from specific socioemotional needs that generate dichotomous behavioral outcomes. For example, in a large-scale study of fourth-grade girls, relational aggression was found to demonstrate a significantly weaker relationship with maladjustment and behavioral problems than overt aggression. Further, relational aggression was less strongly associated with social skill deficits and adjustment problems than was overt aggression (Rhule, Putallaz, Grimes, Kupersmidt, & McKnight, 2001). Interestingly, relational aggression was actually significantly positively related to reports of status and socially effective behaviors. Thus, successful relational manipulation may require a socially savvy and cunning mind. Perhaps this subtype is worthy of further scrutiny by those researchers investigating risk for future deviance and antisocial behavior.

As both chapters suggest, longitudinal studies are needed to tease out the origins and trajectories of girls' aggressiveness and CD. Pepler and Craig underscored the need to better understand the cumulative effects of risk factors for the developmental trajectory of aggression in girls as well as the timing and relative importance of protective factors for the prediction of discontinuity. Keenan et al. accepted this challenge and developed a study that aims to delineate the developmental origins, risk factors, and comorbid conditions related to girls' externalizing patterns. By including measures that assess items like social aggression and quality of maternal relationship, they have taken great strides in trying to unveil the subtleties of normative and pathological development in females.

By complementing the findings of insightful researchers with girls' own perceptions of their social experiences, this inquiry may proceed rapidly. As Keenan et al. proposed, CD may encompass both externalizing and internalizing symptoms in girls. It is essential that we understand the functional role of deviant and aggressive behaviors before we implement preventive strategies that may aggravate related symptoms of depression and anxiety. By concentrating on context and explicitly asking about function, we may eventually empower women to enhance future relationships and provide a healthy model for a whole new generation of girls and boys.

REFERENCES

Gottman, J. M., & Mettetal, G. (1986). Speculations about social and affective development: Friendship and acquaintanceship through adolescence. In J. M. Gottman & J. G. Parker (Eds.), *Conversations of friends: Speculations on affective development.* New York: Cambridge University Press.

Maccoby, E. E. (1998). *The two sexes: Growing up apart, coming together.* Cambridge, MA: Harvard University Press

Paquette, J. & Underwood, M. (1999). Gender differences in young adolescents' experiences of peer victimization: Social and physical aggression. *Merrill-Palmer Quarterly, 45,* 242–266.

Peters, M. F. (1988). Socialization within African-American families. In H. P. McAdoo (Ed.), *Black families,* 2nd edition. Newbury Park, CA: Sage.

Rhule, D., Putallaz, M., Grimes, C. L., Kupersmidt, J., & McKnight, K. (June 2001). *Overt and relational aggression: Victims, aggressors and gender.* Paper presented at the annual meeting of the American Psychological Society, Toronto, Ontario.

Tremblay, R. E. (1991). Aggression, prosocial behavior, and gender: Three magic words but no magic wand. In D. J. Pepler & K. H. Rubin (Eds.), The development and treatment of childhood aggression (pp. 71–78). Hillsdale, NJ: Lawrence Erlbaum Associates.

Part II

GIRLS' PHYSICAL AGGRESSION

3

Gender Differences in the Prevalence of Physically Aggressive Behaviors in the Canadian Population of 2- and 3-Year-Old Children

Raymond H. Baillargeon
Richard E. Tremblay
Université de Montréal

J. Douglas Willms
University of New Brunswick

Gender differences in the prevalence of behavior problems are among the most basic epidemiological issues that can be investigated. These differences can be used to better understand the origins of childhood behavior problems, their timing and sequence, their continuity and discontinuity throughout the life span, and their etiology (Rutter, 1988). Unfortunately, most of our knowledge on gender differences in the prevalence of behavior problems in children is based on studies of samples drawn almost exclusively from clinics or mental health facilities and nonrepresentative samples of the population (for reviews, see Al-Issa, 1982; Eme, 1979, 1984; Gove, 1979; Gove & Herb, 1974; Maccoby & Jacklin, 1974, 1980; Tieger, 1980; Whiting & Edwards, 1973). Hence, little is known about potentially important shifts in gender ratios during childhood.

There have been several epidemiological studies of disruptive behavior disorders in school-age children (for a recent review, see Lahey, Miller, Gordon, & Riley, 1999). In comparison, only a few epidemiological studies have examined behavior problems in children less than 4 years of age (Achenbach, Edelbrock, & Howell, 1987; Cederblad, 1968; Crowther, Bond, & Rolf, 1981; Cullen & Boundy, 1966; Earls, 1980a, 1980b, 1982; Jenkins, Bax, & Hart, 1980; Koot & Verhulst, 1991; Larson, Pless, & Miettinen, 1988; Luk, Leung, Bacon-Shone, & Lieh-Mak, 1991; Macfarlane, Allen, & Honzik, 1954; McGee, Partridge, Williams, & Silva, 1991; Richman, Stevenson, & Graham, 1975, 1982; Sanson, Prior, Smart, & Oberklaid, 1993; Tremblay et al., 1996). Table 3.1 presents an overview of epidemiological studies of physically aggressive behaviors in 2- and 3-year-old children. Two studies were excluded because they used rather broad age groupings lumping together preschool- with school-age children (Cederblad, 1968; Cullen & Boundy, 1966) and another two studies because they did not report statistical tests of gender differences (Earls, 1980b; Tremblay et al., 1996). Other studies have relied on clinical or nonrepresentative samples of the general population (e.g., Anderson, 1983; Bates, Maslin, & Frankel, 1985; Beller & Neubauer, 1963; Campbell & Breaux, 1983; Cornely & Bromet, 1986; Keenan & Shaw, 1994; Long, 1941; Newth & Corbett, 1993; Stallard, 1993), the results of which are subject to well-known biases that make it impossible to generalize to the general population and were thus not reviewed in this chapter.

Epidemiological studies of behavior problems in 2- and 3-year-old children that report on gender differences in the prevalence of physically aggressive behaviors have provided inconsistent findings. Several epidemiological studies did not find gender differences in the prevalence of physically aggressive behaviors (Achenbach et al., 1987; Crowther et al., 1981; Earls, 1980a; Larson et al., 1988; Macfarlane et al., 1954; Richman et al., 1982). For example, Richman et al. (1982) found that 5% and 5.3% of 3-year-old girls and boys, respectively, living in a London Borough were reported by one of their parents, usually the mother, as having frequent and/or severe temper tantrums including kicking. In contrast, other epidemiological studies have found gender differences in the prevalence of physically aggressive behaviors (Luk et al., 1991; Koot & Verhulst, 1991; Sanson et al., 1993). For example, Luk et al. (1991) found that 6% of 3-year-old boys attending preschool facilities in Hong Kong were reported by their preschool teachers as having frequent—at least daily—unprovoked fighting, hitting, biting, or kicking. In comparison, only 1% of 3-year-old girls were reported to manifest these behaviors.

One of the factors that may account for these discrepant results is how *physical aggression* is defined (Tremblay, 2000). Many epidemiological

TABLE 3.1

Overview of Epidemiological Studies of Physically Aggressive Behaviors in Preschool-Age Children

Year	Age (years)	N (girls/N)	Instrument	Informant	Sample	Definition
					Unnamed Study (Achenbach, Edelbrock, & Howell, 1987)[a]	
—	2–3	(140/273)	CBCL/2–3	Mother or father	218 randomly selected clusters comprising 30 households each in 34 residential census tracts of eight communities in the Worcester, Massachusetts, metropolitan area	Total score on the aggressive syndrome scale
					Vermont Child Development Project (Crowther, Bond, & Rolf, 1981)[a]	
January 1974–February 1976	2 3	(11/25) (53/106)	VBC	Day-care teacher	All preschool-age children attending licensed day-care centers in Vermont's most populated county	Frequent struggles or fights with another child or parent (i.e., almost all the time every day to several times a day)
					Martha's Vineyard Child Health Survey (Earls, 1980a)[a]	
1977–1978	3	(47/100)	Semistructured interview with the BSQ	Mother	All children born between June 1974 and July 1975 living in a rural community on an island in the northeastern United States	Frequent tantrums—shouting, screaming, banging, and kicking (i.e., three a day or more or lasting more than 15 minutes)

(continued on next page)

TABLE 3.1 (continued)

Year	Age (years)	N (girls/N)	Sample	Instrument	Informant	Definition
			Unnamed Study (Koot & Verhulst, 1991)[b]			
1974– December 1979	2–2½ 2½–3 3–3½ 3½–4	(52/98) (52/106) (51/106) (51/101)	Random sample of children born between October 15, 1985 and October 14, 1987 drawn from the Zuid-Holland inoculation register and from the Rotterdam municipal health service register	CBCL/2–3	Mother and/ or father	Fights, hits, or attacks people (i.e., sometimes or often)
			Unnamed Study (Larson, Pless, & Miettinen, 1988)[a]			
1986	3	(—/756)	All children born in 1983 to women residing in a designated community health district of Montréal	Mailed CBCL/2–3	Mother or father	T score of 70 or above (i.e., > 90th percentile) on the combined aggressiveness and destructive syndrome
			Unnamed Study (Luk, Leung, Bacon-Shone, & Lieh-Mak, 1991)[b]			
November 1986– July 1987	3	(423/851)	Stratified proportional sampling of preschool facilities for Chinese children in Hong Kong	PBCL	Teacher or child-care worker	Frequent unprovoked fighting, hitting, biting, or kicking (i.e., at least daily)

University of California Control Study (Macfarlane, Allen, & Honzik, 1954)[a]

Date	Age	(n/N)	Measure	Informant	Behavior	Sample
October 1929–March 1931	3 3½	(49/98) (47/88)	Behavior inventory	Mother	Frequent and/or severe temper tantrums—biting, kicking, striking, throwing things, destruction of property, banging head	Representative sample of the Berkeley Survey, which in turn includes every third child born in Berkeley between January 1, 1928 and June 30, 1929

Waltham Forest Study (Richman, Stevenson, & Graham, 1982)[a]

| 1969–1970 | 3 | (363/705) | Semistructured interview with the BSQ | Mother or father | Frequent tantrums—shouting, screaming, banging, and kicking (i.e., three a day or more or lasting more than 15 minutes) | One in four random sample drawn from the Waltham Forest Family Register, which consists of families living in this outer London Borough with a child born after March 1969 |

Australian Temperament Project (Sanson, Prior, Smart, & Oberklaid, 1993)[b]

| 1983–1990 | 2–3 | (—/300) | AQ | Mother | Aggressive and competitive total score | Subsample of 300 families (of children living in the Melbourne metropolitan or outer metropolitan area) of a representative sample of the infant population of the entire state of Victoria |

Note. AQ (Aggression Questionnaire; Arnold, 1988); BSQ (Behaviour Screening Questionnaire; Richman & Graham, 1971); VBC (Vermont Behavior Checklist; Rolf & Hasazi, 1977); CBCL 2/3 (Childhood Behavior Checklist 2–3; Achenbach, Edelbrock, & Howell, 1987); PBCL (Preschool Behaviour Checklist; McGuire & Richman, 1986); [a]No gender differences; [b]Gender differences.

studies have used individual behaviors that refer not only to physical aggression, but to other types of deviant behavior as well (see Table 3.1). It may be that girls are less likely than boys to manifest one, but not another type of deviant behavior. Of course the same problem of definition occurs in other studies where a sum of equally weighted heterogeneous individual behaviors is used to define deviance. In addition, among the few studies that considered individual behaviors that referred exclusively to physical aggression, only the one by Koot and Verhulst (1991) considered more than one such behavior. Most certainly different sources of variance are contributing to the observed prevalence in any individual behavior. It may be that gender differences are present for one, but not another source of variance. Using more than one individual behavior could increase our confidence that the findings apply to the source of variance that is common to all such behaviors. Unfortunately, Koot and Verhulst (1991) compared boys and girls by adding together two of the three response categories (i.e., *sometimes* and *often*). It may be that girls are just as likely as boys to occasionally manifest these behaviors, but they may be less likely than boys to do so frequently or vice versa. Hence, it is difficult to draw any definitive conclusion as to gender differences in the prevalence of physically aggressive behaviors in 2- and 3-year-old children based on the results of past epidemiological studies.

The objective of this report is to test whether 2- and 3-year-old girls in the Canadian population are less likely than boys to frequently and/or occasionally manifest each of three physically aggressive behaviors. The extent to which gender differences may or may not vary with age are also investigated.

METHOD

Sample

The National Longitudinal Survey of Children and Youth (NLSCY) is the first nationwide household survey on child health in Canada. The NLSCY was developed conjointly by Human Resources Development Canada and Statistics Canada. Its target population for the first data collection, in 1994 to 1995, consisted of the population of Canadian children newborn to 11 years of age who lived in private households. The children in each household were selected at random, up to a maximum of four children per household. Children living in institutions (i.e., hospitals, residential facilities where the child has lived for more than 6 months) and on Indian reserves were not targeted by the survey. Children living in the Yukon and Northwest Territories took part in a separate component of the NLSCY. The respondent households for the first collection cycle included 22,831 children. A sample of 963 and 1,000 two-year-old girls and boys, respectively, was surveyed. In addition, a sample of 928 and 1,018 three-year-old girls and boys, respectively, was surveyed.

Instrument

Three physically aggressive behaviors have been included in the NLSCY for 2- and 3-year-old children—namely: (a) Gets into many fights; (b) When another child accidentally hurts him or her (such as bumping into him or her), assumes that the other child meant to do it and reacts with anger and fighting; and (c) Kicks, bites, and hits other children. Each behavior was rated by the Person Most Knowledgeable (PMK) about the child, usually the mother, using a three-point Likert scale: (a) *never or not true*, (b) *sometimes or somewhat true*, and (c) *often or very true*. This information was collected in a face-to-face or telephone interview. Data were collected in November to December 1994 and February to March 1995. In the case of a nonresponse, the household was contacted again in June 1995. Of the 15,570 household selected to participate in the NLSCY, 13,439 responded (i.e., 86.3%).

Sampling Weight and Missing Value

In a clustered sample (i.e., not a simple random sample) such as the NLSCY, each child is assigned a weight that stands for the number of children in the population that he or she represents. We divided each weight by the mean of the weights for children of the same age and gender to get proper estimates of the variance of our estimates. Then for each behavior we eliminated cases with missing values. Note that only a small number of cases was eliminated for that reason, however (i.e., less than 6%). The distribution of children by age and gender is presented in Table 3.2. We used a conservative alpha level (i.e., .01) because our variance estimates are likely to be underestimates of the ones we would have obtained with a simple random sample.

Statistical Model and Goodness-of-Fit Evaluation

The possible effect of gender and age on the prevalence of a physically aggressive behavior can be investigated using logit models (Fienberg, 1980). The outcome of a logit analysis includes the estimate of the conditional probability of a randomly selected child in the Canadian population in 1994 to 1995 being rated in a particular response category given his or her gender and age.

The objective of this model is to reproduce the observed frequencies associated with the different response categories of a physically aggressive behavior. The extent to which this objective is realized can be assessed us-

TABLE 3.2

Distribution of Children by Age and Gender for the First Data Collection (1994–1995) of the National Longitudinal Survey of Children and Youth (NLSCY)

	Gets into many fights?
2-year-old	
Girl	942 (97.8)
Boy	959 (95.9)
3-year-old	
Girl	913 (98.4)
Boy	998 (98.1)
	Reacts with anger and fighting?
2-year-old	
Girl	927 (96.2)
Boy	941 (94.1)
3-year-old	
Girl	900 (96.9)
Boy	981 (96.4)
	Kicks, bites, and hits other children?
2-year-old	
Girl	940 (97.6)
Boy	963 (96.3)
3-year-old	
Girl	913 (98.4)
Boy	998 (98.0)

Note. Percentages of children without missing data appear in parentheses.

ing either the Pearson chi-square statistic, X^2, or the likelihood ratio chi-square statistic, L^2. Both the X^2 and the L^2 have a large sample χ^2 distribution. When the expected frequencies obtained under a particular model are close to the observed frequencies, the X^2 and/or L^2 value are small. In contrast, a large value of X^2 and/or L^2 is indicative of a poor fit of the model to the data. A standard by which to judge whether the X^2 and/or L^2 is large or small is given by the degrees of freedom. The degrees of freedom associated with a particular model can be determined by subtracting the number of independent parameters to be estimated from the number of nonredundant observed frequencies. In the same vein, two hierarchically related models—two models are hierarchically related if one includes all the parameters of the other plus some additional ones—can be compared using the L^2 because it can be partitioned exactly. This is done by subtracting the L^2 of a model based on the larger number of parameters from the model with a smaller number of parameters. The degrees of freedom associated with the resultant L^2 are given by subtracting the corresponding degrees of freedom. A large difference in L^2, compared with the change in the degrees of freedom, suggests that the added parameters of the less restricted model have real significance. In contrast, a drop in L^2 close to the change in the degrees of freedom suggests there is no significant improvement in fit when the less restricted model is chosen to fit the data. In addition, models can be compared using the Bayesian Information Criterion [BIC; $BIC = L^2 - (df)(\log n)$]. The BIC penalizes models with many rather than fewer parameters, and when alternative models are compared, the model with the lowest BIC value is preferred.

Maximum Likelihood Parameter Estimation

Maximum likelihood parameter estimates of the various logit models presented in this chapter were obtained using the expectation maximization (EM) algorithm from a computer program for the analysis of categorical data written by Jeroen K. Vermunt (September 18, 1997). This program is called lEM ("log-linear and event history analysis with missing data using the EM algorithm") and is distributed freely on the World Wide Web (*http://www.kub.nl/faculteiten/fsw/organisatie/departementen/mto/ software2.html*).

RESULTS

Table 3.3 presents the goodness-of-fit statistics for several logit models. First, we considered a logit model that includes both gender and age effects on the prevalence of the physically aggressive behavior. This model ade-

TABLE 3.3

Goodness-of-Fit Statistics for Several Logit Models

Model	Pearson chi-square (X^2)	Likelihood ratio chi-square (L^2)	Degrees of freedom	p^a	BIC
Gets into many fights					
[BA] [BG] [AG]	7.74	7.70	2	.02	−8.80
[BA] [AG]	29.96	31.79	4	.00	−1.20
[BG] [AG]	30.49	30.73	4	.00	−2.25
[B] [AG]	57.91	55.25	6	.00	5.77
Reacts with anger and fighting					
[BA] [BG] [AG]	1.73	1.73	2	.42	−14.73
[BA] [AG]	8.15	8.18	4	.09	−24.74
[BG] [AG]	50.30	50.47	4	.00	17.55
[B] [AG]	57.31	57.39	6	.00	8.02
Kicks, bites, and hits other children					
[BA] [BG] [AG]	1.99	2.01	2	.37	−14.49
[BA] [AG]	26.91	27.44	4	.00	−5.55
[BG] [AG]	22.62	22.88	4	.00	−10.11
[B] [AG]	46.01	47.45	6	.00	−2.03

Note. [BA] refers to the two-way interaction between age and the physically aggressive behavior; [BG] refers to the two-way interaction between gender and the physically aggressive behavior; [AG] refers to the two-way interaction between age and gender; [B] refers to a prevalence effect on the response categories of the physically aggressive behavior; BIC: Bayesian Information Criterion.; $^a p$ value associated to the likelihood ratio chi-square statistic.

quately fits the data, suggesting there is no three-way interaction among gender, age, and physically aggressive behavior (for each behavior, see first row in Table 3.3). Second, we considered a logit model that includes an age but not a gender effect on the prevalence of the behavior. This model does not fit the data except for the second behavior (for each behavior, see second row in Table 3.3). Moreover, for the second behavior, this model represents an increase of 6.45 in L^2 with a corresponding increase of two degrees of freedom from the previous model ($L^2 = 8.18 - 1.73 = 6.45$, df = 4 - 2 = 2, p = .04), suggesting that this model does not represent a significant decrement in fit over the previous model. Together these results suggest there is a significant gender effect on the prevalence of the first and third, but not the second physically aggressive behavior. Third, we considered a logit model that includes a gender but not an age effect on the prevalence of the behavior. This model does not fit the data, suggesting there is an age effect on the prevalence of all three physically aggressive behaviors (for each behavior, see third row in Table 3.3). Finally, we considered a logit model that includes neither a gender nor an age effect on the prevalence of the behavior. Not surprisingly, this model does not fit the data (for each behavior, see fourth row in Table 3.3). Hence, for the first and third physically aggressive behaviors the preferred logit model is one that includes both gender and age effects on the prevalence of the behavior. Note that the BIC associated with this model is the lowest (see Table 3.3). For the second physically aggressive behavior, however, the preferred model is one that includes an age but not a gender effect on the prevalence of the behavior. Note that the BIC is the lowest for this model (see Table 3.3).

**Prevalence of Physically Aggressive Behaviors
in the Canadian Population of 2- and 3-year-old Children**

Figures 3.1, 3.2 and 3.3 present the gender- and age-specific prevalence estimates for the first, second, and third physically aggressive behavior, respectively, under the preferred logit model. As expected, physically aggressive behaviors are quite common in the Canadian population of 2- and 3-year-old children. For instance, 33.1% and 37.7% of 2-year-old girls and boys, respectively, are estimated to occasionally kick, bite, and hit other children (see Fig. 3.3). In addition, a smaller, but substantial number of 2- and 3-year-old children in the Canadian population manifest these behaviors on a frequent basis. For instance, 2.4% and 4.8% of 2-year-old girls and boys, respectively, are estimated to often kick, bite, and hit other children (see Fig. 3.3).

**Gender Differences in the Prevalence of Physically
Aggressive Behaviors in the Canadian Population
of 2- and 3-Year-Old Children**

Figures 3.4, 3.5, and 3.6 show the odds describing gender and/or age effects on the prevalence of the first, second, and third physically aggressive be-

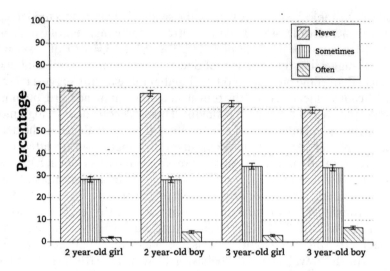

FIG. 3.1.   Gets into many fights: gender- and age-specific prevalence estimates (with 99% confidence intervals) in the Canadian population of 2- and 3-year-old children.

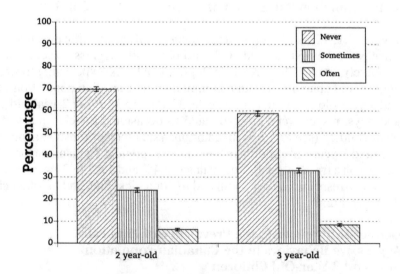

FIG. 3.2.   Reacts with anger and fighting: age-specific prevalence estimates (with 99% confidence intervals) in the Canadian population of 2- and 3-year-old children.

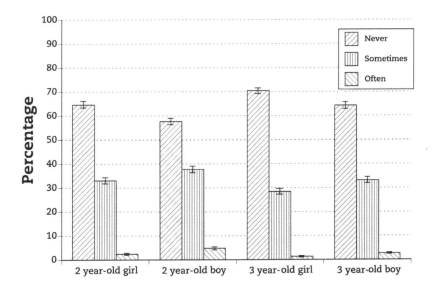

FIG. 3.3.   Kicks, bites, and hits other children: gender- and age-specific prevalence
estimates (with 99% confidence intervals) in the Canadian population
of 2- and 3-year-old children.

haviors, respectively, under the preferred logit model. First, consider the
odds of being rated in Category 2 (i.e., *sometimes or somewhat true*) rather
than in Category 1 (i.e., *never or not true*). For example, the odds of biting,
kicking, and hitting other children were .33 to .65; that is, (.33 / .65) = .51
for 2-year-old girls (see Fig. 3.6). Comparatively, the odds were (.38 / .58) =
.66 for 2-year-old boys (see Fig. 3.6). Hence, girls were estimated to be [1 /
(.51 / .66)] = 1.28 [99% Confidence Interval (CI) = 1.07–1.53] times less
likely than boys to kick, bite, and hit other children sometimes rather than
never. The corresponding odds ratio for the first physically aggressive behavior did not reach statistical significance. Second, consider the odds of
being rated in Category 3 (i.e., *often or very true*) rather than in Category 2.
Girls were estimated to be [1 / (.07 / .16)] = [1 / (.09 / .20)] = 2.27 (99% CI =
1.41–3.66) times less likely than boys to get into many fights often rather
than sometimes (see Fig. 3.4). In addition, girls were estimated to be [1 /
(.07 / .13)] = [1 / (.05 / .08)] = 1.77 (99% CI = 1.01–3.08) times less likely
than boys to kick, bite, and hit other children often rather than sometimes
(see Fig. 3.6).

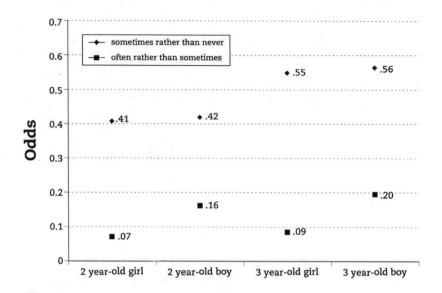

FIG. 3.4. Gets into many fights: odds describing gender and age effects on its prevalence in the Canadian population of 2- and 3-year-old children.

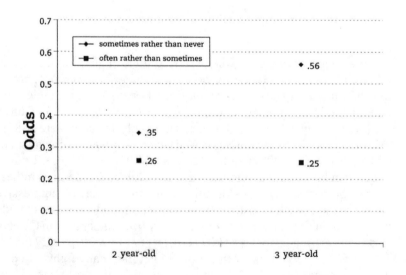

FIG. 3.5. Reacts with anger and fighting: odds describing the effect of age on its
prevalence in the Canadian population of 2- and 3-year-old children.

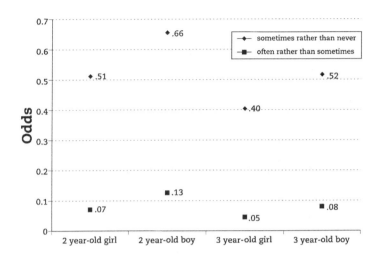

FIG. 3.6.   Kicks, bites, and hits other children: odds describing gender and age effects
on its prevalence in the Canadian population of 2- and 3-year-old children.

Age Differences in the Prevalence of Physically Aggressive Behaviors in the Canadian Population of 2- and 3-Year-Old Children

Three-year-old children were estimated to be $(.55 / .41) = (.56 / .42) = 1.35$ $(99\% \text{ CI} = 1.12–1.62)$ times more likely than 2-year-old children to get into many fights sometimes rather than never (see Fig. 3.4). In addition, 3-year-old children were estimated to be $(.56 / .35) = 1.62$ $(99\% \text{ CI} = 1.34–1.97)$ times more likely than 2-year-olds to react with anger and fighting sometimes rather than never (see Fig. 3.5). In contrast, 3-year-old children were estimated to be $[1 / (.40 / .51)] = [1 / (.52 / .66)] = 1.27$ $(99\% \text{ CI} = 1.06–1.52)$ times less likely than 2-year-olds to kick, bite, and hit other children sometimes rather than never. The odds of being rated in Category 3 rather than Category 2 did not differ between 2- and 3-year-old children.

DISCUSSION

Gender differences in behavior problems such as physical aggression are generally believed to emerge only after the age of 4 to 5 year (Campbell, 1990; Keenan & Shaw, 1997; Tieger, 1980). Implicit in this view is that gender differences are not present in younger children. However, the results from epidemiological studies of physically aggressive behaviors in 2- and 3-year-old children are inconsistent with some studies reporting gender differences. One likely explanation for these inconsistent findings is that the definition of *physical aggression* varied substantially across studies. In fact only a few studies considered individual behaviors that referred exclusively to physical aggression. Among those who did, only one study by Koot and Verlhust (1991) considered more than one such behavior. Unfortunately, it is impossible to say whether the gender differences reported in this study reflect frequent or occasional behavior or both. The aim of the present study was to test whether 2- and/or 3-year-old girls in the Canadian population are less likely than boys to manifest either occasionally, on a frequent basis, or both each of three physically aggressive behaviors.

We found gender differences in the prevalence of two of the three physically aggressive behaviors—fights and kicks, bites, and hits other children—with girls being less likely than boys to manifest these behaviors on a frequent basis. It may be that gender differences in the prevalence of physically aggressive behaviors emerge even before children reach their second birthday, with the genetic and environmental factors responsible for these differences being active early on in the child's life. One factor that is generally believed to cause such differences is a differential in the socialization process. These results are consistent with studies that show that, very early on in the life of the child, socializing agents including parents, caregivers and peers may discourage nontraditional sex-type behaviors like aggression in girls (Fagot, 1984; Fagot & Hagen, 1985; Smetana, 1989). Of course an alternative explanation is that gender differences in physically aggressive behaviors are present from infancy rather than emerging sometimes before the age of 2. Tremblay et al. (1999) found that 37.8% of 17-month-old boys with siblings living in the main urban areas of the province of Québec in 1996 were reported by the PMK, usually the mother, as kicking on a frequent or occasional basis. In comparison, only 25.1% of 17-month-old girls with siblings were reported to manifest this behavior. However, they did not find statistically significant gender differences on any of the other 10 physically aggressive behaviors they considered for 17-month-old children with siblings. According to Gualtieri and Hicks (1985), girls are less vulnerable to negative prenatal, perinatal, and postnatal environmental conditions and mild genetic anomalies; therefore, they are less likely to present neuro-developmental disorders because of their faster development and reduced stress reactivity.

We found no gender differences for one of the three physically aggressive behaviors (i.e., reacts with anger and fighting), however. It may be that this physically aggressive behavior represents a different type of physical aggression—reactive–defensive—than the other two behaviors with girls and boys manifesting similar levels of physical aggression on the reactive–defensive, but not the proactive–offensive type of physically aggressive behaviors. An alternative explanation is that the other two physically aggressive behaviors are biased against girls. For instance, it may be that girls may be less likely to manifest these behaviors not because they are less physically aggressive than boys, but because they are less active than boys (Tieger, 1980). In their review of gender differences in motor activity, Eaton and Enns (1986) found that during childhood boys were generally more active than girls. If so the proactive–offensive would be more susceptible than the reactive–defensive type of physically aggressive behaviors to this kind of mediated effect. Of course other factors could mediate gender differences in physically aggressive behaviors and possibly have the opposite effect (i.e., bias reactive–defensive, but not the proactive–offensive type of physically aggressive behaviors). Unfortunately, these extraneous sources of variance cannot be easily controlled for when considering gender differences on individual behaviors (Thissen, Steinberg, & Gerrard, 1986).

Future research on gender differences in physical aggression needs to distinguish physical aggression—aggression that causes bodily harms—from other socially undesirable behaviors such as disobedience and opposition, as well as between different types of physical aggression (e.g., direct vs. indirect, offensive vs. defensive). In adopting a life-course perspective, researchers planning studies of gender differences in physical aggression should pay special attention to the first 2 years of life, when most children have already manifested physically aggressive behaviors (Tremblay et al., 1999). Researchers studying gender differences in physical aggression face the difficult challenge of identifying and possibly controlling for factors that can mediate gender differences in physical aggression.

REFERENCES

Achenbach, T. M., Edelbrock, C., & Howell, C. T. (1987). Empirically based assessment of the behavioral/emotional problems of 2- and 3-year-old children. *Journal of Abnormal Child Psychology, 15*(4), 629–650.

Al-Issa, I. (1982). Gender and child psychopathology. In I. Al-Issa (Ed.), *Gender and psychopathology* (pp. 53–81). New York: Academic Press.

Anderson, D. R. (1983). Prevalence of behavioral and emotional disturbance and specific problem types in a sample of disadvantaged preschool-aged children. *Journal of Clinical Child Psychology, 12*, 130–136.

Arnold, G. (1988). Familial and temperamental factors in the development of aggression in four year olds. Unpublished master's thesis, La Trobe University.

Bates, J. E., Maslin, C. A., & Frankel, K. A. (1985). Attachment security, mother–child interaction, and temperament as predictors of behavior-problem ratings at age three years. In I. Bretherton & E. Waters (Eds.), *Growing points of attachment theory and research. Monographs of the Society for Research in Child Development* (pp. 167–193, Serial No. 209, Vol. 50, No. 1–2).

Beller, E. K., & Neubauer, P. B. (1963). Sex differences and symptom patterns in early childhood. *Journal of the American Academy of Child Psychiatry, 2,* 417–433.

Campbell, S. B. (1990). *Behavior problems in preschool children: Clinical and developmental issues.* New York: Guilford.

Campbell, S. B., & Breaux, A. M. (1983). Maternal ratings of activity level and symptomatic behavior in a non-clinical sample of young children. *Journal of Pediatric Psychology, 8,* 73–82.

Cederblad, M. (1968). A child psychiatric study on Sudanese Arab children. *Acta Psychiatrica Scandinavica, 44* (Suppl. 200), 1–230.

Cornely, P., & Bromet, E. (1986). Prevalence of behavior problems in three-year-old children living near Three Mile Island: A comparative analysis. *Journal of Child Psychology and Psychiatry, 27,* 489–498.

Crowther, J. H., Bond, L. A., & Rolf, J. E. (1981). The incidence, prevalence, and severity of behavior disorders among preschool-aged children in day care. *Journal of Abnormal Child Psychology, 9,* 23–42.

Cullen, K. J., & Boundy, B. E. (1966). The prevalence of behaviour disorders in the children of 1,000 western Australian families. *The Medical Journal of Australia, 2,* 805–808.

Earls, F. (1980a). Prevalence of behavior problems in 3-year-old children: A cross-national replication. *Archives of General Psychiatry, 37,* 1153–1157.

Earls, F. (1980b). The prevalence of behavior problems in 3-year-old children: Comparison of the reports of fathers and mothers. *Journal of the American Academy of Child Psychiatry, 19,* 439–452.

Earls, F. (1982). Application of DSM–III in an epidemiological study of preschool children. *American Journal of Psychiatry, 139,* 242–243.

Eaton, W. O., & Enns, L. R. (1986). Sex differences in human motor activity. *Psychological Bulletin, 100,* 19–28.

Eme, R. F. (1979). Sex differences in childhood psychopathology: A review. *Psychological Bulletin, 86,* 574–595.

Eme, R. F. (1984). Sex-role stereotypes and the epidemiology of child psychopathology. In C. S. Widom (Ed.), *Sex roles and psychopathology* (pp. 279–316). New York: Plenum.

Fagot, B. I. (1984). The consequences of problem behavior in toddler children. *Journal of Abnormal Child Psychology, 12,* 385–396.

Fagot, B. I., & Hagan, R. (1985). Aggression in toddlers: Responses to assertive acts of boys and girls. *Sex Roles, 12,* 341–351.

Fienberg, S. E. (1980). *The analysis of cross-classified categorical data* (2nd ed.). Cambridge, MA: MIT Press.

Gove, W. R. (1979). Sex differences in the epidemiology of mental disorder: Evidence and explanations. In E. S. Gomberg & V. Franks (Eds.), *Gender and disordered behavior. Sex differences in psychopathology* (pp. 23–68). New York: Brunner/Mazel.

Gove, W., & Herb, T. (1974). Stress and mental illness among the young: A comparison of the sexes. *Social Forces, 53,* 556–565.

Gualtieri, T., & Hicks, R. (1985). An immunoreactive theory of selective male affliction. *Behavioral and Brain Sciences, 8,* 427–441.

Jenkins, S., Bax, M., & Hart, H. (1980). Behaviour problems in pre-school children. *Journal of Child Psychology and Psychiatry, 21,* 5–17.

Keenan, K., & Shaw, D. (1997). Developmental and social influences on young girls' early problem behavior. *Psychological Bulletin, 121,* 95–113.

Koot, H. S., & Verhulst, F. C. (1991). Prevalence of problem behavior in Dutch children aged 2–3. *Acta Psychiatrica Scandinavica, 83*(Suppl. 367), 1–37.

Lahey, B. B., Miller, T. L., Gordon, R. A., & Riley, A. W. (1999). Developmental epidemiology of the disruptive behavior disorders. In H. C. Quay & A. E. Hogan (Eds.), *Handbook of disruptive behavior disorders* (pp. 21–48). New York: Plenum.

Larson, C. P., Pless, I. B., & Miettinen, O. (1988). Preschool behavior disorders: Their prevalence in relation to determinants. *Journal of Pediatrics, 113*, 278–285.

Long, A. (1941). Parents' reports of undesirable behavior in children. *Child Development, 12*, 43–62.

Luk, S. L., Leung, P. W. L., Bacon-Shone, J., & Lieh-Mak, F. (1991). The structure and prevalence of behavioral problems in Hong Kong preschool children. *Journal of Abnormal Child Psychology, 19*, 219–232.

Maccoby, E. E., & Jacklin, C. N. (1974). *The psychology of sex differences.* Stanford, CA: Stanford University Press.

Maccoby, E. E., & Jacklin, C. N. (1980). Sex differences in aggression: A rejoinder. *Child Development, 51*, 964–980.

Mcfarlane, J. W., Allen, L., & Honzik, M. P. (1954). *A developmental study of behavior problems in normal children.* Berkeley, CA: University of California Press.

McGee, R., Partridge, F., Williams, S., & Silva, P. A. (1991). A twelve-year follow-up of preschool hyperactive children. *Journal of the American Academy of Child and Adolescent Psychiatry, 30*, 224–232.

McGuire, J., & Richman, N. (1986). Screening for behaviour problem in nurseries: The reliability and validity of the preschool behaviour checklist. *Journal of Child Psychology and Psychiatry, 27*, 7–32.

Newth, S. J., & Corbett, J. (1993). Behaviour and emotional problems in three-year-old children of Asian parentage. *Journal of Child Psychology and Psychiatry, 34*, 333–352.

Richman, N., & Graham, P. J. (1971). A behavioural screening questionnaire for use with three-year-old children. Preliminary findings. Journal of Child Psychology and Psychiatry, 12, 5–33.

Richman, N., Stevenson, J. E., & Graham, P. J. (1975). Prevalence of behaviour problems in 3-year-old children: An epidemiological study in a London borough. *Journal of Child Psychology and Psychiatry, 16*, 277–287.

Richman, N., Stevenson, J. E., & Graham, P. J. (1982). *Preschool to school: A behavioural study.* London: Academic Press.

Rolf, J. E., & Hasazi, J. E. (1977). Identification of preschool children at risk and some guidelines for primary intervention. In G. W. Albee & J. M. Joffe (Eds.), *Primary prevention of psychopathology* (Vol. 1: The Issues, pp. 121–152). Hanover, NH: University Press of New England.

Rutter, M. (1988). Epidemiological approaches to developmental psychopathology. *Archives of General Psychiatry, 45*, 486–495.

Sanson, A., Prior, M., Smart, D., & Oberklaid, F. (1993). Gender differences in aggression in childhood: Implications for a peaceful world. *Australian Psychologist, 28*, 86–92.

Smetana, J. G. (1989). Toddlers' social interactions in the context of moral and conventional transgressions in the home. *Developmental Psychology, 25*, 499–508.

Stallard, P. (1993). The behaviour of 3-year-old children: Prevalence and parental perception of problem behaviour: A research note. *Journal of Child Psychology and Psychiatry, 34*, 413–421.

Thissen, D., Steinberg, L., & Gerrard, M. (1986). Beyond group-mean differences: The concept of item bias. *Psychological Bulletin, 99*, 118–128.

Tieger, T. (1980). On the biological basis of sex differences in aggression. *Child Development, 51*, 943–963.

Tremblay, R. E. (2000). The development of aggressive behavior during childhood: What have we learned in the past century? *International Journal of Behavioral Development, 24*, 129–141.

Tremblay, R. E., Boulerice, B., Harden, P. W., McDuff, P., Pérusse, D., Pihl, R. O., & Zoccolillo, M. (1996). Do children in Canada become more aggressive as they approach adolescence? In Human Resources Development Canada & Statistics Canada (Eds.), *Growing up in Canada: National Longitudinal Survey of Children and Youth.* (pp. 127–137). Ottawa: Statistics Canada.

Tremblay, R. E., Japel, C., Pérusse, D., McDuff, P., Boivin, M., Zoccolillo, M., & Montplaisir, J. (1999). The search for the age of "onset" of physical aggression: Rousseau and Bandura revisited. *Criminal Behaviour and Mental Health, 9*, 8–23.

Vermunt, J. K. (1997, September, 18). *lEM: A general program for the analysis of categorical data* [computer program]. Tilburg University Press.

Whiting, B., & Edwards, C. P. (1973). A cross-cultural analysis of sex differences in the behavior of children aged three through 11. *The Journal of Social Psychology, 91*, 171–188.

ACKNOWLEDGMENTS

Preparation of this chapter was supported by a research contract from Applied Research Branch, Human Resources Development Canada. We want to thank Elisa Romano for her thoughtful comments on an earlier version of this chapter. We also want to thank Hong Xing Wu for preparing the figures.

4

African-American Girls and Physical Aggression: Does Stability of Childhood Aggression Predict Later Negative Outcomes?

Shari Miller-Johnson
Duke University

Bertrina L. Moore
Marion K. Underwood
The University of Texas at Dallas

John D. Coie
Duke University

Girls are becoming increasingly violent and delinquent especially African-American girls. To illustrate, between 1981 and 1997, whereas the violent crime arrest rate for juvenile males increased by 20%, the rate for young females nearly doubled (Snyder & Sickmund, 1999). Similarly, between 1989 and 1993, juvenile arrests for serious crimes increased by 55% for girls compared with a 33% increase for boys. In addition, although most offenses committed by girls continue to be less serious status offenses, girls are increasingly becoming involved in more serious crimes, such as aggravated assault, gangs, and drug trafficking (Poe-Yamagata & Butts, 1996).

Rates of female delinquency seem to vary by ethnicity. Results from the National Longitudinal Survey of Youth (Office of Juvenile Justice and Delinquency Prevention [OJJDP], 1999) indicate that 8% of all girls ages 12 to

16 in this nationally representative sample had reported committing assault in the past 12 months. More African-American females reported committing assault (12%) than Euro-American (7%) or Hispanic (10%) young women. Among female offenders, African-Americans girls are also more likely to receive a severe disposition and less likely to be referred to mental health facilities than juvenile justice facilities (Bergsmann, 1994). As a result, African-American females make up almost half of those girls in detention, although they only represent 1% of the general female population in the United States. Similarly, in a cross-cultural study of aggression, 8-year-old African-American children were more aggressive than 8-year-old children from other ethnic groups (Osterman et al., 1994). This was especially true for African-American girls, who had the highest levels of both self- and peer-estimated aggression among the girls in the study.

Despite this evidence, few studies to date have explored the developmental functions, antecedents, and consequences of aggression for African-American females. Most of the research on childhood aggression has focused on boys perhaps because base rates of physical aggression are higher for males during the preschool, childhood, and adolescent periods (see Coie & Dodge, 1998; Loeber & Hay, 1997, for reviews of this large research literature). Other investigators seem to have assumed that the development of aggression is similar for girls and boys. However, the evidence suggests that the developmental trajectories for aggression in girls and boys may actually be quite different (Loeber & Stouthamer-Loeber, 1998).

An understanding of the development of aggression in African-American girls is further complicated because many of the theoretical models of antisocial behavior were developed based on work with White samples (e.g., Moffitt, 1993; Patterson, Capaldi, & Bank, 1991). Coie and Dodge (1998) suggested that different developmental models may be needed to understand the development of aggression in ethnic minority groups—in particular, models that acknowledge that growing up as a member of a minority group may necessitate different coping and socialization strategies (Ogbu, 1993). As noted by Coie and Dodge (1998), "Being Black brings numerous social hardships in American society (Ogbu, 1990), and with these hardships, relative risk for aggressive behavior" (p. 815; see Hawkins, Laub, & Lauritsen, 1998, for a more detailed discussion of the relationship between ethnicity and juvenile offending).

Even when researchers have focused on aggression among ethnic minority youth, they have often neglected girls. Frequently studies with African-American samples have included only boys without considering aggression in African-American girls (e.g., Gorman-Smith, Tolan, Loeber, & Henry, 1998; Hudley & Graham, 1993). There may well be more variation within than between ethnic groups, and the forms and functions of African-American girls' and boys' aggression may differ.

This chapter serves two primary goals. First, we review the few studies to date that have explored aggression in African-American girls, with attention to several questions. Why might African-American girls be more aggressive than girls from other ethnic groups? What does current evidence suggest are the developmental consequences of childhood aggression for African-American girls? The majority of this chapter focuses on physical aggression because most longitudinal research to date has assessed this overt form of aggressive behavior (Coie & Dodge, 1998). Furthermore, Pulkinnen (1992; Pulkinnen & Pitkaenen, 1993) found that physical aggression placed girls at greatest risk for long-term problems in comparison with other forms of aggression. We also discuss the as-yet-unexplored question of whether African-American girls engage in more subtle forms of aggression thought to be more characteristic of girls, indirect/relational/social aggression (see Underwood, Galen, & Paquette, 2001, for a discussion of definitional issues).

The second goal is to present longitudinal data on the stability of childhood aggression and maladjustment in adolescence and young adulthood in a sample of African-American girls and boys. With these data, we address four primary questions. Does childhood aggression predict externalizing and internalizing problems for African-American adolescent girls? Is more childhood aggression a stronger predictor for girls or boys? Does the stability of childhood aggression predict the timing and number of arrests for juvenile and adult crimes? Are these predictive relations similar for African-American girls and boys?

WHY MIGHT AFRICAN-AMERICAN GIRLS BE MORE AGGRESSIVE THAN GIRLS FROM OTHER ETHNIC GROUPS?

In this section, we review literature related to race and ethnic differences in aggression and offending behavior. The current research base has not examined this question by gender; therefore, we can only conjecture on how these theories might be extended to African-American females. The predominant view is that racial and ethnic differences in violence are a function of ecological factors such as social, institutional, and community level characteristics (Farrington, Loeber, & Stouthamer-Loeber, in press; Hawkins et al., 1998). Race and poverty are closely intertwined, and the largest detriment to African-American children's socioemotional development is low socioeconomic status (SES). African-American children experience the greatest socioeconomic disadvantage (Guerra, Huesmann, Tolan, Van Acker, & Eron, 1995) and are at higher risk than White children for experiencing an array of socioemotional problems (Gibbs, 1989).

These environmental explanations for higher rates of aggression among African-American youth are numerous, and the evidence seems plentiful. Elliot

(1994) discussed how race becomes especially salient in the transition from adolescence to young adulthood. Young African Americans are left without access to economic and educational opportunities afforded to others in the majority, and young African Americans are thereby denied full adult status in our society. Consequently, African-American youth may become embedded in gangs and a culture supporting violent behavior. Elliot explained that, in this way, delinquent activity becomes a viable source of status attainment. Similarly, Coie and Jacobs (1993) emphasized the broader social context as a determinant of conduct problems. Poverty brings with it a host of factors that may lead to violence, including limited social resources, weak intergenerational ties, a low sense of community belonging, accessibility to guns, and drug dealing. In low-SES communities, there may be a high density of stressed families who find it difficult to provide support and buffer their children against the negative effects of the larger social context. Youth may come to model the behavior that surrounds them in their community. Thus, in low-SES neighborhoods, deviant behavior may not only be normative, but may be a way of survival. Coie and Jacobs (1993) stressed the importance of defining deviance relative to the specific context and the associated norms surrounding deviant behavior.

McLoyd (1990) elucidated processes underlying how low SES impacts the development of African-American children. In her model, poverty diminishes the capacity for involved, supportive, and consistent parenting, thus making parents more vulnerable to the crippling effects of negative life events. Psychological distress is a major mediator between the links of economic hardship and parenting behavior. This psychological distress comes from an excessive number of negative life events, chronic impoverished conditions, and the absence and disturbance of marital bonds. Thus, economic hardship adversely affects children's socioemotional functioning partly due to the impact on how the parent behaves toward the child. Low-SES parents regularly face frustration-producing life events that may deprive them of the patience and understanding required to be nurturing and responsive to their children. In addition, for African Americans living in low-SES neighborhoods (unlike low-SES Whites), poverty is inextricably tied to and complicated by racism. Because of this array of disadvantage, the socioemotional and behavioral problems that African-American children face cannot possibly be solved in the same manner as the problems of impoverished Whites.

A number of studies have examined how living in economically disadvantaged neighborhoods is detrimental to children's mental health. Inner-city low-SES children are more likely to be exposed to neighborhood violence and to be victimized by violence in their communities than their more advantaged counterparts. Several studies (e.g., DuRant, Pendergrast, & Cadenhead, 1994; Fitzpatrick, 1997) have found that victimization and witnessing violence contribute to early aggression, which in turn predicts aggression in subsequent years. Attar, Guerra, and Tolan (1994) found that the total number of stressors experienced by children predicted both concurrent and future aggression. Perhaps the most pervasive effect of low SES is that these children experience more negative life events and believe in the appropriateness of aggressive strategies. Thus, for these children, an aggressive behavioral style may be adaptive for survival (Coie & Jacobs, 1993).

There is inconsistent evidence on the impact of parenting behavior on African-American children's development. In a sample of African-American preschoolers, Travillion and Snyder (1993) found that parents' use of harsh verbal and physical punishment was associated with children's aggressive behavior. Similarly, African-American adolescents who experienced parent derogation/rejection (Taylor, Biafora, Warheit, & Gil, 1997) and severe corporal punishment and discipline (DuRant, Cadenhead, Pendergrast, Slavens, & Linder, 1994) were more likely to be aggressive. In contrast, Deater-Deckard, Dodge, Bates, and Pettit (1996) found that associations between physical discipline and externalizing problems were significant for White families only. They suggested that the link between physical punishment and aggressive behavior may be culturally specific (for a more extended discussion of this subject, see *Psychological Inquiry*, 1997, Volume 8, entire issue).

Psychologically oriented theories focus on issues of racial identity and aggressive behavior. Ward (1995) proposed that African-American racial identity is based on an intimate connectedness, deep concern, and active care for others. This identity of care originated from African traditions of extended kinship networks and has been strengthened in this country by the sense of community provided by African-American churches. Ward (1995) argued that this collectivist, care-taking identity has helped African Americans survive the worst forms of oppression, but that this identity has recently been undermined by larger cultural values emphasizing autonomy and materialism. Consequently, youth are not developing the positive African-American identity of caring and connectedness. Their positive racial identity is further compromised by "the increasing cynicism of many Black teenagers toward a social system that possesses an ideology of social justice, yet offers little more than illusions of equality" (Ward, 1995, p. 177). Because youth may lack the ethic of care that comes with a more positive African-American identity, they fail to realize that aggression against another is aggression against the self.

Xie, Cairns, and Cairns (1999) conducted one of the few studies to examine gender differences in the social environments of African-American youth. They found that aggression was associated with other problems, including low academic competence and unpopularity. Interestingly, both aggressive girls and boys were affiliated with social networks, often with networks made up of other aggressive youth. However, particular qualities of the networks differed by gender. Girls who were aggressive had smaller peer networks than did aggressive boys. In addition, aggressive boys were more central members of their peer networks than nonaggressive boys, whereas aggression was unrelated to network centrality for girls. Together these results imply that, although peer groups may support aggressive behavior for African-American youth of both genders, this effect may not be as strong for aggressive girls because they have fewer affiliations and are less likely to be central members of deviant peer networks.

These theories and research recognize how contextual risk processes impact behavioral factors (i.e., the impact of environmental/ecological factors, parenting behavior, racial identity, and peer social context on aggression). However, these theories do not take into account the special challenges that African-American girls may face in developing a positive sense of self. A positive self-concept might protect African-American girls from problem behavior and help them strive for ambitious goals, in the face of possibly being doubly disadvantaged by their gender and ethnicity. There is incredible diversity in psychological adjustment and developmental outcomes for urban girls (Leadbeater & Way, 1996). We need to know more about what fosters resilience in African-American girls at risk. With this in mind, it is fair to say that childhood aggression and its effects are complex, and any prevention or intervention efforts should consider the ethnicity, SES, and gender of the individuals they are trying to target.

WHAT ARE SOME OF THE DEVELOPMENTAL CONSEQUENCES OF CHILDHOOD AGGRESSION FOR AFRICAN-AMERICAN GIRLS?

Much of the research to date on the developmental consequences of childhood aggression for African-American girls has focused on adolescent childbearing. Peer-rated aggression in the fourth grade predicted adolescent childbearing (Underwood, Kupersmidt, & Coie, 1996). In a subsequent sample from the same locale, childhood aggression also predicted having more children and having them at younger ages (Miller-Johnson, Winn et al., 1999). It is important to note that, although adolescent childbearing is associated with serious disadvantages for mother and child (Bachrach, Clogg, & Carver, 1993; Furstenberg, Brooks-Gunn, & Chase-Lansdale, 1989), outcomes for adolescent mothers are not always negative (Furstenberg, Brooks-Gunn, & Morgan, 1987; Leadbeater & Bishop, 1994). Other evidence suggests that early sexual activity may increase the risk for aggression. Valois, McKeown, Garrison, and Vincent (1995) found that early sexual activity was associated with aggression for African-American girls, and aggression was part of a cluster of risk-taking behaviors including sexual activity and substance use. However, data in this study were concurrent, therefore the direction of effects was not possible to disentangle.

Research strongly suggests that aggressive African-American girls may be at risk for much more than early motherhood. Because many of these aggressive girls have deviant peers who may be in a gang, they may be likely to join gangs. Harper and Robinson (1999) studied a large sample of low-SES African-American adolescent girls to look at risk-taking behaviors associated with gang affiliation. Relative to girls who were nongang members, girls who were part of gangs were more likely to engage in risky sexual activity (earlier age of sexual debut, greater number of sexual partners, and lower frequency of condom use), substance use (more frequent use of cigarettes, alcohol, and marijuana), and violent behavior (frequent weapon carrying, physical fighting, and attacking).

Several reports from our longitudinal study of African-American youth suggest that aggressive girls may be at risk for a variety of later negative outcomes. We describe these investigations in some detail for two reasons. First, it is one of the few longitudinal studies available that focuses on African-American youth and included girls. Second, the data we report later in this chapter are from subsequent work with this sample.

The first of these studies examined whether peer-rated aggression and social rejection in the third grade predicted psychological adjustment at the end of the first year of middle school (Coie, Lochman, Terry, & Hyman, 1992). Outcomes included externalizing problems (self- and parent reports), internalizing problems (self- and parent reports), and adjustment to middle school (self-, parent, and teacher reports). For both girls and boys, third-grade aggression predicted self- and parent reports of externalizing problems and self-reports of internalizing disorders. Although boys were more likely to have difficulty adjusting to school than girls, gender accounted for only 5% of the variance, and the extent to which aggression predicted adjustment problems was similar for girls and boys. Overall the findings demonstrate that both peer rejection and aggression were important predictors of later negative outcomes for both genders. When the investigators examined consensus judgments of externalizing and internalizing disorders (evidence from two of the three sources—self-, teacher, and peer reports), social preference seemed to be a stronger predictor of caseness for girls than for boys. Thus, rejection by peers may be especially relevant for girls in terms of indicating risk for subsequent disorder.

In a subsequent study with the same sample, Miller-Johnson, Coie, Maumary-Gremaud, Lochman, and Terry (1999) examined whether aggression and rejection in the third grade predicted specific types of delinquency at Grades 6, 8, and 10. Participants reported delinquent offenses in response to the National Youth Survey (Elliot, Huizinga, & Ageton, 1985; Elliot, Huizinga, & Menard, 1989). Overall the interaction of peer rejection and aggression did not predict delinquency for girls, and there were fewer predictive relations for girls than boys.

The results show that for girls childhood aggression (and not peer rejection) predicted serious offenses (including felony theft, felony assault, and robbery offenses), whereas peer rejection (and not aggression) predicted more minor offenses. For boys, aggression and rejection together predicted more serious offenses, and aggression predicted all types of delinquent behaviors. The authors interpreted the results as suggesting that early starter models of delinquency may be less relevant for girls (which hardly seems surprising given that early and late starter models were proposed on the basis of research with boys; Loeber, 1990; Moffit, 1993). They also noted that the experience and correlates of social rejection might differ for girls and boys. If rejection among girls is more strongly linked to social isolation and withdrawal than to aggression, girls may be less likely to form deviant peer cliques—or as Xie et al. (1999) found, these cliques may be smaller and aggressive girls may be less central members compared with nonaggressive girls.

THE CURRENT STUDY—A LONGITUDINAL PERSPECTIVE

In the prospective study described here, we examined the stability of childhood aggression as a predictor of externalizing and internalizing problems in adolescence and the timing and number of arrests through young adulthood. Our investigation was guided by several hypotheses. For the stability of aggression, we predicted that aggression would be similarly stable for girls and boys. Most scholars accept that by fourth grade, aggression is a highly stable trait—almost as stable as intelligence (Olweus, 1979). Stability seems high for both girls and boys in most samples (Coie & Dodge, 1998; Huesmann et al., 1984). Still few studies have explored gender differences in the stability of aggression for ethnic minority youth.

We also anticipated that aggression in childhood would predict externalizing and internalizing problems in adolescence and arrest outcomes in young adulthood for both girls and boys. However, we hypothesized that the stability of childhood aggression would be a relatively weaker predictor for girls than boys. For girls physical aggression in childhood is more atypical and deviant than it is for boys. Therefore, the risk for a girl who is rated by peers as physically aggressive in a single year would likely be great to start and perhaps less likely to be increased by being rated as aggressive in subsequent years. Conversely, because physical aggression among boys may be more normative than it is among girls, aggression across multiple years should increase the likelihood of risk for future problems.

METHOD
Participants

The data reported here are from a prospective study examining the development of school and personal adjustment from third grade through young adulthood (Coie, Lochman, Terry, & Hyman, 1992; Coie, Terry, Lenox,

Lochman, & Hyman, 1995). All third graders in 12 elementary schools were administered sociometric measures of peer social status and social behavior in 1984, 1985, and 1986 (N = 1,749; Cohort A: 588; Cohort B: 559; Cohort C: 602). Sociometric surveys were readministered when the students were in the fourth and fifth grades. A subsample was chosen as follows for longitudinal assessment at 2-year intervals. First, participants were assigned to one of five peer-status categories based on the third-grade sociometric measure (i.e., controversial, neglected, popular, average, rejected; see Coie & Dodge, 1988, for scoring details). Children were then randomly selected from the four nonrejected groups within each of the original three cohorts. Attempts were made to include all children with rejected status due to specific research questions pertaining to peer rejection. The sociometric sample was predominantly African American (90%) and of low SES (65% of the children in the school system were eligible for the free or reduced school lunch program). Given problems in interpreting sociometric data on children who are in an extreme minority of a school population (Kupersmidt & Coie, 1990), only African-American participants were included in the longitudinal follow-up, although sociometric data were obtained for all children in the schools.

Measures

Sociometric Survey.   Sociometric surveys were group administered in third-, fourth-, and fifth-grade classrooms. Children received a roster of all the children in their grade and nominated the three students whom they *liked most* and *liked least*. Children also received behavioral descriptions and nominated the three children in their grade who best fit each descriptor. In this study, the single item descriptor for "starts fights, hits other children, or says mean things to them" was used as a measure of physical aggression. Children were allowed to vote for peers of both genders to increase the stability of measurement (Terry & Coie, 1991). Scores were calculated for each child using ratings from all students in a given grade and then standardized within schools. Separate scores were computed for each participant at third, fourth, and fifth grades using ratings from same-grade peers. As expected, examination of the "starts fights" variable showed a higher proportion of males at the upper portion of the distribution. Therefore, this variable was standardized within gender to guarantee identification of similar prevalence rates for girls and boys. Aggressive participants were those who received a standardized "starts fights" score greater than 1.0 standard deviation.

Child Assessment Schedule (CAS).   Youth reported on their externalizing and internalizing symptoms using the Child Assessment Schedule (CAS; Hodges, 1987). The CAS is a semistructured interview that generates psychiatric symptom and diagnostic information. It has demonstrated accept-

able test–retest reliability and internal consistency and compares favorably
with other structured child interviews.

Arrest Status.   Juvenile and adult police records were examined for
the period from 1978 to 1998. All of the participants had reached at least
their 22nd birthday at the time of the final data collection. The date of police
apprehension and an individual's date of birth were used to calculate the age
of offending. In the jurisdiction where the study took place, records were
part of the juvenile court system through age 16. After that time offenses
were included as part of the adult criminal justice system. This report contains offense records through age 22.

The current analyses include children with complete data at the Grades 6,
8, and 10 follow-ups and who had sociometric data for at least two time
points across Grades 3 to 5 ($N = 297$; 53% male). Attrition was due primarily to the inability to locate participants. Additionally, a smaller number of
participants refused to be interviewed. We were able to obtain full sociometric data for 73% of participants at three grades, 15% at only two grades,
and 7% at only one grade; 5% of subjects were retained in a grade prior to
middle school and were deleted from analyses involving sociometric data
across more than 1 year. For the adolescent follow-up assessments, youth
participation rates were 84%, 79%, and 73% at Grades 6, 8, and 10. Analyses were completed separately by gender due to specific questions about the
longitudinal development of aggressive behavior in girls. Outcomes included youth ratings of externalizing and internalizing symptoms at Grades
6, 8, and 10 and arrests through age 22.

RESULTS

We first report on the stability of aggression by gender across Grades 3 to 5.
We then report on externalizing, internalizing, and arrest outcomes by gender as a function of stable aggressive status.[1]

Stable Aggressive Status Across Grades 3 to 5

Stable aggression was defined by using third-, fourth-, and fifth-grade standardized peer ratings and a score cutoff of 1.0 or greater to indicate that a
child was highly aggressive at each of the three grades. Stable aggressive
groups were defined as follows: (a) aggressive at no grades ($N = 230$; 50%
girls); (b) aggressive at 1 grade ($N = 43$; 48% girls); and (c) aggressive at
two or more grades ($N = 36$; 53% girls). Table 4.1 shows the correlations for
peer ratings of aggression across Grades 3 to 5 by gender. Girls and boys

---

[1]Also available were parent ratings of internalizing and externalizing symptoms. Results were generally consistent with child ratings.

TABLE 4.1

Correlations: Peer Ratings of Physical Aggression Across Grades 3 to 5 by Gender

	GR 3	GR 4	GR 5
GR 3	—	.44***	.20*
GR 4	.43***	—	.46***
GR 5	.21*	.49***	—

Note. Correlations in the upper right are for females; those in the lower left are for males; * $p < .05$; ** $p < .01$.

showed similar patterns across the three grades. Correlations were highest between grades that were 1 year apart—in the 0.40 range. However, associations decreased when looking over a 2-year interval (approximately 0.20).

Stability of Aggression as a Predictor of Adolescent Outcomes

Externalizing Symptoms.   Repeated measures analyses of variance (ANOVA) determined whether stable aggressive status (i.e., was a child aggressive at 0, 1, 2, or more grades) predicted externalizing and internalizing symptoms across Grades 6, 8, and 10 (see Table 4.2). For externalizing out-

TABLE 4.2

Stability of Aggression Across Grades 3 to 5 and Youth Reports of Externalizing and Internalizing Symptoms During Adolescence

	Externalizing		Internalizing	
	Females (2,151)	*Males (2,152)*	*Females (2,151)*	*Males (2,152)*
Overall	6.53**	5.80**	0.69	7.35***
Gr 6	1.89	1.64	0.40	3.19*
Gr 8	9.53***	3.76*	0.13	2.88+
Gr 10	2.84+	7.87***	3.62*	6.22**

* $p < .05$; ** $p < .01$; *** $p < .001$; +$p < .10$.

comes, the pattern of results was quite similar for girls and boys. As shown in Fig. 4.1, externalizing symptoms in adolescence increased as a function of stable aggressive status. In other words, the greater the stability of childhood aggression, the higher the level of externalizing symptoms during adolescence. For girls the pattern was most evident at Grade 8. However, for boys this pattern persisted across Grades 6, 8, and 10 and became stronger over time.

Internalizing Outcomes. Girls and boys showed different patterns for persistent aggression as a predictor of internalizing outcomes. As shown in Fig. 4.2, for girls the stability of childhood aggression did not predict the

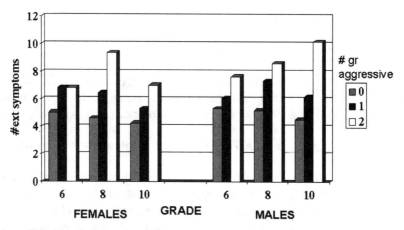

FIG. 4.1.   Stability of childhood aggression and child reports of externalizing

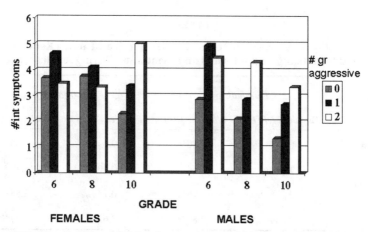

FIG. 4.2.   Stability of childhood aggression and child reports of internalizing symptoms—by gender.

level of internalizing symptoms except at 10th grade (and here the only significant contrast was the difference between girls who were aggressive at no grades and girls who were aggressive at two or more grades). However, for boys stable childhood aggression predicted internalizing symptoms at Grades 6, 8, and 10. Therefore, persistent childhood aggression predicted later internalizing symptoms for boys, but not for girls.

Arrest Outcomes. For both girls and boys, stable aggressive status was a significant predictor of the total number of arrests through age 22 (girls: $F(2,151) = 5.27$, $p < .01$; boys: $F(2,152) = 6.53$, $p < .01$). However, the arrest patterns differed somewhat by gender in terms of whether the child was aggressive at zero, one, two, or more grades. For girls there were no significant differences in the number of arrests between girls who were aggressive at one or two grades. In other words, once a girl was aggressive at one grade, it did not impact the number of arrests (arrest totals: girls—aggressive no grades – 1.00; aggressive one grade – 3.04; aggressive two or more grades – 2.37). However, for boys, the greater the stability of childhood aggression, the greater the number of arrests through age 22 (arrest totals: boys—aggressive no grades – 3.92; aggressive one grade – 5.91; aggressive two or more grades – 10.12). Therefore, once girls were aggressive for at least one grade, they were arrested more often than those who were never aggressive. However, for boys the number of arrests increased as a function of the stability of childhood aggression.

We also examined the timing of the first arrest for girls and boys as a function of stable aggression using survival analyses (Singer & Willet, 1991). These analyses generated curves that indicate the proportion of girls and boys who avoided being arrested as a function of stable aggression across Grades 3 to 5. A robust relationship was found between stable aggressive status and the timing of arrest for both females (Wilcoxon χ^2 (2, $N = 154) = 12.78$, $p < .01$) and males (Wilcoxon χ^2 (2, $N = 155) = 23.91$, $p < .001$). However, as shown in Figs. 4.3 and 4.4, the survival function suggests differences in the timing of the first arrest by gender. Girls who were aggressive at two or more grades did not first get arrested until about age 14. Girls who were aggressive at only one grade also began to get arrested at about the same age—however, at a much slower rate than girls who were more persistently aggressive. In contrast, boys who were aggressive at two or more grades began to get arrested as early as age 8 and continued to be arrested for the first time at a steep rate through the teen years. Those boys who were aggressive at only one grade began to first get arrested at a later age—about 16 years old.

DISCUSSION

Overall the findings supported many of our hypotheses. As shown in other studies (e.g., Huesmann et al., 1984; Pulkinnen & Putkaenen, 1993), child-

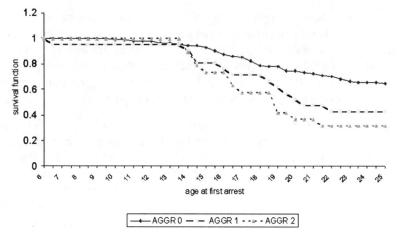

FIG. 4.3.   Stability of aggression and timing of firest arrest—females.

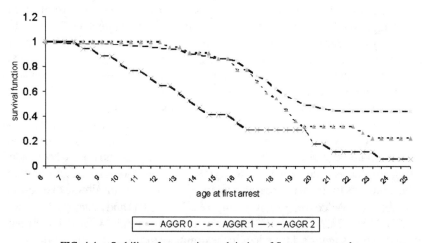

FIG. 4.4.   Stability of aggression and timing of firest arrest—males.

hood aggression was similarly stable for African-American girls and boys. The stability of childhood aggression predicted externalizing outcomes for girls as well as for boys, particularly at Grade 8. However, the stability of childhood aggression was not a significant predictor of internalizing problems for girls, whereas it was for boys. Similarly, for girls being rated as aggressive did predict arrests, but stability seemed less essential than for boys. Once a girl was aggressive at one grade during childhood, she was at higher risk for more frequent arrests regardless of whether she was aggressive in subsequent grades. The timing of the first arrest was also later for girls than for boys.

These results are the first to show the stability of physical aggression during childhood for African-American girls. These findings fit with previous work on primarily male samples showing that aggression is a fairly stable behavior (Coie & Dodge, 1998; Olweus, 1979). Indeed the correlations across third through fifth grades were virtually identical for girls and boys. Not surprisingly, the stability of aggressive behavior was highest across contiguous grades. This information is important to know in terms of building and testing models for the development of aggressive behavior in African-American girls.

Our findings on externalizing problems join the body of evidence showing that childhood aggression is a strong predictor of later negative outcomes (Coie & Dodge, 1998). Contrary to our hypotheses, the pattern of results was similar for girls and boys—namely, the greater the stability of childhood aggression, the higher the level of adolescent externalizing problems. These results suggest that persistent aggressive behavior during childhood is an important risk factor for later externalizing problems for both girls and boys. Although we concur with others as to the importance of more subtle types of aggression in females (Crick et al., 1999; Underwood et al., in press), these data suggest that physical aggression in girls remains a useful indicator of risk for subsequent behavior problems. Our findings confirm earlier work by Pulkinnen (1992) showing that physical aggression predicted long-term problems for girls. Additional study is needed to determine whether more subtle forms of aggression in girls also predict negative long-term outcomes.

These findings also build on previous work showing that stable aggression predicts an array of problematic outcomes during adolescence for African-American females. In our earlier work, we found that stable aggressive behavior during childhood was a robust predictor of teen childbearing among females (Miller-Johnson et al., 1999). Specifically, the probability of having a baby increased from 0.28 for those never aggressive to 0.41 for those aggressive at one grade level to 0.55 for those aggressive at two or more grades. Similarly, for boys the probability of reporting getting a girl pregnant increased in a linear fashion from 0.35 for those who were never aggressive to 0.49 for those who were aggressive at one elementary grade to 0.63 for those who were aggressive at two or more grades (Miller-Johnson, Winn, Coie, Maumary-Gremaud, Hyman, Terry, & Lochman, 2003). Therefore, the stability of childhood aggression may be a useful criterion to indicate risk for a variety of negative outcomes during the teen years.

These findings also suggest that, although aggression is a fairly stable construct, many children do not persist in their aggressive behavior across the elementary school years. For example, the correlation from third to fifth grade was in the 0.20 range for both girls and boys. Similarly, of the children who were aggressive during at least one grade, more than half were aggressive at only one grade. These findings suggest that aggressive behavior is not persistent for all girls and boys. Future research might identify characteristics related to the resistance of aggression over time.

For internalizing symptoms, stable aggression during childhood predicted internalizing symptoms for boys, but not for girls. Our findings on males are consistent with Patterson and Capaldi's (1990) mediational model of depressed mood in boys with conduct problems. They proposed a number of factors that may mediate ties between antisocial behavior and depression. First, social skills deficits associated with antisocial behavior may increase the risk for depression. These social deficits may also be exacerbated by interpersonal conflict, which leads to rejection by peers, teachers, and parents. Furthermore, academic problems and peer difficulties may also lead to depressed mood. This model warrants replication with females to better understand the ties between conduct problems and internalizing symptoms in girls.

Our results on arrest outcomes are applicable to ongoing discussions of the relevance of early and late starter pathways for girls (Silverthorn & Frick, 1999; Webster-Stratton, 1996; Zoccolillo, 1993). Those boys who were aggressive at two or more grades during childhood showed a distinct pattern of multiple arrests and arrests at relatively early ages beginning at about age 8. In contrast, those girls who were most stably aggressive during childhood did not begin to be arrested until much later—at about age 14. These results provide partial support for Silverthorn and Frick's (1999) conceptualization of developmental trajectories to antisocial behavior for girls. Specifically, they proposed a delayed-onset pathway in females that is analogous to the childhood-onset pathway in boys. Although girls may have predisposing characteristics that are similar to those found in early starting boys (e.g., family dysfunction, cognitive deficits), their antisocial behavior is delayed until the teen years. Indeed our findings suggest that antisocial behavior, at least defined in terms of arrest, was manifested later in girls compared with boys. What remains unknown, however, is whether other forms of antisocial behavior (e.g., dating violence, substance use) also show a delayed onset for girls compared with boys. At the same time, we did find evidence for early starting antisocial behavior, in the form of physically aggression, by the third grade. Furthermore, this early physical aggression was predictive of persistent externalizing problems through adolescence. Clearly, there is a need for additional study to further our understanding of developmental trajectories for antisocial behavior among girls.

We must qualify our results with several caveats. As with most longitudinal studies, there was attrition in the sample. In addition, arrest data only reflected those youth who were actually apprehended. We tried to buffer against this by including self-report data, and, as noted previously, the pattern of findings for parent ratings was quite similar. One strength of this study is its focus on an African-American sample of both girls and boys in a prospective, longitudinal design.

Our work was also limited to physical aggression. It remains unclear whether these findings generalize to subtler behaviors more commonly found in girls, such as indirect/relational/social aggression (Underwood et al., in press). Most of the work on the subtle forms of aggression have been done with Euro-American girls (Crick et al., 1999; Lagerspetz & Björkqvist, 1994). One important direction for future work is the degree to which girls from other minority ethnic groups engage in indirect/relational/social forms of aggressive behavior. Given that African-American girls appear to be more physically aggressive than other girls (Osterman et al., 1994), does this mean they resort less often to these more subtle behaviors? Are African-American girls also more aggressive across these different forms of aggression? How are these various forms of aggressive behavior related to each other? Do these types of aggression predict later negative outcomes? Related to this is the question of whether African-American girls perceive social aggression as being hurtful, and whether they use different methods of social aggression than girls of other ethnic groups.

In general, there is a dearth of interventions that address the specific needs of girls. Even scarcer are strategies tailored to girls' diverse ethnic and contextual backgrounds (Acoca, 1999). Our review of the literature, combined with these findings, has some implications for intervention efforts. First, physically aggressive girls appear to be at high risk for externalizing problems during adolescence, similar to boys. Examining stable aggression as a predictor may give us empirically derived guidelines to help select groups for intervention. For boys the best use of resources may be to target those who are more stably aggressive. For girls even 1 year of being rated as aggressive may confer risk, which suggests that maybe all girls rated as aggressive should be targeted for intervention.

A recent set of guidelines on gender-sensitive intervention strategies was also put forth by the Office of Juvenile Justice and Delinquency Prevention (1998), and many of these build on the literature reviewed in this chapter. Prevention efforts for high-risk girls need to attend to the health and reproductive needs of African-American females. This includes providing information on women's health, birth control options, sexually transmitted diseases, and health care services. Interventions also need to be sensitive to the socioeconomic and contextual issues faced by many African Americans, such as decreased educational and economic opportunities and lack of access to conventional sources of status attainment. Intervention strategies might promote positive life skills, such as exposing girls to positive role models, developing career and job skills, and providing tutoring and other specialized academic services as needed. Intervention staff would also benefit from training in gender- and ethnic-specific issues, including adolescent female development, sensitivity to cultural issues, and stereotypes regarding gender and race. We hope that empirical research begins to evaluate the effectiveness of intervention programs for African-American girls to promote the most positive outcomes for these young women and protect them and their children from the risks associated with childhood aggression.

ACKNOWLEDGMENTS

This research was supported by Grants R01 MY390140 and K05MH00797 from the Prevention Branch of the National Institute of Mental Health to the fourth author, and a FIRST award (#55992) from the National Institute of Mental Health and a grant from the Timberlawn Psychiatric Research Foundation to the third author. We are grateful to the staff and children of the Durham, North Carolina schools for their cooperation in this longitudinal study.

REFERENCES

Acoca, L. (1999). Investing in girls: A 21st century strategy. *Juvenile Justice. Journal of the Office of Juvenile Justice and Delinquency Prevention, 6*, 3–13.
Attar, B. K., Guerra, N. G., & Tolan, P. H. (1994). Neighborhood disadvantage, stressful life events, and adjustment in urban elementary school children. *Journal of Clinical Child Psychology, 23*, 391–400.
Bachrach, C. A., Clogg, C. C., & Carver, K. (1993). Outcomes of early childbearing: Summary of conference. *Journal of Research on Adolescence, 3*, 337–348.
Bergsmann, I. (1994). Establishing a foundation: Just the facts. *1994 Juvenile female offenders conference: A time for change* (pp. 3–14). Lanham, MD: American Correctional Association.
Coie, J. D., & Dodge, K. A. (1998). Aggression and antisocial behavior. In N. Eisenberg (Ed.), *Handbook of child psychology* (pp. 779–862). New York: Wiley.
Coie, J. D., & Jacobs, M. R. (1993). The role of social context in the prevention of conduct disorder. *Development and Psychopathology, 5*, 263–275.
Coie, J. D., Lochman, J., Terry, R., & Hyman, C. (1992). Predicting early adolescent disorder from childhood aggression and peer rejection. *Journal of Consulting and Clinical Psychology, 60*, 783–792.
Coie, J. D., Terry, R., Lenox, K., Lochman, J., & Hyman, C. (1995). Childhood peer rejection and aggression as predictors of stable patterns of adolescent disorder. *Development and Psychopathology, 7*, 697–713.
Crick, N. R., Werner, N. E., Casas, J. F., O'Brien, K. M., Nelson, D. A., & Grotpeter, J. K., & Markon, K. (1999). Childhood aggression and gender: A new look at an old problem. In D. Bernstein (Ed.), *Gender and motivation. Nebraska symposium on motivation* (Vol. 45, pp. 75–141). Lincoln, NE: University of Nebraska Press
Deater-Deckard, K., Dodge, K. B., Bates, J. E., & Pettit, G. S. (1996). Physical discipline among African American and European American mothers: Links to children's externalizing behaviors. *Developmental Psychology, 32*, 1065–1072.
DuRant, R. H., Cadenhead, C., Pendergrast, R. A., Slavens, G., & Linder, C. W. (1994). Factors associated with the use of violence among urban black adolescents. *American Journal of Public Health, 84*(4), 612–617.
DuRant, R. H., Pendergrast, R. A., & Cadenhead, C. (1994). Exposure to violence and victimization and fighting behavior by urban black adolescents. *Journal of Adolescent Health, 15*, 311–318.
Elliott, D. S. (1994). Serious violent offenders: Onset, developmental course, and termination—The American Society of Criminology 1993 Presidential address. *Criminology, 32*, 1–21.

Elliott, D. S., Huizinga, D., & Ageton, S. S. (1985). *Explaining delinquency and drug use.* Newbury Park, CA: Sage.

Elliott, D. S., Huizinga, D., & Menard, S. (1989). *Multiple problem youth: Delinquency, substance use, and mental health problems.* New York: Springer-Verlag.

Farrington, D. P., Loeber, R., & Stouthamer-Loeber, M. (in press). How can the relationship between race and violence be explained? In D. F. Hawkins (Ed.), *Violent crimes: The nexus of ethnicity, race and class.* New York: Cambridge University Press.

Fitzpatrick, K. M. (1997). Aggression and environmental risk among low-income African American youth. *Journal of Adolescent Health, 21,* 172–178.

Furstenberg, F. F., Brooks-Gunn, J., & Chase-Lansdale, L. (1989). Teenaged pregnancy and childbearing. *American Psychologist, 44,* 313–320.

Furstenberg, F. F., Brooks-Gunn, J., & Morgan, S. P. (1987). *Adolescent mothers in later life.* Cambridge, MA: Cambridge University Press.

Gibbs, J. T. (1989). Black American adolescents. In J. T. Gibbs & L. N. Huang (Eds.), *Children of color* (pp. 179–223). San Francisco: Josey-Bass.

Gorman-Smith, D., Tolan, P. H., Loeber, R., & Henry, D. B. (1998). Relation of family problems to patterns of delinquent involvement among urban youth. *Journal of Abnormal Child Psychology, 26*(5), 319–333.

Guerra, N. G., Huesmann, L. R., Tolan, P. H., Van Acker, R., & Eron, L. D. (1995). Stressful events and individual beliefs as correlates of economic disadvantage and aggression among urban children. *Journal of Consulting and Clinical Psychology, 63*(4), 518–528.

Harper, G. W., & Robinson, W. L. (1999). Pathways to risk among inner city African American adolescent females: The influence of gang membership. *American Journal of Community Psychology, 27*(3), 383–404.

Hawkins, D. F., Laub, J. H., & Lauritsen, J. L. (1998). Race, ethnicity, and serious juvenile offending. In R. Loeber & D. P. Farrington (Eds.), *Serious and violent juvenile offenders* (pp. 30–46). Thousand Oaks, CA: Sage.

Hodges, K. (1987). Assessing children with a clinical interview: The Child Assessment Schedule. In R. J Prinz (Ed.), *Advances in behavioral assessment of children and families* (pp. 203–233). Greenwich, CT: JAI Press.

Hudley, C., & Graham, S. (1993). An attributional intervention to reduce peer-directed aggression among African American boys. *Child Development, 64*(1), 124–138.

Huesmann, L. R., Eron, L., Lefkowitz, M. M., & Walder, L. (1984). Stability of aggression over time and generations. *Development Psychology, 20,* 1120–1134.

Kupersmidt, J. B., & Coie, J. D. (1990). Preadolescent peer status, aggression, and school-adjustment as predictors of externalizing problems in adolescence. *Child Development, 61,* 1350–1362.

Lagerspetz, K. M., & Björkqvist, K. (1994). Indirect aggression in boys and girls. In L. R. Huesmann (Ed.), *Aggressive behavior: Current perspectives. Plenum series in social /clinical psychology* (pp. 131–150). New York: Plenum.

Leadbeater, B. J., & Bishop, S. J. (1994). Predictors of behavior problems in pre-school children of inner-city Afro-American and Puerto Rican adolescent mothers. *Child Development, 65,* 638–648.

Leadbeater, B. J., & Way, N. (1996). Introduction. In B. J. Leadbeater & N. Way (Eds.), *Urban girls* (pp. 1–12). New York: New York University Press.

Loeber, R. (1990). Development and risk factors of juvenile antisocial behavior and delinquency. *Clinical Psychology Review, 1,* 1–41.

Loeber, R., & Hay, D. (1997). Key issues in the development of aggression and violence from childhood to early adulthood. *Annual Review of Psychology, 48,* 371–410.

Loeber, R., & Stouthamer-Loeber, M. (1998). Development of juvenile aggression and violence: Some common misconceptions and controversies. *American Psychologist, 53,* 242–259.

McLoyd, V. C. (1990). The impact of economic hardship on black families and children: Psychological distress, parenting, and socioemotional development. *Child Development, 61*(2), 311–346.

Miller-Johnson, S., Coie, J. D., Maumary-Gremaud, A., Lochman, J., & Terry, R. (1999). Relationship between childhood peer rejection and aggression and adolescent delinquency, severity and type among African American youth. *Journal of Emotional and Behavioral Disorders, 7*, 137–147.

Miller-Johnson, S., Winn, D., Coie, J., Maumary-Gremaud, A., Hyman, C., Terry, R., & Lochman, J. (1999). Motherhood during the teen years: A developmental perspective on risk factors for childbearing. *Development and Psychopathology, 11*, 85–100.

Miller-Johnson, S., Winn, D., Coie, J., Maumary-Gremaud, A., Hyman, C., Terry, R., & Lohman, J. (2003). *Risk factors for adolescent paternity among African American males.* Unpublished manuscript.

Moffitt, T. E. (1993). Adolescence-limited and life-course-persistent antisocial behavior: A developmental taxonomy. *Psychological Review, 100*, 674–701.

Ogbu, J. U. (1990). Overcoming racial barriers to equal access. In I. Goodlad & P. Keating (Eds.), *Access to knowledge: An agenda for our nation's schools* (pp. 59–89). New York: College Entrance Examination Board.

Ogbu, J. U. (1993). Differences in cultural frame of reference. *International Journal of Behavioral Development, 16*, 483–506.

Office of Juvenile Justice and Delinquency Prevention. (1998). *Guiding principles for promising female programming. Inventory of best practices.* Washington, DC: Author.

Office of Juvenile Justice and Delinquency Prevention. (1999). *1999 National report series: Minorities in the juvenile justice system.* Washington, DC: Author.

Olweus, D. (1979). Stability of aggressive reaction patterns in males: A review. *Psychological Bulletin, 86*(4), 852–875.

Osterman, K., Björkqvist, K., Lagerspetz, K. M., Kaukiainen, A., Huesmann, L. R., & Fraczek, A. (1994). Peer and self-estimated aggression and victimization in 8-year-old children from five ethnic groups. *Aggressive Behavior, 20*, 411–428.

Patterson, G. R., & Capaldi, D. M. (1990). A mediational model for boys' depressed mood. In J. Rolf, A. S. Masten, D. Cicchetti, K. H. Neuchterlein, & S. Weintraub (Eds.), *Risk and protective factors in the development of psychopathology* (pp. 141–163). New York: Cambridge University Press.

Patterson, G. R., Capaldi, D. M., & Bank, L. (1991). An early starter model for predicting delinquency. In D. J. Pepler & K. H. Rubin (Eds.), *The development and treatment of childhood aggression* (pp. 139–168). Hillsdale, NJ: Lawrence Erlbaum Associates.

Poe-Yamagata, E., & Butts, J. A. (1996). *Female offenders in the juvenile justice system. Statistics summary.* Washington, DC: Office of Juvenile Justice and Delinquency Prevention.

Pulkinnen, L. (1992). The path to adulthood for aggressively inclined girls. In K. Björkqvist & P. Niemëla (Eds.), *Of mice and women: Aspects of female aggression* (pp. 113–121). San Diego CA: Academic Press.

Pulkinnen, L., & Pitkaenen, T. (1993). Continuities in aggressive behavior from childhood to adulthood. *Aggressive Behavior, 19*, 249–263.

Silverthorn, P., & Frick, P. J. (1999). Developmental pathways to antisocial behavior: The delayed-onset pathway in girls. *Development and Psychopathology, 11*, 101–126.

Singer, J. D., & Willet, J. B. (1991). Modeling the days of our lives: Using survival analysis when designing and analyzing longitudinal studies of duration and timing of events. *Psychological Bulletin, 5*(1), 268–290.

Snyder, H. N., & Sickmund, M. (1999). *OJJDP statistical briefing book*. Washington, DC: Office of Juvenile Justice and Delinquency Prevention.

Taylor, D. L., Biafora, F. A., Warheit, G., & Gil, A. (1997). Family factors, theft, vandalism, and major deviance among a multiracial/multiethnic sample of adolescent girls. *Journal of Social Distress and the Homeless, 6*(1), 71–87.

Terry, R., & Coie, J. D. (1991). A comparison of methods for defining sociometric status among children. *Developmental Psychology, 27*, 867–880.

Travillion, K., & Snyder, J. (1993). The role of maternal discipline and involvement in peer rejection and neglect. *Journal of Applied Developmental Psychology, 14*, 37–57.

Underwood, M. K., Galen, B. R., & Paquette, J. A. (2001). Top ten challenges for understanding aggression and gender: Why can't we all just get along? *Social Development, 10*, 248–266.

Underwood, M. K., Kupersmidt, J. B., & Coie, J. D. (1996). Childhood peer sociometric status and aggression as predictors of adolescent childbearing. *Journal of Research on Adolescence, 6*(2), 201–223.

Valois, R. F., McKeown, R. E., Garrison, C. Z., & Vincent, M. L. (1995). Correlates of aggressive and violent behaviors among public high school adolescents. *Journal of Adolescent Health, 16*, 26–34.

Ward, J. V. (1995). Cultivating a morality of care in African American adolescent: A culture-based model of violence prevention. *Harvard Educational Review, 65*(2), 175–186.

Webster-Stratton, C. (1996). Early onset conduct problems: Does gender make a difference? *Journal of Consulting and Clinical Psychology, 64*, 540–551.

Xie, H., Cairns, R. B., & Cairns, B. D. (1999). Social networks and configurations and in inner-city schools: Aggression, popularity, and implications for students with EBD. *Journal of Emotional and Behavioral Disorders, 7*(3) 147–156.

Zoccolillo, M. (1993). Gender and the development of conduct disorder. *Development and Psychopathology, 5*, 65–78.

Commentary:
New Research Approaches
to the Study of Aggression

Lea Pulkkinen
University of Jyväskylä

AGE-RELEVANT MEASUREMENT OF AGGRESSION

From the early days of the 20th century, the loose or imprecise use of psychological terminology has been recognized as a problem (Block, 2000). The concept of *aggression* is no exception as Tremblay (1991) showed. In the so-called *jingle-jangle problem* the *jingle fallacy* refers to the situation in which the same term is used for different entities, whereas in the jangle fallacy, different terms are used for the same underlying construct (Block, 2000).

In the two chapters reviewed here, an exact operational definition of *aggression* has been the goal. Baillargeon, Tremblay, and Willms (chap. 3) measured *physical* aggression of 2- and 3-year-old children in terms of three items rated (mostly by mothers) on a 3-point scale (1 = *never or not true*; 2 = *sometimes or somewhat true*; and 3 = *often or very true*): (a) Gets into many fights; (b) When another child accidentally hurts him/her (such as bumping into him/her), assumes that the other child meant to do it, and then reacts with anger and fighting; and (c) Kicks, bites, hits other children. The results are analyzed for each item separately without forming a scale for physical aggression. Miller-Johnson, Moore, Underwood, and Coie (chap. 4), in contrast, say that they have measured the physical aggression of third graders (and again when they were in the fourth and fifth grades) by means of an item: "Starts fights, hits other children, or says mean things to them." The method used was peer nomination, according to which children were asked to nominate three children who best fit the description. Aggressive participants at each grade were those who received a standardized aggression score greater than 1.0 standard deviation from the mean.

Throughout the Results section of their chapter, Miller-Johnson et al. described their findings using the general term (childhood) *aggression*, but in the title, Table 4.1, and partly in the Discussion, the term *physical aggression* was used. The third component of the item, however, concerns verbal aggression. Physical and verbal aggression correlate highly as other studies show, but labeling the measured variable only on the basis of physical aggression is not warranted.

All the variables in the Baillargeon et al. chapter concern physical aggression, but there is a problem in their developmental relevance. Although it is good that the second item tries to tap defensive, reactive aggression, one may question of how well a 2-year-old child is able to attribute intentions to another individual's behavior as supposed by the second item. Perhaps the item reflects an adult reaction that is projected onto small children. The Person Most Knowledgeable (PMK) who was asked to rate the child's behavior had to make the interpretation of the attribution. Possibly this process explained why the results for this item differed from the results of the other items in a sense that there were no gender differences. However, the results for the two other items *fights* and *kicks* differed from each other in the sense that getting into many fights increased from age 2 to 3, but kicking, biting, and hitting decreased. One may argue that the age typicality of these items differed; getting into fights as a sequence of behaviors is more typical of older children than of babies or small toddlers.

The operationalization of aggression presupposes sensitivity to mental processes and typical behaviors at the age in question. Detailed observational studies, as conducted by Goodenough (1931), Dawe (1934), Jersild and Markey (1935), Appel (1943), Koch (1942), Must and Sharpe (1947), and Mandel (1959) at the time when the empirical study of aggression began are needed for the construction of measures. For instance, Goodenough studied children ages 7 months to 8 years and found nearly 2,000 different outbursts of anger on the basis of mothers' recordings. Mandel (1959) listed 2,205 different aggressive responses in the behavior of 9 to 16-year-old boys in a boarding school. I personally learned a lot from these studies when I reviewed them for my doctoral dissertation (Pitkänen, 1969).

These old studies provide a great deal of descriptive material concerning conflicts between toddlers. The successions of aggressive events have been classified, and the frequencies of different categories have been recorded. Physical aggression is displayed earlier than verbal aggression. Although the former decreases and the latter increases with age (Goodenough, 1931; Koch, 1942), the frequency of different types of acts within each category varies with age (Jersild & Markey, 1935). Furthermore, children have conflicts mostly with those of the same sex and age; aggression toward adults is relatively infrequent. One child does not behave aggressively toward one person only; the number of different targets correlates highly with the frequency of quarrels. Boys tend to project hostility on the environment when in conflict with adults, but toward the other person when in conflict with other children.

The use of different aggression indicators at different ages causes problems for the comparability of findings across ages, but making such comparisons is the essence of longitudinal studies. Perhaps it may be possible to secure international agreement on a conceptual analysis project based on the findings of both previous and ongoing studies, which results in improved consensus on age-relevant measures of aggression. The various aspects of aggression (Pitkänen, 1969; Pulkkinen, 1987, 1996; Tremblay, 2000) could be measured by means of subscales. These aspects would include the intention of the aggressor (i.e., whether the aggression is defensive [reactive] or offensive [proactive]); direct and indirect ways of expressing aggression; different expressive modalities (physical, verbal and facial); intensity of the aggression; and the aggressor's tendency to escalate a conflict once started. In view of the seriousness of aggression and violence for the future security of mankind, systematic joint efforts for gaining conceptual clarity on aggression, and the methodology of its measurement, should surely be encouraged.

CULTURE-SPECIFIC CYCLES OF MALADJUSTMENT

Miller-Johnson et al. demonstrated a continuity from childhood aggression to externalizing problem behaviors and arrests. Although the authors said that aggression in childhood was "rather stable," the stability coefficient was only .20, which is much less than that quoted in other studies (e.g., Cairns & Cairns, 1994). Low stability may be due to the low reliability of aggression as measured by a single variable, which may also explain inconsistencies in the findings. The conclusions reached by this study could have been drawn with greater caution, especially in view of the minimal use of statistical tests. The analysis of data based on single variables also raises doubts about reliability in the Baillargeon et al. study. Little, Cunningham, Shahar, and Widaman (in press) recommended following a procedure (parceling) according to which a construct such as aggression is operationalized by three relevant item combinations.

The increasing number of longitudinal studies indicates a continuity in behavior problems from childhood to adulthood. Less is known about how children's behavioral patterns develop. For instance, it is known that hyper-activity during the preschool years combined with aggressive behavior is strongly linked to later antisocial behavior (Rutter, Giller, & Hagell, 1998). Yet whether hyperactivity and aggression are developmentally independent characteristics or whether they develop interactively under certain risk con-ditions should be further investigated. Aggression may begin a cycle of maladaptation as shown by Kokko and Pulkkinen (2000): Physical aggres-sion at age 8 preceded school maladjustment at age 14, and school malad-justment was both directly and indirectly—via problem drinking and/or lack of occupational alternatives—linked to long-term unemployment. The accumulation of problems in social functioning often comprises antisocial behavior (Rönkä, Kinnunen, & Pulkkinen, 2000).

Females and males may be involved in different types of maladaptation cycles, and the typical cycles may also vary in different subcultures. More information should be collected on differences in male and female cycles of maladaptation, as well as on vulnerability factors in different subcul-tures. For instance, media violence and availability of guns and drugs may increase vulnerability to aggression and crime among individuals living in the high-risk conditions of African-American youth. A vulnerability fac-tor has little effect at low risk, but a detrimental effect at high risk (Tiet et al., 1998).

APPLIED STUDY FOR THE PREVENTION OF AGGRESSION

To prevent aggression and other aspects of externalizing problem behav-iors, we need to understand how causal mechanisms operate. Miller-John-son et al. suggested the selection of specific groups for intervention. The authors referred to a set of guidelines on gender-sensitive intervention strategies put forth by the American Office of Juvenile and Delinquency Prevention. It would be interesting to know how these strategies have been developed. In general, there are not many well-known intervention studies carried out. Their scarcity is related, on the one hand, to the fact that basic research has not been able to suggest or identify effective protective factors against aggression among people living in high-risk conditions. Therefore, there is no good empirical basis for the development of interventions. On the other hand, the low valuation of applied research in human sciences concerning, for instance, the development of intervention strategies is ob-vious in many countries, as evaluated on the basis of funding opportunities. In technical sciences, applied study is more highly valued because techni-cal innovations are seen as increasing the gross national product (GNP). It is not yet sufficiently recognized that social innovations might also have a strong impact on national economies. For the future of mankind, social innovations may be even more important than technical innovations in view of the high technological level already reached.

REFERENCES

Appel, M. (1943). Aggressive behavior of nursery school children and adult procedures in dealing with such behavior. *Journal of Experimental Education, 11*, 185–199.

Block, J. (2000). Three tasks for personality psychology. In L. R. Bergman, R. B. Cairns, L.-G. Nilsson, & L. Nystedt (Eds.), *Developmental science and the holistic approach* (pp. 155–164). Mahwah, NJ: Lawrence Erlbaum Associates.

Cairns, R. B., & Cairns, B. D. (1994). *Lifelines and risks.* London: Harvester Wheatsheaf.

Dawe, H. (1934). An analysis of two hundred quarrels of preschool children. *Child Development, 5*, 139–157.

Goodenough, F. (1931). *Anger in young children.* Minneapolis: University of Minnesota Press.

Jersild, A., & Markey, F. (1935). Conflicts between preschool children. *Child Development Monographs, 21.*

Koch, H. (1942). A factor analysis of some measures of the behavior of preschool children. *Journal of General Psychology, 27*, 257–287.

Kokko, K., & Pulkkinen, L. (2000). Aggression in childhood and long-term unemployment in adulthood: A cycle of maladaptation and some protective factors. *Developmental Psychology, 36*, 463–472.

Little, T. D., Cunningham, W. A., Shahar, G., & Widaman, K. F. (in press). To parcel or not to parcel: Exploring the question, weighing the merits. *Structural Equation Modeling.*

Mandel, R. (1959). *Die Aggressivität bei Schülern.* Bern: Huber.

Must, M., & Sharpe, D. (1947). Some influential factors in the determination of aggressive behavior in preschool children. *Child Development, 18*, 11–28.

Pitkänen, L. (1969) *A descriptive model of aggression and nonaggression with applications to children's behaviour.* Jyväskylä: Jyväskylä Studies in Education, Psychology and Social Research, Whole Nr. 19.

Pulkkinen, L. (1987). Offensive and defensive aggression in humans: A longitudinal perspective. *Aggressive Behavior, 13*, 197–212.

Pulkkinen, L. (1996). Proactive and reactive aggression in early adolescence as precursors to anti- and prosocial behavior in young adults. *Aggressive Behavior, 22*, 241–257.

Rutter, M., Giller, H., & Hagell, A. (1998). *Antisocial behavior by young people.* Cambridge, MA: Cambridge University Press.

Rönkä, A., Kinnunen, U., & Pulkkinen, L. (2000). The accumulation of problems of social functioning as a long-term process: Women and men compared. *International Journal of Behavioral Development, 24*, 442–450.

Tiet, Q. Q., Bird, H. R., Davies, M., Hoven, C., Cohen, P., Jensen, P. S., & Goodman, S. (1998). Adverse life events and resilience. *Journal of American Academy of Child and Adolescent Psychiatry, 37*, 1191–1200.

Tremblay, R. E. (1991). Aggression, prosocial behavior, and gender: Three magic words but no magic wand. In D. J. Pepler & K. H. Rubin (Eds.), *The development and treatment of childhood aggression* (pp. 71–78). Hillsdale, NJ: Lawrence Erlbaum Associates.

Tremblay, R. E. (2000). The development of aggressive behaviour during childhood: What have we learned in the past century? *International Journal of Behavioral Development, 24*, 129–141.

Part III

THE SOCIAL NATURE OF GIRLS' AGGRESSION

5

The Development
of Aggressive Behaviors
Among Girls: Measurement
Issues, Social Functions,
and Differential Trajectories

Hongling Xie
Beverley D. Cairns
Robert B. Cairns
Center for Developmental Science,
University of North Carolina at Chapel Hill

Over the past 30 years, the developmental trajectories and functions of physical aggression have been largely clarified in various longitudinal investigations (e.g., Cairns & Cairns, 1994; Farrington, 1991; Magnusson & Bergman, 1990). Modest to high levels of continuity of physically aggressive behaviors have been reported (e.g., Cairns & Cairns, 1994; Olweus, 1979; Pulkkinen, 1998), and the magnitude depends on the length of time between two assessment points. The development of physically aggressive behaviors is also supported by a person's social relationships and social interaction within peer networks (e.g., Cairns, Cairns, Neckerman, Gest, & Gariépy 1988; Dishion, Andrews, & Crosby, 1995; Farmer, 2000; Farmer & Rodkin, 1996; Giordano, Cernovich, & Pugh, 1986; Luthar & McMahon, 1996; Rodkin, Farmer, Pearl, &Van Acker, 2000; Xie, Cairns, & Cairns, 1999). Finally, physical aggression in childhood and adolescence yields robust predictions of subsequent maladjustment such as school dropout, teen parenthood, and criminal behaviors (e.g., Cairns, Cairns, & Neckerman, 1989; Ensminger & Slusarcick,

1992; Farrington, 1986; Serbin, Peters, McAffer, & Schwartzman, 1991; Stattin & Magnusson, 1989).

Over a decade ago, the Cairns and their colleagues (Cairns, Cairns, Neckerman, Ferguson, & Gariépy, 1989) reported that, in addition to confrontational strategies such as physical aggression, children and adolescents also used nonconfrontational strategies for interpersonal control and anger expression. They called such nonconfrontational behaviors social aggression. This includes gossiping, social ostracism, and social isolation. A significant gender difference was found in middle childhood and early adolescence, with girls using social aggression more often than boys. About the same time, Lagerspetz and her colleagues (Lagerspetz, Björkqvist, & Peltonen, 1988) also reported a similar gender difference in subtly aggressive behaviors they labeled *indirect aggression*. Earlier, Feshbach and colleagues (Feshbach, 1969; Feshbach & Sones, 1971) found that girls were more likely than boys to use indirect aggression (e.g., ignoring, avoidance) to a newcomer during a laboratory observation session. More recently, increased attention has been given to these subtle forms of aggression (e.g., Crick & Grotpeter, 1995; Galen & Underwood, 1997; Kaukiainen et al., 1999; Xie, 1998). Compared with physical aggression, much less is known about the social processes and developmental properties of subtly aggressive behaviors.

In this chapter, we focus on the social functions and developmental predictions of social and physical aggression among girls, but findings on boys are included to provide a necessary comparison. Four issues are examined: (a) characteristics of subtly aggressive behaviors and corresponding measurement strategies, (b) interactional properties of social aggression compared with physical aggression, (c) social functions and peer social dynamics of socially aggressive behaviors, and (d) developmental predictions of criminal behaviors associated with social and physical aggression. Gender differences in the developmental trajectories of aggression are identified. Implications for prevention and future research are discussed.

In examining these issues, qualitative and quantitative data from the Carolina Longitudinal Study (CLS; Cairns & Cairns, 1994) are used. The CLS involved 695 participants first seen in Grade 4 (Cohort I, $n = 220$) and Grade 7 (Cohort II, $n = 475$). Twenty-five percent of the sample was African American, which represents the proportion of African-American population in the communities selected from a mid-Atlantic state. Participants were interviewed annually until high school graduation and at 2- or 4-year intervals into adulthood. Regardless of their locations and living circumstances, effort has been made to track each and every one of these participants. High levels of retention have been achieved over the years (.87 – .99).

SOCIAL AGGRESSION:
DEFINITION AND DEVELOPMENTAL FUNCTIONS

Definition and Differentiation

Given that different terms have been used to label subtle aggressive behaviors (i.e., social aggression, indirect aggression, and relational aggression), a clarification of definition is necessary. Their primary differences and similarities on operationalization and primary measurement strategies are summarized in Table 5.1.

Social aggression refers to actions that cause interpersonal damage and are achieved by nonconfrontational and largely concealed methods that employ the social community (Cairns et al., 1989; Xie, 1998). It includes gossiping, social exclusion, social isolation, social alienation, writing notes about someone, talking about someone behind his or her back, stealing friends or romantic partners, triangulation of friendship or romantic relationship, and telling secrets/betrayal of trust. Two characteristics of socially aggressive behaviors should be noted: (a) it is nonconfrontational, and (b) it uses social relationships or the social community as a vehicle to attack. Narrative reports of interpersonal conflicts have been used to assess gender differences and developmental changes. Gender differences were assessed by the proportions of socially aggressive conflicts as a function of different gender combinations of the actors in the conflicts (i.e., female–female, female–male, male–female, and male–male). Developmental changes were assessed in a similar manner by comparing the proportions of socially aggressive conflicts reported at different ages.[1]

Underwood and colleagues (e.g., Galen & Underwood, 1997) later used the term *social aggression* to also include negative facial expressions and body gestures. Vignettes, narratives, questionnaires, and laboratory observations were employed to assess gender differences in the perception of socially aggressive behaviors and adolescents' experience of social aggression.

Feshbach and colleagues (Feshbach, 1969; Feshbach & Sones, 1971) used the term *indirect aggression* to refer to behaviors such as ignoring, avoiding, and excluding others from social interchanges during a laboratory observation session. Indirect aggression in these sessions was confrontational in the sense that the perpetrator was present. Gender differences in social interaction were identified. Later Lagerspetz and colleagues used the term *indirect aggression* to refer to a somewhat different set of aggressive

---

[1]A socially aggressive conflict was coded when social aggression was the primary exchange in the conflict.

TABLE 5.1

A Comparison of Different Definitions

Different Terms	Behavior Examples	Confrontational Behavior	Nonconfrontational Behavior	Involvement of Social Others	Primary Measurement Strategies
Social aggression (e.g., Cairns)	Social alienation, gossip, isolation, writing/passing notes, & stealing friends		All	Always	Narrative reports of conflict
Social aggression (e.g., Underwood)	Gossip, exclusion, negative facial expression, & body gestures	Some	Some	Sometimes	Narratives, observations, & vignette
Indirect aggression (e.g., Lagerspetz)	Gossip, becoming someone else's friend, & social isolation		All	Most of the time	Peer rating
Indirect aggression (e.g., Feshbach)	Ignoring, avoiding, & excluding	All		Sometimes	Laboratory observation
Relational aggression (e.g., Crick)	Threatening to terminate a friendship, ignoring, social exclusion, & gossip	Most	Some	Sometimes	Peer nomination & teacher rating

strategies, in which the harm was indirectly achieved and the perpetrator remained unidentified (Lagerspetz & Björkqvist, 1994; Lagerspetz et al., 1988). Individual differences in indirect aggression were assessed by peer ratings on five behaviors: "Tells untruth behind the back," "Starts being somebody else's friend as revenge," "Tries to get the other on his or her side," "Says to others: 'Let's not be with him or her'," and "Takes revenge in play." Similar to social aggression, indirect aggression as used by Lagerspetz and her colleagues referred to nonconfrontational behaviors. Indirect aggression differs from social aggression, however, in that the perpetrator does not have to use the social community as a means to attack.

Relational aggression refers to behaviors that harm others through manipulation or damage to social relationships or feelings of acceptance and inclusion (e.g., Crick, 1997; Crick & Grotpeter, 1995). Individual differences in relational aggression are usually assessed by the Peer Nomination Instrument. Five behaviors were included in the measure: "When mad, gets even by keeping the person from being in their group of friends," "Tells friends they will stop liking them unless friends do what they say," "When mad at a person, ignores them or stops talking to them," "Tries to keep certain people from being in their group during activity or play time," and "Tries to make other kids not like a certain person by spreading rumors about them" (Crick, 1997). In some reports of factor analysis, the last item—gossip/rumor—also loaded on overt aggression (physical and verbal aggression) and was excluded from relational aggression (e.g., Crick & Grotpeter, 1995). Note that these behaviors can be either confrontational or nonconfrontational. Some of these behaviors (e.g., gossip) involve the social community, whereas others (e.g., threatening to end a friendship, ignore) do not.

Why Nonconfrontational Behaviors?

The question arises as to why we refer to social aggression exclusively as nonconfrontational and socially mediated. The answer lies in the unique features associated with nonconfrontational compared with confrontational behaviors. The use of a nonconfrontational strategy enables the perpetrator to conceal or obscure his or her identity, whereas the use of confrontational aggression makes the identity of the perpetrator clear to both the victim and other individuals. As a result, carrying out confrontational aggression runs two risks: direct revenge or escalation by the victim, and punishment by the authorities. In contrast, nonconfrontational behaviors such as social aggression minimize these risks (see also Cairns & Cairns, 1994; Lagerspetz & Björkqvist, 1994). The damage of such actions may be largely delayed in time and transformed in context. As a result, the chances of revenge by the victim and punishment by the authorities may be largely reduced.

The effectiveness of nonconfrontational aggression depends on the use of social networks as a vehicle for attack. The damage to the victim is not automatic and requires mediation through other individuals in the social community. For a social attack to be effective, the perpetrator has to engage the participation and help of other individuals within the social networks. As a result, the use of nonconfrontational aggression may involve more complicated social dynamics than confrontational aggression. It may also require the processing and utilization of more complicated social information.

The use of nonconfrontational aggression requires more advanced cognitive and social skills. For a social attack to be effective, a person needs accurate knowledge of the networks of interpersonal relationships and subtle skills of manipulating social relationships. It was found that high levels of indirect aggression were associated with high levels of social intelligence, whereas confrontational aggression (i.e., physical aggression and verbal aggression) was not (Kaukiainen et al., 1999).

It seems reasonable to expect that nonconfrontational aggressive behaviors develop later in life than confrontational aggressive behaviors given the prior consideration. Longitudinal research has reported that physical aggression emerges early in development (e.g., Tremblay et al., 1999). Verbal aggression emerges at a later point when children start verbal communication. A rapid increase in socially aggressive behaviors has been documented during the transition from childhood to adolescence (e.g., Björkqvist, Lagerspetz, & Kaukiainen, 1992; Cairns & Cairns, 1994). By early to middle adolescence, gossiping becomes the most frequently reported form of social aggression (Paquette & Underwood, 1999).

The unique features of nonconfrontational aggression may require unique assessment strategies. The possibility that a perpetrator's identity could be concealed and obscured in using nonconfrontational aggression brings a measurement challenge to the forefront—namely, how to measure individual differences on such subtle and disguised behaviors when personal identity is concealed. Given the unique features of socially aggressive behaviors, assessment strategies should be carefully considered to avoid the risk of losing the subtlety of such a phenomenon (see also Cairns, 1986).

The Development of Social Aggression: Adaptive Functions

Three important developmental questions deserve attention: (a) Why do individuals use nonconfrontational behaviors of social aggression? (b) Why is there a substantial increase during early adolescence? (c) Why do adolescent girls report more use of social aggression than adolescent boys?

The Development of Social Aggression: Theoretical Proposals.
From a frustration–aggression perspective, Dollard, Doob, Miller, Mowrer, and Sears (1939) proposed that aggression cannot always be directly expressed because of the threat of punishment. They also noted that the inhibition of aggression does not necessarily reduce the motivation to aggress. Instead displacement may occur, which involves aggressing against a target associated with a weaker threat of punishment (see also Zillman, 1978). Given that social aggression may fulfill the motivation without changing the target, it seems to be a reasonably effective strategy to express anger while reducing the threat of retaliation and punishment.

In social learning theory, Bandura (1973) proposed that, through modeling and direct feedback (i.e., reward or punishment), a person learns social rules and standards to guide his or her behaviors. He also noted that individuals engage in a variety of neutralization strategies by which self-condemnation for aggression is minimized. These actions include diffusion and displacement of responsibility, justification of aggression in terms of higher principles, and dehumanization of the victim. Social aggression may enable the perpetrator to successfully neutralize self-condemnation by diffusing and displacing responsibility when his or her identity can be obscured behind the fabric of social networks. Spreading gossip can also be easily rationalized as "telling the truth."

More recently, an effect/danger ratio explanation was offered. According to Björqvist (1994), the effect/danger ratio is the expression of a subjective estimation of the likely consequences of an aggressive act. The aggressor assesses the ratio between the effect of the intended strategy and the possible danger involved—whether physical, psychological, or social. The objective is to maximize the ratio. Although believed to be effective, physical aggression puts a person at great risk for direct retaliation. Indirect aggression, in contrast, may be equally effective with minimal danger of a counterattack. The effect/danger ratio of verbal aggression may stand between physical and indirect aggression. Hence, indirect aggression represents the most desirable strategy based on the effect/danger ratio.

The Development of Social Aggression During Early Adolescence.
Previous longitudinal and cross-sectional studies (Cairns & Cairns, 1994; Cairns et al., 1989; Eder & Sanford, 1986; Lagerspetz & Björkqvist, 1994) reported a significant increase in social aggression during late childhood and early adolescence. One must wonder why. Both individual and social contextual factors may help explain this developmental spurt.

Social-cognitive development from childhood to adolescence may facilitate the use of social aggression. Nonconfrontational aggressive strategies require the utilization of more complicated social information and commonly occur in adult interpersonal interactions. This suggests that social aggression is a more advanced strategy and develops later in life (e.g., Björkqvist et al., 1994). During late childhood and early adolescence, children experience an increase in their cognitive ability and social-cognitive skills (e.g., Inhelder & Piaget, 1958; Keating, 1990). Their ability to understand another's perspective and information in the broader social networks makes the nonconfrontational aggressive strategy more feasible at this period of development.

Further, the increased salience of popularity, social status, and romantic relationships may have a powerful effect on interpersonal exchanges. Extracurricular activities make the issue of popularity and social status more salient in middle school (e.g., Eder, Evans, & Parker, 1995). Participation in highly visible extracurricular activities such as cheerleading for girls and athletic teams for boys is related to increased popularity and peer status (Eder & Kinney, 1997). During middle school, a visible social hierarchy develops, and affiliation with popular girls becomes an important avenue for promoting one's peer status (e.g., Eder, 1985). Competition for friends, a romantic partner, and social visibility or status may generate interpersonal conflicts that evoke the use of social aggression.

Gender Difference in Socially Aggressive Behaviors.   Why do girls use social aggression more often than boys? It has long been noted that physical confrontation may be more accepted by society for males than for females. The differential social sanctions against physical aggression may contribute to girls' reliance on nonconfrontational aggressive strategies instead of direct confrontations.

It should be noted that gender difference in social aggression increases during late childhood and early adolescence, when sexual dimorphism takes place (Björkqvist et al., 1992; Cairns & Cairns, 1994; Xie, 1998). Greater physical strength of boys after puberty, compared with girls (e.g., Hoyenga & Hoyenga, 1979), enables boys to compete and confront more physically and may bias their estimation of the danger of retaliation. Hence, boys are more likely to continue using physical aggression after puberty than girls, who may rely more on nonconfrontational aggression as a practical matter. Further, during puberty social role differences in males and females (including the expression of anger and interpersonal control) may become more dominant, with greater social sanctions against females' use of physical aggression. Hence, it is likely that biological development converges with social role expectations during puberty to support more differentiated aggression expression between males and females.

Girls tend to be more concerned with social status and relationships than boys (e.g., Rosenberg & Simons, 1975). To undermine another person's social status, one must manipulate both the opinions and relationships of others. Direct confrontational strategies such as physical or verbal aggression may not be effective given the range and type of damage they inflict. Merten (1997) demonstrated how girls in junior high school were able to indirectly undermine another girl's increased popularity and turn others against her by telling others that she talks about people behind their backs.

The effectiveness of social aggression is also perceived differently by boys and girls. The differential effectiveness is likely related to gender differences in the use of social aggression. Galen and Underwood (1997) found that when presented with a social aggression vignette, girls reported a greater degree of hurtfulness than boys. Girls perceived social aggression to be as hurtful as physical aggression, but boys perceived social aggression to be less hurtful than physical aggression.

Gender differences in friendships and close relationships may also contribute to the observed gender differences in social aggression. Compared with friendships among boys, friendships among girls tend to focus more on intimacy and mutual support, with a higher degree of self-disclosure (e.g., Berndt, 1982; Blyth & Foster-Clark, 1987; Maccoby, 1990). Greater demand for intimacy and mutual support may increase the likelihood of interpersonal conflicts related to friendship loyalty and social exclusion (Eder & Hallinan, 1978). High levels of self-disclosure may make girls more vulnerable to gossip and betrayal (see also Maccoby, 1998). Merten (1997) illustrated how the notes exchanged between friends could later be used to discredit one another.

In summary, the development and gender differences of social aggression reflect the simultaneous operation of several correlated factors: (a) sexual dimorphism during puberty, (b) social-cognitive development, (c) changes in peer social networks and social dynamics, and (d) gender differences in social roles and social relationships. To be sure, the use of social aggression serves adaptive functions for the perpetrator. It reduces the opportunity for revenge and punishment while effectively undermining the other person's social status and social relationships.

INDIVIDUAL DIFFERENCES IN SOCIAL AGGRESSION: METHODOLOGICAL ISSUES

Two tasks are required to adequately assess individual differences in socially aggressive behaviors: (a) record the occurrence of such behavior, and (b) identify the individual(s) responsible for that behavior. These two assessment tasks can be essentially reduced to one for confrontational aggression given the direct link between a confrontational act and a person's identity. Yet for nonconfrontational behaviors of social aggression, these two tasks are not always resolvable when the identity of a person can be disassociated with his or her disguised acts. Traces of social aggression may be detected after a certain period of time, but the identity of the perpetrator may remain difficult to track. The primary challenge for researchers is to make a precise link between the individual and the disguised act.

Measurement Strategies

Teacher Ratings. In assessing physically aggressive and disruptive behaviors, evaluations from teachers are often included. Previous research indicates that teacher ratings are highly reliable and informative (e.g., Achenbach, McConaughy, & Howell, 1987; Xie, Mahoney, & Cairns, 1999) because teachers can base their ratings on observations across multiple contexts over a substantial period of time (see also Cairns & Green, 1979). One potential limitation of teacher ratings may be the gender bias and personal belief that girls tend to use subtle aggression and boys use physical aggression. Another limitation may result from teachers' limited knowledge of subtle aggressive behaviors in students' social interactions.

Peer Ratings. Peer ratings have been used to assess individual differences in aggressive behaviors. For instance, Lagerspetz and Björkqvist (1994) asked each participant to rate his or her classmates on how the classmates would react when they became angry at a peer. Each child was asked to evaluate every classmate of the same gender. Options of behavioral reactions were provided to the participant for physical aggression, verbal aggression, and indirect aggression. The strength of this measure is that each participant receives ratings from all the same-gender peers in the class. The weaknesses are: (a) some participants may not be able to make an accurate rating, (b) ratings may be affected by the rater's social relationship with the classmate being rated, and (c) the general reputation of the classmate may affect the raters' judgment.

Peer Nominations. Peer nominations have also been used to assess individual differences in aggressive behaviors. For instance, in a group administration setting, Crick (1997) asked each participant to nominate three classmates for a described behavior. Items were designed to assess physical aggression, verbal aggression, and relational aggression. To adjust for different numbers of participants, nomination scores received by each participant were then standardized within the appropriate social unit such as the class or school.

Although efficient, this measurement strategy suffers from several limitations. First, this standardization procedure for peer nominations eliminates the opportunity to examine developmental changes of aggressive behaviors because the mean scores of every age group have been set to 0. Second, it may be ineffective to identify subtle aggressive behaviors such as gossip. If an aggressor can be hidden behind group processes, an effective social aggressor may not be publicly recognized for his or her bad behavior. As a result, it may identify only those who are not highly skilled in concealing their aggressive acts. Third, nominations may be influenced by social stigma (e.g., Kenny, 1991). When a child is perceived by peers to be disruptive and high in physical aggression, he or she may be nominated because of social stigma or the salience of his or her disruptive behavior rather than subtly aggressive behaviors (see also Crick et al., 1999). Finally, a child may have been nominated for gossiping behavior as a result of character defamation by others. When a rumor is told in a class or school that Child A always talks about other people behind their backs, it is likely that Child A will receive high scores of peer nominations for gossiping.

Self-Report. Many studies have used self-reports to assess individual differences in social behaviors. Previous research, however, has found that self-reports often fail to show high levels of correspondence with measures from outside the self (e.g., Achenbach et al., 1987; Cairns & Cairns, 1994; Xie, Mahoney, & Cairns, 1999). The primary function served by self-perceptions and self-evaluations is adaptive and toward a positive self-image (e.g., Brown & Dutton, 1995; Cairns & Cairns, 1994; Epstein, 1973; Greenwald, 1980; Kenrick & Stringfield, 1980; Sedikides & Strube, 1997; Taylor & Brown, 1994; Xie, Mahoney, & Cairns, 1999). When a domain is specific or involves public knowledge, self-reports are more likely to be aligned with information from outside the self (e.g., Marsh, Walker, & Debus, 1991; Skaalvik & Rankin, 1994). When a domain is general or private or a behavior is hard to justify, self-reports are more likely to be distorted (e.g., Leung, 1996).

Given the disguised nature of subtle aggression, it is likely that the perpetrator will deny his or her aggressive actions. A low correspondence between self-reports and others' reports has been reported (Lagerspetz et al., 1988; Xie, Cairns, & Cairns, 2002a). The discrepancy between self-reports and others' reports may be further exacerbated by the difficulty for others to observe a disguised behavior. Although self-report may be limited by self-denial, when a person admits such an act, it may be highly valid.

Direct Observation. Behavior observations can be conducted by trained observers either inside the laboratory or in natural contexts such as classrooms or playgrounds. Feshbach and her colleagues (Feshbach, 1969; Feshbach, & Sones, 1971) observed the social interactions between a newcomer and a pair of children who were acquainted. They found that girls were more likely to ignore the newcomer than boys were. The advantage of using direct observations is the validity and accuracy of linking the perpetrator with his or her behaviors. Laboratory settings, however, may pose limitations on observing concealed behaviors such as gossiping which requires the manipulation of social communities and the existence of more than one social context for such behavior to follow its natural course.

Behavior observations in natural settings transcend the limitation of a laboratory setting in the sense that natural settings provide more opportunities for social interactions with peers (see also Pepler & Craig, 1995). Pepler and her colleagues (Pepler, Craig, & Roberts, 1998) video- and audiotaped children's social interactions on the playground. They were able to record both prosocial and antisocial behaviors, as well as gossiping behaviors when two or more children talked about another child. Hart and his colleagues also used observations of children's behaviors on the school playground to assess individual differences in relational aggression (McNeilly-Choque, Hart, Robinson, Nelson, & Olsen, 1996). Even natural observations may be somewhat limited in the type of context observed because the natural course of socially aggressive behaviors often moves through multiple contexts over a substantial period of time—sometimes days or weeks.

Narrative Measures.   Narratives of interpersonal conflicts reported by children and adolescents in semistructured interviews provide another avenue to assess socially aggressive behaviors and their interactional processes. The first step toward the establishment of an appropriate measure for individual differences of social aggression starts from an understanding of the natural course of socially aggressive behaviors in interpersonal exchanges.

Cairns and Cairns (1994) asked participants to report two recent interpersonal conflicts (one with a same-gender peer and the other with an opposite-gender peer). A standard protocol was used to elicit the details. The interview started with, "Has anyone bothered you recently or caused you any trouble or made you mad?" It was then followed by standard probes: "Who was it?" "How did it start?" "What happened?" "What did you do?" "How did it end?" "Did anything else come of it?" On the basis of narrative reports, the aggressive acts and perpetrator's identity were coded (Xie, 1998). A peer-narrative measure was computed according to the number of times a child was identified as the perpetrator of socially aggressive strategies in their peers' conflict reports. This measurement strategy differs from peer nomination in the sense that a researcher codes a child's aggressive acts in conflict exchanges reported by the child's peers.

The strength of narrative measure is that the researcher codes socially aggressive behaviors. Consider a scenario of social alienation: "Jane told me that Wendy said something bad about me." From the participant's perspective, Jane was a loyal friend who provided valuable and protective information. From Jane's perspective, she was simply telling the truth. From Wendy's perspective, Jane was alienating her relationship with the participant. However, it is possible that Wendy does not know that it was Jane who was talking. Using peer nominations or self-report, Jane's social alienating behavior might not be identified. In this case, the independent judgment by the researcher becomes the key to identify Jane's aggressive behavior. Another strength of the narrative strategy is the unique opportunity to examine social interactional processes of social aggression (Xie, Swift, Cairns, & Cairns, 2002b). It takes substantial time and multiple relationships for socially aggressive acts to become effective. This unique feature of social aggression makes it difficult to study its interactive patterns and interpersonal processes by using traditional methods of behavioral observation. In this regard, narrative accounts of interpersonal exchanges may bear unique information.

Narrative measures also encounter a couple of limitations. First, it is time- and effort-consuming because it involves narrative coding. Second, the reported conflicts are likely to be salient events, and individual difference measures have only limited range (i.e., many individuals were not identified as aggressive).

Relations Among Different Measures

How do these different measures of subtle aggressive behaviors relate to each other? Do they yield similar outcomes? Here we compare the empirical findings yielded by different measures on three aspects: gender differences of subtle aggressive behaviors, relations between subtly aggressive behaviors and physically aggressive behaviors, and intercorrelations among different measures.

Gender Differences.   Consistent patterns of gender differences on subtly aggressive behaviors are found with diverse assessment strategies: peer ratings (e.g., Lagerspetz et al., 1988), teacher ratings (e.g., McNeilly-Choque et al., 1996), self-reports (e.g., Xie et al., 2002a), behavior observations (e.g., Feshbach, 1969; McNeilly-Choque et al., 1996), and narrative measures (Cairns et al., 1989; Xie, 1998). In these studies, girls are often found to use subtle aggression (including social, indirect, or relational aggression) more than boys. Peer nominations, however, tend to yield negligible or reversed gender differences in the mean levels of relational aggression (e.g., McNeilly-Choque et al., 1996; Rys & Bear, 1997; Tomada & Schneider, 1997). Some reported more girls than boys in the top end of nomination scores (e.g., Crick & Grotpeter, 1995; Rys & Bear, 1997), whereas others reported more boys than girls in the top end (e.g., Crick, Casa, & Mosher, 1997; Tomada & Schneider, 1997). The reasons for such a discrepancy could have been multiple, among which may be the effect of reputation stigma on peer nominations of relational aggression.

Subtle Aggression and Physical Aggression. It is expected that when a person's general reputation and disruptive actions play a role in the assessment, a highly positive correlation may be found between subtly aggressive behaviors (e.g., social aggression, indirect aggression, relational aggression) and physically aggressive behaviors. Teacher ratings, peer ratings, and peer nominations seemed to yield high levels of correlation (e.g., Crick et al., 1997; Kaukiainen et. al., 1999). Low to modest levels of correlations between subtle and physical aggression were found in direct observations, peer-narrative measures, and self-reports (e.g., McNeilly-Choque et al., 1996; Pepler et al., 1998; Xie et al., 2002a).

Intercorrelations. Teacher ratings and peer nominations of relational aggression tend to correlate with each other at a moderate to high level (e.g., Crick et al., 1997). These two measures, however, have only modest correspondence with observational measures (e.g., McNeilly-Choque et al., 1996). A reliable, albeit low, correlation was found between self-report and peer ratings or peer-narrative measures (e.g., Lagerspetz et al., 1988; Xie et al., 2002a). The cross-assessment correlations are lower for subtle aggression than for physical aggression (e.g., Lagerspetz et al., 1988; McNeilly-Choque et al., 1996). This finding is of no surprise given the subtlety of the disguised acts and the ambiguity of a perpetrator's identity (Cairns & Cairns, 1994; Xie, Mahoney, & Cairns, 1999).

In summary, it is important for researchers to become aware of the strength and potential limitations of different measurement strategies. The sophistication and subtlety of the methodology must match the sophistication and subtlety of the phenomenon under investigation. Assessment of individual differences cannot be separated from the understanding of the natural course of social behaviors in interpersonal exchanges because human behavior takes its course in social interchanges and serves important functions in regulating social relationships.

SOCIAL AGGRESSION: INTERACTIONAL PROPERTIES

The unique features of socially aggressive behavior in interpersonal social interactions deserve a closer examination. Given its nonconfrontational nature, a successful social attack requires the assistance of other individuals. It was speculated earlier that social aggression serves important adaptive functions for the perpetrator. It may help obscure the perpetrator's identity and reduce the risk of direct revenge and punishment by authorities (Cairns et al., 1989; Cairns & Cairns, 1994; Lagerspetz et al., 1988). Narrative reports of conflicts with peers from the Carolina Longitudinal Study (Cairns & Cairns, 1994) have been used to identify the interactional properties of social aggression.

The Role of a Third Party

In reports of interpersonal conflicts among children and adolescents, we often encountered scenarios of social aggression, including social alienation ("Jane told me that Wendy said something bad about me") and gossiping ("They started the rumor that I stole a whole bunch of money from my mama's pocket"). If it takes two to fight, it takes at least three to gossip. We found that the vast majority of conflicts using physical aggression have a dyadic structure, but the majority of conflicts involving social aggression have a triangular structure or even more complicated structures (Xie, 1998). The participation of other individual(s) in the social community is critical for social aggression.

Concealment of the Perpetrator's Identity

One advantage of using social aggression is that the perpetrator may conceal or obscure his or her identity behind the social process. Among all the social attacks reported in the seventh grade, we found that about 10% of the time the victim had no clue who the perpetrator was. In another 10% or so, it was not clear whether the perpetrator's identity was revealed (Xie et al., 2002b). These were the times that a social attack reached the victim and hence got reported. Here is one participant's report:

> Cara found a rumor was going around about her stealing money from her mom; when asked about the person who did it, Cara replied: "They never did find out, … they said that Jenny said it, and Jenny said that Diane said it, but then um then, Jenny said that Amy said it, then Amy said that Angie said, and Angie said that Amy said, and Amy said that Jenny said it, so we never did find out who said it.…"

Reduced Risk of Counterattack

Another advantage of using social aggression is that the likelihood of direct revenge becomes largely reduced. Without knowing the perpetrator's identity, a victim would have a hard time committing revenge. Even when the perpetrator's identity was revealed, we found that the likelihood of physical or verbal counterattack against social aggression was substantially lower than the counterattacks against physical aggression (Xie et al., 2002b).

In addition to avoid counterattack from the victim, the perpetrator may use these tactics to set up negative exchanges of physical or verbal aggression among other individuals while eliminating the perpetrator's liability. Approximately one fifth of social aggression led to verbal or physical aggression between the victim and other individuals not involving the perpetrator. One report from a seventh-grade boy illustrates this point: "... See people, they like to see a good fight and you know, they just like to see a fight and they'll say like, he talked about your mother and all stuff like that...."

Punishment/Intervention by Authorities

The third speculated advantage of social aggression is the decreased chance of punishment by the authorities. In the reported conflicts, we found that teachers were less likely to intervene in social-aggression conflicts than in physical-aggression conflicts (Xie & Cairns, 2001). The difference may reflect several key features of the interactional process. First, the acts of social aggression are often hidden rather than open. It is more difficult for the school authorities to detect. Second, compared with physical aggression, students may be less likely to enlist the school authorities to intervene in negative exchanges of social aggression. Third, even when teachers have knowledge about the negative exchanges, they may be more likely to intervene in physical aggression than social aggression.

SOCIAL AGGRESSION: PEER SOCIAL NETWORKS AND SOCIAL FUNCTIONING

Given the unique features of social aggression in social interactions, we next examine the social processes involved. Mapping out the social processes and social functions served by socially aggressive behavior may be an important step toward understanding its roles in human development.

Social Networks and Social Aggression

Measures of peer social networks were built into the Carolina Longitudinal Study from the beginning. During individual interviews, participants were asked, "Are there some people in your class who hang around together a lot?" "Who are they?" "How about you? Do you have a group that you hang around with?" According to the reports of peer groups from all respondents within a grade, a composite social cognitive map was generated to identify social groups (Cairns, Gariépy, & Kindermann, 1991; Cairns, Perrin, & Cairns, 1985). A network centrality index was employed to assess the degree of embeddedness of an individual in the social networks. There were three levels: high, medium, and low. We found an association between network centrality and the use of social aggression (e.g., Xie et al., 2002a). Children and adolescents of low centrality in the peer social networks were least likely to use social aggression compared with other children and adolescents (see Fig. 5.1 for illustration).

Why is social network centrality positively associated with the use of social aggression? The association may reflect, among other things, the dynamic processes of shifting alliance in peer social networks during early adolescence. First, adolescents may use social aggression as a way to undermine others' social status and for themselves to achieve high prominence in social networks (see also Merten, 1997). Goodwin (1990a) demonstrated how girls restructure alignments in their groups by telling a given member about the wrongdoing committed by an absent party against the listener.

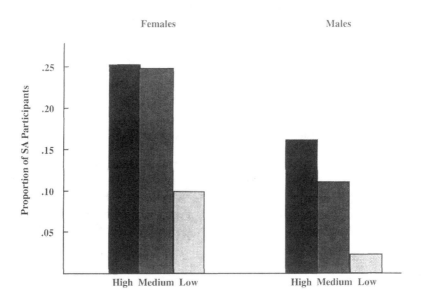

FIG. 5.1.   Social network centrality and the use of social aggression
in interpersonal conflicts.

Second, adolescents who are more central in the social networks may be more successful in the use of social aggression. The use of social aggression requires a person to be solidly embedded in his or her social networks. An effective social attack cannot be achieved without a connection to the social networks. Conversely, the more deeply a person is embedded in the fabric of relationship network, the more effective the social attack.

Third, compared with peripheral members in peer social networks, central figures may also encounter more conflict themes of social status and social relations. On one hand, they are likely to play a prominent role in the dynamics of group inclusion and exclusion (see also Adler & Adler, 1995). On the other hand, their prominent and central status makes them a more likely target for jealousy and competition. As a result, children and adolescents at the center of the networks are more likely to engage in social aggression.

When Social Aggression Fails

In over 700 reports from the fourth and seventh grade, we encountered several incidents where an act of social aggression obviously failed to inflict the designated damage. Although there were only a handful of such cases, they provided valuable insight on the critical elements for an effective social attack. Not surprisingly, these reports often came from someone other than the target victim. It happened when the perpetrator approached but failed to convince the listener. The perpetrator's act was then revealed. Here is a report from a seventh-grade girl: "I was mad at Robin because you know she was lying about Nancy. She (Robin) said that she (Nancy) called Michelle and me name-stuff like that." In the earlier part of the interview, the participant named Nancy as one of her two best friends. A seventh-grade boy reported a similar scenario: "She's (Vickie) been talking about Katie and I told Katie about it.... I believe Katie a lot more than Vickie.... Katie is my good friend."

Targeting someone who is a solid member of a dominant group in the social network may also bear a higher risk. Mary, a fourth-grade girl, said the following about a recent conflict:

> When Cindy started telling all these things about Stella, I told her not to do it, ... cause if you're going to go ahead and talk about somebody, you know you're not gonna have any friends, cause you know many people like that friend and you don't, so who's gonna like you, if you don't like her. So I told her to stop and I just ignore her most of the time.

Social network analysis indicated that Stella was a secondary member in the most nuclear group in the class. She was also reported by Mary as "many people like that friend." Interestingly, Mary was in the same peer group as Cindy, but their group only had a secondary status in the class.

Mary's reluctance might result from her consideration of the threat of a greater counterattack by the dominant group. When the interviewer asked Mary how she felt about it, she replied: "I didn't feel pretty good, because, you know, Stella was my friend too. I just don't like people talking about other people cause ... they're going to talk back if you do that."

Social Dynamics and Interpersonal Behaviors

The analysis of conflict narratives suggests that variations in social behaviors cannot be exclusively attributed to individual differences. Broader social dynamics may play a significant role in a specific pattern of interpersonal exchanges. A conflict of social isolation and friendship rejection illustrates this point:

> Ellen, a fourth-grade participant, found herself being refused by a group of girls to play jump rope. She also noticed that her best friend—Katherine—tried to avoid her. It turned out that the group had just lost or ostracized two girls and Katherine was made a member. The girls in that group did not approve of Katherine and Ellen being together anymore. In the end, Katherine told Ellen that she would start sitting with that group of girls for lunch and she did not like Ellen anymore.

The negative social interchanges between Katherine and Ellen were largely affected by the changing social dynamics in the broader social networks. Two girls were suddenly out of a group, creating a vacancy. Katherine was offered the spot, but at a price: She had to break up her friendship with Ellen. The use of subtle interpersonal strategies such as social aggression is a reflection of the kind of social dynamics unfolding in the broader social framework. An examination of the natural course of socially aggressive behavior and its social basis is essential in our effort to understand its development.

Functions of Socially Aggressive Behavior

Socially aggressive behavior can be destructive and inflict serious damage on its victims. It may serve other functions for social groups as well, particularly as a tool for social information transfer. Consensus social judgments of the character or qualities of other persons can be useful in protecting individuals from victimization, and they become one of the bonds that hold groups of individuals together in cohesive units (see also Adler & Adler, 1995; Goodwin, 1990b). Social groups may become attacking groups. In the seventh grade, Kelly reported a conflict between three core members of her group (including Kelly) and another girl who was affiliating with the group, but behaving in an unacceptable manner:

> Well, Lori has made a big shuffle between me and Michelle and Stephanie.... We had-
> n't (haven't) really done anything about it yet, but we are planning on (it). We were
> trying to think about what we were going to say and how we were going to say it, so we
> wouldn't make it sound real mean or anything.... Ok, during PE, she would ignore
> people and then when something happened with the group she was staying with, she
> would get back in with others that she had been ignoring, and that really bothered us
> because she would do that about every day.

The discussion of Lori's behavior and the planning of how to express group disapproval would certainly hurt Lori's social status. Consensus judgment of Lori's behavior, however, might help strengthen group bonds and clarify behavioral norms. Social information transfer can also be used as a tool to restructure social relationships (see also Goodwin, 1990b).

Qualitative research efforts in sociology and anthropology have also shown that gossip helps communicate social information and clarify social norms in addition to promoting group cohesion (e.g., Eder & Enke, 1991; Eder & Sanford, 1986; Fine, 1986; Illich, 1982). At the individual level, gossip may also be viewed as a way to project a positive self-image by discrediting others (e.g., Besnier, 1989; Paine, 1967) and establish dominance and control (see Artz, chap. 6, this volume).

It has also been proposed that various social functions of gossip may differ at different developmental stages. Gottman and Mettetal (1986) recorded dyadic conversations between friends in laboratory settings. They found that gossip in early childhood was mainly used to promote group solidarity. In middle childhood, gossip gained another function—clarifying group norms. By adolescence, gossip became an avenue for solving interpersonal problems.

Social Aggression Beyond Adolescence

It should be noted that the use of socially manipulative strategies is not confined to adolescent girls. It may help level the playing field at a critical time in development—puberty—when girls are, on the average, at a disadvantage physically to boys. It provides an effective, socially condoned, nonconfrontational strategy. Once the strategy emerges, it can become perfected and, for many, used throughout the life course. As males enter adulthood and the pressure against the use of physical forces increases, they may also rely on nonconfrontational methods as their primary strategy of interpersonal control (see Björkqvist et al., 1994).

In summary, an effective social attack relies on assistance from other individuals in the social networks. Socially aggressive behaviors are influenced by broader social dynamics in the peer networks. Such behaviors may play important roles for groups, such as maintaining group cohesion and determining social dominance of an individual within the group and in the network.

AGGRESSION AND DEVELOPMENTAL PREDICTIONS OF CRIMINAL BEHAVIORS

Previous longitudinal research has shown that childhood physical aggression is a significant predictor of subsequent criminal arrests (e.g., Farrington, 1991; Magnusson & Bergman, 1990). It remains to be determined whether early social aggression is linked to subsequent criminal behaviors. Given that most previous studies focus on boys, it is also important to identify possible gender differences in the developmental trajectories leading to criminal behaviors.

Social Aggression and Criminal Behavior

Using peer-narrative measures, we identified socially and physically aggressive behaviors in Grades 4 and 7. Participants in the Carolina Longitudinal Study were followed into their adulthood. Criminal records from the State Bureau of Investigation (SBI) of North Carolina were obtained for 95% of the participants who remained in North Carolina when they were in their early 20s.

Consistent with previous research, the use of physical aggression in peer conflicts was positively associated with the number of arrests, and the effect of physical aggression on later criminal arrests was more pronounced among males than among females. Social aggression failed to predict later criminal arrests (Xie, 1998). Why?

Answers to this question require an examination of the developmental processes that link physical aggression to subsequent maladjustment. Consistent with the holistic and interactive perspective on human development, it has been found that physical aggression alone does not significantly increase the risk for developmental maladjustment (e.g., Magnusson & Bergman, 1990). Only when combined with other risk factors (e.g., poor academic performance) does physical aggression become an antecedent for problematic outcomes. In other words, it is not physical aggression by itself that predicts future maladjustment, but the at-risk configuration in which physical aggression is embedded.

The next step is to determine whether social aggression is related to concurrent developmental risks in other areas of development. We found that social aggression was related to neither poor academic competence nor low popularity. In contrast, physical aggression was related to both (Xie et al.,

2002a). Therefore, unlike physical aggression, social aggression alone is not related to risk factors in other areas of development. Hence, it does not provide robust predictions of future maladjustment.

The failure of social aggression to predict subsequent developmental problems is consistent with reports from other longitudinal studies. Pulkkinen (1992) found that girls who were high in negative facial expressions during childhood generally did not go on to have problems in early adulthood. They even achieved higher levels of education than nonaggressive girls. In contrast, physically aggressive girls tended to encounter multiple problems later in life, including lower levels of academic achievement. In their ethnographic work, Adler and Adler (1998) also noted that preadolescents (ages 8–12) who were involved more in group dynamics of inclusion and exclusion mastered the manipulative techniques earlier and were more successful in their peer interactions. Taken together, these results suggest that subtly aggressive behaviors may serve different developmental functions from physical aggression.

Developmental Trajectories and Criminal Behavior

Hostile aggressive behaviors were also captured by teacher ratings in the Carolina Longitudinal Study. Each year teacher ratings of aggression were obtained by using the Interpersonal Competence Scale (Cairns, Leung, Gest, & Cairns, 1995). An aggression factor was identified, which included *fight*, *get in trouble at school*, and *argue*. These annual ratings of aggression enabled us to track developmental trajectories over time.

Based on the SBI records of criminal arrests, three groups were identified: those who were not arrested, those who were arrested for nonviolent crimes only, and those who were arrested for violent crimes. The developmental trajectories of aggression among these three groups were compared. A hierarchical linear modeling procedure was employed.

Estimated trajectories are shown in Fig. 5.2.[2] For boys, both the nonviolent crime group and the violent crime group showed heightened levels of aggression from childhood to late adolescence compared with the no-crime group. There was no significant difference between the two crime groups.

Among girls, the nonviolent crime group had consistently higher aggression scores than the no-crime group. The violent-crime group of girls, however, showed a different developmental pattern. They displayed a normative

---

[2]Participants who were arrested had been more likely to drop out of school by the end of Grade 11. As a result, a higher proportion of teacher ratings were missed for the crime groups than for the no-crime group. To avoid a biased estimation, developmental trajectories were only examined from Grade 4 to Grade 10. The two cohorts were combined for analysis.

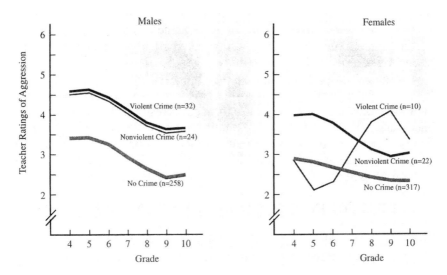

FIG. 5.2.   Differential developmental trajectories of teacher ratings of aggression
as a function of gender and crime.

level of aggression in childhood, which was followed by increasing levels
of aggression from early to late adolescence. Notice that all other groups
displayed a decrease during this period. This finding is similar to Stattin and
Magnusson's (1990) Swedish sample report, where physical aggression
among girls was not significantly related to adulthood criminal arrests until
early adolescence (i.e., age 13).

Why did girls arrested for a violent crime show such an increased level of
aggression during adolescence? One possible explanation is that, during
early adolescence when most girls start to use nonconfrontational strategies
as the primary method of interpersonal control and manipulation, those
who fail to conform by utilizing physical force may represent a group of
particularly troubled and deviant girls.

Individuals develop in a web of social relationships, however, so emerging social events and social relationships during adolescence may offer a
more plausible explanation. Previous research has shown that romantic
partners and close affiliates play a significant role in female deviant behaviors. Magnusson, Stattin, and Allen (1985) demonstrated that affiliation
with older males and the adoption of deviant behavioral norms serve as the
linkage between the early maturation status of adolescent girls and their
subsequent deviant behaviors. Similarly, in a Finish cohort, Lea Pulkkinen
and her colleagues (Rönkä, Kinnunen, & Pulkkinen, 2001) were able to
show that affiliation with deviant partners at age 27 was predictive of

women's subsequent social adjustment problems at age 36. In the Carolina Longitudinal Study, we also found that the characteristics of affiliated peers appeared more important in predicting teen motherhood than teen fatherhood (Xie, Cairns, & Cairns, 2001).

Two important points should be noted: (a) The unique trajectories followed by violent girls may reflect emerging events and social relationships later in development as opposed to a fixed effect resulting from early experiences; and (b) the high levels of continuity among violent boys may be an illusion of early fixedness, but in reality reflect the continuing dynamics of selective affiliation and accumulative effects of social contextual factors over development (see also Aguilar, Sroufe, Egeland, & Carlson, 2000).

IMPLICATIONS FOR PREVENTION AND INTERVENTION

Several aspects of the development of aggressive behaviors bear significant implications for prevention and intervention. Although social aggression fails to follow the same pattern as physical aggression in its association with developmental problems, it has a powerful impact on peer social dynamics that in turn often increases negative exchanges of physical and verbal aggression among children and adolescents. On the basis of the issues and findings discussed previously, four implications can be gencrated for prevention and intervention of aggressive behaviors.

First, aggression is not an individual affair, but an interactional and social one. Both the individual and peer social networks should be simultaneously included for prevention and intervention (Cairns & Cairns, 1994; Farmer, 2000). The development of aggressive behaviors is largely maintained by synchronous interactions between the individual and social others and is also influenced by peer social dynamics. Interpersonal competitions for popularity, social status, dominance, friendship, and romantic relationships often produce intense negative exchanges among individuals. Any prevention effort leading to a successful outcome should not leave out the social structure and social context.

Second, different aggressive behaviors can be used interchangeably, and their development is not isolated. The prevention should not target one specific form of aggression alone. Of special interest is that subtle forms of social aggression, having once become effective, often lead to open confrontations of physical and/or verbal aggression among other individuals. Although physical aggression is often the primary focus of prevention and intervention, the interactional and social processes of social aggression speak for the importance of situating physical aggression in the context of concrete interpersonal exchanges, specific conflict issues, and history of relationships.

Third, prevention efforts must be sensitive to the developmental aspects of aggressive behaviors. Different strategies are required for different developmental points in the lives of children. For instance, social aggression becomes much more prominent during adolescence than during early childhood. This developmental change, to a large extent, is associated with interpersonal issues emerging during adolescence, such as romantic relationships, hierarchical social status, and more sophisticated group inclusion and exclusion. Given that new relationships and behaviors emerge in the course of development, prevention and intervention efforts should not be limited to the early years.

Finally, teachers and other school authorities need to be aware of the social networks and social dynamics in the class or school. Extra attention should be paid to subtle negative exchanges of social aggression because such behavior is often ignored and receives little intervention until it escalates into major conflicts of open arguments or physical fights.

IMPLICATIONS FOR FUTURE RESEARCH

Methodology lies at the heart of any scientific endeavor. Theoretical proposals, the research task, and the nature of the phenomenon under investigation should guide the selection of an appropriate methodology. It has been 70 years since Lewin (1931) pointed out the danger of focusing on psychological variables without identifying the milieu of their operation. Cairns (1979) also stated that, "By focusing on individual *differences* in characteristics, instead of the development of *actual* interchange characteristics, only meager information as been obtained on the course of development of relevant social behaviors" (p. 391). Nonetheless, studies of the development of social behavior continue to focus on individual differences without adequate attention to social interactional processes (see also Maccoby, 1984).

What can be gained by a simultaneous analysis of the social process and individual differences? Knowledge of behavioral development may be advanced in three ways. First, such an approach helps identify the interpersonal social processes that give rise to a specific behavioral exchange. Earlier in this chapter, we reported that a third party or the involvement of other individuals in the social community was critical for the completion of a social attack. Some exchanges of physical and/or verbal aggression arose from socially aggressive behavior initiated by a third party.

Second, a simultaneous analysis of the social process and individual differences of social behaviors is critical in gaining insight into how individual differences arise in social interactions. For example, Maccoby (1998) pointed out that gender differences in children's social behaviors become prominent in dyadic or group interactions. Gender differences in social behaviors may not be found when the social context (i.e., the interaction partner) is left out and only individual difference measures are considered.

Third, attention to the dynamic processes of individual development increases the understanding of how behavioral reorganization occurs in development and avoids overattributing developmental continuity to individual tendencies and/or the fixed effect of early experience. Longitudinal studies have revealed modest to high levels of continuity of aggressive behaviors (i.e., primarily physical aggression) from childhood to adulthood (e.g., Cairns & Cairns, 1994; Olweus, 1979). The empirical evidence of developmental continuity of aggression is often interpreted as the manifestation of an individual trait and/or a fixed effect of early experience (e.g., Moffitt, 1993; Silverthorn & Frick, 1999). The fact that most aggressive children do not grow up to be aggressive adults has often been ignored (see also Loeber & Stouthamer-Loeber, 1998). Dynamic social interchanges and relationships ensure that behavioral reorganization is possible given certain social supports in close social relationships.

CONCLUDING COMMENTS

The development of social and physical aggression seems to share common principles despite different forms. Aggressive actions occur in social interactions and serve important functions in regulating interpersonal relationships. These behaviors in turn are largely influenced by the actions of others and the dynamics of social relationships (Cairns, 1979). In the case of social aggression, embeddedness in the peer social networks is essential for an effective social attack. Socially aggressive strategies may serve adaptive and important functions for the individual and social group. Together with research on physical aggression and bullying behaviors (e.g., Cairns et al., 1988; Farmer, 2000; Giordano et al., 1986; Luthar & McMahon, 1996; Pepler & Craig, 1995; Rodkin et al., 2000; Salmivalli, Huttunen, & Lagerspetz, 1997; Sutton & Smith, 1999), the empirical evidence indicates that the development of aggressive behaviors is supported by the peer social context including close social affiliations and social dynamics in the networks. It should be noted that these principles and findings seem to transcend gender boundaries.

Bidirectional and dynamic influences between the individual and others suggest that behavior reorganization can occur at any point of development. Socially aggressive behavior emerges during middle childhood and early adolescence as a result of the operation of several correlated factors, including sexual dimorphism during puberty, a child's increased social cognitive skills, and changes in peer social dynamics. Developmental trajectories are not fixed by early experience. Females arrested for a violent crime in early adulthood may not have shown heightened levels of aggression until adolescence. Risk factors are not confined to childhood nor are windows of opportunity. On developmental novelty and change, Cairns (2000) wrote, "The first three years of life are important, but so are the next three, and so are the transition years of youth. At each developmental stage, new behaviors and functions emerge" (p. 59).

ACKNOWLEDGMENTS

The preparation of this chapter was supported by funds from Spencer Foundation and NIMH (MH45523 and MH61293). We thank our colleague, Thomas W. Farmer, for his constructive comments.

REFERENCES

Achenbach, T. M., McConaughy, S. H., & Howell, C. T. (1987). Child/adolescent behavioral and emotional problems: Implications of cross-informant correlations for situational specificity. *Psychological Bulletin, 101,* 213–232.

Adler, P. A., & Adler, P. (1995). Dynamics of inclusion and exclusion in preadolescent cliques. Social *Psychology Quarterly, 58,* 145–162.

Adler, P. A., & Adler, P. (1998). *Peer power: Preadolescents culture and identity.* New Brunswick, NJ: Rutgers University Press.

Aguilar, B., Sroufe, L. A., Egeland, B., & Carlson, E. (2000). Distinguishing the early-onset/persistent and adolescence-onset antisocial behavior types: From birth to 16 years. *Development and Psychopathology, 12,* 109–132.

Bandura, A. (1973). *Aggression: A social learning analysis.* New York: Holt.

Berndt, T. J. (1982). The features and effects of friendship in early adolescence. *Child Development, 53,* 1447–1460.

Besnier, N. (1989). Information withholding as a manipulative and collusive strategy in nukulaelae gossip. *Language in Society, 18,* 315–341.

Blyth, D. A., & Foster-Clark, F. S. (1987). Gender differences in perceived intimacy with different members of adolescents' social networks. *Sex Roles, 17,* 689–718.

Björkqvist, K. (1994). Sex differences in physical, verbal, and indirect aggression: A review of recent research. *Sex Roles, 30,* 177–188.

Björkqvist, K., Lagerspetz, K. M. J., & Kaukiainen, A. (1992). Do girls manipulate and boys fight? *Aggressive Behavior, 18,* 117–127.

Björkqvist, K., Österman, K., & Lagerspetz, K. M. J. (1994). Sex differences in covert aggression among adults. *Aggressive Behavior, 20,* 27–33.

Brown, J. D., & Dutton, K. A., (1995). Truth and consequences: The costs and benefits of accurate self-knowledge. *Personality and Social Psychology Bulletin, 21,* 1288–1296.

Cairns, R. B. (1979). *Social development: The origins and plasticity of interchanges.* San Francisco: Freeman.

Cairns, R. B. (1986). Phenomena lost: Issues in the study of development. In J. Valsiner (Ed.), *The individual subject and scientific psychology* (pp. 97–112). New York: Plenum Press.

Cairns, R. B. (2000). Developmental science: Three audacious implications. In L. R. Bergman, R. B. Cairns, L.-G. Nilson, & L. Nystedt (Eds.), *Developmental science and the holistic approach* (pp. 49–62). Mahwah, NJ: Lawrence Erlbaum Associates.

Cairns, R. B., & Cairns, B. D. (1994). *Lifelines and risks: Passages of youth in our time.* New York: Cambridge University Press.

Cairns, R. B., Cairns, B. D., & Neckerman, H. J. (1989). Early school dropout: Configurations and determinants. *Child Development, 60,* 1437–1452.

Cairns, R. B., Cairns, B. D., Neckerman, H. J., Ferguson, L. L., & Gariépy, J.-L. (1989). Growth and aggression: I. Childhood to early adolescence. *Developmental Psychology, 25,* 320–330.

Cairns, R. B., Cairns, B. D., Neckerman, H. J., Gest, S., & Gariépy, J.-L. (1988). Social networks and aggressive behavior: Peer support or peer rejection? *Developmental Psychology, 24,* 815–823.

Cairns, R. B., Gariépy, J.-L, & Kindermann, T. (1991). *Identifying social clusters in natural settings.* Unpublished manuscript, University of North Carolina at Chapel Hill.

Cairns, R. B., & Green, J. A. (1979). How to assess personality and social patterns: Ratings or observations? In R. B. Cairns (Ed.), *The analysis of social interaction: Methods, issues, and illustrations* (pp. 209–226). Hillsdale, NJ: Lawrence Erlbaum Associates.

Cairns, R. B., Leung, M.-C., Gest, S. D., & Cairns, B. D. (1995). A brief method for assessing social development: Structure, reliability, stability, and developmental validity of the Interpersonal Competence Scale. *Behaviour Research and Therapy, 33*(6), 725–736.

Cairns, R. B., Perrin, J. E., & Cairns, B. D. (1985). Social structure and social cognition in early adolescence: Affiliative patterns. *Journal of Early Adolescence, 5,* 339–355.

Crick, N. R. (1997). Engagement in gender normative versus nonnormative forms of aggression: Links to social-psychological adjustment. *Developmental Psychology, 33,* 610–617.

Crick, N. R., Casas, J. F., & Mosher, M. (1997). Relational and overt aggression in preschool. *Developmental Psychology, 33,* 579–588.

Crick, N. R., & Grotpeter, J. K. (1995). Relational aggression, gender, and social-psychological adjustment. *Child Development, 66,* 710–722.

Crick, N. R., Werner, N. E., Casas, J. F., O'Brien, K. M., Nelson, D. A., Grotpeter, J. K., & Markon, K. (1999). Childhood aggression and gender: A new look at an old problem. In D. Bernstein (Ed.), *Gender and motivation. Nebraska symposium on motivation* (Vol. 45, pp. 75–141). Lincoln, NE: University of Nebraska Press.

Dishion, T. J., Andrews, D. W., & Crosby, L. (1995). Antisocial boys and their friends in early adolescence: Relationship characteristics, quality, and interactional process. *Child Development, 66,* 139–151.

Dollard, J., Doob, L. W., Miller, N. E., Mowrer, O. H., & Sears, R. R. (1939). *Frustration and aggression.* New Haven, CT: Yale University Press.

Eder, D. (1985). The cycle of popularity: Interpersonal relations among female adolescents. *Sociology of Education, 58,* 154–165.

Eder, D., & Enke, J. L. (1991). The structure of gossip: Opportunities and constraints on collective expression among adolescents. *American Sociological Review, 56,* 494–508.

Eder, D., Evans, C. C., & Parker, S. (1995). *School talk: Gender and adolescent culture.* New Brunswick, NJ: Rutgers University Press.

Eder, D., & Hallinan, M. T. (1978). Sex differences in children's friendships. *American Sociological Review, 43,* 237–250.

Eder, D., & Kinney, D. A. (1997). The effect of middle school extracurriculum activities on adolescents' popularity and peer status. *Youth & Sociology, 26*, 298–324.

Eder, D., & Sanford, S. (1986). The development and maintenance of interactional norms among early adolescents. In P. Adler & P. Adler (Eds.), *Sociological studies of child development* (pp. 283–300). Greenwich, CT: JAI Press.

Ensminger, M. E., & Slusarcick, A. L. (1992). Paths to high school graduation or dropout: A longitudinal study of a first-grade cohort. *Sociology of Education, 65*(2), 95–113.

Epstein, S. (1973). The self-concept revisited: Or a theory of a theory. *American Psychologist, 28*, 404–416.

Farmer, T. W. (2000). Social dynamics of aggressive and disruptive behavior in school: Implications for behavior consultation. *Journal of Educational and Psychological Consultation, 11*, 299–322.

Farmer, T. W., & Rodkin, P. C. (1996). Antisocial and prosocial correlates of classroom social positions: The social network centrality perspective. *Social Development, 5*, 174–188.

Farrington, D. P. (1986). Stepping stones to adult criminal careers. In D. Olweus, J. Block, & M. Radke-Yarrow (Eds.), *Development of antisocial and prosocial behavior: Research, theories, and issues* (pp. 359–384). New York: Academic.

Farrington, D. P. (1991). Childhood aggression and adult violence: Early precursors and life outcomes. In D. J. Pepler & K. H. Rubin (Eds.), *Development and treatment of childhood aggression* (pp. 5–29). Hillsdale, NJ: Lawrence Erlbaum Associates.

Feshbach, N. D. (1969). Sex differences in children's modes of aggressive responses toward outsiders. *Merrill-Palmer Quarterly, 15*, 249–258.

Feshbach, N. D., & Sones, G. (1971). Sex differences in adolescent reactions to newcomers. *Developmental Psychology, 4*, 381–386.

Fine, G. A. (1986). The social organization of adolescent gossip: The rhetoric of moral evaluation. In J. Cook-Gumperz, W. Corsaro, & J. Streeck (Eds.), *Children's worlds and children's language* (pp. 405–423). Berlin: Mouton.

Galen, B. R., & Underwood, M. K. (1997). A developmental investigation of social aggression among children. *Developmental Psychology, 33*, 589–600.

Giordano, P. C., Cernkovich, S. A., & Pugh, M. D. (1986). Friendship and delinquency. *American Journal of Sociology, 91*, 1170–1201.

Goodwin, M. H. (1990a). Tactical uses of stories: Participation frameworks within girls' and boys' dispute. *Discourse Processes, 13*, 33–71.

Goodwin, M. H. (1990b). *He-said-she-said: Talk as social organization among Black children*. Bloomington, IN: Indiana University Press.

Gottman, J., & Mettetal, G. (1986). Speculations about social and affective development: Friendship and acquaintanceship through adolescence. In J. Gottman & J. Parker (Eds.), *Conversations of friends: Speculations on affective development* (pp. 192–237). New York: Cambridge University Press.

Greenwald, A. G. (1980). The totalitarian ego: Fabrication and revision of personal history. *American Psychologist, 35*, 603–618.

Hoyenga, K. B., & Hoyenga, K. T. (1979). *The question of sex differences: Psychological, cultural, and biological issues*. Boston: Little, Brown.

Illich, I. (1982). *Gender*. New York: Pantheon.

Inhelder, B., & Piaget, J. (1958). *The growth of logical thinking from childhood to adolescence*. New York: Basic Books.

Kaukiainen, A., Björkqvist, K., Lagerspetz, K., Osterman, K., Salmivalli, C., Rothberg, S., & Ahlbom, A. (1999). The relationships between social intelligence, empathy, and three types of aggression. *Aggressive Behavior, 25*, 81–89.

Keating, D. P. (1990). Adolescent thinking. In S. S. Feldman & G. R. Elliott (Eds.), *At the threshold: The developing adolescent* (pp. 54–89). Cambridge, MA: Harvard University Press.

Kenny, D. A. (1991). A general model of consensus and accuracy in interpersonal perception. *Psychological Review, 98,* 155–163.

Kenrick, D. T., & Stringfield, D. O. (1980). Personality traits and the eye of the beholder: Crossing some traditional philosophical boundaries in the search for consistency in all the people. *Psychological Review, 87,* 88–104.

Lagerspetz, K. M. J., & Björkqvist, K. (1994). Indirect aggression in girls and boys. In L. R. Huesmann (Ed.), *Aggressive behavior: Current perspectives* (pp. 131–150). New York: Plenum.

Lagerspetz, K. M. J., Björkqvist, K., & Peltonen, T. (1988). Is indirect aggression typical of females? Gender differences in aggressiveness in 11–12-year-old children. *Aggressive Behavior, 14,* 303–315.

Leung, M.-C. (1996). Social networks and self enhancement in Chinese children: A comparison of self reports and peer reports of groups membership. *Social Development, 5,* 146–157.

Lewin, K. (1931). Environmental forces in child behavior and development. In C. Murchison (Ed.), *A handbook of child psychology* (pp. 94–127). Worcester, MA: Clark University Press.

Loeber, R., & Stouthamer-Loeber, M. (1998). Development of juvenile aggression and violence: Some common misconceptions and controversies. *American Psychologist, 53,* 242–259.

Luthar, S., & McMahon, T. (1996). Peer reputation among inner city adolescents: Structure and correlates. *Journal of Research on Adolescence, 6,* 581–603.

Maccoby, E. E. (1984). Socialization and developmental change. *Child Development, 55,* 317–328.

Maccoby, E. E. (1990). Gender and relationships: A developmental account. *American Psychologist, 45,* 513–520.

Maccoby, E. E. (1998). *The two sexes: Growing up apart, coming together.* Cambridge, MA: Belknap Press/Harvard University Press.

Magnusson, D., & Bergman, L. R. (1990). A pattern approach to the study of pathways from childhood to adulthood. In L. N. Robins & M. Rutter (Eds.), *Straight and devious pathways from childhood to adulthood* (pp. 101–115). Cambridge, England: Cambridge University Press.

Magnusson, D., Stattin, H., & Allen, V. (1985). Biological maturation and social development: A longitudinal study of some social processes of mid-adolescence to adulthood. *Journal of Youth and Adolescence, 14,* 267–283.

Marsh, H. W., Walker, R., & Debus, R. (1991). Subject-specific components of academic self-concept and self-efficacy. *Contemporary Educational Psychology, 16,* 331–345.

McNeilly-Choque, M. K., Hart, C. H., Robinson, C. C., Nelson, L. J., & Olsen, S. F. (1996). Overt and relational aggression on the playground: Correspondence among different informants. *Journal of Research in Childhood Education, 67,* 2417–2433.

Merten, D. E. (1997). The meaning of meanness: Popularity, competition, and conflict among junior high school girls. *Sociology of Education, 70,* 175–191.

Moffitt, T. E. (1993). Adolescence-limited and life-course-persistent antisocial behavior: A developmental taxonomy. *Psychological Review, 100,* 674–701.

Olweus, D. (1979). Stability of aggressive reaction patterns in males: A review. *Psychological Bulletin, 86,* 852–875.

Paine, R. (1967). What is gossip about? An alternative hypothesis. *Man, 2,* 278–285.

Paquette, J. A., & Underwood, M. (1999). Gender differences in young adolescents' experiences of peer victimization: Social and physical aggression. *Merrill-Palmer Quarterly, 45,* 233–258.

Pepler, D. J., & Craig, W. M. (1995). A peek behind the fence: Naturalistic observations of aggressive children with remote audiovisual recording. *Developmental Psychology, 31,* 548–553.

Pepler, D. J., Craig, W. M., & Roberts, W. L. (1998). Observation of aggressive and nonaggressive children on the school playground. *Merrill-Palmer Quarterly, 44,* 55–76.

Pulkkinen, L. (1992). The path to adulthood for aggressively inclined girls. In K. Björkqvist & P. Niemëla (Eds.), *Of mice and women: Aspects of female aggression* (pp. 113–122). San Diego: Academic Press.

Pulkkinen, L. (1998). Levels of longitudinal data differing in complexity and the study of continuity in personality characteristics. In R. B. Cairns, L. R. Bergman, & J. Kagan (Eds.), *Methods and models for studying the individual* (pp. 161–183). San Diego: Academic Press.

Rodkin, P. C., Farmer, T. W., Pear, R., & Van Acker, R. (2000). Heterogeneity of popular boys: Antisocial and prosocial configurations. *Developmental Psychology, 36,* 14–24.

Rönkä, A., Kinnunen, U., & Pulkkinen, L. (2001). Continuity in problems of social functioning: A cumulative perspective. *Journal of Adult Development, 8,* 161–171.

Rosenberg, F. R., & Simons, R. G. (1975). Sex differences in the self-concept in adolescence. *Sex Roles, 1,* 147–159.

Rys, G. S., & Bear, G. G. (1997). Relational aggression and peer relations: Gender and developmental issues. *Merrill-Palmer Quarterly, 43,* 87–106.

Salmivalli, C., Huttunen, A., & Lagerspetz, K. M. J. (1997). Peer networks and bullying in school. *Scandinavian Journal of Psychology, 38,* 305–312.

Sedikides, C., & Strube, M. J. (1997). Self-evaluation: To thine own self be good, to thine own self be sure, to thine own self be true, and to thine own self be better. In M. P. Zanna (Ed.), *Advances in Experimental Social Psychology* (pp. 209–269). New York: Academic Press.

Serbin, L. A., Peters, P. L., McAffer, V. J., & Schwartzman, A. E. (1991). Childhood aggression and withdrawal as predictors of adolescent pregnancy, early parenthood, and environmental risk for the next generation. *Canadian Journal of Behavioural Science, 23,* 318–331.

Silverthorn, P., & Frick, P. J. (1999). Developmental pathways to antisocial behavior: The delayed-onset pathway in girls. *Development and Psychopathology, 11,* 101–126.

Skaalvik, E. M., & Rankin, R. J. (1994). Gender differences in mathematics and verbal achievement, self-perception, and motivation. *British Journal of Educational Psychology, 64,* 419–428.

Stattin, H., & Magnusson, D. (1989). The role of early aggressive behavior in the frequency, seriousness, and types of later crime. *Journal of Consulting and Clinical Psychology, 57,* 710–718.

Stattin, H., & Magnusson, D. (1990). The role of early aggressive behavior in the frequency, seriousness, and types of later crime. *Journal of Consulting and Clinical Psychology, 57,* 710–718.

Sutton, J., & Smith, P. K. (1999). Bullying as a group process: An adaptation of the participant role approach. *Aggressive Behavior, 25,* 97–111.

Taylor, S. E., & Brown, J. D., (1994). Positive illusions and well-being revisited: Separating fact from fiction. *Psychological Bulletin, 116,* 21–27.

Tomada, G., & Schneider, B. H. (1997). Relational aggression, gender, and peer acceptance: Invariance across culture, stability over time, and concordance among informants. *Developmental Psychology, 33*, 601–609.

Tremblay, R. E., Japel, C., Perusse, D., McDuff, P., Boivin, M., Zoccolillo, M., & Montplaisir, J. (1999). The search for the age of "onset" of physical aggression: Rousseau and Bandura revisited. *Criminal Behaviour and Mental Health, 9*, 8–23.

Xie, H. (1998). *The development and functions of social aggression: A narrative analysis of social exchange in interpersonal conflicts.* Unpublished dissertation, University of North Carolina at Chapel Hill.

Xie, H., Cairns, R. B., & Cairns, B. D. (1999). Social networks and social configurations in inner-city schools: Aggression, popularity, and implications for students with EBD. *Journal of Emotional and Behavioral Disorders, 7*, 147–156.

Xie, H., & Cairns, B. D. (2001, April 19–22). The development of social aggression: Peer social networks and interactional processes. In T. Earls & T. Farmer (Chairs), *The social context of aggression: The Robert B. Cairns memorial symposium.* Paper symposium at the biennial meetings of the Society for Research in Child Development (SRCD), Minneapolis, MN.

Xie, H., Cairns, B. D., & Cairns, R. B. (2001). Predicting teen motherhood and teen fatherhood: Individual characteristics and peer affiliations. *Social Development, 10*, 488–511.

Xie, H., Cairns, R. B., & Cairns, B. D. (2002). The development of social aggression and physical aggression: A narrative analysis of interpersonal conflicts. *Aggressive Behavior, 28*, 341–355.

Xie, H., Mahoney, J. L., & Cairns, R. B. (1999). Through a looking glass or a hall of mirrors? Self-ratings and teacher-ratings of academic competence over development. *International Journal of Behavioral Development, 23*, 163–183.

Xie, H., Swift, D. J., Cairns, B. D., & Cairns, R. B. (2002). Aggressive behaviors in social interaction and developmental adaptation: A narrative analysis of interpersonal conflicts during early adolescence. *Social Development, 11*, 205–224.

Zillman, D. (1978). *Hostility and aggression.* Hillsdale, NJ: Lawrence Erlbaum Associates.

6

To Die For:
Violent Adolescent Girls'
Search for Male Attention

Sibylle Artz
University of Victoria

Over and above any genetic, constitutional or biological predisposition that may underlie the observed differences between males and females in aggressive behavior, there is something about the way we socialize boys and girls and the different expectations we have for males and females in our society that contributes in an important way to the differential incidence of antisocial aggression in these two groups of human beings. (Eron, 1992, p. 96)

I entered academia and the formal world of research and evaluation in 1992, after working for more than 23 years as a child and youth care worker in direct practice with children and families. Many of the clients I worked with had problems with violence and aggression, but most who engaged in overt and multiple acts of aggression and violence were males. The number of violent females whom I encountered during my years in direct practice was so small that I can still individually name them. Thus, when I was asked in 1993 by a Southern Vancouver Island school district to help them find ways to deal with a growing problem with violent school girls—with girls physically attacking and harming each other—I was intrigued. This was the first time in my experience that violent girls were being singled out as a category—a group that needed attention. I immediately agreed to work with the district, but not as an external expert whose role it was to get to the bottom of the problem and from there suggest solutions that others would carry out, but as a member of a collaborative research-focused team. I believed this to be important because I wanted district personnel to be intimately involved in the formulation of an understanding of this phenomenon because it was their stated intention to create prevention and intervention programs based on the proposed research. Given my child and youth background, with its focus on the holistic care and psychosocial development of children, youth, and their families, I also wanted to include an education-based researcher in this endeavor. Thus was formed a research partnership among Dr. Ted Riecken, Faculty of Education, University of Victoria, myself, and the school district. Together we undertook a series of interconnected studies that we called *A Community-Based Violence Prevention Project.*[1]

A COMMUNITY-BASED VIOLENCE PREVENTION PROJECT

The research undertaken in this project was guided by two principles: community-based participation and direct involvement in the research process by those the project sought to serve, and a commitment to empirically evaluate the effect of our programs. Therefore, the research dimensions of the project were twofold: (a) work with the schools was grounded in the participant-based program evaluation model developed by Barnsley, Ellis, and Jacobson (1986) and involved lay researchers in all facets of program evaluation; and (b) evaluations were based on a pre- and posttest outcome measures to determine the interventions' effects.

This meant that each school participated with the university-based researchers to assess local needs; define individual project objectives; set goals; design, develop, and/or choose evaluation tools (a participant-based approach); conduct preprogram surveys, observations, and interviews; and implement programs and conduct postprogram surveys, observations, and interviews (a pre–posttest outcome measures approach). From the outset, an overall objective of the project was to teach and train school and community workers in basic research strategies to demystify such research and assist them in making program evaluation an ongoing part of program delivery. The project encompassed research using quantitative and qualitative approaches—that is, we conducted paper-and-pencil surveys, systematic observations, and structured and semistructured interviews; took field notes; and produced both descriptive statistics and phenomenological accounts. Further, all the data we gathered included both male and female samples, and all our analyses were gender based.

Finally, although most of the research we undertook was coconceived, I took the lead in one particular area—that which focused on the life worlds and practices of school girls who use violence. To better understand how

[1]This project was described in Artz and Riecken (1997) *and* Artz, Riecken, MacIntyre, Lam, & Maczewski (2000).

girls engaged in and made sense of their use of violence, I first undertook a year-long ethnographic study. I was assisted by six key informants, all girls who identified themselves as engaged in violence against other girls and on some (rare) occasions against boys, and who agreed to explain, uncover, and explore their use of violence so that I and others could better understand it. These girls wanted to be helpful. As one girl emphatically stated, "Violence is wrong, and I've never beat up anybody I didn't have to." Her dilemma and that of her five co-informants was that she did not like violence, but in particular instances she thought it the only "right thing to do."

As I worked with my key informants to deepen my understanding of girls' lived experience of using violence, I became more and more involved in the local community in trying to unravel school-based violence and girls' participation in it. I am now involved in working with girls who are incarcerated for their use of violence as well as with school girls. I have been assisted in my research not only by my six initial key informants, but also by their teachers, counselors, and community workers, and by graduate students and other interested researchers.

I have added seven additional school girls, three who use violence (against other girls) and four who do not, and seven school boys, three who use violence (against other boys) and four who do not, to my group of key informants. I have gathered data, together with my research team (Artz, Blais, & Nicholson, 2000), from eight incarcerated girls who use violence and seven incarcerated boys who use violence and from their custody workers and support staff, including professional staff such as nurses, psychiatrists, drug and alcohol counselors, and teachers. This is a work in progress. What follows after a brief summary of the literature on girls and violence is a description of what I have learned so far about aggressive and violent girls from the girls and from those who live and work with them.

DELVING INTO THE LITERATURE
ON GIRLS' USE OF VIOLENCE

The literature on girls' use of violence suggests that girls who use violence seem to have in common with boys who use violence lives lived for the most part in families characterized by conflict and interpersonal violence between parents and among siblings and by violence directed by parents toward their children (Artz, 1998; Chesney-Lind & Shelden, 1998). Also present in many of the families of violent children, male and female, are problems with substance use, divorce, abandonment by a primary caregiver, death of a primary caregiver, problems with stepparents', and frequent moves often brought about by marriage breakups and/or financial difficulties. Also for either sex violent children and youth and those who engage in a wide variety of deviant and criminal behaviors frequently experience difficulties with school and peers and often feel lonely and isolated (cf. Flowers, 1990; Lipsey & Derzon, 1998; Varma & Marinos, 1999). The literature on violent children (cf. Augimeri, Webster, Koegl, & Levene, 1998; Whithecomb, 1997) is consistent in identifying factors related to aggression and violence in children:

- Family and social factors such as socioeconomic deprivation and poverty; harsh and inconsistent parenting; marital discord; spousal, parental, and sibling violence; poor parental mental health; physical and sexual abuse; and alcoholism, drug dependency, and other substance misuse.
- Neurologically based problems with cognitive functioning including low scores on IQ tests and discrepancies in performance and verbal IQ scores, speech language disorders, and mental illnesses such as schizophrenia, depression, attention deficit and hyperactivity disorders (ADD and ADHD), and psychosis and psychopathy.
- Personality factors such as early signs of impulsivity and aggression.
- Exposure to trauma through personal experience with family, street, and excessive media violence.

As the literature continually confirms and Whithecomb (1997) pointed out, only rarely, and only in the case of children who suffer from specific and serious mental disorders such as schizophrenia, depression, attention deficit and hyperactivity disorders (ADD and ADHD), and psychosis, does a single causative factor exist that can definitively explain aggression and violence in children. Rather,

[for] the majority of children who commit violent acts ... a single causative factor cannot be identified ... [instead] most are exposed to a number of adverse environmental experiences over a period of time. The greater the number of such experiences and the earlier the age at which they were first exposed, the more likely it is that they will themselves become perpetrators. Unfortunately, many neurocognitive and family/social factors tend to affect the same individuals, even acting with one another to increase the likelihood that the affected individual will finally become a perpetrator. (p. 440)

That being said, the literature also points out that, prior to the 1970s, most theorists and researchers treated females as incidental to the study of violence, crime, and delinquency (Artz, 1998; Berger, 1989; Chesney-Lind & Shelden, 1998). For the most part, crime, delinquency, and especially violence were considered masculine forms of behavior, and females who participated were considered aberrant. As Blum (1998) noted in her book, *Sex on the Brain,*

... at a 1995 conference on crime and genetics, when scientists [geneticists] were asked how much energy went into figuring out male versus female aggression, their reply was that the difference was so accepted, such a given, that it really didn't make for interesting research. (p. xiv; brackets added)

Evidence to the contrary has of course been mounting over the years (cf. Berger, 1989; Björkqvist & Niemëla, 1992; Chesney-Lind & Shelden, 1998, for overviews). There is also a growing concern that current theories that explain violence, crime, and delinquency do not readily apply to the involvement of girls, nor do they provide insight into the continuing increase in the number of girls being charged with assault (Artz, 1998; Chesney-Lind & Shelden, 1998; Reitsma-Street, 1999). As Reitsma-Street (1999) stated, "most approaches to explaining delinquency [including violence] and to designing interventions have been developed by males about boys" (p. 340). She further stated,

Delinquency theories on youth predict that those most alienated, marginalized, and devalued by adults and societal institutions would be most delinquent. Despite the gains of the women's movement, girls remain more marginalized and devalued than boys (Bourn, McCoy, & Smith, 1998; Brown & Gilligan, 1992; Holmes & Silverman, 1992; Jiwani, 1998; Lees, 1997). The girls, therefore, should be more delinquent than boys. The reverse is true .... (p. 341)

A GENDERED UNDERSTANDING
OF PARTICIPATION IN VIOLENCE

Evidence for girls' lesser involvement in all forms of crime including violent crime abounds. In British Columbia, the province in which I conduct my research, the charge rates for violent crimes for girls have risen from 2.2 per 1,000 females ages 12 to 17 in 1988 to a high of 5.6 per 1,000 in 1996 and appear to be declining somewhat since 1997, when the rate dipped to 5.3 per 1,000. For boys ages 12 to 17, the charge rates for violent crime were 8.5 per 1,000 in 1988, reached a high of 16.2 per 1,000 in 1994, and declined thereafter to 14.3 in 1997 (BC Police Services Branch, 1998). In the schools with which I have been involved, in 1994, 20.9% of female students ages 13 to 17 and 51.9% of male students ages 13 to 17 reported they had beaten up another kid at least once or twice (Artz, 1998). These numbers declined significantly after 4 years of violence prevention programming in the schools in which we worked—by 50% for girls and 22% for boys (Artz, Riecken, MacIntyre, Lam, & Maczewski, 2000). Clearly, boys continue to outstrip girls with respect to self-reported involvement in violence.

When, in the context of the *Community-Based Violence Prevention Project*, we examined self-reported gender differences among school girls and school boys who use violence and among school girls and school boys who do not, we found that the violent school girl thinks and behaves in many ways much like the violent school boy. She misuses drugs and alcohol and smokes at similar rates, she retaliates against her parents, she steals from stores as often as he does, she lies as often, and she endorses and justifies aggression to the same degree that he does. She also enjoys similar pastimes (mostly partying), and she affiliates with the same social groups (head bangers, rappers, and skates). Also along with the violent school boy, the violent school girl damages property just for fun, breaks into a place just to look around, damages school property on purpose and carries a weapon, although at lower rates than the violent school boy does. Along with the violent school boy, the violent school girl ranks her family as significantly lower in importance than do other groups and reports not being understood by her parents at higher rates than do nonviolent school girls and boys. However, there are some significant differences between violent school girls and boys.

The violent school girl places the least importance of all four groups (violent girls, violent boys, nonviolent girls, nonviolent boys) on her relationship with her mother. She reports significantly higher rates than all others of fear of sexual assault, being talked into having sex with a boyfriend when this is not what she wants, and physical assault at home. In keeping with her fears, she also reports significantly higher rates of physical and sexual abuse and being victimized by "a group or gang of kids" than all others. At the same time, she, along with her nonviolent female peers, endorses friendship, being loved, concern and respect for others, forgiveness, honesty, politeness, generosity, and being respected at levels significantly higher than those reported by all males, violent and nonviolent. Additionally, again along with her nonviolent female peers, she reports significantly higher levels of concern for AIDS, child abuse, racial discrimination, teenage suicide, the environment, drug abuse, youth gangs, native–White relationships, and violence against women. Finally, the violent school girl reports significantly higher levels of concern than all other groups for the unequal treatment of women and violence in schools (Artz, 1998). She is at once more socially conscious and more brutalized than the violent school boy and the least connected to her family. As Reitsma-Street (1999) pointed out, despite the changing times, the violent girl and the girl otherwise in conflict with the law continues to be the most "devalued, but still pro-social" participant in our society (p. 340).

The explanation for girls' use of violence is not as straightforward as it is for boys. Unlike boys who use violence, girls who use violence are more prosocial, more concerned with violence as a social issue, more open to shifting away from violent behavior, and far less committed to violence as a way of being even while making use of violence (Artz, Riecken, MacIntyre, Lam, & Maczewski, 2000). The challenge in understanding girls' use of violence, especially girl–girl use of violence, at least in part is making sense of this paradox.

UNRAVELING GIRLS' USE OF VIOLENCE

As I have pondered this paradox over the years, I have noted that the girls with whom I have discussed their use of violence bring me back again and again to three organizing principles in their lives. These principles may help explain the girls' contradictory stance despite their sharing with boys histories of deprivation, neglect, abandonment, abuse, family disruption, family violence, family based substance misuse, and the like. These organizing principles are their: (a) constant immersion in sexual objectification, (b) sense of mistrust and misogyny, and (c) view of friendships or relationships as alliances of power. These three principles appear to keep girls locked into their stance that attacking other girls is the "right thing to do" even while decrying violence.

SEXUAL OBJECTIFICATION

Being Thin, Having a Perfect Body

For girls, especially girls who use violence, the dominant theme is still that what counts for girls is not capacities and capabilities, but their looks. Girls and women are still deeply immersed in what Fuss (1992) identified as the "homospectatorial look."[2] As Fuss pointed out, females are purposefully and systematically inducted by the multibillion dollar fashion, cosmetics, and arts and entertainment industries into becoming subjects who are desired by men. As she stated:

> Playing on the considerable social significance attributed to a woman's value on the heterosexual marketplace, women's fashion photography [in all its many forms] scopophilically poses its models as sexually irresistible subjects, inviting its female viewers to consume the product by (over) identifying with the image. (p. 90)

Females learn early in life to view themselves through men's eyes and to treat their bodies as objects for consumption that must first of all appeal to men. The girls who participated in our studies spoke about having to be like "a supermodel ... like underweight, like [with] a perfect body, so pretty" to be socially accepted, and they spoke about the need to be appealing to boys.

---

[2]Set up in such a way as to create a love of being looked at.

Pretty Power

As one school girl explained to me, girls compete for *pretty power*. The *prettiest* girl becomes the most powerful girl because she is seen as being desirable by the boys; this then helps in making her sought after by girls. This hierarchy sets girls up to compete against each other based on appearance and assigns the greatest power to those deemed the most beautiful. Accordingly, a girl's *look* is her most important asset and all else is secondary. The more desirable a girl's look, the greater is her social currency. As a girl in custody explained, "They judge people by their looks. Probably if some ugly [girl] came in here, they'd be like 'eeu'. If you're prettier it's easier to get accepted." If a girl is considered ugly by her peers (male or female), she is targeted for abuse. As another girl in custody told me,

> Like ... I'm the ugly one right now and there's Ashley [the girl with the most power] who's the pretty one ... there's two or three girls in here. These girls don't like these other girls ... and one of them will say to [the girls they don't like], "Oh shut up!" And everybody's all talking and stuff ... and they'll jump right in after them and fight and stuff.... It's like I'm sitting there and then all of them just start jumping me and kicking me and punching me and stuff like that .... It's like a majority thing ....

Custody workers also talked about the pretty power hierarchy in action. They mentioned an ongoing "competitiveness of the girls for the boys' attention," and noted that girls moved through their day in custody well aware that they were being "watched—literally watched by the boys," and focused mainly on "always the next relationship with a boy. It's always trying to please boys."

Sexualized Name Calling

Teachers, school counselors, and administrators made similar observations and reported that most conflicts involving adolescent girls had to do with clothes, sexual name calling, and boys. Sometimes the adults whom these young women encounter in their daily lives contribute to the sexual objectification they experience. An example of this was provided by a school principal who had been asked by a 13-year-old female student for help in dealing with a male teacher who one day in class had asked her, "Is that bun on your head supposed to match the two on your chest?" The male teacher, when confronted, said that he was, "Only joking, and what's the big deal?" The kinds of experiences described here are not isolated incidents. In a survey of students in Grades 8 to 10 conducted in a Gulf Islands secondary school in 1999, 66% of girls in Grade 9 reported experiencing sexual harassment in the past 6 months. (Grade 9 boys also reported experiencing sexual harassment, but at the much lower rate of 19%.)[3]

When describing girls in negative terms, both the girls and boys who participated in our studies used language that sexually objectified females. The most frequently used putdowns were *slut* and *bitch*. Also popular were *skag*, *ho*, (derived from *whore*), and *fatass*. Such putdowns were used to describe girls who were singled out as targets for social ostracism and/or violence either covert or overt. I first learned in my 1996 study that in most but not all cases the key informants beat up other girls primarily because they saw these girls as threatening their relationships with boys. On occasion they also engaged in physical battles with other girls and sometimes boys to defend their status and uphold their reputations. Chiefly they felt justified in attacking other girls if they believed that these girls deserved to be beaten because they were sexually provocative or promiscuous and could therefore be construed as *sluts*. They also felt justified in attacking those who attempted to attach this label to them. Here is one key informant's description of the dynamics involved:

> Like on the third day of school and I'm walking out on the thing and she's like giving me dirty look and I'm like, whatever, okay, and then a couple of days later, I'm walking out and I hear this, "Fucking slut," and I turn around and say, "What the hell is that for?" and we kinda get in an argument and then I walked away. The next day it's, "There goes the bitch," and I'm like this is a grade eight talking to a grade ten. And then at the dance she pushed me and I go, "Nice fucking outfit!" and then she went and told the vice-principal and then about a week went by and like I hadn't talked to her or anything and I was standing in the hall talking to my friend and I hear, "Kiss my ass!" so I said, "Say it to my face!" and so she did and then it was just like a reflex and I just went like that (motions a backhand smack) and I backhanded her. I should have punched her. She pissed me off so badly.

Sexualized Violence

Each time my research colleagues and I (Artz, 1998; Artz, Blais, & Nicholson, 2000) investigated girls' use of violence, we found that female violence was largely sexualized violence directed at other girls. Creighton and Farr (1999), working on a related project in the same area that we are working in, interviewed 133 youth (75 female and 58 males) for their report, *Sexpectations: Youth Perceptions on the Causes of Sexual Assault, Report 2—Target Audience Research, Project Respect*, and also found clear indications that,

---

[3]Survey results of student population Gulf Islands Secondary School. Unpublished report prepared by SWOVA, Saltspring Island, BC.

The link between being labeled a slut and being targeted for sexualized violence is clearly demonstrated by some youth's beliefs. That is, some teens feel that guys are sexually "entitled" to certain girls and that these girls (labeled as sluts) have lost the right to say "no" or that they don't mean "no." The teens agreed that nobody deserves to be sexually assaulted, however many stated that sluts are "asking for it." (p. 4)

When I asked my 1996/1998 key informants to define the word *slut*, I was told that,

It's like girls can be called sluts if they have sex, but guys are rewarded. If a girl's to go and do it with fifty guys, then they're called a slut or something, but if a guy's going to do it with fifty girls then like, it's "Right on!" Like guys get rewarded and girls get beat up or pushed around or talked about like rumors or something.

I was given an example of a girl who, in the minds of the three girls who were discussing her, was a slut because,

She wears clothes that don't fit her, and we have every right to call her a slut. No offence [in this case to me, the interviewer] but she's a slut. She slept with people at the beginning of the year, and then she was denying it, she's got a screw loose.

Creighton and Farr (1999) were given the following definitions of the term *slut*.

- A girl that will get with a guy (a boy's definition)
- A slut has a short skirt and screws anything that walks and has a penis (a boy's definition)
- Being a slut means getting someone else to solve your problems with sexual attention (a girls' definition). (pp. 4–5)

Creighton and Farr also found that,

A girl with big breasts, a girl with many guy friends, a girl seen merely talking to another girl's boyfriend may be labeled a slut .... (p. 5)

The boys we interviewed divided the girls into two categories—the good girls and the sluts who are dirty girls and deserve what they get (Artz, Blais, & Nicholson, 2000). One boy explained the difference in type this way:

... say it's a ... Christian school girl, square girl, nice girl, and doesn't ask for anything to be brought upon her. Doesn't really want to have anything to do with the lifestyle that other people are living. People should respect that, [but] If the girl's selling sex and if she wants to be into things, then she's going to get beat up. Someone's going to make [the girl] sell sex for them and [she] pretty much knows that when she gets into the business. So, [she] brings it on [herself].

This boy also stated that girls, particularly *good* girls, couldn't really be trusted to live by the codes that boys are expected to live by, especially the code of not *ratting*—that is, telling adults about any rule-breaking, deviant, or delinquent behaviors that young people were engaging in because it is *normal* for good girls to be afraid and weak, therefore they find it necessary to tell someone about things that scared them. *Bad* girls, however, should, as he saw it, be required to live by the same code that boys must follow because they have chosen to stray into a lifeworld normally reserved for males, therefore brought on themselves any punishment that they receive for breaking the code. As he explained:

> [The code] applies to girls in one way, and that's if they choose to live like guys. Say if some girl decides to be a hooker and then she rats out, she's going to get the same as a guy would get.

MISTRUST AND MISOGYNY

Mistrust of females and misogyny were evident everywhere in the way in which the youth participants talked about girls in the studies I conducted and coconducted. During the interviews, two points of view about girls' violence emerged: (a) girls' fights are "so silly" and therefore not worth bothering with, and (b) girls' violence is "so much worse" than boys' violence. Both points of view frame girls' engagement in violence as somehow inferior to boys' engagement in violence. Further, both girls' "silly" behavior and girls' "worse" behavior are seen by teachers, counselors, and custody workers as reasons that girls are much harder to work with than boys.

Girls' Fights Are So Silly

Middle-school boys told us that:

> Girls fight about boys and stupid things like I heard you say blah, blah, blah, usually it's stupid stuff—about boys and what they say about each other.

This was echoed by statements made by middle-school girls—that,

> Girls fight over little sappy things like who's prettier than who, popularity, guys.

For these students, male violence was seen as being more real, and more serious. One male student summed it up this way:

> I think boys have a bigger ego to support. Girls fight over boys and stupid things ... a lot of things that are pointless.

Another male student said,

> I just think that boys try to be more macho than girls and think they're better than girls
> … or they think if they're tough they'll be more popular ….

Female students had similar explanations. As one girl put it,

> I think guys flaunt it, they think it's more macho.

Girls Are So Much Worse

Those young people who talked about girls being *so much worse*, talked about girls being more vicious and girls carrying grudges for longer periods of time than boys. They also noted that girls seem to have sudden and inexplicable changes of mood and allegiance. For these young people, boys' approach to conflict were seen as more stable, predictable, and right. As one school girl explained,

> There's more equality now between girls and guys. And the guys think that if we're
> going to have equality, then we gotta be equal with *them* …. We were having this discussion in English class, and the guys think that girls are wimps because whenever
> they get in a fight they don't just duke it out, they just cry and about a month later they
> finally talk to each other, and then they cry again and they get all sappy and they're
> friends. Or they hate each other one day, and the next day they're friends. Guys are just
> like, "All we do is duke it out and then go for a beer."

As a girl in custody explained,

> Girls are mean. Girls are like in here for a week before, they'll do it [victimize] mentally…. Like it's totally about power. They'll victimize them [other girls] and then
> they'll like beat them up. With guys, they'll like throw everything that they're doing
> down and then like, "Let's go!" And they'll fight and it's over. With girls it's like
> weeks and weeks ….

Another girl in custody noted,

> It's weird, 'cause I always thought that girls should stick together. It's not like that
> anymore. Girls hate each other more than guys hate each other … [In the past] girls
> were friends more. They didn't like fight physically over something stupid as their
> boyfriend breaking up with them and then going out with their best friend. They just
> got into a little spat about it and then that was it. Now it can escalate and one girl can
> end up getting stabbed or something. It's just like insane. Girls, it's just like scandals. I like just watch who I'm friends with. It's bad…. We give each other bad
> names … like slut ….

Even a girl who had a generally more favorable view of girls stated,

> I like it better with girls. Girls are bitches though. That's the one thing I have to say. When you've got eight girls together, they're bitches. One of them PMSing and the others are like, "Don't fucking take it out on us. We'll beat you." That's how bad it gets sometimes ....

In discussing girls' use of violence, one custody worker compared girls' use of violence with boys' use of violence in the following way:

> A lot of the time, girls will come in here and they'll be so afraid of the other girls that even if they're living in a different unit, they'll stay in their room, so if all these girls are living in the same unit .... What kind of meaner? They're very degrading to each other, like the real bad bully, like guys will say, "fuck you," or "you're an asshole," but the girls get right down to the nitty gritty, like they'll make up stories about each other about screwing the other guys—as dirty as they can get, that's how dirty they'll get. Girls are just way more degrading. The boys are more physical. People are way more concerned about girl-to-girl violence.

Girls Are Harder to Work With

In discussing the claim that girls are harder to work with than boys, a number of workers (not all) stated that they would rather work with boys than girls. A variety of reasons were offered to explain this preference:

> [Boys are] more easily programmed. They ... can be demanding, but not as much as I found the girls at the beginnin g.... They understand what the rules of the game of the day were.
>
> Females can be the worst saints and sinners .... They are both sides of the spectrum. I don't see any moderation. Females can be quite nasty, and they can be quite nice depending on the problem.
>
> Females seem to be like they're erratic, like they're all over the place like we're not really sure what they're going to do next when they're upset. They remind me of a little rocket, they're kind of going off in all different directions.
>
> I find girls to be very demanding .... They have to be corrected on a lot of things .... Flighty attitudes of brushing you off, not listening, turning away, rather be talking to their friends than listening to you.
>
> Pop culture is way more prevalent with females, especially music.
>
> If two males residents are going to fight, they do. That's it. If two female residents are going to fight, there's this huge planning process that goes into it and whispering among the girls and note writing. The female residents are always a lot more sneaky and underhanded.

These findings echo those of Baines and Alder (1996), who pointed out, "A frequently heard lament among youth workers and administrators in juvenile justice and related areas is that 'girls are more difficult to work with.'" They also pointed out that this lament has been documented in Germany and Australia by Kersten (1990) and in England by Hudson (1989). Chesney-Lind and Okamoto (2000) also noted that, "Research has found that many (but not all) people who work in the juvenile justice system typically prefer working with boys, and routinely stress the 'difficulty' of working with girls" (p. 20). They in turn cited Alder (1997), who noted that girls in youth-serving systems are frequently unfavorably compared with boys in the system who are seen as easier to deal with because they are more "open, honest and less complex" than their more "hysterical, manipulative, verbally aggressive and untrusting" female counterparts (p. 21).

This unfavorable comparison between males and females was highlighted in the popular press in Canada by Margaret Wente (2000), a well-known columnist who compared the two pop music icons, Eminem (a.k.a. Marshall Mathers), who exalts violence against women with lyrics like,

> My little sister's birthday, she'll remember me
> For a gift I had 10 of my boys take her virginity
> And bitches know me as a horny-ass freak
> Their mother wasn't raped, I ate her cunt in her sleep,

and Britney Spears, who dresses in pig tails and knee socks and sings lyrics like, "Hit me baby one more time." Wente's contention was that Spears was "so much worse" than Eminem because Eminem in his wide appeal to nice teenage boys from the suburbs ....

> addresses a major problem in Western culture which is how to channel young men's natural aggression now that war and hunting are obsolete. Sports sops up some of it, but mostly, the current approach is to declare that male aggression is deviant and try to suppress it. No wonder young men like to get together in large groups and yell dirty words. Parents everywhere should be relieved that boys with attention deficit disorders and anger management issues can, like Eminem, amount to something after. And I honestly think that he and his ilk are far more wholesome than Britney Spears, an invitation to pedophilia if ever I saw one ... Britney makes child porn look cute. (Wente, 2000, p. A17)

This comparison suggests, among other things, that male violence against women is a normal outcome of natural male aggression, whereas female sexuality posing in a girlish guise is an invitation to pedophilia and violence against women. In other words, when men beat women and otherwise express aggression and violence this fits with a normal course of events, but when women are sexually abused and beaten they probably "asked for it." Thus, male involvement in violence is normal and, as Wente says, "wholesome." Female involvement in violence, even their involvement in being sexually and physically victimized, is self-generated. Such beliefs create ongoing challenges for anyone working with youth, female or male. Young women who are exposed to this kind of thinking must struggle with the negative message about their ultimate worth and implied culpability in their own abuse. Young men who are exposed to such thinking will find no reason to refrain from violence, particularly sexualized violence against women.

In all the studies I have been involved in, girls' replies to questions about what it was like to be a girl were largely negative. The first time I asked this question of three girls who met with me to discuss girls' use of violence, I was told, "The guys here degrade you." I was then provided with stories about the sexual harassment and sexual abuse they had experienced. Of my six original key informants, four had experienced sexual abuse. The girls focused on their fears of pregnancy because women who give birth "just look like a mess" and "If I was a man I don't know if I'd wanna be attracted to her anymore." Girls also talked about the restrictions they face as girls, with fewer options for involvement in sports and other recreational activities and greater demands to be involved in household chores. Mostly they preferred the company of males and were in constant competition with females for male attention. When asked about their relationships with other girls, they described changing alliances rather than friendships—that is, attachments to others based on affection and esteem.

RELATIONSHIPS AS ALLIANCES OF POWER

When my six original key informants discussed their friendships, they each described a best friend with whom they had frequent altercations. One girl's best friend lured her to a corner store where others were waiting to beat her up because she appeared to have been flirting with the one of the girls' boyfriends. The girl explained,

> That's the kind of friendship we have, she wanted to see me get pushed around, and I would love to see her get pushed around.

She also described other female friends as tough and willing to beat up others, even kill for her. As she further explained,

> There's a whole bunch of girls that I know that are in gangs, and they're pretty nice, it's just staying off their bad side, 'cause they can do serious damage to you.

Another girl who identified friends as being "the most important thing in her life" also talked about the difficulties she had with her many friendships because her friends often became her enemies. To illustrate this point, she gave the following example:

Janet Williams, she was my friend and we were enemies first and she didn't like my friends, so she'd always get me into trouble. Like, there was a new girl who came and we said this and that about each other and we got mad at each other, so we hated each other for two years, and then the new girl left and we found out what she did, that she said these things about each other to us, so we apologized for everything, so we were friends. But then she didn't like that I liked Todd, and she didn't like my clothes, so she called me out and that's how we had a big fight [watched by more than 100 spectators].

Other girls, nonviolent school girls and girls in custody, had similar stories. One girl who was serving time for sexually assaulting another girl told us,

Personally, like I can't say that I like everybody, right? So I have my share of girls that I totally hate .... My share of girls that I victimize .... I victimize a girl because she pissed me off, or she did something ... that I want to get her back for .... Like she looks at me the wrong way ... [or like the girl I assaulted] she told a lie about my boyfriend ....

A nonviolent school girl—that is, a girl who had never physically assaulted another girl—described the girl–girl dynamics she experienced as follows:

Girls fight over who's prettier, about popularity, about boys ... I think we're all in constant competition with each other because a lot of us have the same taste. All of us like one person. Say one guy is good looking, we're all in a fight over who's getting who .... If all the girls are fighting for this one really popular guy and one girls gets him, everyone will think she's more popular too. That's one of the reasons we all fight over the same popular guy. It gives you just that much more status if you have this guy .... Everyone wants to have lots of money, good grades, be known, have a good guy to hang off, to hang off the arm of.

Having a "good guy to hang off the arm of" is important to social survival and determines rank on the *pretty power* hierarchy. If the choice is between maintaining a friendship with a female friend and trumping that friend's status by winning the competition for the most desirable male, these girls are willing to sacrifice their female friendships. They will maintain their female friendships only as long as these assist them with gaining male attention. As one girl said she only *bothers* with her *best friend* because this friend facilitates access to boys.

In his article, *The Meaning of Meanness: Popularity, Competition, and Conflict Among Junior High School Girls*, Merten (1997) elaborated on the strong connection between girl–girl meanness and girl–girl competition for male attention in popular girls' quests to achieve a social status that allows them to dominate other girls through the formation of alliances. Merten found that the preservation of the status quo of the established girls, who monopolized the most popular boys and high-prestige roles such as cheerleader, was central to these alliances. The high-status girls were willing to accept other girls in their clique, but only if these girls did not overreach their grasp by attempting to bump the established girls from their perches at the top. If any girl involved in the dynamics of the group lost the support of her allies because she overreached her designated status, she was shunned and subjected to a number of forms of meanness like whispering campaigns, name calling, and other forms of bullying. Even the highest status girl was vulnerable to demotion if her popularity became too great because, for example, too many males found her attractive, thus leaving a smaller competitive field for the rest. As Merten pointed out, "competition-conflict to gain or preserve popularity was an ever-present undercurrent in the interpersonal relationships of the clique ..." (p. 185).

Missing in these stories is a sense of caring and relational focus so often attributed to girls (Brown & Gilligan, 1992; Gilligan, 1982; Gilligan, Lyons, & Hanmer, 1990; Gilligan, Ward, & Taylor, 1988). Gilligan and her colleagues conducted research at two independent high schools for girls and one independent co-educational high school and consistently found that adolescent girls are strongly motivated by relational concerns and a desire to help others even on occasion at the expense of self. Although these researchers never claimed that all girls approach life from a relational and caring perspective, they stated that more girls than boys show an inclination to avoid relational conflict to preserve their relationships. Such an orientation to self and world was not evident in how the participants in the various studies described here portrayed themselves and their connections to others. As one girl said,

> Like there's status. I'm one of the girls, I have to admit, that sort of runs the place. If I tell one of the girls to do something, she'll do it for me. The other ones they're younger, not little, but mouthy, and we don't like them. So it's me and [she names three girls] right now are pretty much whatever. We'll like mouth everybody off and it's fun .... It's kind of a status thing ....

Educated in Romance

Were it not for the fact that Merten's (1997) research participants came from a social milieu that matched the privilege enjoyed by the girls who took part in the research conducted by Gilligan and her colleagues, it may be possible to argue that violent school girls and particularly violent girls in youth custody suffer from excessive deprivation and therefore cannot afford to care because they are too busy trying to survive. Yet Merten's research participants, the *dirty dozen* (a label applied to their clique by several of their teachers), suffered no such deprivation.

The nonphysically violent school girls who participated in our studies also suffered none of the deprivation usually identified as contributing to risk and violence, but nevertheless understood and lived by the rules of the pretty power hierarchy. Could it be that when we seek to understand girls' use of violence especially toward other girls, we must look beyond the well-documented risk factors (cf. Andrews, 1996; Galambos & Tilton-Weaver, 1998; McCord & Tremblay, 1992) into the contributions to violence made by the social construction of gender and particularly gender politics?

In their book, *Educated in Romance*, Holland and Elsenheart (1990), provided excellent evidence for the need to further explore gender politics. Their study exposed a pervasive culture of romance grounded in a high-pressure peer system that propels women into a world where their attractiveness to men counts most. Holland and Elsenheart focused on looking into why so many women enter college with strong academic backgrounds and firm career goals, but leave with dramatically scaled-down ambitions, and found that female peer culture demands conformity to the romance rule. In middle schools, secondary schools, and custody centers, the same rules seem to apply. The "same as it ever was" male-focused messages about what is really important for females seem to be prevailing, at least for those on the margins if not beyond. Such messages continue to undermine girls' experiences of capability and autonomy (Orenstein, 1994). These messages also severely marginalize girls whose sexual preference may not be heterosexual.

Devaluing Things Feminine

The general devaluing of things feminine by girls and boys, as well as many workers and teachers, appears to be closely related to and reflective of what Baines and Alder (1996) suggested is "the general construction of gender as binary opposites, with the feminine being subordinated to and therefore devalued, relative to the masculine" (p. 474). This devaluing of the feminine is not a new phenomenon. It has long been recognized and been the subject of much discussion and research. It is important to this discussion of girls' use of violence because of the contribution that this devaluing makes to girl–girl violence. Violence against women in all its forms, including girl–girl violence, is grounded in socially tolerated oppression of women by men.

Oppressed Group Behavior

If a part of what drives girls' violence toward other girls is explained by the oppression of women by men, and if that oppression fuels violent girls' need to gain status and power through attracting the male gaze, we must help girls differentiate between a healthy sexual attraction, if indeed their preference is heterosexual, and a narrowly defined competition for male attention. Girls who buy into the need to hold the male gaze as their ticket to social status, and who in the process accord themselves and other girls so little intrinsic value that they will physically harm and even kill another girl to preserve their connection to males, are exhibiting classic oppressed group behavior. The hallmark of such behavior is an "attitude of adhesion to the oppressor" (Friere, 1971, p. 30), which demands that those who are dominated by an oppressive group (i.e., a group that both defines and controls access to success) work solely toward fulfilling the roles assigned to them by the dominant group. Adhesion to the oppressor is sometimes enacted through horizontal violence—that is, violence against other members of the oppressed. Such horizontal violence is sanctioned especially when an oppressed group member deviates from the expected norms. Girls who seek to carefully control other girls' access to dominant boys; victimize other girls emotionally, physically and sexually; and bully and shun other girls in search of male attention may feel powerful, but in the end are powerless because they are always in a dependent position.

WHAT IS TO BE DONE?

In attempting to understand what is to be done, I first listened to the suggestions provided by the girls. Here is one 15-year-old school girl's explanation and prescription:

> Girls who get into trouble probably have some sort of self-confidence problems, and they need to figure out who they are, like by going to counseling. And like I think they should get community work, not just community hours. They should do something which is working within the community, doing something constructive instead of just sweeping grounds or whatever, something they can learn from instead of the punishment type thing, something they might want to carry on after it's all done .... And their parents need counseling, their fathers need help, they're like the main source of the problem and their mothers need something like a "Speak Out" group, a group where you get together with a bunch of people and learn to tell your feelings and thoughts and things instead of just being in a corner and being quiet. The mothers need to learn to be their own person and not be ordered around by their husband or being pushed around by their husband. If they're not being pushed around then they can get out of the situations they're in .... And the victims need help, they need to get their self-conscious built, or their self-esteem built, because most people don't try to steal other people's boyfriends and go around calling people sluts and whatnot. There's gotta be something wrong there. Seems to me that those people are doing things the wrong way, trying to get on top in a negative way, and then they get pounded on. When you're a teenager you're in kind of a conflict position where you have to keep your own position and not let people put you down.

Through my own and my colleagues' work on violence prevention (Artz, 1998; Artz & Riecken, 1997; Artz, Riecken, MacIntyre, Lam, & Maczewski, 2000), we learned that girls—especially those who are encouraged to participate in designing and implementing violence prevention programming—are far more receptive to making changes in their behavior than boys. Girls told us they wanted to be listened to and respected. They also wanted to be liked and to belong. Girls in custody gave us similar messages. As one girl put it,

> I need control. I need respect from others. I need concern for other people around me....

The girls whom we interviewed told us they found themselves wanting to be responsive to workers who:

- are friendly and nice
- provide information that helps them with their problems, including counseling and medication
- listen to them and take the time to talk
- cut them some slack and joke around with them
- make it safe for them to show how they feel
- are sensitive to them when they are experiencing hard times
- are consistent and fair. (Artz, Blais, & Nicholson, 2000, p. 34)

Others who concern themselves with meaningful programming for girls suggest that this must include a focus on gender-specific risk factors, such as dealing with the multiple abuses faced by girls, knowledge development in the areas of female health, practical assistance with education, employment and housing, and, most important, the promotion of a sense of efficacy and personal empowerment derived from something other than defeating other girls while seeking to attract males (Chesney-Lind, 1998). Chesney-Lind also pointed out that vital to the success of any program is cultural specificity. As she noted,

> Programs must also be scrutinized to assure that they are culturally specific as well as gender specific, since girls' lives are colored by their culture and their gender (and sometimes triply marginalized by age, gender and race as a result). (Chesney-Lind, 1998, p. 33)

Olasfsdottir (1996) suggested that only when we remove both boys and girls from the possibility of perpetuating the traditional sex roles can we unravel and prevent the continuation of males' oppression of females. She suggested that before we can hope to successfully integrate and co-educate the sexes, we must first practice a sex-segregated pedagogy. The segregated pedagogy she described consists of a girls' pedagogy that includes individual work that allows each girl to see herself as autonomous from the group demands so often placed on girls; *dare* training that provides girls with freedom to move, make noise, and enjoy their bodies; training in mistakes that removes the pressure to exhibit learned helplessness and perfectionism; and training in *pain and blood* (i.e., training that both legitimizes feelings of pain without overemphasizing female dependency on others to deal with their pain). The boys' pedagogy includes social training in self-discipline, exercises in intimacy that legitimate caring, and promoting brotherhood through peaceful and collaborative approaches to work and problem solving rather than through the formation of competing groups.

Until we remove ourselves from the ongoing game that Rozak and Rozak (1970) identified as *playing masculine and feminine* that locks us into a system that rewards masculinity with power and femininity with security bestowed by masculine power, we remain in a state of unfinished revolution (Anderson, 1991). In our theories as well as in our practice, we need to constantly deconstruct stereotypes wherever we find them. If we are committed to violence prevention, we especially need to deconstruct gender stereotypical notions bound up in the dynamics of girl–girl violence. Further, given the connection between girl–girl violence and male power, it is limiting to work with violent girls in the absence of working with the boys who are their reference group.

We must refrain from working as if groups of people were discrete units or entities. Gender problems are by definition relational problems. Currently these problems are grounded in cultural representations that serve to keep stereotypical versions of gender and power in place. In our debates and actions, we have not progressed much beyond theories of gender that either exaggerate and oppose male–female differences or attempt to argue that we are really all the same under the skin. The exaggeration of difference serves to alienate women from men and lock us into a contest over *betterness* and dominance. The negation of the differences keeps us from recognizing the special needs of either gender group and diverts attention away from a critical analysis of power relations. Both create a kind of false consciousness in that they support the assumption that there is a group of *all women* and *all men* about whom we can pass judgment. Both essentially support the status quo (Hare-Mustin & Mareck, 1994).

Our problem seems to be that we are still engaged in trying to find a "unified field theory of gender" even at a time when quantum mechanics and postmodernism have amply demonstrated that such a quest is akin to searching for the pot of gold at the end of the rainbow. I think we need to start again with a willingness to accept partiality, multiplicity, randomness, incoherence, and uncertainty. Gender cannot ultimately be pinned down.

As Hare-Mustin and Mareck suggested, "constructing gender is a process... as observers of gender we are also its creators" (p. 70). In working to create gender-sensitive prevention and intervention, we need to work out and work through our personal assumptions and critically analyze our own social conditions and gender relations along with those of our clients. If it is true that the social construction of gender is central to our engagement in aggression and violence, we must begin with a redefined notion of gender and power to develop meaningful and effective strategies for violence prevention. This is the next step in my work in progress and the first challenge in the development of programming.

REFERENCES

Alder, C. (1997). *"Passionate and willful" girls: Confronting practice*. Paper presented to the annual meeting of the Academy of Criminal Justices Sciences, Louisville, KY.
Anderson, D. (1991). *The unfinished revolution*. Toronto, Ontario: Doubleday Canada Limited.
Artz, S. (1998). *Sex power and the violent school girl*. Toronto, Ontario: Trifolium Books/Teachers College Press.
Artz, S., Blais, M., & Nicholson, D. (2000). *Developing girls' custody units draft report*. Submitted to the Department of Justice Canada.
Artz, S., & Riecken, T. (1997). What, so what, then what?: The gender gap in school-based violence and its implications for child and youth care practice. *Child and Youth Care Forum, 26*(4), 291–304.
Artz, S., Riecken, T., MacIntyre, I., Lam, E., & Maczewski, M. (2000). Theorizing gender differences in receptivity to violence prevention programming in schools. *The BC Counsellor, 22*(1), 7–36.
Augimeri, L., Webster, C., Koegl, C., & Levene, K. (1998). *EARL-20B: Early assessment risk list for boys, Version 1, Consultation Edition*. Toronto, Ontario: Earlscourt Family Centre.
Baines, M., & Alder, C. (1996). Are girls more difficult to work with? Youth workers' perspectives in juvenile justice and related area. *Crime and Delinquency, 42*(3), 467–485.
B.C. Police Services Branch. (1998). Youth crime. *BC Crime Trends, Issue #2*. Victoria, BC: Ministry of Attorney General.
Berger, R. (1989). Female delinquency in the emancipation era: A review of the literature. *Sex Roles, 21*, 375–399.
Björkqvist, K. & Niemëla, P. (1992). New trends in the study of female aggression. In K. Björkqvist & P. Niemëla (Eds.), *Of mice and women: Aspects of female aggression*. San Diego: Academic Press.
Blum, D. (1998). *Sex on the brain: The biological differences between men and women*. New York: Viking.
Bourne, P., McCoy, L., & Smith, D. (1998). Girls and schooling: Their own critique. *Resources for Feminist Research, 26*, 55–68.
Brown, L., & Gilligan, C. (1992). *Meeting at the crossroads*. New York: Ballentine.

Chesney-Lind, M. (1998, September). *What to do about girls? Promising perspectives and effective strategies.* Paper prepared for the International Community Corrections Annual Research Conference, Washington, DC.

Chesney-Lind, M., & Sheldon, R. (1998). *Girls delinquency, and juvenile justice.* Pacific Grove, CA: Brooks/Cole.

Creighton, G., & Farr R. (1999). *Sexpectations: Youths perceptions of sexual assault report 2—Target audience research, Project Respect.* Report Submitted to Victoria Women's Sexual Assault Centre, Victoria, British Columbia.

Eron, L. D. (1992). Gender differences in violence: Biology and/or socialization? In K. Björkqvist & P. Niemëla (Eds.), *Of mice and women: Aspects of female aggression* (pp. 89–97). Orlando, FL: Academic Press.

Flowers, R. (1990). *The adolescent criminal: An examination of today's juvenile offender.* Jefferson, NC: McFarland & Company.

Fuss, D. (1992). Fashion and the homospectatorial look. *Critical Inquiry, 18*(4), 713–737.

Gilligan, C. (1982). *In a different voice: Psychological theory and women's development.* Cambridge, MA: Harvard University Press.

Gilligan, C., Lyons, N., & Hanmer, T. (Eds.). (1990). *Making connections: The relational world of adolescent girls at Emma Willard School.* Cambridge, MA: Harvard University Press.

Gilligan, C., Ward, J., & Taylor, J., & Bardige, B. (1988). *Mapping the moral domain.* Cambridge, MA: Harvard University Press.

Hare-Mustin, R., & Mareck, J. (1994). Gender and the meaning of difference: Postmodernism and psychology. In A. Herrmann & A. Stewart (Eds.), *Theorizing feminism: Parallel trends in the humanities and social sciences* (pp. 49–76). Chicago, IL: Westview.

Holland, D., & Elsenheart, M. (1990). *Educated in romance.* Chicago and London: The University of Chicago Press.

Holmes, J., & Silverman, E. (1992). We're here, listen to us! A survey of young women in Canada. Ottawa, Ontario: Canadian Advisory Council on the Status of Women.

Hudson, A. (1989). Troublesome girls: Towards alternative definitions and policies. In M. Cain (Ed.), *Growing up good: Policing the behavior of girls in Europe* (pp. 197–242). London: Sage.

Jiwani, Y. (1998). Violence and the girl child: Out of the public purse. *Kinesis*, November 17–18.

Kersten, J. (1990). A gender specific look at patterns of violence in juvenile institutions: Or are girls really "more difficult to handle?" *International Journal of Sociology of the Law, 18*, 473–493.

Lipsey, M., & Derzon, J. (1998). Predictors of violent or serious delinquency in adolescence and early adulthood: A synthesis of longitudinal research. In R. Loeber & D. Farrington (Eds.), *Serious & violent juvenile offenders: Risk factors and successful interventions* (pp. 86–105). Thousand Oaks, CA: Sage.

Merten, D. (1997). The meaning of meanness: Popularity, competition, and conflict among junior high school girls. *Sociology of Education, 70*, 175–191.

Olafsdottir, P. M. (1996). Kids are both boys and girls in Iceland. *Women's International Studies Forum, 19*(4), 357–369.

Orenstein, P. (1994). *Schoolgirls: Young women, self-esteem and the confidence gap.* New York: Doubleday.

Reitsma-Street, M. (1999). Justice for Canadian girls: A 1990s update. *Canadian Journal of Criminology, 41*(4), 335–363.

Rozak, T., & Rozak, B. (Eds.). (1970). *Masculine and feminine.* New York: Harper & Row.

Survey results of student population Gulf Islands Secondary School. Unpublished report prepared by SWOVA, Saltspring Island, British Columbia.

Varma, K., & Marinos, V. (2000). How do we best respond to the problem of youth crime? In J. Roberts (Ed.), *Criminal justice in Canada: A reader* (pp. 221–232). Toronto: Harcourt Brace Canada.

Whithecomb, J. (1997). Causes of violence in children. *Journal of Mental Health, 6*(5), 433–442.

Wente, M. (2000, October 28). Eminem and Britney: Who scares you more? *The Globe and Mail,* p. A17.

Commentary:
The Importance of Social
Context and Relationships
in Female Aggression

Pierrette Verlaan
Research Center on Behaviour Disorders
Sherbrooke University

Despite a great deal of research, the prevailing controversy about sex differences in the nature, causes, and course of aggressive behavior is far from resolved. More important, the mechanisms by which sociocultural factors interface with individual differences in the development of female aggression remains poorly understood. The authors of the two preceding studies provide valuable and diverse perspectives on some of the current issues relevant to the study of girlhood aggression. Giving voice to girls who engage in aggressive behavior, the studies by Xie and the Cairns (chap. 5) as well as by Artz (chap. 6) touch on key issues in our conceptualization of what female aggression is all about and how it develops from childhood through adolescence. Their contributions highlight a complex interplay of interpersonal and social factors influencing girls' life experiences.

Xie and the Cairns provided a wealth of thought-provoking material on the social functions and developmental predictions of social and physical aggression among girls. Interestingly, the study starts by deploring the fact that no consensus has been reached to adequately identify the more subtle, nonconfrontational forms of aggressive behavior that the Cairns labeled *social aggression* more than a decade ago (Cairns, Cairns, Neckerman, Ferguson, & Gariépy, 1989). Xie and her colleagues sharpened the definitions for different aggressive behaviors (i.e., indirect aggression, relational aggression, and social aggression) that largely pertain to nonconfrontational acts of social exclusion (i.e., shunning, avoiding, negative facial expressions), betrayal of trust (i.e., telling others' secrets, stealing friends), and character defamation (i.e, rumor spreading, gossiping, writing nasty notes). The clarification of terms helps the field tremendously and can be seen as a tentative step toward consensus building. However, as Xie and her colleagues rightly pointed out, typologies of aggressive behaviors are only as good as the measurement taken. This attention to measurement is particularly relevant: As Bartlett (2002) recently reported, when similar methodologies of assessment are used to identify social, indirect, and relational forms of aggression, there are no significant differences among these constructs. Hopefully this new insight on the substantial overlap in these constructs can serve to diminish the controversy surrounding this field of research.

An important contribution of both the Xie et al. and Artz studies is the reminder that girls' aggressive development is linked to their social contexts and peer social dynamics. Popularity, social status, and particularly relationships are central to girls' lives. Close relationships can protect girls from victimization and promote group cohesion. However, aggression in close relationships can also be a cruelly effective tool to harm others. The secrets exchanged in close relationships can be used in shifting alliances to put down and discredit others. Xie and her colleagues pointed out that effective social attacks rely on the perpetrators' ability to mobilize the peer group against the victim. Clearly a dominant or popular status within the social network is critical in achieving successful harm to another.

Xie, Cairns, and Cairns proposed that girls engage in nonconfrontational violence out of fear of retaliation from victims and authority as well as to conceal their identity. I would also add that because the use of overt confrontational strategies of aggression is condemned by most girls' cultures, engagement in physical fighting is most likely to elicit retaliation from the peer milieu, particularly social exclusion and defamatory remarks from other girls. Because relating and connecting define girls' social worlds, the fear of isolation and loss of relationships and status may have powerful inhibiting effects on girls' use of confrontational forms of aggression. Thus, it is socially safer and ultimately more profitable for girls to take out their fears, anxieties, and anger in such a way that their aggression is hidden within a group context and looks unintentional. Furthermore, social aggression is an acceptable stereotypically feminine way to exert strong feelings of anger and also keep other girls in the social community in line.

Artz's study on high-aggressive girls reinforced many of the valid points that Xie and the Cairns made about the importance of social networks and relationships. From a feminist perspective, Artz suggested that girls' aggression is best understood in the context of other gender issues, including the girls' own sense of powerlessness. She stated that girls' aggression is grounded in socially tolerated oppression of women by men. Girls are born into a culture of symbols and socialization practices that teach the lesser importance of characteristics or behaviors associated culturally with women. Therefore, high-aggressive girls learn that power resides for the most part in aggression (that they have often witnessed) and rules have their source in those who have the power to impose them. Because girls have been taught that their power comes from being nice and pleasing others, girls learn to internalize their own capabilities and capacities and view them as unimportant. In that sense, Artz noted "that girls learn early in life to view themselves through men's eyes and to treat their bodies as objects for consumption that appeal to them."

Within this gender socialization framework, female power and dominance is obtained by *social currency* obtained with regard to *male attention*. Thus, male attention directed toward other females poses a particular risk to girls' social standing. In other words, high-aggressive girls feel justified to attack if they believe that other girls are being sexually provocative, promiscuous, or a threat to their relationships with boys. Rumors, jealousy, and competition over real or potential boyfriends were the issues most likely to ignite a fight among the aggressive teenage girls interviewed by Artz. These girls indicated that the ethic of revenge is often accompanied by the assumption that victims deserve their treatment. This connection is consistent with theories that point to frustration-aggression and negative intention cuing working together to develop, maintain, and exacerbate acts of aggression. The extent to which girls buy into messages about women's inferiority and see status as something to be gained through male relationships, supports their inclination to judge each other harshly. The social interactions that these girls build around a constant battle for dominance, social status, relationship exclusivity, and vengeance are similar to the social processes outlined in the Xie et al. study. Both studies stress that understanding this dynamic is crucial in resolving aggression among girls.

Where does the collective message of Artz and Xie and her colleagues leave us for prevention and intervention? For one, both studies demand a wider range of research approaches than are typically used with males. Although girls are not always made of sugar, spice and all that's nice, most of them are less likely to engage in the physical behaviors described in most empirical investigations on childhood aggression to date. When boys' aggression gets out of hand, we intervene. What intervention is possible for a type of aggression that has not, as yet, a unified definition in science? What intervention is possible if our society pretends that girls' aggression has no serious consequences?

As a first step, I agree with Xie and her colleagues that attending to the lack of prevention or intervention strategies related to the use of nonconfrontation aggression is urgently recommended. I think part of our work is to help people understand that these aggressive strategies are as harmful as fistfights and can have long-lasting effects. Adults, including teachers, often see these forms of aggressive behavior, but do not take them seriously, nor do they intervene to address the problem.

A second pressing issue put forth by Xie and her colleagues is that intervention strategies should comprise both an individual and a group approach because relationships and peer social dynamics determine girls' aggressive behaviors. Girls depend on close, intimate friendships to get them through life. The trust and support of these relationships provide girls with emotional and psychological safety nets. By understanding the nature of girls' relationships and placing girls' aggression in a social context, we can help girls learn to resist the pressures to conform to stereotypes and rid them of the fiction that they must always be friends with everyone. Thus, any prevention effort leading to a successful outcome should not leave out the social structure and social context in girls' lives.

Finally, extra attention is also required to address the negative perceptions of youth workers toward young aggressive girls. As emphasized in Artz study and elsewhere (e.g., Adler & Baincs, 1996), aggressive girls are generally viewed as mistrusting, demanding, sneaky, and more complex to work with than aggressive boys. It is possible that the lack of knowledge of girls' social dynamics and traditional gender role beliefs, specifically those implying that girls are supposed to be nice, nurturing, and contain their feelings (especially anger), account for some of negative perception of these girls by youth workers. Because relationship problems and poor self-images are at the forefront of aggressive girls' problems, it is important for youth workers to build respectful and empowering relationships with these young girls (Way, 1995).

More than any other time in history, girls are looking for ways to define themselves. To prevent girls from purposely hurting others, parents, teachers, and youth workers must acknowledge that strong-willed and independent girls, as well as those who are shy and timid, need to fit in, be liked, and have a place in the social group and school community. We must show girls that conflict-free relationships do not usually exist, and that when they acknowledge their aggressive tendencies, they can move beyond them to negotiate conflicts and define relationships in healthy ways.

Within the fields of research and clinical practice focused on aggressive girls, there is a need for more in-depth explorations of adequate prevention and intervention strategies, which in turn depend on the development of adequate theoretical models and empirical rigor that take into account social and individual influences on girls' development and adjustment.

REFERENCES

Alder, C., & Baines, M. (Eds.). (1996). *And when she was bad? Working with young women in juvenile justice and related areas.* Hobart, AUS: National Clearinghouse for Youth Studies.

Bartlett, N. (2002). *Physical and relational aggression and victimisation among children: The role of familial and individual factors.* Unpublished doctoral dissertation. Concordia University, Montreal, Canada.

Cairns, R. B., Cairns, B. D., Neckerman, H. J., Ferguson, L. L., & Gariépy, J.-L. (1989). Growth and aggression: 1. Childhood to early adolescence. *Development Psychology, 25,* 320–330.

Way, N. (1995). "Can't you see the courage, the strength I have?" Listening to urban adolescent girls speak about their relationships. *Psychology of Women Quarterly, 19,* 107–128.

Part IV

AGGRESSIVE GIRLS
IN TREATMENT

7

Girls Growing up Angry: A Qualitative Study

Kathryn S. Levene
Earlscourt Child and Family Centre

Kirsten C. Madsen
The Hospital for Sick Children

Debra J. Pepler
York University and The Hospital for Sick Children

Although a rich research base informs the field of childhood aggression, few studies have focused specifically on the development and treatment of girls' aggression. Treatments that were primarily developed for and evaluated with boys have been applied to girls (Brestan & Eyberg, 1998). This lack of scientific and clinical attention to the precise nature of girls' aggression has been explained in terms of low prevalence rates (Offord, Boyle, & Racine, 1991; Steiner & Dunne, 1997) and assumptions about the greater societal burden associated with the antisocial consequences for boys (Robins, 1986). Yet there are indications that girls with an early aggressive history are prone to experience major problems over the lifespan. These problems are both similar to and different from those encountered by boys (Robins, 1986). For example, childhood aggression is linked to poor school motivation, premature school leaving (Pulkinnen, 1992), and drug use (Cairns & Cairns, 1994) in both boys and girls. For girls, truancy and running away are particularly problematic issues (Schlossmann & Cairns, 1993) as are the cluster of gender-specific problems associated with sexual development (Caspi, Lynam, Moffitt, & Silva, 1993), early sexual activity (Lenssen, Doreleijers, Van Dijk, & Hartman, 2000; Ray & English, 1995), and teen pregnancy (Quinton, Pickles, Maughan, & Rutter, 1993; Schlossman & Cairns, 1993). There may also be intergenerational links, in that an early aggressive history is associated with girls having offspring who exhibit early signs of behavior and health problems (Serbin, Moskowitz, Schwartzman, & Ledingham, 1991).

Although the negative trajectories of aggressive and antisocial girls and boys are equally concerning, it is girlhood aggression that has yet to be investigated. As one step toward constructing a foundation for understanding girlhood aggression, we embarked on a qualitative inquiry to uncover prominent themes by eliciting the views of clinic-referred girls and their parents. Their narratives, as suggested in the following quote,[1] proved to be powerful and rich sources of information.

> Mother 12: My daughter is a wonderful child … it's crazy 'cause everywhere when she meets kids and other parents, they love her. But sometimes you think nobody would ever believe that there's this demon on the other side. She will, you know, just run at me, clawing, yelling, screaming "you fucking bitch," "you stupid *racist name.*" Whatever. Like everything, the works. She just calls her dad and says "you asshole," like constantly. So, yeah, I'm very concerned about her anger, she erupts, the volatility, the intensity of her anger when she lets loose.

In the 1990s, girlhood aggression emerged as a topic of importance for the Earlscourt Child and Family Centre (ECFC), an urban treatment agency for aggressive and antisocial children under the age of 12 and their families. In late 1996, the Centre implemented the first reported gender-specific program for this population, the Earlscourt Girls Connection (EGC). A developmental model informs the central theoretical framework for this program. According to this theory, development is shaped by the interaction of risk and protective factors that exist within the individual, family, and community (Rutter, 1985). This qualitative study aims to inform the relatively untapped area of inquiry of girlhood aggression through listening to girls and their parents as they discuss what they consider to be salient risk factors. In the following section, the qualitative methodology that was applied is discussed.

METHOD

Participants

Participants were recruited from families admitted to the EGC, a multifaceted, family-focused treatment program for girls under 12 years of age who are exhibiting serious behavior problems. Sixteen families took part in this exploratory investigation: 10 mother-led, 1 father-led, and 5 two-parent families. Information was collected from 37 persons—21 parents and 16 girls. The study group composition was stratified to reflect the EGC popu-

---

[1]Families and family members are identified numerically in this discussion to distinguish family groupings while avoiding any identifying information. Whenever there are identifying names or locations in quoted portions of transcripts, they are replaced by starred nonidentifying words or phrases.

lation with regard to two- and single-parent families and families from Euro-Canadian and visible-minority backgrounds. The girls ranged in age from 7 to 13 years. Families whose daughters were younger than 7 years of age were excluded based on the level of articulation required of the girls. Although the structure of the study imposed some limits on the process of recruitment (e.g., age, stratification), we attempted to enlist consecutive admissions to the program to avoid bias in the sampling procedure. Adult participants signed a consent document for themselves and their daughters that informed them of the nature of the study and assured them that participation was not linked to provision of treatment.

Measures

At admission, child behavior problems were assessed using the Standardized Client Information System (SCIS; Offord, Boyle, & OACMHC, 1996)—a measure adapted from the Child Behavior Checklist (CBCL; Achenbach, 1991). A girl was considered suitable if she was rated by her parent as falling within the clinical range for conduct problems, oppositional defiant problems, and/or externalizing behaviors on this rating scale (70 or higher).[2] The Family and Household section of the SCIS, also completed by the parent, was another source of information.

Description of Sample

The families' admission profile provides useful information on the challenges encountered by the families and the vulnerabilities of the young girls. With one exception, all the girls had some level of learning difficulty, including seven (44%) who were experiencing a serious academic lag of an undetermined source. At least one fifth of the girls (3) had experienced serious physical problems since birth. Seven (44%) girls had witnessed violence directed at their mothers. Sexual abuse had been alleged by four (25%) of the girls. Five (31%) had been physically abused, and one (6%) had been both physically and sexually abused. On the Child Behavior rating scale of the SCIS, the group mean scores, based on the mothers' ratings, were in the clinical range for total externalizing behavior problems (73) and just below the clinical cut-off (67) for attention deficit problems. Scores for depression and problems with social relations were both within the clinical range, and the group mean score for internalizing behavior problems was just below the clinical cutoff (66). Fathers' ratings of their daughters were similar.

---

[2]Within a normally distributed sample, 2 out of 100 children score 70+, 3 children out of 1,000 score 80+, and 1 child out of 10,000 scores 90+ (Offord et al., 1996).

Participants mirrored the EGC population with regard to single-parent (69%) and visible-minority (21%) families. In 13 (81%) of the families, there had been a marital separation, and the majority has remained as single-parent households. Five (32%) of the current households were dual-parent families, including three biological fathers. In half of the families, one parent had or was currently struggling with substance abuse or chronic depression. Ten families (63%) were experiencing financial strain. Annual income for the majority of the families was under $30,000. A sizable number of families were in receipt of government financial assistance and subsidized housing. There were also some indications of resiliency in the families, such as a parent pursuing a career, a family improving their home, and a family engaging in creative activities.

Procedure

The 37 individuals were interviewed at a location chosen by parents, usually at ECFC. Separate but parallel semistructured interview formats guided the parent and child interviews. Meetings generally lasted for 1½ to 2 hours with parents and 1 hour with the girls. Interviewers were matched with participants on the basis of gender. All interviews were audiotaped and transcribed.

Qualitative research methodology (McCracken, 1988) directed our developmental and analytical efforts. The first level of coding began with the first two authors independently reading transcripts while listening to the audiotaped interviews to highlight important utterances and code them into categories. Once this process was completed, coding was discussed until complete agreement was achieved. Two additional coders—experts in the fields of childhood aggression and qualitative inquiry—coded four interviews as a further check on reliability and agreed with the authors' coding. The subsequent level of coding involved the use of the qualitative computer program, QSR NUD*IST (1997), a program used to sort, index, and analyze data. This program was then used to make interconnections between coded observations in each transcript. Based on a thorough consideration of relevant literature, the researchers then isolated common themes, identified themes that interacted with one another, and compared responses of informant groups. Several salient themes emerged from this investigative and interpretative phase, which allowed us to identify variables that may play key roles in the development of girlhood aggression. Some of the observations are consistent with informed thinking about the pathways of behaviorally troubled young girls.

FINDINGS

In undertaking this study, our premise was that members of families in which a daughter was displaying behavior problems would be able to identify factors they perceive as key in influencing the development of girlhood aggression. In their narratives, family members primarily emphasized risk factors and spoke sparingly of protective factors. This imbalance is probably the result of the participants being individuals who were seeking help with serious problems and who had little sense of what has buffered their experiences. Six areas of possible risk emerged from their wide-ranging discussions: early difficulties, family relationships, abuse, school, peer relationships, and community. In the following sections, we highlight these themes, illustrate them with quotations from the transcripts, and discuss possible implications for investigation, prevention, and intervention.

Early Difficulties

A poor early start in life characterized this group of young girls. From birth one fifth of the girls had experienced serious physical problems requiring extensive hospitalizations and intrusive levels of specialized care. Others were described as *difficult*, *cold*, and *colicky* infants.

Mother 11:   When I brought her home everyday was a nightmare. We were so tired. She did not sleep at all. Really you had to get all your energy in her. Sometimes at 5 o'clock in the morning, we were in the rocker ... she did not sleep until 6 o'clock. We took our turns, one time was my husband, one time was me. I was sleeping, he was awake. She was a very difficult baby ... I could never manage to have a routine like with my other babies. One moment she wanted to eat *now* and another moment she would just sleep for 10 minutes. Somehow I went shopping and had to be back quickly because she was crying. She wanted to eat again and again. She was never satisfied. I did breast feeding for 9 months. I could feed her for 20 minutes until I was almost falling asleep. She was just happy and then she started with the second one and then there was the bottle after.

Many parents articulated a link between the early onset of their daughters' problems and later social adjustment problems. Parents also identified constitutional factors that had become apparent over the preschool years, including ADD, ADHD, learning disabilities, and speech problems, as possibly predisposing their daughters to behavioral difficulties. Mother 2 identified undetected ADHD as a substantial risk factor for girls; she believed that undiagnosed ADHD had set her daughter on a problematic pathway for several years. In contrast, her son was diagnosed early with ADHD and received appropriate resources. There is research to support her view. Early ADHD problems in preschool girls are predictive of conduct problems by age 8—a relationship that is stronger for girls than for boys (Bates, Bayles, Bennett, Ridge, & Brown, 1991). Loeber and Keenan (1994) concluded that

ADD girls may be more likely to become conduct disordered than ADD boys. These findings may, in part, be the result of girls being diagnosed and treated later than boys. There is some evidence that girls exhibit behaviors that fit more into the attention deficit sphere than the realm of hyperactivity (Berry, Shaywitz, & Shaywitz, 1985). As such their behaviors may not be overtly disruptive and may garner less attention or understanding than those of their male counterparts with regard to their potential seriousness.

The prevalence of early difficulties in the lives of these girls was notable, and one mother associated it with her daughter's *loss of childhood*. In their narratives, parents associated the difficulties in caring for and interacting with their challenging infants and toddlers as setting the stage for future problems. Such difficult beginnings likely increase the short- and long-term risks for disrupted parent–child relationships.

Summary

Development in girls' early years emerged as a potentially important area for future research. The early years of these troubled girls' lives were characterized as disrupted and burdened by a range of risk factors, the most prominent being physical, temperamental, and constitutional problems, which in turn had potential detrimental effects on the developing parent–child relationship. This early period of vulnerability may also be an optimal time for the introduction of preventive steps to address possible risk factors. The themes that emerged from this study suggest the importance of enhancing the professional education of those individuals who work with young girls and their parents (e.g., teachers, hospital personnel, early childhood educators, general practitioners) with regard to their understanding and responses to families in which a daughter is experiencing severe early problems (e.g., ADHD). Girls who exhibit what are viewed as non-normative behaviors in their early years may also be in a particularly vulnerable position within their families and communities. Public and professional education regarding gender-based expectations may be an avenue for changing expectations to encompass the reality of girlhood development.

Family Relationships

Problematic family relationships were a primary theme in the interviews. A picture emerged, mainly from maternal narratives, of mothers bearing the brunt of the girls' problem behaviors and aggression. They also appeared to be highly aware of and sensitive to expressions of mother–daughter conflict. This likely occurred, at least in part, because they tended to be primary and often sole caregivers. In addition, another layer of problematic family relationships emerged as the mothers talked about their own families of origin.

Mothers' Family of Origin.   With few exceptions, the mothers spoke of their own complex and difficult childhood experiences and how these influenced their lives. Their formative years were characterized by troubling experiences: numerous foster placements, *failing* in adoptive families, both having and caring for dysfunctional parents, and, for some, profound abuse at the hands of parents and siblings. These mothers' efforts to be effective parents and have positive and rewarding relationships with their daughters are especially striking given their primary experiences and models.

> Mother 9:   My family was very dysfunctional, let's put it that way. My father was a drunk; he used to beat the crap out of my mother constantly. By the time I was 5, I was suffering from severe malnutrition. Never went to school. My teeth were rotted out of my mouth. The government stepped in, first they took my brother, then they came and took me. I was put in a foster home for a year, then I was transferred to another foster home and they adopted me by the time I was 8. At first everything seemed to be okay. The point is that I remembered who my family was, even at 6, 7, and 8. I mean I can remember things down to 3 and 4, and I was very uncomfortable at first because I didn't know them, obviously. They had children of their own. But eventually I thought I adjusted pretty well. It came to a point, though, in my teenage years, where the trouble started.

A strained mother–daughter relationship was also a cross-generational theme. More often than not, there was marked conflict or serious parenting issues in the mother's family of origin, which were primarily, but not solely, restricted to the mother and maternal grandmother relationship. Mother 16 spoke about her difficult childhood and her distant relationship with her own mother:

> Mother 16:   I had a hard time because my parents moved almost every year. From about 10 through 14 their economic situation went down every year, and in an alcoholic home you don't bring friends home. My mother would be in her room and the blinds would be closed. In the house there was a feeling of, you wouldn't know if my mother was drunk, whether she'd be depressed, or whether they would be fighting. It was a very awful situation. For my daughter, it's completely the opposite. She comes home and I'm there.

Mothers who had had difficult childhoods spoke about their efforts to create a better home for their daughters. Often this was coupled with expressions of disappointment and anger with regard to what they viewed as their *wasted* efforts to provide a better life for their daughters.

Current Families.   Themes of separation and loss were pervasive in
the maternal narratives about current family groupings. For single-parent
families within a clinic-referred population, separation and loss are associated with many other risk factors such as parental conflict, witnessing
spousal violence, and a profound sense of loss that may have influenced
the development of girlhood aggression in these families. There is evidence of the importance of the parental relationship and its effect on the
lives of young children (Jaffe, Wolfe, Wilson, & Zak, 1986).

Based on the assumption that parents provide primary role models for
their children, offspring may learn their primary caregivers' aggressive
behaviors (Bandura, 1977). Given the predominance of mother-led family
groupings in this study and the importance of same-sex modeling for girls,
it is likely that the girls learned from their mothers' interactional and
parenting styles. There is some evidence that girls who experience harsh,
punitive parenting from their mothers are more likely to display aggressive and antisocial behaviors (Johnson & O'Leary, 1987; Simons, Johnson, Beaman, & Conger, 1993). In one instance, it was the father who
exerted a major influence in his daughter's maladjustment in that he condoned his daughter's *warrior* behaviors and served as a powerful, aggressive model with displays of behaviors such as extreme *road rage*.

Mothers.   Instances of mother–daughter conflict and problematic
parenting issues appeared throughout the maternal narratives. Having a
daughter with a difficult temperament sometimes translated into early
mother–daughter conflict, which, over time, seemed to worsen. Mothers often felt incapable of dealing with their daughters. Mother 12 recalled problem interactions when her daughter was 3 years old:

> Mother 12:   I remember people telling me they remember me trying to get her up the
> hill kind of thing and her fighting you know, like lying in the street, just
> lying there and screaming. I wouldn't know what to do, so I would sit
> down on the street and wait. It was awful.

As the girls developed, parenting issues came to the forefront, especially
as parents tried to set effective limits. The mothers generally viewed their
daughters as being difficult children; to a lesser degree, they saw themselves
as being deficient in their parenting. Patterson and his colleagues (1992) described a coercive interactional cycle that serves as a foundation for the development and maintenance of aggressive and antisocial childhood
behaviors. The inadvertent reinforcement of problem behaviors fuels the
cycle that is likely to be repeated and escalate into increasingly problematic
interactions. This pattern was prominent in the mothers' descriptions of

parenting the girls. They tended to use ineffective disciplinary techniques such as yelling, *telling her off*, or *giving in*, thus unintentionally reinforcing their daughters' negative behaviors. One stepfather described a repetitive pattern of escalating coercive interactions between his wife and stepdaughter that had developed as a result of his wife trying to overcompensate for her daughter's physical disabilities and her ex-husband's punitive parenting. The daughter in some ways maintained this cycle by reminding her mother that she had failed to protect her from the father's wrath. In some instances, as noted next, the parent has some awareness of her contribution to the problem:

> Mother 14: I'm very, sometimes inconsistent. Which is wrong I think, you know. But when she misbehaves I just tell her off. It all depends what's going on in my little world at that time. Sometimes I'm PMS'n, and I find that's the worst time in my life.

Another aspect of coercive mother–daughter relationships is overnegotiation. Since the inception of the program, EGC staff have noted that this seems to be a potent variable in problem adult–girl interactions. As suggested in the following quote, the girl may be viewed as being in charge and directing the interactive cycle:

> Mother 16: I had years of that myself, where I'd say: "Come on do your homework" and she'd mess about, you know goof about and eventually I would have to say: "You have to do your homework now before anything." Because what would happen is she'd go and twist my arm a little bit more because I'm the parent, but she'd go: "Okay, but I want to watch TV and can I have a cookie?" Like this and I'll go: "Okay"—and you know and we'd be doing homework at 8 o'clock at night. It would be very stressful and literally there would be tears. It would just be awful. You can ask her to do something, but she'll just pretend and just wander off and she'll just go and do something else. Sometimes thoughtlessness and other times it's just not being mature.

Later in the interview, this mother indicated that on occasion she has resorted to *smacking* her daughter after a series of negative interactions. Unfortunately, it is not uncommon for the problem interactions to escalate. The cumulative pressures experienced by parents who participated in this study seem immense, with each stress adding exponentially to their load. Given their own models and childhood experiences and their current stresses, it is not surprising that these parents get caught in the coercion trap.

There was also evidence of poor parent–girl boundaries that appeared in different forms over the course of the interviews. For example, some parents shared explicit details of their own childhood abuse traumas with their young daughters. In other families, there was marked role reversal. Mother 3, having become a mother at age 15, was emotionally unprepared for parenting. She treated her very young daughter as a companion and referred to her as her *shadow*.

> Mother 3:   I don't know. I think she is mature. She tries to be mature for like the situation we have. You know, just me and her, and she tries to be strong. If I get a bill she'll say, "Oh okay are you gonna pay that?" And yeah, like it's scary though. I'm like, "You know you don't have to worry about things like that, it's me." Then she says, "Well you know, I want to make sure you know."

In these entwined relationships, the mothers do not seem to be aware of or understand the problems that arise when the parent does not assume an effective adult role. The issue of unclear boundaries was also reflected in statements in which mothers would ascribe negative adult intent to their daughters' behaviors (e.g., *controlling*, *bitch*). Such complaints are perhaps not surprising given the evidence of coercive interactions, household unpredictability, and the girls' caregiver roles within their families.

In reviewing the narratives, a pattern emerged of mothers talking a great deal about their relationships with their daughters and the girls saying little about these relationships. This pattern contrasted with the girls' more voluble and generally positive discussions of their fathers.

Fathers.   Loss of the father, usually as a result of marital disengagement, emerged as a salient theme in the mother and daughter narratives. Loss was considered to be a factor that contributed to both onset and maintenance of the girls' behavior problems. The girls highlighted separation from or absence of the father as a source of distress and upheaval. Girl 7 talked about her sadness that her father was not only absent, but also unavailable. In the following quote, Girl 14 hinted at the complex family issues that get stirred up when considering her noncustodial father:

> Interviewer: Do you ever see your dad?

> Girl 14:   Yeah. Just once a month but he never calls me. My mom says, "Don't waste your time on him. When he gets old, gets old and weary and comes asking for you, then you can say 'no'."

Although there is little research on fathers of aggressive girls, there is some evidence (Kavanagh & Hops, 1994) that having an antisocial father may be predictive of aggression in girls. According to the mothers participating in this study, the majority of the noncustodial fathers had been or continued to be involved in antisocial activities (e.g., substance abuse). The nature of paternal influence on the development of girlhood aggression is likely exerted through several complex factors, including not having a father present, mother's (overt and covert) responses to the father, knowledge of father's antisocial behaviors, and his unacceptable conduct when he does have contact (e.g., driving while drunk). Fathers in the two-parent families were generally prosocial and supportive, although often unavailable due to work demands.

The girls provided a different picture of their fathers. They were mainly positive about them and spoke about loving and missing their absent or unavailable fathers. The three girls who were decidedly negative about their fathers had been exposed to various forms of abuse involving their fathers. Abuse did not necessarily figure in negative judgments. Girl 13 spoke fondly of her father, who had, when he lived with the family, pounded her head against a wall. Even when fathers were largely unavailable, they were viewed positively by their daughters. The following quote illustrates this finding and hints at the girl's view of her mother:

> Girl 15: Even though he is working all the time, he always spends time with me on the weekend and we have a lot of fun together. My dad never leaves me out, even when my sister was born.

There are some intergenerational parallels for this finding. Some of the mothers expressed positive regard for their own fathers regardless of their dysfunctional histories. Despite her father's long-term problems with alcoholism, spousal abuse, and neglect, Mother 9 reported that she gets along with him and views her mother as having the problems.

Siblings. Because children in the same household are usually exposed to a similar family environment and interact with each other in close quarters, it is not surprising that the sibling relationships of the girls included in this study are often highly conflictual. Sibling conflict may have particular relevance for girls' behavior problems given their isolation, the amount of time they spend within the family, as well as the expectation that they may take on a caregiver role. Patterson (1986) illustrated how, in general, aggressive boys regularly engage in fighting behavior with siblings and learn aggressive strategies from their siblings. Similar processes may promote problem behaviors in girls (Pepler & Sedighdeilami, 1998). The home can serve as a high-intensity training arena in aggressive behavior for troubled girls as their caregiver role affords many opportunities to try out aggressive control tactics with siblings.

A range of sibling interactions was identified as contributing to the problems experienced by the girls. Girl 2 was extremely angry with her mother because she sometimes had to lock herself in the bathroom after school until her mother returned to avoid her brother's aggression and getting into physical fights. Father 11 thought that his daughter was negatively influenced by a sister who "has a lot of problems to control her temper." Sibling competition for mother's limited resources is often another source of pressure.

In unfavorably comparing their problematic daughters with siblings, some parents seemed to heighten sibling conflict as well as their own misperceptions. For example, Mother 9 was more critical and verbally aggressive with her daughter than with her son, although both exhibited serious behavior problems:

> Mother 9: She thinks that he gets more attention than she does, which isn't the case, but that's what she feels anyways. I have a tendency to yell at her more than at him. And then, like I told her, I said: "I don't really have any problems with *brother*. That's the point. I'm not yelling at him a whole lot. As with you, I have more to worry about—you're a girl. There's things that you're not supposed to be doing and when you do them it irritates me—obviously I'm going to yell. I have no other choice but to. If you are doing something wrong and I don't think it's proper, then I'm going to yell." But she really hates that when I do it.

Sibling dynamics probably play an important role in the development of aggression in young girls, but there has been little research in this area. We speculate that girlhood aggression frequently plays out behind the *closed doors* of the family, where aggressive girls spend most of their childhood hours (Pepler & Craig, 1999).

Summary

Whether rooted in the presence of mothers or absence of fathers or an interaction of these factors, it was the same-sex relationship that emerged in this exploratory study as playing a dominant role in the evolution of a risk trajectory for girlhood aggression. A struggle for control typified most of the mother–daughter relationships—a struggle that may have started with infancy. There were several themes that warrant further investigation, particularly the complex nature of mother–daughter and family relationships for girls who develop conduct problems.

With regard to interventions, the narratives were rich in highlighting possible areas to explore, such as the importance of expending clinical effort to develop ways to improve and strengthen mother–daughter relationships and evaluate the role of intergenerational issues that may interfere with mothering. For example, adult labeling of a young girl as bossy and controlling may serve as a red flag, signaling coercive processes.

The majority of the girls had noncustodial fathers who, according to the mothers, have generally played a problematic role. Issues were also identified with regard to the availability of fathers in two-parent families. In contrast, it was notable that, with few exceptions, the girls were well disposed to their fathers. Research that addresses the role and influence of fathers in the lives of aggressive and antisocial girls is decidedly lacking and warrants attention. There are also possible clinical directions to explore. Although it is often difficult to engage noncustodial fathers, clinicians might explore creative ways to involve them and promote the development of a healthy father–daughter bond. Clinicians need to pay close attention to the cognitions and experience of this group of troubled young girls regarding their fathers.

We have found that parent training, grounded in social interactional principles, seems to provide the most effective approach, to date, for interrupting the coercive cycle (Kazdin, 1987) with families whose daughters are growing up angry (see, e.g., Levene, 1997). Examining the gender-specific aspects of the coercive cycle may enhance both our understanding and interventions. With regard to preventive efforts, there may be some points of intervention where various systems that deal with estranged parents (e.g., courts, public education) could become productively involved in addressing the needs of young girls and their families.

Abuse

For this group of girls, abuse presented in a variety of forms. Our understanding of the depth and complexity of abusive experiences for girls is insufficient, but we do know that they seriously interfere with normal development (Lynch, 1988). In some cases, there was clear evidence of direct verbal, physical, and sexual assault and domestic assault. In other instances, very young girls have carried the burden of detailed knowledge of their parents' abusive childhoods. Although there were examples of the mothers being physically assaultive with their partners and verbally aggressive with their daughters, physical forms of abuse were generally male initiated. Girl 6 and her sister lived in a generally abusive environment in which their parents were frequently involved in physical fights. The stepfather had been incarcerated several times, and the incident described next led to another imprisonment.

> Mother 6: He followed me out and when I went to go back in the apartment he stuck his foot in the door and I said, "What do you want?" He says, "I want my fucking bag." I kicked the bag out in the hall. I didn't even get my back turned around to get the door shut and to get his foot out of the door when he had that crowbar out.

Summary

Family members reported that individuals and systems (e.g., immediate and extended family systems, health system) contributed to their daughters' experiences of abuse. Sexual abuse poses a particular risk factor for girls and is highly represented in the early histories of delinquent girls (Chesney-Lind, 1989). Much work remains to be done in the areas of prevention and treatment of girlhood abuse that continues to occur at unacceptable levels (see Trocme & Wolfe, 2001). Enhanced efforts based on adequate prevention, treatment, and research are needed to address this issue thoroughly.

School

With one exception, academic difficulties contributed to their daughters' difficulties. This is confirmed in the EGC clinic-referred population, where mathematics has been identified as a particular area of deficit (Michel, 2000). Problematic relationships with teachers were specifically noted as catalysts for girls' behavioral difficulties. Parents thought that their daughters' early negative attitudes about school and learning difficulties were influential in the development of behavior problems. For some parents, there was a profound sense of hopelessness about their ability to forestall a negative school trajectory.

> Mother 8: Maybe if I knew a little more about how to treat children with a learning disability. I think part of her behavior is because she has a learning disability. She doesn't think like other children. Like at the school—other children know they must learn.

> Interviewer: Is there anything that you really worry about with regards to her?

> Mother 13: (crying) She's not learning you know, she doesn't like school.

Some parents highlighted the interaction between other stresses and school problems. Mother 4 indicated that her ex-husband's unpredictable visits had a direct impact on their daughter's behavior at school the day after a failed visit:

> Mother 4: I've heard her in the background because they will call me while she is having her temper tantrum. I've never seen it and the stuff they tell me, it breaks my heart. I'll be crying. They told me that she would go to the office, throw herself down and start knocking things off the principal's desk, the secretary's desk. And the strength in her! They said sometimes they would have to have two teachers trying to hold her. I'm thinking at the

time, she was six-years-old, and I'm thinking how difficult can she be, but the rage that is in her, they just can't hold her.

Although some parents identified school as a source of their daughters' initial difficulties, most indicated that problematic behaviors had been evident prior to school entry. What changed perhaps is that school personnel and classmates were confirming that the girls were exhibiting conduct problems, and these problems were interfering with functioning in ever widening circles of engagement. Mother 2's prior concerns about her daughter's socializing problems coalesced when her difficulties escalated at school and the girl started stealing and lying. Some of the girls experienced informal suspensions from school, requiring that their parents take time off work to care for their daughters. Overall the families judged the school system to be a nonsupportive institution.

As the girls progressed through school, their early academic difficulties were usually compounded by behavior problems. Longitudinal research on aggressive girls reveals that their schoolwork continues to suffer as they move through the grades (Pulkkinen, 1992). These early school problems may, in part, explain why aggressive girls are at risk for school dropout (Schlossman & Cairns, 1993) and high levels of unemployment in adolescence and adulthood (Friedman, Kramer, & Kreisher, 1999; Hill, Howell, Hawkins, & Battin-Pearson, 1999; Pulkkinen, 1992; Robins, 1986; Zoccolillo, 1993). They are also at risk for early pregnancy (Quinton et al., 1993; Schlossman & Cairns, 1993).

Summary

There is research to support our concerns about the relationship between poor school achievement and problems over the lifespan for girls who have an early aggressive history. Family members who participated in the study shared this perspective. Researchers and educators need to direct their attention to the role of the education system in improving the lot of aggressive young girls. There are many possible directions to explore, such as enhanced teacher training regarding gender-specific learning styles and specialized tutoring (Michel, 2000).

Peers

Parents displayed an awareness of the interactional effects of risk factors, particularly early behavior problems and problematic peer relationships. Difficult peer relationships were a consistent and primary theme throughout the narratives and were associated with the onset of behavioral difficulties for girls. Parents linked their daughters' social isolation with the onset of aggressive behavior.

Research indicates that aggressive girls typically face social rejection by other girls (Serbin, Marchessault, McAffer, Peters, & Schwartzman, 1993), play alone on the margins of the playground, or sometimes play with boys in mixed groups (Serbin et al., 1993). Parents reported that their daughters were rarely asked to other children's homes to play, and that peers rarely wanted to spend out-of-school time with them. Isolated from their peer groups, these girls miss the positive socialization experiences that occur in girls' friendships. The aggressive girls interacted primarily with their mothers, siblings, or younger children. One mother talked about providing informal child care for her neighborhood because she was desperate for her daughter to have after-school playmates.

Consistent with research (Pepler & Sedighdeilami, 1998; Whitney & Smith, 1993), the girls often reported being bullied by other girls and by boys. Girl 16, whose interview revealed experiences of frequent victimization, graphically described how she lost a tooth when a boy pushed her into a pole while she was on her bike. The idea that clinic-referred, aggressive girls are being bullied may appear paradoxical. A group of children who are both bullies and victims has, however, been identified in the literature (Besag, 1989; Olweus, 1978). Aggressive girls' experiences of victimization are often overlooked, as was the case for Girl 9 who was viewed by adults as the aggressor in conflicts with peers.

Girl 9:   If I cry they make fun of me.

Interviewer: And that upsets you? So why were you crying?

Girl: Because they beat me up, (inaudible) it's not fair.

For example, the catalyst for the referral to EGC of one girl was not the fact that she was the frequent object of teasing and rejection by her peers, but was instead her physical attack on a boy in the schoolyard. The following quote suggests the complicated and less obvious nature of social methods of aggression:

Interviewer: Before I begin the interview, is there anything you would like to talk about that's on your mind?

Girl 15:   It was in the schoolyard and it was last year, and there was a girl, Mary, who came to our school. She was in Grade 2 and she was nice and everything. Another girl came named Anne and played with me and Mary as a friend. So Mary went up to her and said, "Will you be my friend?" And they would play and all that stuff. So I went up to them and said, "Can I be your friend?" Another girl, Sally, said "Ya," but Mary said, "Don't be her friend."

There is evidence that both similarities and differences are evident in girls' and boys' aggression (Björkqvist, Lagerspetz, & Kaukanianen, 1992; Lagerspetz, Björkqvist, & Peltonen, 1988). Boys and girls exhibit verbal aggression at similar levels. In general, however, boys engage in more direct physical aggression and girls engage in more indirect aggression. Exclusion and gossiping, for example, represent powerful forms of indirect aggression that adults may not judge to be particularly maladaptive or aggressive. The degree of pain and disruption is less visible than that suffered through physical aggression. Research suggests that girls consider these forms of aggression to be as hurtful as physical aggression (Galen & Underwood, 1997). Social exclusion is increasingly recognized as an element of bullying particularly associated with the aggressive interactions between girls (Madsen, 1997). Social methods of aggression may evoke overt as well as covert retaliation.

The lack of concordance between parent and daughter reporting regarding the girl's social isolation was a consistent finding. Although girls usually did not acknowledge that they were isolated from peers, the motif of peer rejection was prominent in their parents' accounts.

> Mother 15:   She'll tell you that, "Oh, I got lots of friends," but she'll come home really sad from school and she'll talk about how she'll run out and want to play with the girls and they reject her. Lots of rejection.

In some instances, the girls' isolation was diminished through having younger friends who typically have less sophisticated expectations for friends and may tolerate more immature social skills than same-age children. Association with younger peers may solve some immediate problems, but provide problematic learning experiences for aggressive girls who have had little exposure to the skill building that occurs in same-age children's groups. In turn, this inappropriate learning may further alienate them from their peers.

Summary

There is a decided gap in our understanding of the factors that contribute to problematic peer relationships—a key risk area for girls. The nature of girls' socializing difficulties is complex and is likely influenced by social expectations about gendered behaviors. The issue of indirect and social aggression in association with girlhood aggression (see Crick & Grotpeter, 1995) merits our attention and deserves to be the focus of gender-specific research as discussed in other chapters in this volume (see, e.g., Xie, Cairns, & Cairns, chap. 5). This area has the potential for valuable research in both prevention and intervention.

Community

For many of the families interviewed, day-to-day life is a struggle. The theme of family isolation was woven into the narratives. The girls typically spent most of their time in their small, intense family units that were, in turn, often disconnected from the community. Mother 2, for example, found that her family was not welcome in some local churches because her children were disruptive.

For some families, the theme of abuse extended to the high-risk neighborhoods in which they lived. In two of the instances of alleged sexual abuse, the perpetrator was a neighbor. Both cases went to court and were dismissed, leaving the families feeling profoundly unprotected and unsupported. The mothers identified the abuse and its consequences as triggers for their daughters' troubled behaviors.

As a result of limited financial resources, the majority of families reside in neighborhoods they view as dangerous. The quality of the neighborhood was, for some parents, identified as contributing to their daughters' behavior problems:

Interviewer: And what upsets her the most do you think?

Mother 4:   That she doesn't get to do child things 'cause she's always indoors. I shouldn't say always, but I don't think she spends enough time outdoors. So, I just know I spent a lot of time outdoors growing up. But the thing is—the neighborhood we live in now—I just I don't know many people and I'm a very quiet person. I keep to myself a lot so I don't know the people in the neighborhood and what their kids are like. I'm not really impressed with the neighbors. I shouldn't judge but, from what I see, I'm not impressed. I don't like her hanging out with them kind of thing. I'm very protective that way, so she tends to play by herself.

Not unlike their daughters, the mothers were often isolated with little time or energy to devote to maintaining friendships. Some mothers reported that they only had *needy* friends who were not a reliable source of support. Extended family members generally provided little positive support and sometimes were involved in a negative manner. In families where there was a spouse, that person was usually the mother's sole intimate.

Summary

Poverty is a known risk factor for the development of aggressive behaviors (Dubow & Ippolito, 1994; Levene et al., 2001) and may have an accentuated impact on aggressive girls (Rosenbaum, 1989). In this study, it was not raised as a key issue, but was indirectly highlighted as families talked about dangerous neighborhoods, exposure to abusive neighbors, inadequate housing, isolation, and the struggle to improve career opportunities. Effective case management requires that attention be paid to the multisystemic stressors that influence the lives of at-risk families. Interventions need to address risk factors and augment protective elements of family life and family members' individual strengths.

CONCLUSION

This exploratory inquiry raises questions for future research into the lives of aggressive young girls and their families and related treatment programs. Of course, there are limits to qualitative inquiry, which seeks mainly to identify rather than investigate principal risk factors. The benefits of this form of exploratory research with an understudied phenomenon is that it helps isolate possible key risk variables and helps investigators and clinicians understand what the risk factors mean to the people who are subject to them. It is a necessary approach mainly because it helps ground new and conventional statistically based research in the actualities of the lives lived by the girls and their families. Understanding the life histories of young girls who grow up to be aggressive and antisocial is critical for those working in the child-serving field. This can be accomplished through a range of research, clinical, and prevention activities, some of which were proposed throughout this chapter. In closing, we highlight the importance of undertaking specific future research directions: longitudinal studies of girlhood aggression and specialized treatment programs, and development and evaluation of gender-specific prevention initiatives. Research and treatment efforts would also benefit from a focus on both risk and protective factors in terms of identification of salient factors and an evidence-based approach to building on strengths (see Levene et al., 2001).

ACKNOWLEDGMENTS

This study was made possible through the generous support of the Hospital for Sick Children Foundation. Special thanks to Judith Globerman, Faculty of Social Work, University of Toronto; Kenneth Goldberg, Executive Director, Earlscourt Child and Family Centre; and Earlscourt Girls

Connection staff Sarah Smart, Joelle Therriault, Josephine Mazzucca, Michelle Walsh, Erin Rajca, and Margaret Walsh. The authors would particularly like to thank the families who participated in this study for their willingness to tell their stories and contribute to a greater understanding of girlhood aggression.

REFERENCES

Achenbach, T. M. (1991). *Manual for the Child Behavior Checklist and 1991 profile.* Burlington, VT: Department of Psychiatry, University of Vermont.

Bandura, A. (1977). *Social learning theory.* Englewood Cliffs, NJ: Prentice-Hall.

Bates, J. E., Bayles, K., Bennett, D. S., Ridge, B., & Brown, M. M. (1991). Origins of externalizing behavior: Problems at eight years of age. In D. J. Pepler & K. H. Rubin (Eds.), *The development and treatment of childhood aggression* (pp. 93–120). Hillsdale, NJ: Lawrence Erlbaum Associates.

Berry, C. A., Shaywitz, S. E., & Shaywitz, B. A. (1985, November). Girls with attention deficit disorder: A silent minority? A report on behavioral and cognitive characteristics. *Pediatrics, 76*(5), 801–809.

Besag, V. E. (1989). *Bullies and victims in schools.* Milton Keynes, [England]; Philadelphia: Open University Press.

Björkqvist, K., Lagerspetz, K. M. J., & Kaukiainen, A. (1992). Do girls manipulate and boys fight? Developmental trends in regard to direct and indirect aggression. *Aggressive Behavior, 18*, 117–127.

Brestan, E. V., & Eyberg, S. M. (1998). Effective psychosocial treatments of conduct-disordered children and adolescents: 29 years, 82 studies and 5,272 kids. *Journal of Clinical Child Psychology, 27*(2), 180–189.

Cairns, R. B., & Cairns, B. D. (1994). *Lifelines and risks: Pathways of youth in our time.* New York: Cambridge University Press.

Caspi, A., Lynam, D., Moffitt, T., & Silva, P. (1993). Unraveling girls' delinquency: Biological, dispositional, and contextual contributions to adolescent misbehavior. *Developmental Psychology, 29*, 19–30.

Chesney-Lind, M. (1989). Girls' crime and women's place: Toward a feminist model of female delinquency. *Crime and Delinquency, 35*(1), 5–29.

Crick, N. R., & Grotpeter, J. K. (1995). Relational aggression, gender, and social-psychological adjustment. *Child Development, 66*, 710–722.

Dubow, E. F., & Ippolito, M. F. (1994). Effects of poverty and quality of the home environment on changes in the academic and behavioral adjustment of elementary school-age children. *Journal of Clinical Child Psychology, 23*, 401–412.

Friedman, A., Kramer, S., & Kreisher, C. (1999). Childhood predictors of violent behavior. *Journal of Clinical Psychology, 55*(7), 843–855.

Galen, B. R., & Underwood, M. K. (1997). A developmental investigation of social aggression among children. *Developmental Psychology, 33*(4), 589–600.

Hill, K., Howell, J., Hawkins, J., & Battin-Pearson, S. (1999). Childhood risk factors for adolescent gang membership: Results from the Seattle social development project. *Journal of Research in Crime and Delinquency, 36*(3), 300–322.

Jaffe, P., Wolfe, D., Wilson, S. K., & Zak, L. (1986). Family violence and child adjustment: A comparative analysis of girls' and boys' behavioural symptoms. *American Journal of Psychiatry, 143*, 74–77.

Johnson, P., & O'Leary, D. (1987). Parental behavior patterns and conduct disorder in girls. *Journal of Abnormal Child Psychology, 15*(4), 573–581.

Kavanagh, K. H., & Hops, H. (1994). Good girls? Bad boys? Gender and development as contexts for diagnosis and treatment. In T. H. Ollendick & R. J. Prinz (Eds.), *Advances in clinical child psychology*, (pp. 45–79). New York: Plenum.

Kazdin, A. (1987). Treatment of antisocial behavior in children: Current status and future directions. *Psychological Bulletin, 102*(2), 187–203.

Lagerspetz, K. M., Björkqvist, K., & Peltonen, T. (1988). Is indirect aggression typical of females? Gender differences in aggressiveness in 11- to 12-year-old children. *Aggressive Behavior, 14*(6), 403–414.

Lenssen, V., Doreleijers, T., Van Dijk, M., & Hartman, C. (2000). Girls in detention: What are their characteristics? A project to explore and document the character of this target group and the significant ways in which it differs from one consisting of boys. *Journal of Adolescence, 23*, 287–303.

Levene, K. S. (1997). The Earlscourt Girls Connection: A model intervention. *Canada's Children, 4*(2), 14–17.

Levene, K. S., Augimeri, L. K., Pepler, D. J., Walsh, M. M., Webster, C. D., & Koegl, C. J. (2001). *Early assessment risk list for girls, EARL-21G (version 1-consultation version)*. Toronto: Earlscourt Child and Family Centre.

Loeber, R., & Keenan, K. (1994). The interaction between conduct disorder and its comorbid conditions: Effects of age and gender. *Clinical Psychology Review, 14*, 497–523.

Lynch, M. (1988). The consequences of child abuse In K. Browne, C. Davies, & P. Stratton (Eds.), *Early prediction and prevention of child abuse* (pp. 203–211). Chichester: Wiley.

Madsen, K. C. (1997). *Differing perceptions of bullying.* Unpublished doctoral dissertation, University of Sheffield, England.

McCracken, G. D. (1988). *The long interview.* Newbury Park, CA: Sage.

Michel, M. M. (2000). *Earlscourt Child and Family Centre: Report to the Altamira Foundation.* Internal report.

Offord, D. R., Boyle, M. H., & Ontario Association of Children's Mental Health Centres (OACHMHC). (1996). *Standardized Client Information System* (SCIS). Toronto: OACHMHC.

Offord, D. R., Boyle, M. H., & Racine, Y. A. (1991). The epidemiology of antisocial behavior in childhood and adolescence. In D. J. Pepler & K. H. Rubin (Eds.), *The development and treatment of childhood aggression* (pp. 93–120). Hillsdale, NJ: Lawrence Erlbaum Associates.

Olweus, D. (1978). *Aggression in schools: Bullies and whipping boys.* Washington, DC: Hemisphere.

Patterson, G. R. (1986). The contribution of siblings to training for fighting: A microsocial analysis. In D. Olweus, J. Block, & M. Radke-Yarrow (Eds.), *Development of antisocial and prosocial behavior: Research, theories, and issues* (pp. 235–261). Orlando, FL: Academic Press.

Patterson, G. R., Reid, J. B., & Dishion, T. (1992). *A social learning approach: Vol. 4. Antisocial boys.* Eugene, OR: Castalia.

Pepler, D., & Sedighdeilami, F. (1998). *Aggressive girls in Canada* (Government Document W-98-30E). Applied Research Branch Strategic Policy Human Resources Development Canada.

Pepler, D. J., & Craig, W. (1999, February). Aggressive girls: Development of disorder and outcomes. LaMarsh Report #57. Toronto: LaMarsh Centre for Research on Violence and Conflict Resolution, York University.

Pulkkinen, L. (1992). The path to adulthood for aggressively inclined girls. In K. Björkqvist & P. Niemëla (Eds.), *Of mice and women: Aspects of female aggression* (pp. 113–121). San Diego, CA: Academic Press.

Quinton, D., Pickles, A., Maughan, B., & Rutter, M. (1993). Partners, peers, and pathways: Assortative pairing and continuities in conduct disorder. *Development & Psychopathology, 5*(4), 763–783.

QSR NUD*IST 4 [Computer software]. (1997). Melbourne Victoria, Australia: Qualitative Solutions and Research Pty Ltd. (ACN 357 213).

Ray, J., & English, D. (1995). Comparison of female and male children with sexual behavior problems. *Journal of Youth and Adolescence, 24*(4), 439–451.

Robins, L. (1986). The consequences of conduct disorder in girls. In D. Olweus, J. Block, & M. Radke-Yarrow (Eds.), *Development of antisocial and prosocial behavior: Research, theories, and issues* (pp. 385–414). Orlando FL: Academic Press.

Rosenbaum, J. L. (1989). Family dysfunction and female delinquency. *Crime & Delinquency, 35*, 31–44.

Schlossman, S., & Cairns, R. B. (1993). Problem girls: Observations on past and present. In G. H. Elder, J. Modell, & R. D. Parke (Eds.), *Children in time and place: Developmental and historical insights* (pp. 110–130). Cambridge: Cambridge University Press.

Serbin, L. A., Marchessault, K., McAffer, V., Peters, P., & Schwartzman, A. E. (1993). Patterns of social behavior on the playground in 9–11-year-old girls and boys: Relation to teacher perceptions and to peer ratings of aggression, withdrawal and likability. In C. Hart (Ed.), *Children on the playground* (pp. 162–183). New York: SUNY Press.

Serbin, L. A., Moskowitz, K. S., Schwartzman, A. E., & Ledingham, J. E. (1991). Aggressive, withdrawn, and aggressive/withdrawn children in adolescence: Into the next generation. In D. J. Pepler & K. H. Rubin (Eds.), *The development and treatment of childhood aggression* (pp. 55–70). Hillsdale, NJ: Lawrence Erlbaum Associates.

Simons, R. L., Johnson, C., Beaman, J., & Conger, R. D. (1993). Explaining women's double jeopardy: Factors that mediate the association between harsh treatment as a child and violence by a husband. *Journal of Marriage and the Family, 55*, 713–723.

Steiner, H., & Dunne, J. E. (1997). Summary of the practice parameters for assessment of treatment of children and adolescents with conduct disorder. *Journal of the American Academy of Child and Adolescent Psychiatry, 29*, 44–52.

Trocme, N., & Wolfe, D. (2001). *Child maltreatment in Canada: Selected results from the Canadian incidence study of reported child abuse and neglect.* Ottawa, Ontario: Minister of Public Works and Government Services, Canada.

Whitney, I., & Smith, P. K. (1993). A survey of the nature and extent of bullying in junior/middle and secondary schools. *Educational Research, 35*(1), 3–25.

Zoccolillo, M. (1993). Gender and the development of conduct disorder. *Development and Psychopathology, 5*, 65–78.

8

Girls in the Juvenile Justice System: Risk Factors and Clinical Implications

Leslie D. Leve
Patricia Chamberlain
Oregon Social Learning Center

Conduct disorder (CD) is the second most common psychiatric disorder in girls, with population rates varying from 0.8% to 16% (Zoccolillo, 1993). Further, one half of the girls who have five or more conduct symptoms have a second, nonexternalizing diagnosis (e.g., major depression or schizophrenia), suggesting high comorbidity rates for girls with conduct problems (e.g., Loeber & Keenan, 1994; Robins & Price, 1991). Short- and long-term outcomes for antisocial girls include internalizing problems and mental health disorders, early pregnancy, future arrests, school dropout, drug problems, health-risking sexual behavior, welfare dependence, and mortality (Bardone, Moffitt, & Caspi, 1997; Keenan, Loeber, & Green, 1999; Lewis, Yeager, Cobham-Portorreal, Showalter, Anthony, 1991; Pajer, 1998; Pawlby, Mills, & Quinton, 1997; Robins & Price, 1991; Zoccolillo & Rogers, 1991). Because antisocial behavior has such negative consequences for the girl and society, effective treatment programs must be developed and implemented in adolescent populations. In this chapter, we review the theory and research on antisocial behavior in girls, and we present preliminary data from a randomized clinical treatment trial aimed to reduce antisocial behavior in girls in the juvenile justice system. We conclude by highlighting sexual behavior and peer relations as specific areas for future intervention work.

SEX DIFFERENCES IN ADOLESCENT ANTISOCIAL BEHAVIOR

Surprisingly few published studies examine CD and its psychosocial outcome behaviors in girls. Those studies that have been conducted suggest that there are almost no sex differences in behavioral dysfunction in the first 4 years of life, more boys than girls (approximately 3:1) are given a CD diagnosis in middle childhood, and the high boy to girl ratio diminishes from preadolescence to adolescence (American Psychiatric Association, 1994; Keenan & Shaw, 1997).

The magnitude of sex differences in aggression may depend on how *aggression* is defined. Peer nomination, self-report, and observational studies suggest that social/relational/indirect aggression, which is delivered circuitously, verbally, or nonverbally (rather than physically and overtly), may be more characteristic of girls than boys (Björkqvist, Lagerspetz, & Kaukiainen, 1992; Cairns, Cairns, Neckerman, Ferguson, & Gariepy, 1989; Crick, Casas, & Ku, 1999; Crick & Grotpeter, 1996; Underwood, 1998). For example, research conducted in Finland by Björkqvist and colleagues (1992) suggested that 11- and 15-year-old girls tended to use indirect means of aggression, whereas the boys tended to employ direct strategies. Additionally, sex-role prohibitions against physical aggression are stronger for girls, and physically aggressive girls are more disliked by their peers than are physically aggressive boys (Pepler, 1995).

There are different long-term outcomes for boys and girls who engage in antisocial behavior. Robins and Price (1991) found that, regardless of other types of psychiatric problems, conduct problems in girls predicted poor long-term outcomes such as internalizing disorders, early pregnancy, and high use of social services. Similarly, Lewis et al. (1991) found that for a sample of incarcerated boys and girls, significantly fewer of the girls were rearrested in adulthood (71% vs. 95% of the boys). However, long-term outcomes for the girls were poor. Of 21 participants in the original sample, 15 did not complete high school, 4 were prostitutes, 19 attempted suicide (with 1 success), 15 had serious drug problems, 13 had been involved in seriously violent relationships with men, and 1 died of AIDS. These studies suggest there are sex differences in the expression and outcomes of antisocial behavior. In the next section, we present research on four common correlates of antisocial behavior in girls: association with deviant peers, engagement in risky sexual behavior, teen pregnancy, and early parenthood.

COMMON OUTCOMES AND CORRELATES
OF ANTISOCIAL BEHAVIOR IN GIRLS

Association With Deviant and Prosocial Peers

Research suggests that adolescent girls who show antisocial behavior tend to associate with deviant peers (Dishion, 2000), which may indirectly relate to adolescent motherhood because peers shape the social world (Cairns, Cairns, & Neckerman, 1989). For example, in a longitudinal sample of boys, Capaldi (1991) found that the level of antisocial behavior and the association with deviant peers in the fourth grade contributed to sexual intercourse by the ninth grade. Further, adolescents with externalizing and internalizing co-occurring symptoms are at the greatest risk for engaging with a deviant peer group and demonstrating sexual promiscuity (Dishion, 2000).

To investigate the nature of adolescent friendships in girls, Giordano, Cernkovich, and Pugh (1986) identified 13 dimensions of adolescent friendship and examined the presence of these in adolescents with varying degrees of delinquency. In terms of caring, trust, and patterns of self-disclosure, they found no significant differences across increasing levels of delinquency. However, girls were more likely to self-disclose and characterize their relationships as caring and trusting than boys. Delinquent youths reported receiving more tangible rewards from their friendships than did their less delinquent counterparts. Interestingly, girls reported that they were just as likely as boys to get drugs from friends and hang out in unsupervised settings. Girls reported higher levels of contact than boys. Regardless of delinquency level, the long-term stability of friendships did not vary significantly. Delinquent youths reported higher levels of peer influence and loyalty (i.e., sticking together given trouble) than did less delinquent groups, but had higher levels of conflict imbalance, jealousy, and competition. This finding has been replicated in a study of normative and antisocial boys' friendships (Dishion, Andrews, & Crosby, 1995).

These findings refute the notion that delinquent girls are lonely social misfits; they are at least as peer-oriented as boys and nondelinquent girls. Giordano et al. (1986) argued that delinquent girls have adopted a set of values that define antisocial activities as appropriate and that their friendship styles encourage or mutually reinforce delinquent behavior. There has been consistent empirical support for the powerful role of negative (or deviant) peer relations in the development and maintenance of delinquency (e.g., Elliott, Huizinga, & Ageton, 1985). In addition, there is accumulating evidence to suggest that girls with conduct problems may be at risk for lacking positive peer relationships. For example, Woodward and Fergusson (1999) found that the group of girls in the highest 10% of conduct problems had the lowest self-rating of positive peer attachment as rated on the Inventory of Parent and Peer Attachment (Armsden & Greenberg, 1987).

Rutter and colleagues (Quinton & Rutter, 1988; Rutter, Quinton, & Hill, 1990; Zoccolillo, Pickles, Quinton, & Rutter, 1992) documented the central importance of positive social relationships on the adult adjustment for girls. They investigated the impact of a set of mediating variables on continuities and discontinuities in social functioning over time (into adulthood) for a sample of institutionally reared (IR) children and a matched sample of noninstitutionally reared (NR) children. The emotional support of a nondeviant spouse proved to be a powerful protective factor to counter the ill effects of disrupted upbringing for IR boys and girls. However, IR girls were more likely than NR girls to marry deviant males (52% vs. 19%), although IR boys were not significantly more likely than NR boys to marry deviant females (27% vs. 17%). For IR participants, deviant behavior in childhood and adolescence were unrelated to marital support. In summary, deviant adolescent girls are capable of having caring relationships—they just tend to have them with deviant males.

Findings from these studies and others (e.g., Weissberg, Caplan, & Harwood, 1991) strongly suggest that effective treatment programs for high-risk girls should emphasize developing peer relationships with nondelinquent youths, building individual competencies (e.g., how to relate to prosocial peers), and creating environments that promote such competencies. Our preliminary data (presented later) confirm this treatment approach and have led us to propose an intervention component targeting the encouragement of prosocial peer relations using a skills-trainer model (see expanded description later in this chapter).

Engagement in Risky Sexual Behavior

A related outcome of antisocial behavior is engagement in health-risking sexual behaviors such as having sex without protection or having multiple sexual partners (Capaldi, Stoolmiller, Clark, & Owen, 2002; Woodward & Fergusson, 1999). Metzler, Noell, Biglan, Ary, and Smolkowski (1994) examined mechanisms of peer and parental influence on sexual risk-taking behavior, hypothesizing that family variables (e.g., positive family involvement, coercive family interactions, and poor parental monitoring) related to involvement with deviant peers, which in turn related to risky sexual behavior. As predicted, the largest direct predictor of risky sexual behavior was association with deviant peers. The relationship between having deviant peers and engaging in risky sexual behavior has been replicated elsewhere (e.g., Whitbeck, Yoder, Hoyt, & Conger, 1999). As predicted, low parental monitoring and high levels of coercive family interaction predicted higher levels of association with deviant peers. The hypothesized model fit equally well for girls and boys. However, girls reported higher levels of sexual risk-taking and less positive involvement with their families than boys (Metzler et al., 1994).

Other researchers have revealed a relationship between risky sexual behavior and parental monitoring (e.g., Miller, Forehand, & Kotchick, 1999), and between association with delinquent peers and low rates of contraception and high rates of sexually transmitted diseases (Underwood, 1998). Furthermore, some studies have found a strong link between parental monitoring and adolescent antisocial behavior (e.g., Griffin, Botvin, Scheier, Diaz, & Miller, 2000). These findings suggest that adolescent girls who are disconnected from their families and associate with delinquent peers are at risk for engaging in risk-taking sexual behaviors.

Pawlby et al. (1997) compared 100 inner-city girls, 50 of whom were identified as being high risk on the basis of current or recent involvement with the Social Services Department as a result of serious family difficulties. Analyses suggest that high-risk girls began dating earlier (12.5 years vs. 13.4 years) and were more likely to have had a sexual relationship (61% vs. 32%), to have had more sexual partners (4.8 vs. 3.3), and to have been pregnant (17% vs. 4%) than control girls. High rates of sex-partner change increase the risk of contracting a sexually transmitted disease because a greater number of partners increases the likelihood that any one partner will be infected (Ericksen & Trocki, 1992; Padian, Hitchcock, Fullilove, Kohlstadt, & Brunham, 1990). Pawlby also found that, of those girls in a current relationship (high-risk $n = 19$; control $n = 17$), more high-risk girls engaged in sexual intercourse (79% vs. 29%), did not protect against unwanted pregnancies (37% vs. 6%), did not engage in a discussion of contraception use (73% vs. 0%), had known their boyfriend for 2 weeks or less before dating him (68% vs. 35%), and had met him by hanging around on the streets (63% vs. 18%). In summary, a girl's delinquency not only relates to her entree into a sexual relationship, but her sexual behaviors may put her at increased risk for contracting a sexually transmitted disease (STD).

In conjunction with parent-training programs that increase parental supervision and decrease coercive family interaction, interventions that increase knowledge about STD protection and improve communication skills may successfully decrease risky sexual behavior and improve overall outcomes (including a reduction in unplanned pregnancy rates). We elaborate on such an intervention later in this chapter.

Teen Pregnancy

Numerous researchers have found a relationship between aggressive behavior or police contacts during childhood and adolescent childbearing status (Capaldi, Crosby, & Stoolmiller, 1996; Crockett, Bingham, Chopak, & Vicary, 1996; Underwood, 1998). Zoccolillo and Rogers (1991) found that, 2 to 4 years postdischarge, girls with CD had a 50% pregnancy rate (vs. 8% statewide). Woodward and Fergusson (1999) found that girls in the highest 10% of their sample for conduct problems had a pregnancy rate 5.3 times higher ($p < .001$) than those in the lowest 50% of the sample. Similarly, in a sample of girls diagnosed with CD prior to age 18, almost 60% experienced a teenage pregnancy, with the CD preceding the pregnancy in every case (Kovacs, Krol, & Voti, 1994).

Teen pregnancy is also related to peer reputation and status. Underwood, Kupersmidt, and Coie (1996) examined the frequency and timing of adolescent childbearing as a function of aggression and peer sociometric status. Peer nominations were made for status (i.e., popular, average, rejected, neglected, and controversial) and aggression when girls were in the fourth grade. Eleven years later (with 79% of the original sample still residing in the area), one half of the aggressive girls had become mothers (vs. 25% of the nonaggressive girls, $p <$ .05). Controversial girls (i.e., liked by some, disliked by others) also had a 50% childbearing rate (a significantly higher rate than any of the other sociometric groups). Underwood and colleagues also found that aggressive and controversial girls gave birth earlier than those in other groups and controversial girls had more children than those in other sociometric groups. Overall, these results suggest that aggression in girls is a strong predictor of adolescent pregnancy/motherhood and peer relations play a mediating role in this relationship.

Early Parenthood and the Intergenerational Cycle of Antisocial Behavior

Pregnant, adolescent girls are at risk for multiple, cascading negative effects. Being an adolescent mother constrains social, academic, and work opportunities. Adolescent motherhood has been associated with serious educational, financial, and relationship problems (Furstenberg, Brooks-Gunn, & Chase-Lansdale, 1989) and, in turn, negative effects on psychological functioning (Brown, Adams, & Kellam, 1981). The earlier that adolescent mothers have their first child, the more negative the effects appear to be on the mother. For example, if mothers are 15 years or younger at the time they give birth, they complete 1½ years less schooling than those who bear their first child later in adolescence (Moore, Hofferth, Caldwell, & Waite, 1979).

The children of adolescent mothers are also at risk for negative outcomes. In particular, mothers with a history of severe antisocial behavior as adolescents put the next generation at risk in multiple ways. As adults, women who were antisocial as adolescents are more likely than nonantisocial girls to affiliate with antisocial men (Quinton & Rutter, 1988); to be in violent, abusive relationships (Rosenbaum & O'Leary, 1981); to get divorced (Rosenbaum, 1989); and to exhibit poor parenting skills (Capaldi & Patterson, 1991). These outcomes result in a greatly increased risk for a child to behave in an aggressive and antisocial manner. For example, the Oregon Youth Study (Capaldi, 1991) followed a sample of at-risk boys for 10 years beginning when they were in the fourth grade. In that sample, mothers who gave birth to their first child by age 20 were twice as likely to have sons with early arrest records (before age 14; 35% vs. 18%). Having an antisocial mother may put a child at greater risk than having an antisocial father because the association between biological mother convictions and adoptee convictions is stronger than that for biological father convictions especially for girls (Mednick, Gabrielli, & Hutchings, 1996).

In their follow-up of IR girls ($n = 81$) and boys ($n = 90$), Rutter and Quinton (1984) found that women who experienced severe breakdowns in their upbringing were more likely (than those who had not) to have significant difficulties raising their children; an appreciable minority gave up care of their children to other people. In contrast, IR men rarely had their children taken into care. The IR girls were significantly more likely than controls (41% vs. 5%) to become teenage parents; the difference was smaller for boys (9% vs. 2.5%).

More broadly, there is evidence in the psychiatric literature that women with chronic and/or recurring problems tend to transmit problems to their offspring. In addition to genetic explanations, there are two primary psychosocial mechanisms through which this transmission is hypothesized to occur. First, disturbed or deviant mothers are more likely to provide their children with poor parenting (Hare & Shaw, 1965; Keller et al., 1986; Lyons-Ruth, Zoll, Connell, & Grunebaum, 1989). Second, such mothers tend to marry men who have severe psychiatric, personality, or substance abuse problems (Merikangas & Spiker, 1982; Westen, Ludolph, Misle, Ruffins, & Block, 1990; Zoccolillo et al., 1992) and/or who are violent (Lewis et al., 1991), although the selection of a nondeviant male partner has been shown to have a protective effect (Rutter & Quinton, 1984).

Andrews, Brown, and Creasey (1990) found that daughters of troubled women experienced a range of their own problems. Daughters of mothers with chronic problems reported three times more early trauma experiences than daughters whose mothers had no disorder or who had only one episode. Daughters of mothers with chronic problems also reported significantly more physical and/or sexual abuse by their mothers' partners. In summary, the presence of conduct problems in adolescent girls is increasingly recognized as a significant problem that is likely to negatively affect their adult adjustment (Robins & Price, 1991; Zoccolillo et al., 1992) and the adjustment of their offspring. Reducing the risky sexual behaviors that cause unplanned adolescent pregnancies may interrupt the intergenerational cycle of antisocial behavior.

TREATMENT IMPLICATIONS

Given the seriousness of the problems that antisocial girls encounter (and the potential intergenerational effects of these problems), it is critical that we focus on girls in our longitudinal research on the development of CD.

Further, given the dearth of well-controlled studies that focus on interventions for antisocial girls (with a few notable exceptions; e.g., Chalmers & Townsend, 1990), our work has focused on developing an intervention program for antisocial adolescent girls involved in the juvenile justice system.

It is widely acknowledged that adolescent girls who are involved in the juvenile justice system are not treated comparably to their male counterparts (Bloom, 1998; Chesney-Lind, 1998). Several researchers have noted that these girls tend to be ignored by the system or dealt with more harshly for less serious crimes than boys (Chesney-Lind, 1999). There may be numerous reasons for this: the perception that females are criminal "lightweights" (Giordano & Cernkovich, 1997), the attitudes of social control agents in male-dominated juvenile justice systems (Schlossman & Cairns, 1991), or the characterization of females being difficult to work with because they are emotionally demanding ("emotional hypocrisies"; Zanarini & Gunderson, 1997). The upshot is that systems typically lack appropriate resources geared to girls' needs.

There is evidence to suggest that, as a group, adolescent girls are also short-changed by community service delivery systems. Girls tend not to be referred to or make use of mental health, social service, or educational delivery systems as often as boys (Offord, Boyle, & Racine, 1991); their utilization rates of these services are lower than for any other group (i.e., younger girls and younger and older boys). Adolescent girls are also more likely than boys to be incarcerated for minor offenses (Chesney-Lind, 1988), although they commit fewer and less serious offenses than boys (Ageton & Elliott, 1978). Chesney-Lind's review showed that, despite the relatively minor nature of their offenses, a higher proportion of adolescent girls than boys end up in adult jails nationwide.

RELEVANCE TO THIS STUDY

Considering the scarcity of scientific research on girls' antisocial behavior and the lack of research-based treatment techniques for antisocial girls, the paucity of information is grave. The next section presents data from a randomized clinical intervention with a sample of teenage girls referred from the juvenile justice system. We describe an experimental intervention targeting girls' delinquent, aggressive (overt and relational), and antisocial behaviors by providing placement and structured treatment in a well-supervised setting where consistent, nonviolent discipline is used. Contact with delinquent peers is minimized through close supervision. Hypothesized short-term (proximal) outcomes include decreased contact with deviant peers, increased academic performance, and more stable (vs. disrupted) placements. Hypothesized longer term (distal) outcomes include decreased delinquency and drug use, increased positive relationships with spouse/partner, increased school/grade completion, and increased occupational opportunities. We present preliminary evidence in support of some of the hypothesized proximal outcomes in the next section and conclude with an expanded treatment model that might further improve delinquent girls' psychosocial and health outcomes.

TREATMENT FOSTER CARE:
OVERVIEW OF THE EXPERIMENTAL INTERVENTION

Treatment Foster Care (TFC) is a family-based alternative to residential, institutional, and group care for children and adolescents with significant behavioral, emotional, and mental health problems.[1] Rivera and Kutash (1994) defined TFC as a service that provides treatment to troubled children within private homes of trained families. The TFC model was first seen in the United States in the mid-1970s as an alternative to institutional placements and has grown steadily within the child welfare, juvenile justice, and mental health systems. TFC is now one of the most widely used forms of out-of-home placement for children and adolescents with severe emotional and behavioral disorders and is considered to be the least restrictive form of residential care (Kutash & Rivera, 1996; Stroul, 1989).

The Oregon TFC model is theoretically based using social learning theory as a specified treatment approach to target factors identified by research as relating to the development, maintenance, and escalation of antisocial behavior and delinquency. OSLC began providing TFC services in 1983. We received county, state, and federal funding to use the approach with a variety of children and adolescents, including those leaving the state mental hospital, developmentally delayed adolescents, severely emotionally disturbed 3- to 17-year-olds, and female juvenile offenders. We conducted three controlled clinical trials to test the efficacy of the approach compared with standard community-based treatments such as Group Care (GC) programs (Chamberlain, Mooreland, & Reid, 1992; Chamberlain & Reid, 1991, 1998). Outcomes at 1 year posttreatment are reported in Chamberlain and Reid (1998) and Eddy and Chamberlain (2000) and suggest that TFC boys spend more time in their assigned placements, less time incarcerated, more time with their natural families, and less time as runaways. Further, TFC boys demonstrated greater decreases in official criminal referral rates than GC boys 1 year posttreatment. Differences in self-report of criminal

---

[1]In the literature, TFC has been referred to as Therapeutic Foster Care, Specialized Foster Care, and Foster Family-Based Care. All of these terms refer to the same service, which in this chapter is called Treatment Foster Care (TFC).

behavior were also found, with TFC boys reporting less engagement in
criminal activity than GC boys.

A Study of Girls Referred to TFC

Adolescent girls referred to TFC from the juvenile justice system appear to
have some unique treatment needs. We are currently conducting a clinical
trial with 12- to 17-year-old adolescent girls referred from the juvenile justice system. Girls are randomly assigned to TFC or GC. All participating
girls have been screened by their local juvenile justice department staff and
have been recommended for placement in out-of-home care owing to
chronic and severe delinquency. After they are referred to the study, we obtain consent to participate from each girl and her guardian. Our assessment
includes multimethod, multiagent measures of criminal behavior, mental
health, history of trauma/abuse, parenting practices experienced, educational history and level, substance use, sexual history, and relational/so-
cial/indirect aggression. The study is ongoing, with 61 girls enrolled as of
April 2001 (30 TFC; 31 GC) and a targeted full sample size of 100.

In addition to providing TFC girls with close supervision of their whereabouts and peer associations, consistent discipline, and a positive relationship with a mentoring adult, we train foster parents to track and give
consequences for relational/social aggression and encourage the girls' involvement in prosocial activities in the community. Training and supervision for foster parents includes helping them avoid taking the girls' indirect
aggression personally (e.g., pitting family members against each other) and
teaching them to avoid extensive arguing and power struggles.

Risk Factors for Girls. We have found some key differences in the
characteristics of boys and girls who are referred to us from the juvenile justice system. Risk factors from our prior study of boys referred to our program and from the girls referred to our current study thus far are presented in
Table 8.1. As can be seen in the table, the girls referred for treatment come
from more chaotic families than the boys referred for treatment.

These findings are congruent with previous work showing that antisocial
girls come from adverse and dysfunctional backgrounds. For example, it is
a well-replicated finding that antisocial girls tend to originate from nonin-
tact families with a history of numerous parental changes (e.g., Calhoun,
Jurgens, & Chen, 1993; Henry, Moffitt, Robins, Earls, & Silva, 1993). Further, our work replicates findings that delinquent girls come from families
involved in criminal activity. Similar to our study, other studies show that
76% of delinquent girls had at least one family member with a previous ar-

TABLE 8.1

Sample Description and Risk Factors for Boys and Girls at Baseline[a]

Risk Factor	Boys (N = 79)	Girls (N = 61)	Sig.
Ethnicity			*
Non-Hispanic White	83.5 (66)	77.0 (47)	
African American	5.1 (4)	1.6 (1)	
American Indian	2.5 (2)	6.6 (4)	
Hispanic	7.6 (6)	3.3 (2)	
Other	1.3 (1)	11.5 (7)	
Age in years	14.4	15.1	**
Single-parent family at present (%)	57.0	71.2	ns
Adopted (%)	9.1	8.2	ns
Family income less than $10,000 (%)	37.3	35.7	ns
Number of crimes committed (by self)	13.5	13.1	ns
Mom was convicted of crime (%)	21.6	46.7	**
Dad was convicted of crime (%)	31.3	63.2	**
At least one parent convicted of crime (%)	41.1	70.0	**
At least one sibling institutionalized (%)	20.0	37.3	*
Experienced physical abuse (documented) (%)	5.7	65.6	**
Experienced sexual abuse (documented) (%)	6.8	72.1	**
Attempted suicide (%)	2.6	58.3	**
Characterized as heavy drug or alcohol user (%)	9.3	82.0	**
Pregnant at least once (%)	N/A	29.3	
Number of prior treatment placements	1.33	3.03	**
Adolescent's report of days in detention year			
Prior to baseline	73	72	ns
Ran away at least once (%)	73.7	91.7	

[a]Unless otherwise noted, data are from referral agent and/or parent; * $p < .05$; ** $p < .01$.

rest (Rosenbaum, 1989), and 64% of delinquent girls reported that a relative had been incarcerated (Bergsmann, 1989).

We also found evidence of sex differences in the rates of symptoms for mental health disorders. The percentage of boys and girls in the clinical (vs. the normal) range on the Brief Symptom Inventory (BSI; Derogatis, 1975) at the beginning of the study is shown in Table 8.2. Girls had significantly higher scores than boys on almost all of the scales measured.

Preliminary Short-Term Outcomes for Girls.   Approximately 12 months after the randomized placement into TFC/GC groups, we measured the proximal outcomes of placement disruptions and criminal referrals. A primary goal of the TFC approach has been to provide girls with a stable, safe community placement. The number of days girls spent in various settings during the 12 months pretreatment and the 12 months posttreatment is presented in Table 8.3. There were no significant differences between girls' whereabouts during the pretreatment period. Although it is premature to run significance tests on our outcome data because our sample size when split by group is still somewhat small at follow-up (GC = 17; TFC = 22) and our data collection is still underway, results on approximately one third of the final sample suggest that TFC girls appear to be spending more days in treatment and fewer days in locked-up settings between treatment and

TABLE 8.2

Percentage of Boys and Girls at Earliest Wave With Clinical Diagnoses[a]

Diagnosis	Boys at Baseline (N = 79)	Girls at Baseline (N = 49)
Depression	8%	19% *
Anxiety	11%	26% *
Paranoid/psychotic	10%	20%
Somatization	5%	20% **
Hostility	4%	13% *
General psychopathology	1.3%	16% **

[a]Clinical diagnoses are based on the Brief Symptom Inventory (Derogatis, 1975). For boys, the BSI data were first collected at baseline and for girls at baseline plus 3 months. Clinical cutoff: t score > 63. χ^2 tests of significance = 1 df in each case.
* $p < .05$.
** $p < .01$.

TABLE 8.3

**Days in Treatment, Lockup, at Home,
or on the Run Between GC and TFC Girls**

	12 Months Pretreatment M (SD)		12 Months Posttreatment M (SD)	
Situation	GC	TFC	GC	TFC
Treatment	66 (84)	89 (110)	126 (112)	223 (120)
Lockup	106 (93)	74 (86)	65 (102)	30 (85)
At home	115 (116)	142 (122)	112 (102)	75 (103)

Note. GC (*n* = 17). TFC (*n* = 22).

12-months following treatment. These differences are important in that antisocial girls are notoriously difficult to keep in treatment settings. Our data provide a preliminary suggestion that TFC is more effective at keeping girls in their appropriate placement and out of lockup, thereby providing a more stable family environment.

TFC also aims to reduce arrest rates. Preliminary data from those who have completed the 12-month follow-up show that the rates of criminal referrals appear to be dropping for girls in both the GC and TFC conditions. TFC girls reduced their average number of criminal referrals in a 12-month period from fivefold, whereas GC girls reduced by fourfold (significance tests were not conducted because our data collection is still underway).

Risky Sexual Behavior.   Although preliminary outcomes suggest that there may be some positive effects associated with participation in TFC, there are indications that problem patterns remain that are likely to undermine girls' long-term adjustment. Given that the TFC intervention has not specifically targeted the reduction of risky sexual behavior, we did not find the lack of a differential reduction in such behaviors between the TFC and GC girls to be surprising. Preliminary baseline and 12-month follow-up data for a number of risking sexual behaviors are shown in Table 8.4. The variables in Table 8.4 were selected because engagement in these sexual practices increases the risk for health-related problems such becoming pregnant or contracting an STD. The percentage of girls who engage in these health-risking sexual behaviors is strikingly high especially given that many of the girls in the sample were in detention or treatment hospitals for some of the time, thus limiting their access to engage in sexual relations of any kind. There were no significant differences between the TFC and GC

TABLE 8.4

Percentage of Girls Who Engaged in Health-Risking Sexual Behaviors at Baseline ($n = 61$) and at the 12-month Follow-up ($n = 38$)

Health-Risking Sexual Behavior	%
Baseline	
Had sexual intercourse at least once	90
Had sexual intercourse with someone known less than 24 hours	40
Had sexual intercourse with someone who injects drugs	28
Never or rarely used safe-sex practices when having intercourse	37
Had sexual intercourse with three or more partners in a 12-month period	46
Never/almost never discussed safe-sex practices with new sexual partners	27
12-Month Follow-up	
Had sexual intercourse at least once	84
Had sexual intercourse with someone known less than 24 hours	32
Had sexual intercourse with someone who injects drugs	8
Never or rarely used safe-sex practices when having intercourse	29
Had sexual intercourse with three or more partners in a 3- to 6-month period[a]	18
Never/almost never discussed safe-sex practices with new sexual partners	27

[a]In the 12-month follow-up, this question was asked about the prior 3 or 6 months; thus, the rate may not be directly comparable to the baseline rate.

girls in their health-risking sexual behavior scores at baseline or follow-up and no Group x Pre–post difference score interactions.

Next, we formed a composite score of health-risking sexual behavior by aggregating the following items: having sexual intercourse with someone known less than 24 hours, having sexual intercourse with a user of injected drugs, percentage of time that safe-sex practices are used during intercourse, number of sexual partners, and the percentage of time safe-sex practices are discussed with a new sexual partner. Scores for each of the five items were collapsed into a scale with values ranging from 0 to 1, and then a mean of the five items was computed. Internal consistency for the health-risking sexual behavior composite was acceptable (interitem alpha = .67), and baseline health-risking sexual behavior correlated significantly with 12-month health-risking sexual behavior ($r = .39$, $p < .05$). Preliminary correlational analyses show that engagement in health-risking sexual behavior at baseline was related to concurrent self-reports of contraction of a sexually transmitted infection ($r = .32$, $p < .05$) and self-reported sexually transmitted infections at the 12-month follow-up ($r = .42$, $p < .05$). This provides external validity to our construct by suggesting that girls who engage in health-risking sexual behavior are in fact more likely to be diagnosed with a sexually transmitted infection at a later point in time. Further, engagement in health-risking sexual behavior at baseline related to poorer physical health at the 12-month assessment ($r = -.27$, $p < .05$).

Expanding the Treatment Model to Target Health-Risking Sexual Behavior

Although our results are preliminary (based on our partial sample), they suggest that we can improve the long-term health outcomes for antisocial girls if we can reduce their engagement in health-risking sexual behavior. Because the GC and TFC girls still demonstrated substantial health-risking sexual behaviors 12 months into our current study, we believe that the TFC intervention effects could be bolstered by a specific intervention component that targets health-risking sexual behavior. The key to reducing health-risking sexual behavior in delinquent girls may lie in two domains, neither of which were specifically targeted in our current study: girls' positive relationships with their female peers and girls' knowledge of and comfort in discussing safe sex practices.

Friendships With Other Girls. Our preliminary data provide some evidence to suggest that having nondeviant female friends may protect against engagement in health-risking sexual behaviors. We see a negative trend between the girls' engagement in health-risking sexual behavior and her self-reported positive peer relationships ($r = -.36$, $p < .10$) as measured by the Inventory of Parent and Peer Attachment–Peer Scale (Armsden & Greenberg, 1987). This suggests that girls who engage in health-risking sexual behavior report low levels of positive qualities in their friendships (these friendships may be with deviant or nondeviant peers). Furthermore, associating with deviant friends was inversely related to the percentage of time the girls used protective methods when engaging in sexual relations with a new partner ($r = -.48$, $p < .01$). As presented earlier in this chapter, other researchers have found similar relationships between the peer network and risky sexual behavior. For example, Underwood (1998) found that the number of friends and frequency of peer interaction positively predicted the avoidance of pregnancy.

Many high-risk girls report that their boyfriend is their best friend. Pawlby et al. (1997) compared high-risk and control girls, finding that 41% of the high-risk girls identified their current boyfriend as their best friend; none of the control group girls identified their current boyfriend as their best friend ($p < .003$). Girls who do not have a female friend to talk with about dating and sexuality may be at greatest risk (e.g., Underwood, 1998). In our TFC and GC samples, 33% and 47% reported that their best friend was someone other than a female peer at baseline and 12-months, respectively (i.e., their best friend was a boyfriend or an adult). There were no significant differences between TFC and GC girls for having a female peer as a close friend, and the intervention had no effect on increasing the number of participants reporting a female best friend. By implementing an intervention to improve girls' close relationships with nondeviant female peers, we may be better able to protect against health-risking sexual behavior.

Knowledge and Comfort in Discussing Sexual Behaviors. Our preliminary data also suggest that engagement in health-risking sexual behavior is related to increased discomfort in discussing safe sex practices ($r = .45$, $p < .01$). Similarly, adolescent girls report embarrassment as a primary factor in rejecting contraceptive methods (St. Lawrence, 1993). Furthermore, some adolescent girls in our sample had inaccurate beliefs about methods for preventing the contraction of STDs; less than half the sample correctly identified condoms without spermicide as protective against STDs (see Table 8.5).

Other studies have shown similar misconceptions about how AIDS is transmitted. For example, 45% of the participants in one adolescent sample thought that a person must have many different sexual partners in order to be at risk for AIDS (St. Lawrence, 1993). Programs to increase knowledge of protective methods are well established, and many studies have shown that increasing knowledge reduces the likelihood of contracting an STD (e.g., NIMH Multisite HIV Prevention Trial Group, 1998).

One existing program documented the successes in helping mothers discuss sexuality and STDs with their adolescents (Lefkowitz, Sigman, & Kitfong Au, 2000). In this study, mothers of 11- to 15-year-olds were randomly assigned to either an intervention or delayed control group. In the intervention group, mothers received two training sessions in which a group leader discussed qualities of successful communication about dating and sexuality: listening, providing support and encouragement, and asking open-ended questions about sexuality. The intervention sessions included

TABLE 8.5

**Percentage of Girls Who Rate the Following Methods as "Helping
Protect People From Getting a Sexually Transmitted Disease"**

| | Rated as Protecting Against STDs | |
Method	Baseline	12-month Follow-up
Condom with spermicide	59%	55%
Condom without spermicide	43%	37%
Birth control pill	13%	11%
Spermicide alone	12%	8%
Withdrawal	3%	8%
Rhythm	2%	3%
IUD	2%	8%
Diaphragm	12%	18%
Sponges	5%	5%
Cervical cap	12%	13%
Female condom	38%	38%

Note. Only condoms with and without spermicide and female condoms help protect against contracting HIV and other STDs.

instruction, role playing, and homework assignments. In the follow-up assessment, Lefkowitz and colleagues found that adolescents in the intervention group indicated more comfort in talking to their mother about conflict and sexuality issues and talked more often about sexuality; there was a suggestion that the girls in the intervention group also demonstrated improved knowledge about AIDS. Additionally, mothers in the intervention group modified their communication skills so that they asked more open-ended questions, discussed dating and sex more, and behaved in a less judgmental manner than mothers in the control group. Thus, it is possible to teach mothers how to discuss sexuality with adolescents in a way that increases the adolescent's comfort and communication.

Given the importance of close female friends, another effective intervention approach might be to teach delinquent adolescent girls how to talk about sexuality and STDs with their female peers. Increasing the comfort level may be particularly important for girls who have experienced group care settings; one study showed that youths who lived in congregate care facilities had more negative attitudes toward condoms than youths living with families even after controlling for behavior problems (McMillen, Auslander, Stiffman, Elze, & Thompson, 2000).

Potential Intervention Strategies

Female Peers as Skills Trainers. Recruiting skilled young women to participate in weekly sessions with study girls may increase positive relations with female peers and increase comfort and knowledge about sexuality. Similar to a peer mentoring approach, the skills trainer would serve as a role model for appropriate prosocial behavior, and the participant could confide in her about issues surrounding family life or sexuality. Further, to facilitate prosocial peer relations outside of the intervention program, the skills trainer could help the participant identify a nondeviant girl in the community with whom to participate in social events. The skills trainer could engage in role playing and problem-solving discussions with the participant about how to begin friendships outside of the current peer network (or within the current peer network if it includes some nondeviant peers). The skills trainer would thus serve as a prosocial peer and use a behavior-based approach to help the girl learn skills to acquire other nondeviant female friends.

Behavior-Based Sexual Risk Reduction. A second function of skills trainers could be to discuss sexuality and STDs with the participants to increase their knowledge of risk and protective factors and their comfort in discussing sexuality. Modeling the work of Belcher et al. (1998) and Lefkowitz et al. (2000), the skills trainer could hold one-on-one sessions to review information about STD transmission and risk behaviors, discuss the prevalence of STDs, clarify misconceptions, and describe HIV antibody testing procedures and locations. Using Miller's Motivational Enhancement Interviewing Model (Miller, Zweben, DiClemente, & Rychtarik, 1992), girls could also be presented with their answers (and the correct answers) to an STD knowledge scale. These procedures would allow the girl to come to her own conclusions about her thoughts and behavior while eliciting personally relevant discussions with the skills trainer.

To sensitize girls about health-risking sexual behavior, the skills trainer could work with each girl to identify antecedents of unsafe sexual situations and problem solve around methods to reduce such risks by performing specific acts such as carrying condoms or staying in a group setting to reduce pressure. The skills trainer could also use role playing to increase communication skills and comfort level and could provide practice with the correct application of a condom on an anatomical model. Thus, this approach relies on behavior-based strategies such as role playing similar to the existing components of the TFC program, but targets decision making around sexuality.

Belcher et al. (1998) evaluated the effectiveness of such an approach by conducting a randomized intervention trial with 74 women at risk for contracting HIV or other STDs. Using a single-session, skill-based, sexual-risk reduction approach, they found that the intervention significantly increased rates of condom use: The behavioral skills training group increased condom used from 22% (baseline) to 66% (3-month follow-up), whereas the education-only control group increased usage from 27% to 43%. This suggests that behavior-based, sexual-risk reduction approaches may be a promising addition to the current TFC program.

Computer-Assisted Technologies.   A third strategy for reducing health-risking sexual behavior in adolescent girls could be to use interactive computer simulations of dating and romantic relationship situations. Paired with parent training and the skills trainer approach, the computer-assisted interactions could enhance role playing and provide real-life scenarios where healthy/unhealthy decisions could be made (and their respective consequences could be learned). Computer simulations targeting the reduction of health-risking sexual behaviors have been or are currently being developed and show promising results (e.g., Lightfoot, 2001; Noell, Ary, & Duncan, 1997; Pacifici, Stoolmiller, & Nelson, 2001). For example, Pacifici and colleagues developed the interactive "Virtual Date," involving a branching story about a teenage date, with three contingency points at which the participant chooses between two alternatives. Combined with an instructional component, intervention participants whose initial attitudes in favor of coercive sexual relations were at or above the mean showed a differential decrease in sexual coercion attitudes following the intervention compared with a control group. An added benefit to computer-assisted technologies is that they can be a cost-effective way to increase comfort and knowledge about sexuality.

Summary

Our data show that girls referred for treatment by the juvenile justice system already have fairly severe histories of antisocial behavior and come from at-risk family backgrounds. Although our data collection is still underway, our randomized trial suggested that (similar to our results for boys) TFC holds promise to reduce antisocial behavior in at-risk adolescent girls.

However, our effectiveness in reducing health-risking sexual behaviors is less clear. Facilitating friendships with nondeviant female peers and providing a peer-administered behavior-based program aimed at increasing knowledge and comfort around sexuality may improve our current program. Demonstrating a reduction in health-risking sexual behaviors could protect the girls from a variety of potential health problems (STDs, HIV, and poor physical health) and decrease the number of unplanned pregnancies and early parenthood.

In a cost-effectiveness evaluation of violence prevention programs and other approaches to reducing criminal and at-risk behavior in youth (Aos, Phipps, Barnoski, & Leib, 1999), the OSLC TFC program for boys was among the approaches that resulted in the greatest savings to taxpayers (an average of $27,000 per boy in saved criminal justice and victim costs). This savings resulted from decreased arrest and incarceration rates for the participants. The impact of TFC led it to be chosen as 1 of 10 Blueprint for Violence Prevention programs by the Center for the Study and Prevention of Violence at the University of Colorado (Elliott, 1998) and as 1 of 9 national Exemplary Safe and Drug-Free Schools Programs by the U.S. Department of Education in 2001. Although the cost-effectiveness of the TFC program for girls is still under evaluation, we anticipate similar taxpayer savings as in the boys treatment program, with saving in domains such as the criminal justice system, STD treatment clinics, and medical costs associated with high-risk pregnancies and deliveries. Adding modules to TFC interventions for girls that promote healthy sexual and social development may further enhance the participant's outcomes and the program's overall cost-effectiveness.

ACKNOWLEDGMENTS

Support for this research was provided by grants from NIMH (MH 37911, MH 54257, MH 59127, MH 60195) and from NIMH and the Office of Research on Minority Health (MH 46690). The authors would like to thank John Reid, Kevin Moore, Rachel Whaley, and Courtenay Paulic for their contributions to this work and Matthew Rabel for his editorial assistance.

REFERENCES

Ageton, S. S., & Elliott, D. S. (1978). *The incidence of delinquent behavior in a national probability sample of adolescents. The National Youth Survey* (Report No. 3). Boulder, CO: Behavioral Research Institute.
American Psychiatric Association. (1994). *Diagnostic and statistical manual of mental disorder* (4th ed.). Washington, DC: Author.

Andrews, B., Brown, G. W., & Creasey, L. (1990). Intergenerational links between psychiatric disorder in mothers and daughters: The role of parenting experiences. *Journal of Child Psychology & Psychiatry & Allied Disciplines, 31*(7), 1115–1129.

Aos, S., Phipps, P., Barnoski, R., & Leib, R. (1999). *The comparative costs and benefits of programs to reduce crime: A review of national research findings with implications for Washington State.* Olympia, WA: Washington State Institute for Public Policy.

Armsden, G. C., & Greenberg, M. T. (1987). The Inventory of Parent and Peer Attachment: Individual differences and their relationship to psychological well being in adolescence. *Journal of Youth and Adolescence, 16*, 427–454.

Bardone, A. M., Moffitt, T. E., & Caspi, A. (1997). Adult mental health and social outcomes of adolescent girls with depression and conduct disorder. *Development and Psychopathology, 8*, 811–829.

Belcher, L., Kalichman, S., Topping, M., Smith, S., Emshoff, J., Norris, F., & Nurss, J. (1998). A randomized trial of a brief HIV risk reduction counseling intervention for women. *Journal of Consulting and Clinical Psychology, 66*(5), 856–861.

Bergsmann, I. R. (1989). The forgotten few: Juvenile female offenders. *Federal Probation, 53*(1), 73–78.

Björkqvist, K., Lagerspetz, K. M. J., & Kaukiainen, A. (1992). Do girls manipulate and boys fight? *Aggressive Behavior, 18*, 117–127.

Bloom, M. (1998). Primary prevention and foster care. *Children and Youth Services Review, 20*(8), 667–696.

Brown, C. H., Adams, R. G., & Kellam, S. G. (1981). A longitudinal study of teenage motherhood and symptoms of distress: The Woodlawn Community Epidemiological Project. In R. G. Simmons (Ed.), *Research in community and mental health: A research annual* (pp. 183–213). Greenwich, CT: JAI Press.

Cairns, R. B., Cairns, B. D., & Neckerman, H. J. (1989). Early school dropout: Configurations and determinants. *Child Development, 60*, 1437–1452.

Cairns, R. B., Cairns, B. D., Neckerman, H. J., Ferguson, L. L., & Gariepy, J. L. (1989). Growth and aggression: I. Childhood to early adolescence. *Developmental Psychology, 25*, 320–330.

Calhoun, G., Jurgens, J., & Chen, F. (1993). The neophyte female delinquent: A review of the literature. *Adolescence, 28*(110), 461–471.

Capaldi, D. M. (1991). The co-occurrence of conduct problems and depressive symptoms in early adolescent boys: I. Familial factors and general adjustment at Grade 6. *Development and Psychopathology, 3*, 277–300.

Capaldi, D. M., Crosby, L., & Stoolmiller, M. (1996). Predicting the timing of first sexual intercourse for adolescent males. *Child Development, 67*, 344–359.

Capaldi, D. M., & Patterson, G. R. (1991). Relation of parental transitions to boys' adjustment problems: I. A linear hypothesis. II. Mothers at risk for transitions and unskilled parenting. *Developmental Psychology, 27*, 489–504.

Capaldi, D. M., Stoolmiller, M., Clark, S., & Owen, L. (2001). Heterosexual risk behaviors in at risk young men from early adolescence to young adulthood: Prevalence, prediction, and STD contraction. *Developmental Psychology, 38*, 394–406.

Chalmers, J. B., & Townsend, M. A. R. (1990). The effects of training in social perspective taking on socially maladjusted girls. *Child Development, 61*, 178–190.

Chamberlain, P., Moreland, S., & Reid, K. (1992). Enhanced services and stipends for foster parents: Effects on retention rates and outcomes for children. *Child Welfare, 5*, 387–401.

Chamberlain, P., & Reid, J. B. (1991). Using a specialized foster care community treatment model for children and adolescents leaving the state mental hospital. *Journal of Community Psychology, 19,* 266–276.

Chamberlain, P., & Reid, J. (1998). Comparison of two community alternatives to incarceration for chronic juvenile offenders. *Journal of Consulting and Clinical Psychology, 6,* 624–633.

Chesney-Lind, M. (1988). Girls in jail. *Crime and Delinquency, 34*(2), 150–168.

Chesney-Lind, M. (1998). *What to do about girls? Promising perspectives and effective strategies* (Executive summary). Manoa, HI: University of Hawaii Press.

Chesney-Lind, M. (1999). Challenging girls' invisibility in juvenile court. *Annals, AAPSS, 564,* 185–201.

Crick, N. R., Casas, J. F., & Ku, H. (1999). Relational and physical forms of peer victimization in preschool. *Developmental Psychology, 35*(2), 376–385.

Crick, N. R., & Grotpeter, J. K. (1996). Children's treatment by peers: Victims of relational and overt aggression. *Development and Psychopathology, 8,* 367–380.

Crockett, L. J., Bingham, C. R., Chopak, J. S., & Vicary, J. R. (1996). Timing of first sexual intercourse: The role of social control, social learning, and problem behavior. *Journal of Youth & Adolescence, 25*(1), 89–111.

Derogatis, L. R. (1975). *Brief Symptom Inventory.* Foothill Ranch, CA: NCS Pearson.

Dishion, T. J. (2000). Cross-setting consistency in early adolescent psychopathology: Deviant friendships and problem behavior sequelae. *Journal of Personality, 68*(6), 1109–1126.

Dishion, T. J., Andrews, D. W., & Crosby, L. (1995). Antisocial boys and their friends in early adolescence: Relationship characteristics, quality, and interactional process. *Child Development, 66,* 139–151.

Eddy, J. M., & Chamberlain, P. (2000). Family management and deviant peer association as mediators of the impact of treatment condition on youth antisocial behavior. *Journal of Consulting and Clinical Psychology, 5,* 857–863.

Elliott, D. S. (Ed.). (1998). *Blueprints for violence prevention.* Boulder, CO: Institute of Behavioral Science, Regents of the University of Colorado.

Elliott, D. S., Huizinga, D., & Ageton, S. S. (1985). *Explaining delinquency and drug use.* Beverly Hills, CA: Sage.

Ericksen, K. P., & Trocki, K. F. (1992). Behavioral risk factors for sexually transmitted diseases in American households. *Social Science & Medicine, 34*(8), 843–853.

Furstenberg, F. F., Brooks-Gunn, J., & Chase-Lansdale, L. (1989). Teenaged pregnancy and childbearing. *American Psychologist, 44,* 313–320.

Giordano, P. C., & Cernkovich, S. A. (1997). Gender and antisocial behavior. In D. M. Stoff, J. Breiling, & J. D. Maser (Eds.), *Handbook of antisocial behavior* (pp. 496–510). New York: Wiley.

Giordano, P. C., Cernkovich, S. A., & Pugh, M. D. (1986). Friendship and delinquency. *American Journal of Sociology, 91,* 1170–1201.

Griffin, K. W., Botvin, G. J., Scheier, L. M., Diaz, T., & Miller, N. L. (2000). Parenting practices as predictors of substance use, delinquency, and aggression among urban minority youth: Moderating effects of family structure and gender. *Psychology of Addictive Behaviors, 14*(2), 174–184.

Hare, E. H., & Shaw, G. K. (1965). A study in family health: II. A comparison of the health of fathers, mothers, and children. *British Journal of Psychiatry, 111,* 467–471.

Henry, B., Moffitt, T., Robins, L., Earls, F., & Silva, P. (1993). Early family predictors of child and adolescent antisocial behaviour: Who are the mothers of delinquents? *Criminal Behaviour and Mental Health, 3,* 97–118.

Keenan, K., Loeber, R., & Green, S. (1999). Conduct disorder in girls: A review of the literature. *Clinical Child & Family Psychology Review, 2*, 3–19.

Keenan, K., & Shaw, D. (1997). Developmental and social influences on young girls' early problem behavior. *Psychological Bulletin, 121*(1), 95–113.

Keller, M. B., Beardslee, W. R., Dorer, D. J., Lauori, P. W., Samuelson, H., & Klerman, G. R. (1986). Impact of severity and chronicity of parental affective illness on adaptive functioning and psychopathology in children. *Archives of General Psychiatry, 43*, 930–937.

Kovacs, M., Krol, R. S. M., & Voti, L. (1994). Early onset psychopathology and the risk for teenage pregnancy among clinically referred girls. *Journal of the American Academy of Child & Adolescent Psychiatry, 33*(1), 106–113.

Kutash, K., & Rivera, V. R. (1996). *What works in children's mental health services?* Baltimore, MD: Paul H. Brookes.

Lefkowitz, E. S., Sigman, M., & Kit-fong Au, T. (2000). Helping mothers discuss sexuality and AIDS with adolescents. *Child Development, 71*(5), 1383–1394.

Lewis, D. O., Yeager, C. A., Cobham-Portorreal, N. K., Showalter, B. A., & Anthony, B. A. (1991). A follow-up of female delinquents: Maternal contribution to the perpetuation of deviance. *Journal of the American Academy of Child and Adolescent Psychiatry, 30*(2), 197–201.

Lightfoot, M. (2001, March 30). HIV prevention using technologies with delinquent youth. *Computer Retrieval of Information on Scientific Projects, Abstract Display* [On-line]. Available: http://crisp.cit.nih.gov

Loeber, R., & Keenan, K. (1994). Interaction between conduct disorder and its comorbid conditions: Effects of age and gender. *Clinical Psychology Review, 14*(6), 497–523.

Lyons-Ruth, K., Zoll, D., Connell, D., & Grunebaum, H. U. (1989). Family deviance and family disruption in childhood: Associations with maternal behavior and infant maltreatment during the first two years of life. *Development and Psychopathology, 1*, 219–236.

McMillen, J. C., Auslander, W. F., Stiffman, A. R., Elze, D., & Thompson, R. (2000, November). *Living situation and peer influences on attitudes toward condoms among US teenagers in the foster care system.* Paper presented at the annual meeting of the American Public Health Association, Boston, MA.

Mednick, S. A., Gabrielli, W. F., Jr., & Hutchings, B. (1996). Genetic factors in the etiology of criminal behavior. In J. Muncie, E. McLaughlin, & M. Langan (Eds.), *Criminal perspectives: A reader* (pp. 67–80). Bristol, PA: The Open University.

Merikangas, K. R., & Spiker, D. G. (1982). Assortive mating among inpatients with primary affective disorder. *Psychological Medicine, 12*, 753–764.

Metzler, C. W., Noell, J., Biglan, A., Ary, D., & Smolkowski, K. (1994). The social context for risky sexual behavior among adolescents. *Journal of Behavioral Medicine, 17*, 419–438.

Miller, K. S., Forehand, R., & Kotchick, B. A. (1999). Adolescent sexual behavior in two ethnic minority samples: The role of family variables. *Journal of Marriage and the Family, 61*, 85–98.

Miller, W. R., Zweben, A., DiClemente, C. C., & Rychtarik, R. G. (1992). *Motivational enhancement therapy manual: A clinical research guide for therapist treating individuals with alcohol abuse and dependence* (DHHS Publication No. 92–1894). Rockville, MD: National Institute on Alcohol Abuse and Alcoholism.

Moore, K. A., Hofferth, S. L., Caldwell, S. B., & Waite, L. J. (1979). *Teenage motherhood: Social and economic consequence* (Document # 1146-7). Washington, DC: Urban Institute.

NIMH Multisite HIV Prevention Trial Group. (1998). The NIMH Multisite HIV Prevention Trial: Reducing HIV sexual risk behavior. *Science, 280,* 1889–1894.

Noell, J., Ary, D., & Duncan, T. (1997). Development and evaluation of a sexual decision-making and social skills program: "The choice is yours—preventing HIV/STDs." *Health Education & Behavior, 24*(1), 87–101.

Offord, D. R., Boyle, M. C., & Racine, Y. A. (1991). The epidemiology of antisocial behavior in childhood and adolescence. In D. J. Pepler & K. H. Rubin (Eds.), *The development and treatment of childhood aggression* (pp. 31–54). Hillsdale, NJ: Lawrence Erlbaum Associates.

Pacifici, C., Stoolmiller, M., & Nelson, C. (2001). Evaluating a prevention program for teenagers on sexual coercion: A differential effectiveness approach. *Journal of Consulting & Clinical Psychology, 69,* 552–559.

Padian, N., Hitchcock, P., Fullilove, R., Kohlstadt, V., & Brunham, R. (1990). Report on the NIAID Study Group: Part I. Issues in defining behavioral risk factors and their distribution. *Sexual Transmitted Diseases, 17,* 200–204.

Pajer, K. A. (1998). What happens to "bad girls?" A review of the adult outcomes of antisocial adolescent girls. *American Journal of Psychiatry, 155*(7), 862–870.

Pawlby, S. J., Mills, A., & Quinton, D. (1997). Vulnerable adolescent girls: Opposite-sex relationships. *Journal of Child Psychology and Psychiatry, 38*(8), 909–920.

Pepler, D. J. (1995, April). *Aggression and gender: Self and peer perceptions.* Paper presented at the meeting of the Society for Research on Child Development, Indianapolis, IN.

Quinton, D., & Rutter, M. (1988). *Parenting breakdown: The making and breaking of inter-generational links.* Aldershot, England: Avebury.

Rivera, V. R., & Kutash, K. (1994). Therapeutic foster care services. In V. R. Rivera & K. Kutash (Eds.), *Literature series on the components of a system of care.* Tampa, FL: Research and Training Center for Children's Mental Health, University of South Florida, Florida Mental Health Institute.

Robins, L. N., & Price, R. K. (1991). Adult disorders predicted by childhood conduct problems: Results from the NIMH Epidemiologic Catchment Area Project. *Psychiatry, 54,* 116–132.

Rosenbaum, A., & O'Leary, K. D. (1981). Marital violence: Characteristics of abusive couples. *Journal of Consulting and Clinical Psychology, 49,* 63–71.

Rosenbaum, J. L. (1989). Family dysfunction and female delinquency. *Crime and Delinquency, 35,* 31–44.

Rutter, M., & Quinton, D. (1984). Long-term follow-up of women institutionalized in childhood: Factors promoting good functioning in adult life. *British Journal of Developmental Psychology, 2,* 191–204.

Rutter, M., Quinton, D., & Hill, J. (1990). Adult outcome of institution-reared children: Males and females compared. In L. N. Robins & M. Rutter (Eds.), *Straight and deviant pathways from childhood to adulthood* (pp. 135–157). Cambridge: Cambridge University Press.

Schlossman, S., & Cairns, R. B. (1991). Problem girls: Observations on past and present. In G. H. Elder, Jr., R. D. Park, & J. Modell (Eds.), *Children in time and place: Relations between history and developmental psychology* (pp. 110–130). New York: Cambridge University Press.

St. Lawrence, J. S. (1993). African-American adolescents' knowledge, health-related attitudes, sexual behavior, and contraceptive decisions: Implications for the prevention of adolescent HIV infection. *Journal of Consulting and Clinical Psychology, 61*(1), 104–112.

Stroul, B. (1989). *Community-based services for children and adolescents who are severely emotionally disturbed: Therapeutic foster care.* Washington, DC: CASSP Technical Assistance Center, Georgetown University Child Development Center.

Underwood, M. K. (1998). Competence in sexual decision-making by African-American, female adolescents: The role of peer relations and future plans. In A. Colby & J. James & D. Hart (Eds.), *Competence and character through life* (pp. 57–87). Chicago: The University of Chicago Press.

Underwood, M. K., Kupersmidt, J. B., & Coie, J. D. (1996). Childhood peer sociometric status and aggression as predictors of adolescent childbearing. *Journal of Research on Adolescence, 6*(2), 201–223.

Weissberg, R. P., Caplan, M., & Harwood, R. L. (1991). Promoting competent young people in competence-enhancing environments: A systems-based perspective on primary prevention. *Journal of Consulting & Clinical Psychology, 59*(6), 830–841.

Westen, D., Ludolph, P., Misle, B., Ruffins, S., & Block, J. (1990). Physical and sexual abuse in adolescent girls with borderline personality disorder. *American Journal of Orthopsychiatry, 60*(1), 55–66.

Whitbeck, L. B., Yoder, K. A., Hoyt, D. R., & Conger, R. D. (1999). Early adolescent sexual activity: A developmental study. *Journal of Marriage & the Family, 61*(4), 934–946.

Woodward, L. J., & Fergusson, D. M. (1999). Early conduct problems and later risk of teenage pregnancy in girls. *Development & Psychopathology, 11*(1), 127–141.

Zanarini, M. C., & Gunderson, J. G. (1997). Differential diagnosis of antisocial and borderline personality disorders. In D. M. Stoff, J. Breiling, & J. D. Maser (Eds.), *Handbook of antisocial behavior* (pp. 83–91). New York: Wiley.

Zoccolillo, M. (1993). Gender and the development of conduct disorder. *Development and Psychopathology, 5,* 65–78.

Zoccolillo, M., Pickles, A., Quinton, D., & Rutter, M. (1992). The outcome of childhood conduct disorder: Implications for defining adult personality disorder and conduct disorder. *Psychological Medicine, 22,* 1–16.

Zoccolillo, M., & Rogers, K. (1991). Characteristics and outcome of hospitalized adolescent girls with conduct disorder. *Journal of the American Academy of Child and Adolescent Psychiatry, 30*(6), 973–981.

Commentary:
The Treatment of Aggressive
Girls: Same But Different?

Wendy M. Craig
Queen's University

This book has highlighted the lack of empirically based information on the developmental trajectories of aggressive girls. Researchers have consistently underestimated the prevalence of aggression in girls, as well as the long-term sequella such as teen pregnancy, truancy, running away, early sexual activity, and intergenerational risks for their children. The chapters in this book have begun to fill a significant gap in our understanding through their focus on girls' aggression. Although we are now beginning to understand the mechanisms and processes associated with the development of aggression in girls, there is a paucity in our current understanding of effective treatments for girls with aggressive behavior problems. The two chapters in this section highlight the importance of addressing girls' aggression while underscoring a critical question: Should treatments for girls be the same or different than those for boys? The four themes highlighted in these chapters addressing the treatment of girls' aggression include: (a) the need for a developmental contextual perspective in understanding girls' aggression, (b) the significance and salience of relationships for assessing girls' aggression, (c) designing treatment to target the risky social contexts that may facilitate the development of aggression in girls, and (d) identifying relevant outcomes in the treatment of girls' aggression.

In their review of the research, both groups of authors noted that aggressive girls' problems develop early and that they experience problems in many different contexts. A developmental-contextual perspective identifies the changing nature of aggression, as well as the salience of different social contexts in development. Hence, it is important to consider the interaction of individual risk factors and the social contexts in which the risks are exposed. Both studies highlight the early difficulties experienced by aggressive girls in the family, which transfer with age to other contexts, such as the peer group and school. For example, data from the qualitative study conducted by Levene and her colleagues (chap. 7) with highly aggressive girls ages 7 to 12, indicate that family interactions were characterized by coercive interactional cycles, high levels of conflict between mother and daughter, and problematic boundaries in relationships. In addition, there was a subset of girls who had experienced significant risk at home, including allegations of sexual abuse, witnessing violence in the home, and physical abuse. Also, a majority of the girls were from single-parent families and were living under financial strain (i.e., on welfare or lived in subsidized housing). Thus, as with aggressive boys, the family context for aggressive girls is an environment that may serve to promote their aggressive tendencies rather than inhibit them. However, unlike boys, aggressive girls may have a same-sex role model of aggressive behavior in their primary caregiver—their mothers—and it is with their mothers that many aggressive and coercive interactions unfold. For aggressive girls, the mother–daughter relationship appears to be a significant flashpoint. Furthermore, as Leve and Chamberlain (chap. 8) demonstrated, the family context for the aggressive girls in their sample is more chaotic than it is for aggressive boys. Providing a stable family environment through specialized foster care placements was related to decreases in the girls' aggressive behavior problems.

Levene, Madsen, and Pepler identified individual risk factors that aggressive girls may experience from birth (e.g., birth complications, extensive hospitalization, levels of specialized care, and difficult temperaments), as well as in early childhood (attention deficit, learning problems). These individual risk factors are also found in aggressive boys (Pepler & Rubin, 1991). Individual risk factors interact with risk characteristics of the parents and negative environmental circumstances in the family (e.g., mothers suffering from high degrees of stress and low resources to cope with difficult infants). With children's development, parenting challenges and stresses increase, often resulting in a cycle of negative interactions between mothers and their young children. Alternatively, mothers may neglect their children as a coping strategy, which also contributes to attachment problems between mother and baby. The strained parenting capacity of mothers, particularly with difficult infants, can fuel the cycle of negative interactions between mothers and their young daughters. Thus, as in the case of aggressive boys (Moffitt, Caspi, Rutter, & Silva, 2001), aggressive girls experience early difficulties, and these early difficulties may contribute to poor attachment with mothers, poor quality interactions, and early relationship problems in the home. These troubled primary relationships place aggressive girls at risk for the development of a wide range of problem behaviors. The girls' risks may be compounded by exposure to their mothers' negative parenting style. The family context may be particularly salient for girls compared with boys because girls spend more time at home and are more closely tied to their families in times of stress (Maccoby, 1986). Girls tend to assume more caregiving roles with siblings, report more intimacy in friendships, and place more importance on close friendships than boys (Giordano et al., 1986). Finally, the lessons that aggressive girls learn about parenting from their mothers may transfer to their own parenting experiences, which are likely to occur earlier for these girls than for nonaggressive girls. A concern for precocious sexual involvement and parenting is raised by the Leve and Chamberlain study, which identified the high level of risky sexual behavior that aggressive girls engage in, thereby increasing the likelihood of becoming a mother at an early age.

The early relationship problems that aggressive girls experience at home are transferred to the school and peer contexts, raising concerns that relationships may be a flashpoint for girls' aggression. Leve and Chamberlain reported on a randomized clinical trial with a sample of teenage girls referred from the juvenile justice system. In their intervention, they aim to reduce contact with delinquent peers, a proximal target for reducing aggression, as well as promote friendships with same-sex nondeviant peers. Two interesting findings in the Leve and Chamberlain study highlight the problems that troubled girls face in their friendships. First, many aggressive girls identified their best friend as their romantic partner, indicating that they did not have a same-sex best friend with whom they could discuss common adolescent concerns such as intimacy, dating, and sexuality. Second, they found a correlation between having deviant friends and engaging in risky sexual behavior. Conversely, having a positive peer relationship was related to lower levels of health-risking sexual behaviors. Taken together, these findings suggest that friendships and qualities of the friend may not only reduce aggressive behavior, but may also reduce risky sexual behavior in romantic relationships—another potentially risky context for aggressive girls.

Romantic relationships are a unique type of peer relationship, and the risky interactions or behaviors that occur with peers and friends are likely transferred to problematic romantic relationships. An unexpected outcome of Leve and Chamberlain's intervention for aggressive girls was their growing recognition of the significant problems associated with risky sexual behavior (e.g., having intercourse with someone known less than 24 hours, lack of birth control, increased incidence of sexually transmitted behaviors, and early pregnancies). Leve and Chamberlain provided support for the importance of romantic relationships as a critical context for intervention with aggressive girls, particularly in addressing their risky sexual behaviors. Furthermore, they suggested that targeting this domain may serve two important functions: increasing positive relationships with same-sex peers, as well as increasing knowledge and practice related to safe sex practices.

These two chapters provided insights into the developmental trajectories of aggressive girls, as well as highlighted assessment and outcome issues, treatment targets, and methodological diversity. The emerging significance of risky social relationships (mother–daughter relationships, peer relationships, and romantic relationships) emphasizes the importance of assessing these relationships for aggressive girls and designing interventions that target these complex relationships. A challenge facing researchers in evaluating interventions is to identify and assess appropriate outcomes for aggressive girls in childhood, adolescence, and beyond. These negative outcomes for aggressive girls can be different in some respects from those of boys and will likely encompass their troubled relationships. For boys, delinquency and community aggression are important outcomes, whereas for girls critical outcomes may include their risky sexual behavior, choice of partner, and early pregnancy. Because aggressive girls engage in behavior that increases the risk of becoming young parents and having a potentially ill child due to sexual transmitted diseases, we need to develop interventions tailored to the needs of aggressive girls to prevent the cycle of aggressive behavior in the next generation. Drawing from the research presented in the two preceding chapters, we can identify important directions for the development of treatments for aggressive girls: provide early support and education for mothers, develop positive same-sex friendships for girls, and utilize these friendships to promote peer education regarding risky sexual practices in their romantic relationships. Peer education programs for aggressive girls that focus on the development of healthy romantic relationships and sexual behavior may serve as both an important intervention for supporting positive same-sex peer relationships and an important prevention function in diverting girls from troubled romantic relationship trajectories in their adolescence and into adulthood.

From a methodological perspective, the strong experimental design in the Leve and Chamberlain chapter emphasizes the importance of multimethod, multiagent, and multirelationship contexts in assessing and intervening effectively in girls' aggression. In addition, different methodologies, such as the qualitative approach in the study by Levene and her colleagues, can provide insights, depth, and the foundation for identifying potential targets for intervention. The different methodologies presented in these chapters offer unique perspectives on the development of girls' aggression while providing converging empirical evidence on the salient themes in aggressive girls' lives.

In summary, it is likely that the developmental trajectories of aggressive girls and boys are more similar than different; however, the domains of treatment and the outcomes are distinct. For girls and women, relationships are central to their lives, and they are more concerned about relationships and connectedness within those relationships than are boys and men (Fehr, 1996). Relationships across the lifespan can both promote positive development (act as a protective factor for the development of aggression) or serve to reinforce maladaptive behaviors (be a risky context). The unfolding processes within relationships are determined by interactions between a girl's individual characteristics and the individual characteristics of those with whom she interacts. Treatment programs aimed at girls' aggression should target the potential negative processes within relationships. In evaluating these programs, Leve and Chamberlain have set the gold standard of a randomized clinical trial that provides data on the basic processes, as well as the efficacy of treatment, and they have begun to increase our understanding of what type of treatment works for aggressive girls. Both chapters identify the salience and significance of relationships in reducing girls' aggression. If we can promote and develop healthy relationships for these girls, beginning in the family with the mother–daughter relationship, we may be able to facilitate the development of healthy peer and romantic relationships. A strong relationship foundation may prevent aggressive girls from becoming teenage parents and potentially continuing the cycle of aggression. Researchers have finally recognized that some girls have significant aggressive behavior problems, and there is a body of accumulating evidence identifying the salient developmental processes in girls' aggression. Our challenge is to implement this knowledge in developing prevention and intervention programs that uniquely target the salient relationship processes and contexts for girls and begin to address the problem of intergenerational cycles of aggression in our society.

REFERENCES

Fehr, B. (1996). *Friendship processes*. Thousand Oaks, CA: Sage.

Giordano, P. C., Cernkovich, S. A., & Pugh, M. D. (1986). Friendships and delinquency. *American Journal of Sociology, 91*, 1170–1202.

Maccoby, E. E. (1986). Social groupings in childhood: Their relationship to prosocial and antisocial behavior in boys and girls. In D. Olweus, J. Block, & M. Radke-Yarrow (Eds.), *Development of antisocial and prosocial behavior: Research, theories, and issues* (pp. 263–284). Orlando, FL: Academic Press.

Moffitt, T. E., Caspi, A., Rutter, M., & Silva, P. A. (2001). *Sex differences in antisocial behaviour*. Cambridge, England: Cambridge University Press.

Pepler, D. P., & Rubin, K. (1991). *The development and treatment of childhood aggression*. Hillsdale, NJ: Lawrence Erlbaum Associates.

Part V

AGGRESSIVE GIRLS GROW UP

9

Maternal Conduct Disorder and the Risk for the Next Generation

Mark Zoccolillo
Montreal Children's Hospital
McGill University Health Center

Daniel Paquette
University of Montreal

Richard Tremblay
University of Montreal

Conduct disorder is a familial disorder with evidence from twin and adoption studies for both genetic and shared environment effects (Cadoret, Yates, Troughton, Woodworth, & Stewart, 1995; Eley, Lichtenstein, & Stevenson, 1999; Langbehn, Cadoret, Yates, Troughton, & Stewart, 1998; Rutter, 1997; Rutter, Silberg, O'Connor, & Simonoff, 1999). Recent studies have found considerable stability in antisocial behavior from the preschool or kindergarten period onward, suggesting that for some children the preceding period (from birth to preschool) may be an important risk period for the development of persistent antisocial behavior (Caspi, Moffitt, Newman, & Silva, 1996; Nagin & Tremblay, 1999). Given these data, it would seem logical to examine the early family environment, from birth to school age, of children from families with antisocial mothers. Yet there are few such studies (Cassidy, Zoccolillo, & Hughes, 1996; Fagot, Pears, Capaldi, Crosby, & Leve, 1998; Serbin et al., 1998; Wakschlag & Hans, 1999), and little is known about the early family environment of children growing up in families with antisocial mothers.

Why should we understand better the early family environment of children of women who had conduct disorder (CD)? There are several good reasons. First, it is important for understanding the transmission mechanisms of CD across generations. Second, it may help in understanding the comorbidity of

CD with other disorders. Third, by knowing the risk processes, we can develop effective intervention and prevention programs to work with families with antisocial mothers.

From a theoretical perspective, the study of the intergenerational transmission of conduct disorder is an excellent example of nature–nurture integration (Rutter, 1997). In this model, it is how genetic and environmental risk factors fit together that is of paramount importance. This chapter adopts this perspective.

In the first section of this chapter, we discuss the reasons noted earlier for studying the family environment of children of mothers who had CD. In the second section, methodological issues in studying the family environment of these mothers are addressed. In the third section, illustrative data from two data sets are presented. In the last section, some conclusions and suggestions for future research are presented.

WHY SHOULD WE STUDY THE FAMILY ENVIRONMENT OF CHILDREN OF MOTHERS WHO HAD CD

Understanding the Mechanisms for CD Transmission Across Generations

One of the major problems in studies of the family environment of school-age children and adolescents with CD is the difficulty in determining the order of effects because children with CD have considerable effects on the family environment. Ideally, children should be studied from birth onward to better disentangle the order of effects. This raises the practical problem that most children will not develop CD, and any study of random population samples has to be large to have enough children who develop CD. Recruiting families at birth for study, based on a maternal history of CD, makes it possible to obtain a sample of children at increased risk for CD and with a much higher rate of putative risk factors (Martin & Burchinal, 1992; Robins, 1966; Robins, West, & Herjanic, 1975; Serbin et al., 1998).

Another reason is that families with mothers who had CD are likely to experience multiple and extreme adversity given that dysfunction in multiple (but not single) domains most often occurs in adults who have had a history of CD (Robins, 1966; Robins, 1978; Zoccolillo, Pickles, Quinton, & Rutter, 1992; Zoccolillo, Price, Hwu, & Ji, 1998). To understand the effects of multiple or extreme adversity, it is critical to recruit a sufficient number of families with CD mothers. Comparisons to families in adversity, but where the mother does not have CD, can address the question of whether there are specific risk factors found only in families with CD mothers.

A major reason to study families with CD mothers is to control for genetic transmission of the liability to CD to better determine shared environmental effects. Twin and adoption studies are largely consistent in pointing to both genetic and shared environmental effects on CD development (Cadoret, Yates, Troughton, Woodworth, & Stewart, 1995; Langbehn et al., 1998; Rutter, Silberg, O'Connor, & Simonoff, 1999). Two important consequences flow from these findings of nature–nurture interaction. First, because parental CD is associated with most putative environmental risk factors for CD, any rigorous test of environmental hypotheses must include the possibility that the environmental risk factor is only a marker for genetic transmission. Second, the risk factors associated with having a parent with CD would be expected to be largely shared by siblings in the same family (e.g., unresponsive parenting due to drug use or violence in the home due to marital conflict between two antisocial parents). Families with parents with CD are important to study to determine the nature of the shared environmental effects found in genetically informative studies.

It is important to note that twin and adoption studies are not practically suited for examining the early environment effects of antisocial families for two reasons. First, with regard to adoption studies, the effect of interest is the environmental effect: Are children not at genetic risk for CD (unaffected biological parents) raised from birth in families where the adopted mother has CD at increased risk for CD? Obviously this is not an ethically acceptable design. There is also no natural study counterpart because adoptive parents are screened to select out antisocial parents. Furthermore, the interest is in examining the environment from birth onward; retrospective studies from large adoption cohorts are unlikely to have detailed data on the environment in the first few years of life. Second, with regard to twin studies, the focus would be on mothers with CD who had twins. Given even a relatively high prevalence of 10% of mothers with CD (Zoccolillo, 1993) and an expected twin birth rate of 1 in 100 deliveries (Plomin, 1997) would mean only 0.1% of births would be twins of mothers with CD. Recruiting a birth cohort sample of even 100 twins would require screening 100,000 mothers of newborns. Although it is possible in very large twin studies to have enough twins of mothers with CD, it would be desirable to have as good an idea ahead of time as to how antisocial families differ from other families and what are potentially the best variables for study before embarking on large-scale and costly studies.

In the absence of twin and adoption studies, maternal (and paternal) CD can be used as a variable to both control for genetic effects and test for the possibility of gene–environment interactions in randomly selected and high-risk population samples. This would apply in situations where the putative risk factor and parental CD are associated. If the association between a putative risk factor and child CD disappears when controlling for parental CD, it is likely that the relationship was spurious, possible either genetically mediated or through some other associated common risk factor. If the relationship is moderated, it may be due to an underlying gene–environment interaction. If the relationship is not changed at all, then it is evidence for the risk factor being real because controlling for parental CD would also control for a variety of other risk factors. Risk factors that occur in all families with CD and are absent in non-CD families cannot be tested in such a design (and underscores the importance of understanding better the pattern of risk factors in families with parental CD). It is also important to note that this design only partially controls for genetic effects. For example, the effect of prenatal smoking on later antisocial behavior on the child remains even after controlling for measures of adult maternal and paternal antisocial behavior (Wakschlag et al., 1997). Although this suggests that prenatal smoking is not just a marker for families with both antisocial parents and children, such a design cannot rule out other genetic confounds, such as a genetic liability to sensation seeking, which leads to prenatal smoking in the parent (but not measurable antisocial behaviors such as CD) and an increased risk of antisocial behavior in the child through sensation-seeking behavior. In addition, the measurement of CD is only an imperfect measure of the true genotype. Nonetheless, the few minutes invested by researchers and clinicians in ascertaining parental conduct symptoms yields considerable additional useful information.

Few studies have actually controlled for parental antisociality when examining risk factors. Some notable researchers who have done so include the Oregon Social Learning Center group in looking at parenting practices (Reid & Patterson, 1989), Lahey et al. (1988) in examining parental divorce, Robins et al. in the study of socioeconomic status (SES), divorce, and parenting practices (Robins, 1966; Robins, 1978; Robins, Murphy, Woodruff, & King, 1971; Robins, West, & Herjanic, 1975), and Wakschlag et al. (1997) in examining prenatal smoking.

Explaining Co-Morbidity Between CD and Other Disabilities

Conduct disorder co-occurs more often than by chance with a variety of other disorders and dysfunctions. These include attention deficit hyperactivity disorder (ADHD; Jensen, Martin, & Cantwell, 1997), internalizing disorders (Zoccolillo, 1992), suicide attempts (Brent et al., 1993), and neuropsychological deficits (Moffitt & Lynam, 1994).

One potential explanation of co-morbidity is that children of CD mothers are exposed to multiple risk factors that accumulate in these families secondary to the parents' own CD. Having a dysfunction in multiple domains in adult life is relatively specific to having a history of CD (Zoccolillo, Pickles, Quinton, & Rutter, 1992). If these adult dysfunctions are in turn risk factors for various disabilities in children, it would be expected that children of these parents would also show CD plus a variety of co-morbid conditions. For example, CD is associated with both dropping out of high school and smoking (Bardone, Moffitt, Caspi, & Dickson, 1996; Bardone et al., 1998; Boyle et al., 1993; Zoccolillo & Rogers, 1991). Children of CD parents are expected to have increased rates of low educational attainment (because of the parent's low educational status) and respiratory diseases (because of the parent's smoking), along with CD. Neither low educational status nor smoking are specific to CD, but parental CD greatly increases the risk that their children will be exposed to multiple risk factors. To determine whether various forms of co-morbidity with CD are due to co-occurrence of multiple risk factors within families where the parent also had CD, it is important to know which risk factors actually occur in families with CD and the extent to which they explain co-morbidity.

Developing Effective Intervention and Prevention Programs for Families With Antisocial Mothers

Conduct disorder in girls is relatively common, affecting from 5% to 10% of girls (Zoccolillo, 1993). CD is also associated with a variety of poor adult outcomes (Pajer, 1998), such as substance abuse (Hawkins, Catalano, & Miller, 1992), assortative mating with antisocial men (Krueger, Moffitt, Caspi, Bleske, & Silva, 1998), depression (Zoccolillo, 1992), unresponsive parenting (Cassidy, Zoccolillo, & Hughes, 1996; Hans, Bernstein, & Henson, 1999; Serbin, Peters, McAffer, & Schwartzman, 1991), and low educational status (Bardone, Moffitt, Caspi, & Dickson, 1996; Zoccolillo & Rogers, 1991), all of which are risk factors for adverse development in children. However, no early intervention program has specifically targeted children of CD mothers. It may be that the multiple and seemingly intractable problems encountered in these families appear too complicated for any potentially successful intervention. Yet given how common CD is in girls, ignoring these families means ignoring a large proportion of the most at-risk children. Furthermore, much of successful science is learning from mistakes, but one has to make the mistakes first to learn from them. Avoiding this population means nothing will be learned.

One important issue in developing intervention and prevention programs with these mothers is to view the constellation of risk factors for the child as outcomes of the mother's own CD, and not only as current risk factors. For example, there is good evidence for assortative mating for antisocial behavior such that it would be predicted that the fathers of the infants of mothers with CD would be more likely to have CD than infants born to mothers without CD. Having two parents with a history of CD places children at greater risk for adverse outcomes than if only one parent has CD. Preventing assortative mating would reduce the proportion of infants at very high risk. At first reading, it would seem both excessively intrusive and impossible to prevent assortative mating in young adults. However, association with antisocial males is not only a risk factor for the infant, but also for the mother (Zoccolillo & Rogers, 1991). It is also considered acceptable and, to some extent, feasible to prevent children and adolescents from associating with other antisocial adolescents (regardless of gender; Dobkin, Tremblay, Masse, & Vitaro, 1995; Fergusson & Horwood, 1996; Vitaro & Tremblay, 1994). Interventions programs designed to help CD girls in early adolescence make healthy choices of both male and female friends would be both a legitimate and potentially feasible way to reduce later assortative mating, and it would improve outcomes for both mother and child.

Taking into account the family environment of mothers with CD may also help in better estimating the effects of intervention and prevention programs. An example would be a program that reduced prenatal smoking in all mothers. Mothers with CD are more likely to smoke more during pregnancy and their infants are more likely to have other risk factors (such as a biological father who also has CD). Given that CD mothers have other risk factors, it is not expected that reductions in smoking in CD mothers would have as much of an impact on their children as it would children of mothers who do not have CD. Controlling for maternal CD and other risk factors may help in specifically isolating any effects of reducing prenatal smoking.

METHODOLOGICAL ISSUES

There is much to be gained by focusing on mothers with CD and the risk for children of these mothers. Four important methodological issues for researchers and clinicians are addressed next. They are measuring parental antisociality, missing fathers, case finding and controls, and data analysis.

What Measure of Parental "Antisociality" Should Be Used?

Criteria for antisociality should (a) identify those parents where there is significant environmental risk for the child, and (b) identify those parents where there is a significant probability of a genetic component to the parent's antisociality because this measure is used as a control for genetic confounding.

The most inclusive measures that assess parental antisociality are parental CD symptoms—that is, their child and adolescent history of antisocial behavior. There are several good reasons for using conduct (child and adolescent) rather than adult symptoms. First, pervasive and persistent adult antisocial behavior rarely occurs without a previous history of conduct symptoms (Robins, 1966; Zoccolillo, Pickles, Quinton, & Rutter, 1992). Therefore, identifying those parents with conduct symptoms can identify almost all those who will have significant adult antisocial behavior. Second, twin and adoption studies suggest genetic contributions for conduct symptoms or disorder (Eley, Lichtenstein, & Stevenson, 1999; Gjone, Stevenson, Sundet, & Eilertsen, 1996; Langbehn, Cadoret, Yates, Troughton, & Stewart, 1998) ; relying on adult symptoms would potentially misclassify parents with heritable CD symptoms as "not affected," thus underestimating genetic effects. Third, almost all parents would have passed through the age of risk for CD symptoms. However, many young parents would not have had much opportunity to acquire adult antisocial symptoms. In particular, teen mothers, a group with increased rates of CD (Cassidy, Zoccolillo, & Hughes, 1996; Kovacs, Krol, & Voti, 1994; Serbin, Peters, McAffer, & Schwartzman, 1991; Woodward & Fergusson, 1999; Zoccolillo, Meyers, & Assiter, 1997; Zoccolillo & Rogers, 1991), would not have adult symptoms because of their age.

Another important issue is what threshold of conduct symptoms should be used to define *antisociality*. One follow-up study of the adult outcome of CD symptoms found that it was dysfunction in multiple adult domains that was specific to CD (Zoccolillo, Pickles, Quinton, & Rutter, 1992). Adults with dysfunction in one area only (including criminal convictions) were not more likely to have a history of CD. However, studies looking prospectively from CD symptoms to adult problems have found that even one CD symptom increases the risk of a poor outcome (Robins & Price, 1991), and having only two symptoms was associated with pervasive and persistent adult antisocial behavior (Zoccolillo, Pickles, Quinton, & Rutter, 1992). In addition, studies using latent class analysis (which adjusts for measurement error of the specific items for a latent variable) have found considerably more continuity over time (Fergusson, Lynskey, & Horwood, 1996; Zoccolillo, Pickles, Quinton, & Rutter, 1992), suggesting that arbitrarily fixed thresholds of symptoms such as the three needed for a *DSM–IV* diagnosis underidentify individuals with persistent antisocial behavior. Therefore, the best classification system would have to be flexible to examine various thresholds because it is unclear at present what is the best combination and number of symptoms distinguishing *disordered* from *nondisordered* parents.

Finally, which CD symptoms should be used to distinguish disordered from nondisordered mothers? Three important criteria for the choice of symptoms are: (a) that they have been shown to predict an increased risk of a poor adult outcome; (b) that they predict well for females (many studies have only looked at males); and (c) that they measure a broad range of antisocial behaviors so that less seriously affected parents are not misclassified as not affected. For example, in the general population, a substantial minority of men and most women who meet the full *DSM–III* criteria for antisocial personality disorder do not have significant criminal histories (Robins & Regier, 1991). Criteria that focus on criminality would exclude a large proportion of pervasively and persistently antisocial parents.

One set of CD symptoms that meets the prior criteria is the set of symptoms used in *DSM–III* as the child/adolescent symptoms required for a diagnosis of antisocial personality disorder. These symptoms overlap with *DSM–IV* (American Psychiatric Association, 1994) symptoms, but are less oriented toward aggression and criminality. They have also been shown to predict a poor adult outcome in women (Robins & Regier, 1991; Zoccolillo, Price, Hwu, & Ji, 1998; Zoccolillo, Pickles, Quinton, & Rutter, 1992; Zoccolillo & Rogers, 1991).

The Fathers

The second methodological challenge in studying maternal CD as a risk factor in children's development is gathering data on fathers. Fathers are important contributors to the family environment of CD mothers. It is well established that there is assortative mating for antisocial behavior (Krueger, Moffitt, Caspi, Bleske, & Silva, 1998). Therefore, fathers of the children of CD mothers would be more likely to have CD. Measuring the father's antisocial behavior is critical for three reasons. First, if parental antisociality is being used as a control for genetic transmission, it is essential to have measures of antisociality on both parents. Second, it is likely that fathers who are antisocial increase the environmental risk for the child. Although this can be viewed as an independent risk factor, the increased likelihood of choosing an antisocial mate by women with CD can also be viewed as one of the environmental risk factors associated with maternal CD. Third, there is some evidence that the type of mate chosen by women with CD influences the mother's own level of adult dysfunction (Quinton, Rutter, & Liddle, 1984; Zoccolillo, Pickles, Quinton, & Rutter, 1992). The critical issue here is the effect of the father on the mother's function, rather than an added adverse independent environmental effect.

Although it is important to measure paternal psychopathology and paternal contributions to the environment, this is much easier said than done for two reasons. First, a problem that has plagued researchers looking at the effects of parental antisocial behavior on their offspring is that fathers are often missing. Second, true paternity may not be clear. Some ways to address these two problems are discussed next.

There are several ways to reduce the effects of missing fathers. First, it can be assumed that fathers are most likely to be present at birth and that fathers' involvement diminishes over time. Therefore, researchers concerned with studies of paternal CD should collect paternal data as soon as possible—probably during pregnancy if possible or at birth. Second, where fathers are unavailable, information on missing fathers can be obtained from the mothers—an approach used in several studies. It is important to note that the critical level of accuracy of such data varies depending on the use of the data. As a control for the confound of genetic transmission, false positives are of less concern because it is better to overcontrol than to undercontrol. As a measure of prevalence of CD or antisocial personality disorder (ASPD), in these fathers the data are relatively imprecise particularly with regard to comparisons across samples. It is also possible to build into the maternal assessment of paternal antisocial behavior the means to reduce error and test validity of the data. Asking questions during pregnancy or birth, by definition, means that no more than 9 months can have elapsed since contact with the biological father, reducing any effects of time elapsed on memory. The use of multiple questions assessing both a history of CD and adult antisocial symptoms allows a test of the validity of the data by examining whether the expected association between CD and adult antisocial symptoms is found. Allowing the category of *don't know* (rather than just *yes* and *no*) increases the accuracy of the yes-and-no answers. If a broad range of symptoms is included, mothers are more likely to give a definite answer to at least one of the questions. This information can then be combined with information from the same questions from nonmissing fathers to assign the missing father to categories of nonantisocial/antisocial. For example, if an adult criminal conviction in nonmissing fathers is almost always associated with a paternal history of CD, a report by the mother of an adult criminal conviction can be used to assign missing fathers to the CD category when the mother has no information on the father regarding CD symptoms. Third, some statistical techniques can account for missing data. Notably, if missingness is conditional on an independent variable that is not missing (data Missing At Random, to use the terminology of Little & Rubin [1987]) then maximum likelihood techniques can account for missing variables. Because father's absence is in part related to maternal conduct problems, this may be an appropriate technique for certain analyses. The important element is that there are creative ways to maximize the available data on fathers, which can improve the quality of analyses.

The problem of misattributed paternity is a more difficult one. If such misattribution is random, then the estimates may be less precise, but unbiased. Far more problematic is when the misattribution is not at random. Of particular concern is misattribution of paternity to men who are less antisocial than the true fathers, which would result in underestimating genetic contributions to offspring disruptive behaviors. Only DNA testing can unequivocally establish paternity, but such testing is fraught with ethical problems and not generally feasible. One possible mechanism to reduce or at least test for error is to ask the mother about all sexual partners around the time of conception of the study infant and their histories of antisocial behaviors. These data could then be used to decide probabilistically the true genotype of the father.

Examining the Data

What are useful strategies when deciding what data to collect and how to analyze the data? Several issues should be kept in mind by researchers. First, little is known in this area. Research suggests that the family environment of CD mothers differs in many ways from normal environments. One implication of this is that emphasis should be placed initially on informed descriptive studies so that more information can be gathered on how these environments differ. It is only after this information is gathered that specific hypotheses can be generated with regard to which risk factors may be specifically causal for adverse outcomes in the offspring. In addition, it is critical to establish which risk factors differ only in a quantitative way between CD and non-CD mothers and which risk factors may be specific to CD mothers.

Second, researchers should bear in mind the complexity of risk factors in these families and also that this complexity may be generated by relatively simple mechanisms. For example, data suggest that dysfunction in several areas of adult life (such as a poor work history, unstable opposite-sex relationships, criminality, and substance abuse), in the absence of adult-onset major psychiatric disorders, occurs almost exclusively in those with histories of CD (Zoccolillo, Pickles, Quinton, & Rutter, 1992). It would be more parsimonious and in keeping with the data to focus on why CD leads to these constellation of outcomes than to consider individual alternative hypotheses for each separate adult outcome.

One possible model for the development of CD is that it is the number of risk factors (or cumulative risk) that is important rather than any one risk factor. However, it is precisely in those families where parents have a history of CD that multiple risk would be most likely to occur. In investigating the impact of cumulative risk on the development of CD, it is particularly important to assess and control for the association to parental CD.

Third, researchers need to bear in mind longitudinal and intergenerational continuities when examining risk factors. For example, families with CD mothers often live in the most disadvantaged neighborhoods, giving rise to the hypothesis that neighborhoods play a major role in the material disadvantage seen in these families. However, in a long-term (40 some years) study of children with and without CD from a disadvantaged neighborhood, Robins (1966) found that non-CD children were able to move away to better neighborhoods when they became adults because they completed their education and obtained stable jobs. Conversely, CD children often left the neighborhood in young adulthood and drifted away to other parts of the country, but then returned to raise their children in the same poor neighborhood. Hence, childhood CD led to an intergenerational continuity in growing up in a disadvantaged neighborhood.

Fourth, there is considerable linear dependency among many outcomes and CD. The implication of this is that tests of causal hypotheses of particular risk factors and CD in the offspring must control for recognized confounds. For example, the number of CD symptoms linearly predicts: the number of adult antisocial symptoms (Robins & Price, 1991); an increasing probability of a diagnosis of drug dependence (Robins & McEvoy, 1990); an increasing probability of prenatal smoking; and an increasing probability of a lifetime diagnosis of an internalizing disorder (major depression and anxiety disorders; Zoccolillo, 1992). Dose-response relationships between any putative risk factor and offspring behavior may only be a reflection of an association between some other linearly dependent risk factor or a genetic liability in families of CD mothers.

Case Finding and Controls

With a lifetime prevalence of CD of approximately 5% and 10%, random samples of the female adult population must be relatively large to obtain enough cases of CD (Zoccolillo, 1992). However, there are several ways to find women with CD.

One strategy is to screen consecutive births (or admissions to obstetric clinics) to select women with CD. As we note later, it is possible to do so with self-administered questionnaires.

A second way is to find study populations of mothers with relatively high concentrations of women with CD. A number of recent studies have found an association between CD and teen pregnancy (Wakschlag et al., 2000; Woodward & Fergusson, 1999; Cassidy, Zoccolillo, & Hughes, 1996; Kovacs, Krol, & Voti, 1994; Serbin, Peters, McAffer, & Schwartzman, 1991; Zoccolillo, Meyers, & Assiter, 1997; Zoccolillo & Rogers, 1991). Because adolescent mothers are easily identified by age and often attend specific obstetric clinics, they are a relatively accessible population. Another potential sample comprises mothers identified as being of low SES (e.g., attending welfare clinics, clinics in poor neighborhoods, etc.). An important caveat to note is that many teen and low-SES mothers do not have CD (Wakschlag & Hans, 2000). Therefore, neither adolescent pregnancy nor low SES can be used as an index of CD. These factors are useful only to make case finding more efficient.

A key element in the investigation of risk factors in the family environment of mothers with CD is the choice of comparison groups. The choice of comparison groups depends on the type of analysis. If the focus of the analysis is to determine risk factors specific to mothers with CD, it is important to match controls on a variety of confounds such as SES, age, and IQ. High-risk samples such as teen mothers or low-SES mothers are particularly good for this type of study because the non-CD mothers within the sample make for comparison groups already matched on selected variables. If the analysis is focusing on nonspecific risk factors, the number of risk factors, or risk factors that are more frequent among mothers with CD, a random population sample comparing mothers with CD to all other mothers is more appropriate.

ILLUSTRATIVE STUDIES

In this section, results from two ongoing studies are presented to make a number of points. First, CD symptoms are simple to assess in general population samples. Second, in general population or high-risk samples, there are sizable numbers of mothers with CD. Third, many putative risk factors are highly associated with maternal CD. Fourth, a single risk factor (maternal CD) can lead to multiple risks. Fifth, these studies highlight a range of risk factors to be pursued in further research studies.

Data on two samples are presented. The first is a large general population sample of 5-month-old infants and their parents. Data from this sample are used to demonstrate that maternal conduct symptoms can be easily assessed in general population samples with self-administered questionnaires and maternal conduct symptoms are associated with many risk factors. The second sample comprises teen mothers and is used to demonstrate how maternal conduct symptoms are related to maternal prenatal smoking and the appropriate time for intervention.

Study 1: The Longitudinal Study of Child Development in Québec (LSCDQ)

The Longitudinal Study of Child Development in Québec (LSCDQ) is an interuniversity study of a birth cohort of Quebec children to examine risk factors from early infancy onward for disruptive behavior and lack of school readiness in kindergarten. The study is being conducted in collaboration with the Direction Santé Québec (the health survey research service of the government of Québec), a unit of the Institut de la Statistique du Québec. The target population comprises infants who were between 59 and 60 gestational weeks of age during the survey period (1998) representative of the population of Quebec; 2,223 infants were included; and 2,120 will be assessed every 12 months through the first year of elementary school. The data are weighted to account for the stratified selection procedure and non-response. Mothers and fathers of the infants were asked about a variety of psychosocial and health variables and also about their own past history. Full details of the study are described in the cited references (Jette, Desrosiers, Tremblay, & Thibault, 2000; Zoccolillo, 2000) and are available in English on the Web at: http://www.stat.gouv.qc.ca/publicat/sante/index_an.htm

One important aspect of the study is the measurement of a parent's own history of conduct problems and antisocial adult behaviors. The measurement of child/adolescent and adult antisocial behaviors was limited by financial and time constraints to a self-report format (see Appendix 1 for the questions). Because it is important to clearly distinguish between child and adult behaviors, the questions asking about child/adolescent behaviors were prefaced by, "Before the end of high school did you …?" Adult behaviors were prefaced by, "Since leaving or finishing school have you … ?" The mothers were asked about five child/adolescent antisocial behaviors: stealing more than once, more than one fight, arrested by police or in trouble with Youth Protection (the Québec government agency responsible for delinquent or troubled youth) because of misbehavior, truancy at least twice in 1 year, and running away from home overnight. The four adult behaviors for the mothers were: fired from a job, arrested for nontraffic offense, hit or thrown things at spouse, in trouble at work, with the police, or family, or had an accident due to drugs or alcohol.

Table 9.1 shows the prevalence of child and adult antisocial symptoms in the mother. These prevalence data highlight several important findings. First, with the exception of truancy, the prevalence rates of the CD behaviors are all low; most mothers reported none of the symptoms. The truancy rates may be inflated because no exclusion was made for truancy in the last year of school. Second, three or more symptoms is the threshold used for *DSM–IV* CD; 6.1% of mothers met this threshold—a figure in keeping with other prevalence studies of CD in girls (Zoccolillo, 1993). Third, having three or more adult antisocial behaviors was rare (0.3%). Therefore, few if any of these mothers would have met the *DSM–IV* criteria for antisocial personality disorder (APP).

An important question regarding the validity of CD symptoms is whether they predict adult antisocial behaviors. Previous studies have found that adults with multiple adult antisocial symptoms have had histories of CD, and that females with CD are more likely to have adult antisocial behaviors than females without (Bardone, Moffitt, Caspi, & Dickson, 1996; Robins, 1966; Robins & Regier, 1991; Zoccolillo, Pickles, Quinton, & Rutter, 1992; Zoccolillo, Price, Hwu, & Ji, 1998). A cross-tabulation of the number of CD

TABLE 9.1

Conduct and Adult Antisocial Symptoms in Mothers

Variables	Weighted (%)
Conduct symptoms (before the end of high school)	(N = 2,113–2,120)
Stole more than once	17.8
Been in more than one fight that you started	3.3
Involved with youth protection or the police because of own misbehavior	4
Skipped school more than twice in 1 year	47.6
Ran away from home overnight	9.6
Number of conduct symptoms	(N = 2,118)
None	45.1
One	35.8
Two	13
Three	4.4
Four or five	1.7[b]
Adult antisocial behaviors (after finishing or quitting school)	(N = 2,109–2,118)
Fired from a job	9.5
Arrested[a]	1.5
Hit or threw objects at husband/partner	10.6
Trouble at work, with police, with family, or traffic accident due to drugs or alcohol	1.3[b]
Number of adult antisocial symptoms	(N = 2,116)
None	80.9
One	16
Two	2.9
Three or four	0.3[c]

Note. Source: Institut de la Statistique du Québec, ÉLDEQ 1998–2002; [a]Excluding traffic offenses; [b]Coefficient of variation between 15% and 25%, interpret with caution; [c]Coefficient of variation > 25%; estimate is imprecise and given for information only.

and adult antisocial symptoms shows the expected pattern (Table 9.2). For example, 58.9% of mothers with two or more adult antisocial symptoms had at least two conduct symptoms compared with 15.7% of mothers with no adult antisocial symptoms.

Table 9.3 shows the association between the number of maternal CD symptoms and a variety of selected risk factors. The evidence is clear that

TABLE 9.2

Conduct Symptoms by Adult Antisocial Symptoms
for the Mothers,* 1998

	Number of Conduct Symptoms				
Number of adult antisocial symptoms (n)	0	1	2	3–5	Total
Row %					
Column %					
0	844	592	194	75	1705
	49.5	34.7	11.4	4.3	100.0
	88.7	78.4	70.3	58.6	80.8
1	97	145	64	31	337
	28.8	43.0	19.0	9.2^a	100.0
	10.2	19.2	23.2	24.2^a	16.0
2–4	10	18	18	22	68
	14.7^b	26.5^b	26.5^b	32.4^a	100.0
	1.1^b	2.4^b	6.5^b	17.2^a	3.2
Total	951	755	277	128	2110
	45.1	35.8	13.1	6.1	100.0
	100.0	100.0	100.0	100.0	100.0

Note. Institut de la Statistique du Québec, ÉLDEQ 1998–2002; [a]Coefficient of variation between 15% and 25%, interpret with caution; [b]Coefficient of variation > 25%; estimate is imprecise and given for informational purposes only.; * $p < .001$.

TABLE 9.3

Risk Factors (%) by the Number of Maternal Conduct Symptoms, 1998

Variables	Number of Conduct Symptoms (%)				
	0 (955)	1 (759)	2 (275)	3 (129)	p
Socioeconomic Status					
Current age < 20	1.6^c	3.5^b	2.9^c	11.6^c	<0.01
Current age < 25	16.2	25.8	32.0	37.7	<0.001
Had first child when age 19 or younger	7.3	12.9	13.4^b	24.7^b	<0.001
No high school degree	13.5	18.5	18.8	32.2	<0.001
Biological father no longer in the home	7.1	8.6	10.2^b	19.3^b	<.05
Insufficient household income (Statistics Canada definition)	24.5	24	28.4	41.7	<0.01
Substance Use					
Currently daily smoker	14.7	29.1	37.1	40.5	<.001
Used illegal drugs in the past 12 months^a	1.2^c	3.7	4.2^c	13.0^b	<.001
Ever drunk (five or more drinks on one occasion) in past 12 months	9.2	16.2	23.5	31.8	<.001
Prenatal					
Smoked during pregnancy	15	29.4	38.8	50.2	<.001
Used illegal drugs during pregnancy	0.2^c	2.1^c	2.0^c	5.9^c	<.001

Note. Source: Institut de la Statistique du Québec, éLDEQ 1998–2002; [a] From the following list: inhalants; marijuana; cocaine; amphetamines; heroin; opiates; hallucinogens; tranquilizer drugs without a prescription such as barbiturates, ativan, or valium; extasy; [b] Coefficient of variation between 15% and 25%, interpret with caution; [c] Coefficient of variation > 25%; estimate is imprecise and given for informational purposes only.

the infants of the 6% of the mothers who had three or more conduct problems were much more likely to be exposed to a variety of risk factors, including having a teen mother, a mother with less than a high school education, an absent father, poverty, cigarette smoke while in utero, current smoking, and more alcohol and drug use in the home. In addition, depending on the variable, the risk increases with just one symptom of CD. For one item (prenatal smoking), which has been found to be associated with offspring antisocial behavior in a number of studies (Brennan, Grekin, & Mednick, 1999; Fergusson, 1999; Wakschlag et al., 1997; Wasserman, Liu, Pine, & Graziano, 2001), more extensive analyses were carried out using logistic regression. Maternal conduct symptoms were a significant predictor of prental smoking after controlling for maternal adult antisocial symptoms, maternal educational level, maternal self-reported postnatal depression, and low income.

Table 9.4 shows the association between coercive parenting and maternal conduct symptoms on a parenting scale designed specifically for the Quebec study, the Parental Perceptions and Behaviors Regarding the Infant Scale (PPBS). Each item was rated on an 11-point scale, but a frequency distribution of the items suggested the mothers were using the scale dichotomously, generally using the scale point *not at all what I did* for coercive behaviors. The proportion of mothers using this item appears to decrease as the number of conduct symptoms increased (Table 9.4) with the exception of three questions. One question (lost temper) showed a similar trend, but the differences were not significant. The other two items (spanking baby, shaking baby) were rarely endorsed by any of the mothers. However, on other items reflecting maternal warmth (e.g., "I take a really great pleasure in 'talking' [babbling, using baby-talk] with my baby," "I get the impression that my baby is particularly cute compared with other children his/her age," "I often feel the urge to kiss my baby," "I usually feel very great pleasure when holding my baby in my arms," "I feel a very intense joy and I sort of 'melt down' whenever my baby smiles at me"), there were no differences by the number of conduct symptoms (data not shown).

Data on paternal conduct symptoms (stealing more than once, often started fights, arrested, school suspension or expulsion) were also obtained from the father (when not missing), and for a proportion of missing fathers the mother was asked about the father's history of conduct and adult antisocial symptoms (see Appendix 1 for questions). The quantitative association between maternal and paternal conduct symptoms was not straightforward to assess because the probability of an absent father increased with the number of maternal conduct symptoms (Table 9.3). We conducted a simple assessment of the association between paternal and maternal conduct symptoms by examining the association using present fathers. The propor-

TABLE 9.4

Percent of Mothers Reporting "Not At All What I Did" on the Coercive Parenting Scale Items (PPBS) by the Number of Conduct Symptoms, 1998

PPBS Item	Number of Conduct Symptoms (%)				
	0 (935–932)	1 (752–756)	2 (272–275)	3–5 (34–35)	p
I have been angry with my baby when he/she was particularly fussy.	47.0	39.3	39.7	33.2	< 0.01
When my baby cries, he gets on my nerves.	53.0	47.6	47.2	40.2	< 0.05
I have raised my voice or shouted at my baby when he/she was particularly fussy.	63.1	58.6	56.8	47.5	< 0.01
I have spanked my baby when he/she was particularly fussy	95.8	97.3	98.0	96.7	nonsig.
I have lost my temper when my baby/twin was particularly fussy	77.3	75.2	71.6	67.0	nonsig.
I have left my baby alone in his/her bedroom when he/she was particularly fussy.	62.6	54.5	54	41.6	< 0.001
I have shaken my baby when he/she was particularly fussy.	92.1	94.6	92.7	95.4	nonsig.

Note. Source: Institut de la Statistique du Québec, ÉLDEQ 1998–2002.

tion of mothers who had at least two conduct symptoms increased from 12.9% when fathers had no conduct symptoms to 30.7% when fathers had three to four conduct symptoms—a significant difference.

Study 2: The Relationship Among Conduct Disorder, Smoking, and Prenatal Smoking

The relationship among CD, smoking, and prenatal smoking was examined in a sample of teen mothers. This sample was specifically obtained to examine the environment from conception to preschool of children at high risk for conduct disorder. The mothers were recruited from three sites: (a) a public high school for pregnant teens/teen mothers, (b) group homes for girls with behavioral problems, and (c) the Montreal Children's Hospital Adolescent Obstetrics Clinic. In general, the girls were not married, not self-supporting or supported by baby's father, and most had repeated at least one grade of high school. Forty-four percent of the sample met the *DSM–III–R* criteria for CD. One third of the sample had at least one of the following *DSM–III–R* aggressive CD symptoms: started fights, used weapon in fight, or tried to physically hurt someone.

Table 9.5 shows the relationship between CD and prenatal smoking. As the number of CD symptoms increases so does the percentage of mothers who report smoking during the prenatal period. Table 9.6 shows (a) the association between CD and smoking before pregnancy, and (b) the relationship between

TABLE 9.5

Prenatal Smoking and Conduct Symptoms in Adolescent Mothers[a]

Number of Conduct Symptoms (n = 145)	*Smoked During Pregnancy (%)*
0 (19)	31.6
1.00 (35)	42.9
2.00 (27)	55.6
3.00 (25)	60.0
4.00 (15)	80.0
5.00 (13)	76.9
6.00 or more (11)	63.6

[a]Chi-square 13.204 (6); $p < .04$.

TABLE 9.6

**Conduct Disorder, Smoking Before Pregnancy, and Smoking During
Pregnancy Controlling for Smoking Before Pregnancy
in Adolescent Mothers**

Number of Conduct Symptoms	% Who Were Smoking at Least One Cigarette Per Week Before Pregnancy[a] (n = 143)	Smoked During Pregnancy, Among Those Smoking at Least One Cigarette Per Week Before Pregnancy[b] (%) (n = 103)
0 (19)	36.8	85.7
1.00 (35)	58.8	75.0
2.00 (27)	74.1	75.0
3.00 (25)	92.0	65.2
4.00 (15)	86.7	92.3
5.00 (13)	91.7	81.8
6.00 (11)	81.8	77.8

[a]Chi-square 24.039 (6); $p < .001$; [b]Not significant.

smoking before pregnancy and smoking during pregnancy stratified by the number of conduct symptoms. It is clear that CD increases the risk for smoking during pregnancy only through increasing the probability of being a smoker. Once a smoker, however, CD does not increase the risk of smoking during pregnancy because almost all smokers continue to smoke during pregnancy. The implications of this finding are discussed next.

CONCLUSIONS

Methodology

A simple self-administered questionnaire was able to assess conduct symptoms that have considerable construct validity. The prevalence of three or more symptoms is similar to the expected prevalence from other studies, and there is the expected association with adult symptoms. An increasing number of conduct symptoms was also highly associated with a variety of risk factors for adverse child development, and for at least one important variable (prenatal smoking) maternal CD predicted above and beyond adult symptoms and SES. Given that maternal (and paternal) CD symptoms are variables easily and quickly assessed with self-administered questionnaires and strongly related to multiple risk factors, it is clear that future studies of adverse child development (including large-scale epidemiological studies) should include measures of parental CD. Data analysis must also take into account the association among various risk factors and parental CD and account for any confounding when testing particular models of the development of CD.

Risk

There are a number of substantial implications that follow from the findings described earlier. These findings are applicable to experimental designs to test causality and prevention/intervention programs.

First, children of women with CD are exposed to multiple risks from conception onward. In fact, by age 5 months, at least three major putative risk factors for CD are in evidence: antisocial biological father, prenatal exposure to cigarette smoke, and mother with a coercive (hostile) parenting style. These infants also experience more general risk factors such as parents with low educational status. Interventions that begin even in the preschool period occur after the child has been exposed to considerable adversity during a time of rapid development. Viewed from this perspective, intervention that begins with toddlers is not early intervention and certainly not prevention. Intervention and prevention need to be thought as beginning at or even before conception.

Second, research needs to focus on important (although seemingly intractable) risk factors. Two in particular are prenatal smoking and an antisocial biological father. Overcoming the effects of high genetic risk and in utero exposure to tobacco smoke would seem a tall order to even the most comprehensive postnatal prevention programs. There is probably an irreducible limit to what postnatal programs can accomplish. Given this, research in ways to reduce these prenatal risk factors is a priority.

Third, prevention of adverse parenting outcomes of CD should begin in childhood or adolescence. Assortative mating and prenatal smoking are good examples of this. Even most non-CD mothers who smoke at the time of conception continue to smoke, and the differences in rates of prenatal smoking between CD and non-CD mothers are largely explained by differences in preconception smoking rates. This suggests that prevention of prenatal smoking should focus on prevention of initiation of smoking and understanding why girls with CD are much more prone to smoking in the first place. With regard to assortative mating, if viewed as an adult issue, it appears intractable. Nonetheless, there is considerable research on deviant peer selection by boys with CD and evidence that prevention programs for CD in childhood reduce deviant peer selection (Tremblay, Pagani-Kurtz, Masse, Vitaro, & Pihl, 1995; Vitaro, Tremblay, Kerr, Pagani, & Bukowski, 1997). Similar research needs to be carried out with girls to understand why they choose the boys (and later men) they do and how they can be helped to choose nondeviant males.

Fourth, the finding that maternal reports of coercive parenting varies by maternal conduct disorder suggests that the mother's own behavior may play a part in initiating coercive patterns of behavior seen in later years. Other studies have also found a relationship between a history of maternal CD and unresponsive parenting (Cassidy, Zoccolillo, & Hughes, 1996; Hans, Bernstein, & Henson, 1999; Serbin et al., 1998; Wakschlag & Hans, 1999). Studies are needed to clarify how maternal attitudes and parenting from birth onward influence and interact with the infant's behaviors to lead to coercive relationships and disruptive behaviors in the preschool years.

DIRECTIONS FOR FURTHER RESEARCH

Studies of the family environment of parents with a history of CD are few. The advantages and challenges in these studies have already been noted. Some suggestions for further research are noted next.

The Use of Latent Class Modeling

Symptom counts for CD and the artificial threshold of 3 symptoms according to *DSM* criteria do not account for the fact that each symptom varies in sensitivity and specificity (Fergusson, Lynskey, & Horwood, 1996; Zoccolillo, Pickles, Quinton, & Rutter, 1992). The use of such counts and thresholds has resulted in considerable underestimation of continuities between child and adult symptoms.

One technique that is able to correct for the differing sensitivities and specificities of individual symptoms used in classifying individuals into groups (such as the presence/absence of a diagnosis) is latent class analysis (Goodman 1974). With regard to classifying parents into *nonantisocial* versus *antisocial*, LCA is a useful technique because these behaviors are usually measured dichotomously and each symptom differs in sensitivity and specificity (Fergusson, Lynskey, & Horwood, 1996; Zoccolillo, Pickles, Quinton, & Rutter, 1992). These latent classes can be used to measure of a parent's antisociality and then model the association between this true measure and potential risk factors such as prenatal smoking. The advantage of using latent classes is that it is a more accurate method of combining the data from the various antisocial symptoms than simply summing the number of behaviors. Until recently, however, although LCA software programs were able to derive latent classes and model transitions across latent states, using the latent classes as predictor variables was only possible by assigning each individual to his or her latent class using the modal probability, which reintroduced considerable error. However, it is now possible to model the latent classes directly in log-linear models as predictor or response variables, and to model the relationship between two or more latent variables (such as maternal antisociality and offspring disruptive behavior). Useful references include the texts by Hagenaars (1993), Heinen (1996), and Vermunt (1997). Vermunt has a powerful free software program that does log-linear modeling with latent class variables, among many other useful analyses, which is available for downloading at: http://cwis.kub.nl/~fsw_1/mto/mto_snw.htm#software. More recently, Vermunt and Magidson developed a commercial latent class modeling program (Latent GOLD) with a user-friendly interface (information available at www.statisticalinnovations.com).

CD Families as an Important Subject of Study

The study of CD families is both necessary and complex. Nonetheless, there are few studies in this area. What is needed are researchers specifically interested in families with parents with CD and funding agencies willing to subsidize such research. There are precedents for being specifically interested in parents with particular disorders—notably depression and substance abuse. A focus on the broad issue of parents with CD encourages researchers to jointly examine the many risk factors that exist in these families. Understanding the intergenerational transmission of adversity and psychopathology in these families requires theoretical and empirical perspectives and techniques from epidemiology, behavioral genetics, developmental psychology, and classification, among others. Although there may be significant single causal factors, testing any causal theory has to be done in the context of the complexities of life in these families.

Incorporation of CD Questions Into Other Studies

We have demonstrated that parental CD and adult antisocial symptoms can be assessed by a self-administered questionnaire of eight or nine questions (Appendix 1). These questions could be incorporated into other ongoing or planned studies of child development, such as the Canadian National Longitudinal Study of Children and Youth and epidemiological studies of psychiatric disorder in children. The cost would be minimal, but the yield would be substantial. Similarly, studies of high-risk children, whether observational or interventional, would also benefit from incorporating such questions.

Extension to Genetically Informative Designs

Earlier we noted the practical problems in using twin and adoption studies to disentangle gene and environmental effects in families with CD. Nonetheless, once researchers have determined the most important risk factors for study and developed the most effective methods using family studies, efforts should be made to extend the methods to genetically informative designs. One key question that can be addressed without requiring observation from birth is whether heritability estimates for CD differ in twins with CD parents. This would give a better idea of the strength of genetic versus shared environmental effects specific to these families. As to studies from birth, mothers (and fathers where available) of twins from hospitals with large numbers of births can be readily screened using the five conduct disorder symptoms in Appendix 1 and selected for study. Although it would require a large number of births to acquire a large enough sample, the yield from such a study would be substantial in terms of distinguishing true environmental mechanisms.

To conclude, the study of families in which parents had CD is critical to understanding the development and prevention of CD in their offspring and of general theoretical interest as models for the study of nature–nurture integration (Rutter, 1997). These studies are feasible and potentially rich sources of data. What has been lacking is an interest or awareness of the importance of a focus of girls and mothers in the research community in studying such families. Prevention research with these families is also notably absent. It is hoped this chapter has provided both a modest blueprint for such studies and more important, the encouragement to do so.

REFERENCES

American Psychiatric Association. (1980). *Diagnostic and statistical manual of mental disorders*, (3rd ed.). Washington, DC. Author.

American Psychiatric Association. (1987). *Diagnostic and statistical manual of mental disorders*, (3rd ed., rev. ed.). Washington, DC. Author.

American Psychiatric Association. (1994). *Diagnostic and statistical manual of mental disorders*, (4th ed.). Washington, DC: Author.

Bardone, A., Moffitt, T., Caspi, A., & Dickson, N. (1996). Adult mental health and social outcomes of adolescent girls with depression and conduct disorder. *Development & Psychopathology, 8*, 811–829.

Bardone, A., Moffitt, T., Caspi, A., Dickson, N., Stanton, W., & Silva, P. (1998). Adult physical health outcomes of adolescent girls with conduct disorder, depression, and anxiety. *Journal of the American Academy of Child & Adolescent Psychiatry, 37*, 594–601.

Boyle, M. H., Offord, D. R., Racine, Y. A., Fleming, J. E., Szatmari, P., & Links, P. S. (1993). Predicting substance use in early adolescence based on parent and teacher assessments of childhood psychiatric disorder: Results from the Ontario Child Health Study follow-up. *Journal of Child Psychology & Psychiatry & Allied Disciplines, 34*, 535–544.

Brennan, P. A., Grekin, E. R., & Mednick, S. A. (1999). Maternal smoking during pregnancy and adult male criminal outcomes. *Archives of General Psychiatry, 56*, 215–219.

Brent, D. A., Perper, J. A., Moritz, G., Allman, C., Friend, A., Roth, C., Schweers, J., Balach, L., & Baugher, M. (1993). Psychiatric risk factors for adolescent suicide: A case-control study. *Journal of the American Academy of Child & Adolescent Psychiatry, 32*, 521–529.

Cadoret, R. J., Yates, W. R., Troughton, E., Woodworth, G., & Stewart, M. A. (1995). Genetic-environmental interaction in the genesis of aggressivity and conduct disorders. *Archives of General Psychiatry, 52*, 916–924.

Caspi, A., Moffitt, T. E., Newman, D. L., & Silva, P. A. (1996). Behavioral observations at age 3 years predict adult psychiatric disorders. Longitudinal evidence from a birth cohort. *Archives of General Psychiatry, 53*, 1033–1039.

Cassidy, B., Zoccolillo, M., & Hughes, S. (1996). Psychopathology in adolescent mothers and its effects on mother–infant interactions: A pilot study. *Canadian Journal of Psychiatry-Revue Canadienne de Psychiatrie, 41*, 379–384.

Dobkin, P. L., Tremblay, R. E., Masse, L. C., & Vitaro, F. (1995). Individual and peer characteristics in predicting boys' early onset of substance abuse: A seven-year longitudinal study. *Child Development, 66*, 1198–1214.

Eley, T. C., Lichtenstein, P., & Stevenson, J. (1999). Sex differences in the etiology of aggressive and nonaggressive antisocial behavior: Results from two twin studies. *Child Development, 70*, 155–168.

Fagot, B. I., Pears, K. C., Capaldi, D. M., Crosby, L., & Leve, C. S. (1998). Becoming an adolescent father: Precursors and parenting. *Developmental Psychology, 34*, 1209–1219.

Fergusson, D. M. (1999). Prenatal smoking and antisocial behavior [comment]. *Archives of General Psychiatry, 56*, 223–224.

Fergusson, D. M., & Horwood, L. J. (1996). The role of adolescent peer affiliations in the continuity between childhood behavioral adjustment and juvenile offending. *Journal of Abnormal Child Psychology, 24*, 205–221.

Fergusson, D. M., Lynskey, M. T., & Horwood, L. J. (1996). Factors associated with continuity and changes in disruptive behavior patterns between childhood and adolescence. *Journal of Abnormal Child Psychology, 24*, 533–553.

Gjone, H., Stevenson, J., Sundet, J. M., & Eilertsen, D. E. (1996). Changes in heritability across increasing levels of behavior problems in young twins. *Behavior Genetics, 26*, 419–426.

Goodman, L. A. (1974). Exploratory latent structure analysis using both identifiable and unidentifiable models. *Biometrika, 61*, 215–231.

Hagenaars, J. A. (1993). *Loglinear models with latent variables*. Newbury Park, CA: Sage.

Hans, S. L., Bernstein V. J., & Henson L. G. (1999). The role of psychopathology in the parenting of drug-dependent women. *Development and Psychopathology, 11*, 957–977.

Hawkins, J. D., Catalano, R. F., & Miller, J. Y. (1992). Risk and protective factors for alcohol and other drug problems in adolescence and early adulthood: Implications for substance abuse prevention. *Psychological Bulletin, 112*, 64–105.

Heinen, T. (1996). *Latent class and discrete latent trait models*. Thousand Oaks, CA: Sage.

Jensen, P. S., Martin, D., & Cantwell, D. P. (1997). Comorbidity in ADHD: Implications for research, practice, and DSM–V. *Journal of the American Academy of Child & Adolescent Psychiatry, 36*, 1065–1079.

Jette, M., Desrosiers, H., Tremblay, R. E., & Thibault, J. (2000). *Longitudinal Study of Child Development in Quebec (ELDEQ 1998–2002)* (Vol. 1). Quebec: Institut de la statistique du Quebec.

Kovacs, M., Krol, R. S., & Voti, L. (1994). Early onset psychopathology and the risk for teenage pregnancy among clinically referred girls. *Journal of the American Academy of Child & Adolescent Psychiatry, 33*, 106–113.

Krueger, R., Moffitt, T., Caspi, A., Bleske, A., & Silva, P. (1998). Assortative mating for antisocial behavior: Developmental and methodological implications. *Behavior Genetics, 28*, 173–186.

Lahey, B., Hartdagen, S., Frick, P., & McBurnett, K. (1988). Conduct disorder: Parsing the confounded relation to parental divorce and antisocial personality. *Journal of Abnormal Psychology, 97*, 334–337.

Langbehn, D. R., Cadoret, R. J., Yates, W. R., Troughton, E. P., & Stewart, M. A. (1998). Distinct contributions of conduct and oppositional defiant symptoms to adult antisocial behavior: Evidence from an adoption study. *Archives of General Psychiatry, 55*, 821–829.

Little, R. A. & Rubin, D. R. (1987). *Statistical analysis with missing data.* New York: Wiley.

Martin, S. L., & Burchinal, M. R. (1992). Young women's antisocial behavior and the later emotional and behavioral health of their children. *American Journal of Public Health, 82*, 1007–1010.

Moffitt, T. E., & Lynam, D. R. (1994). The Neuropsychology of Conduct Disorder and Delinquency: Implications for Understanding Antisocial Behavior. In D. Fowles, P. Sutker, & S. Goodman (Eds.), *Psychopathy and Antisocial Personality: A Developmental Perspective* (pp. 233–262). Vol. 18 in the series, Progress in Experimental Personality & Psychopathology Research, New York: Springer.

Nagin, D., & Tremblay, R. E. (1999). Trajectories of boys' physical aggression, opposition, and hyperactivity on the path to physically violent and nonviolent juvenile delinquency. *Child Development, 70*, 1181–1196.

Pajer, K. A. (1998). What happens to "bad" girls? A review of the adult outcomes of antisocial adolescent girls. *American Journal of Psychiatry, 155*, 862–870.

Plomin, R. (1997). *Behavioral genetics.* (3rd ed.). New York: W.H. Freeman.

Quinton, D., Rutter, M., & Liddle, C. (1984). Institutional rearing, parenting difficulties and marital support. *Psychological Medicine, 14*, 107–124.

Reid, J., & Patterson, G. (1989). The development of antisocial behaviour patterns in childhood and adolescence. *European Journal of Personality, 3*, 107–119.

Robins, L. N. (1966). *Deviant children grown up.* Baltimore: Williams & Wilkins.

Robins, L. N. (1978). Sturdy childhood predictors of adult antisocial behaviour: Replications from longitudinal studies. *Psychological Medicine, 8*, 611–622.

Robins, L. N., & McEvoy, L. (1990). Conduct problems as predictors of substance abuse. In L. N. Robins & M. Rutter (Eds.), *Straight and deviant pathways from childhood to adulthood* (pp. 182–204). Cambridge, England: Cambridge University Press.

Robins, L. N., Murphy, G. E., Woodruff, R. A. J., & King, L. J. (1971). Adult psychiatric status of black schoolboys. *Archives of General Psychiatry, 24*, 338–345.

Robins, L. N., & Price, R. K. (1991). Adult disorders predicted by childhood conduct problems: Results from the NIMH Epidemiologic Catchment Area project. *Psychiatry, 54*, 116–132.

Robins, L. N., & Regier, D. A. (1991). *Psychiatric disorders in America: The epidemiologic catchment area study.* New York: The Free Press.

Robins, L. N., West, P. A., & Herjanic, B. L. (1975). Arrests and delinquency in two generations: A study of black urban families and their children. *Journal of Child Psychology & Psychiatry & Allied Disciplines, 16*, 125–140.

Rutter, M. (1997). Nature–nurture integration. The example of antisocial behavior. *American Psychologist, 52*, 390–398.

Rutter, M., Silberg, J., O'Connor, T., & Simonoff, E. (1999). Genetics and child psychiatry: II. Empirical research findings. *Journal of Child Psychology & Psychiatry & Allied Disciplines, 40*, 19–55.

Serbin, L. A., Cooperman, J. M., Peters, P. L., Lehoux, P. M., Stack, D. M., & Schwartzman, A. E. (1998). Intergenerational transfer of psychosocial risk in women with childhood histories of aggression, withdrawal, or aggression and withdrawal. *Developmental Psychology, 34*, 1246–1262.

Serbin, L., Peters, P., McAffer, V., & Schwartzman, A. (1991). Childhood aggression and withdrawal as predictors of adolescent pregnancy, early parenthood, and environmental risk for the next generation. *Canadian Journal of Behavioural Science, 23*, 318–331.

Tremblay, R. E., Pagani-Kurtz, L., Masse, L. C., Vitaro, F., & Pihl, R. O. (1995). A bimodal preventive intervention for disruptive kindergarten boys: Its impact through mid-adolescence. *Journal of Consulting & Clinical Psychology, 63*, 560–568.

Vermunt, J. K. (1997). *Log-linear models for event histories.* Thousand Oaks, CA: Sage.

Vitaro, F., & Tremblay, R. E. (1994). Impact of a prevention program on aggressive children's friendships and social adjustment. *Journal of Abnormal Child Psychology, 22*, 457–475.

Vitaro, F., Tremblay, R. E., Kerr, M., Pagani, L., & Bukowski, W. M. (1997). Disruptiveness, friends' characteristics, and delinquency in early adolescence: A test of two competing models of development. *Child Development, 68*, 676–689.

Wakschlag, L. S., Gordon, R., Lahey, B. B., Loeber, R., Green, S., & Leventhal, B. L. (2000). Maternal age at first birth and boys' risk for conduct disorder. *Journal of Research on Adolescence, 10*, 417–441.

Wakschlag, L. S., & Hans, S. L. (1999). Relation of maternal responsiveness during infancy to the development of behavior problems in high-risk youths. *Developmental Psychology, 35*, 569–579.

Wakschlag, L. S., & Hans, S. L. (2000). Early parenthood in context: Implications for development and intervention. In C. Zeanah (Ed.), *Handbook of infant mental health* (2nd ed.).

Wakschlag, L. S., Lahey, B. B., Loeber, R., Green, S. M., Gordon, R. A., & Leventhal, B. L. (1997). Maternal smoking during pregnancy and the risk of conduct disorder in boys. *Archives of General Psychiatry, 54*, 670–676.

Wasserman, G. A., Liu, X., Pine, D. S., & Graziano, J. H. (2001). Contribution of maternal smoking during pregnancy and lead exposure to early child behavior problems. *Neurotoxicology & Teratology, 23*, 13–21.

Woodward, L. J. & Fergusson, D. M. (1999). Early conduct problems and later risk of teenage pregnancy in girls. *Development & Psychopathology, 11*, 127–141.

Zoccolillo, M. (1992). Co-occurrence of conduct disorder and its adult outcomes with depressive and anxiety disorders: A review. *Journal of the American Academy of Child & Adolescent Psychiatry, 31*, 547–556.

Zoccolillo, M. (1993). Gender issues in conduct disorder. *Development & Psychopathology, 5*, 65–78.

Zoccolillo, M. (2000). Parents' health and social adjustment: Part II. Social adjustment. In M. Jette, H. Desrosiers, R. E. Tremblay, & J. Thibault (Eds.), *Longitudinal study of child development in Quebec (ELDEQ 1998–2002).* Quebec: Institut de la statistique du Quebec.

Zoccolillo, M., Meyers, J., & Assiter, S. (1997). Conduct disorder, substance dependence, and adolescent motherhood. *American Journal of Orthopsychiatry, 67*, 152–157.

Zoccolillo, M., Pickles, A., Quinton, D., & Rutter, M. (1992). The outcome of childhood conduct disorder: Implications for defining adult personality disorder and conduct disorder. *Psychological Medicine, 22*, 971–986.

Zoccolillo, M., Price, R. K., Hwu, H. G., & Ji, T. (1998). Antisocial personality disorder: Comparisons of prevalence, symptoms, and correlates in four countries. In C. Slomkowski, P. Cohen, & L. N. Robins (Eds.), *Where and when: Historical and geographic effects on psychopathology* (pp. 249–277). Mahwah, NJ: Lawrence Erlbaum Associates.

Zoccolillo, M., & Rogers, K. (1991). Characteristics and outcome of hospitalized adolescent girls with conduct disorder. *Journal of the American Academy of Child & Adolescent Psychiatry, 30*, 973–981.

10

Girls' Aggression Across the Life Course: Long-Term Outcomes and Intergenerational Risk

Dale M. Stack
Lisa A. Serbin
Alex E. Schwartzman
Department of Psychology, Concordia University

Jane Ledingham
Child Study Centre and Department of Psychology,
University of Ottawa

ABSTRACT

This chapter focuses on girls' aggression across the life course, specifically examining the long-term outcomes of girls' aggression. The participants in the studies discussed herein come from a large disadvantaged, community-based research sample of families—the Concordia Longitudinal Risk Project. This study is unusual: It includes a large sample of girls and boys within each of the risk profiles (e.g., aggressive, withdrawn, aggressive, and withdrawn) based on comparisons to their same-gender peers. This ongoing intergenerational study commenced in 1976–1978 when the participants were elementary school-age children. Currently, these individuals are parents of young children. The chapter is organized temporally through childhood, adolescence, and young adulthood, extending to the early outcomes for the offspring of the aggressive girls. We first describe the trajectories of highly aggressive girls in the Concordia sample in middle childhood, adolescence, and early adulthood. We then examine a number of outcomes predicted from aggression when the girls have become parents, including maternal health, parenting and environment, and developmental and health outcomes for the offspring. We conclude the chapter by positing some important conclusions and implications, and proposing recommendations for intervention and policy based on our results to date.

GIRLS' AGGRESSION ACROSS THE LIFE COURSE: LONG-TERM OUTCOMES

For many years, aggression in girls was a relatively neglected topic in the research literature. This pattern has begun to change as it becomes clear that aggression in girls may predict patterns of negative adolescent and adult outcomes that are distinct from the overt delinquency and other long-term outcomes typical of aggressive boys. Some of the disturbing recent events in Canada and the United States (e.g., chronic bullying in schools leading to child suicides and homicides) that have been reflected in the media illustrate the problems and challenges we face, as well as the serious and often tragic outcomes. Problems of a psychosocial nature in children and families exact a tragic toll; there is a cost for our children, their families, and society in general. Understanding how aggression begins, how it develops, and its stability across the developmental course in both sexes is currently an important focus of longitudinal research projects. In the present chapter, we focus on a Canadian study of long-term sequelae of girlhood aggression in the context of a broad range of negative psychosocial and health outcomes, including difficulties in parenting and the intergenerational transfer of risk to offspring. Moderating influences, contextual factors, and buffers contributing to resiliency in aggressive children as they mature are also examined.

Aggression has traditionally been characterized as a primarily male phenomenon with stability of gender differences observed across the life span. Research attention has been directed toward physical and overt manifestations of aggression, leaving indirect and covert expressions of aggression relatively neglected. The fact that males are considered to be more physically aggressive than females does not imply that females engage in fewer conflictual relations or experience decreased hostility (Björkqvist, 1994; Crick & Grotpeter, 1995). Perhaps as a result of females being generally physically weaker than males, and also due to social constraints, they may develop alternate strategies to achieve their desired ends, engaging in verbal or indirect aggression. These latter forms of aggression have been referred to as *relational*, and include attempts to harm others by means of causing damage to the others' friendships or sense of inclusion in the associated peer group. Developmental change also characterizes girls' aggression. Although they continue to use direct confrontation, emerging adolescent women also tend to exhibit social ostracism as a central feature of their expression of aggression (Cairns, Cairns, Neckerman, Ferguson, & Gariepy, 1989).

If relational forms of aggression are considered together with overt aggression (physical and verbal), the rate of aggressive behavior observed in men and women becomes closer to equal (Crick & Grotpeter, 1995), implying that the variety of forms of aggression should be considered (Fry & Gabriel, 1994). Being sensitive to developmental changes and corresponding variations in the manifestation of aggressive behaviors helps document the continuity of these behavioral tendencies over time.

Evidence to support the contention that a considerable degree of stability exists in aggressive response styles over time is readily available (Elder, Caspi, & Downey, 1986; Farrington, 1994; Huesmann, Eron, Lefkowitz, & Walder, 1984; Moskowitz, Schwartzman, & Ledingham, 1985; Olweus, 1984; Pulkkinen & Pitkanen, 1993). However, consistent differences in the stability of aggression for each gender have not been found. When greater stability in aggression has been shown for males relative to females, explaining these differences has in part been attributed to the ways in which aggression has been defined and assessed (Björkqvist & Niemëla, 1992; Huesmann et al., 1984). Therefore, it is important to examine and study developmental patterns of expression of girls' aggression over time.

One of the ways in which researchers have studied manifestations or expressions of aggression over time is to examine risk-taking behavior. For example, a pattern of high-risk sexual behavior in adolescence has been documented in a number of prospective longitudinal studies of aggressive girls (e.g., Cairns & Cairns, 1994; Scaramella, Conger, Simons, & Whitbeck, 1998; Serbin, Peters, McAffer, & Schwartzman, 1991), including the age of onset of sexual activity and early pregnancy. It may be that early aggression is predictive of high-risk sexual activity for both genders (Capaldi, Crosby, & Stoolmiller, 1996). In boys, however, the established pattern of childhood aggression as a predictor of ongoing delinquency and crime has been of primary interest in the literature (Capaldi, 1992; Conger, Elder, Lorenz, Simons, & Whitbeck, 1994; Farrington, 1991; Magnusson, 1988).

For girls opportunities to engage in criminal activity outside the home may be somewhat limited by their family roles once they become mothers. As such they may be more apt to express their aggression within the family setting. Patterns of sequential comorbidity of conduct disorders with internalizing disorders, such as anxiety and depression, are also reported in girls as they mature. A growing literature from many countries confirms this trajectory. Studies from the United States and the United Kingdom suggest that girls' aggression in childhood may develop into internalizing problems in adolescence and adulthood, such as depression (Robins, 1986;

Zoccolillo, Pickles, Quinton, & Rutter, 1992). These problems continue at least into mid-adulthood. For example, in Finland, aggressive girls grow up to secure lower ranked jobs and have instability in their occupations, frequently changing jobs (Pulkkinen & Pitkanen, 1993). Although the specifics might change in different sociocultural contexts, psychosocial problems, internalizing disorders, and other negative sequelae are consistently reported and persist over time.

A Longitudinal Study of Aggression in Canada

The Concordia Longitudinal Risk Project is a prospective longitudinal study of aggressive girls and boys crossing three generations. It began when the children were in elementary school, and continued throughout their adolescence and into adulthood. As the participants have become parents, we have had the opportunity to study the offspring from the original sample. Findings from the Concordia study have consistently shown relatively high stability of aggression and withdrawal for both girls and boys (Moskowitz et al., 1985; Serbin, Moskowitz, Schwartzman, & Ledingham, 1991; Serbin, Peters, & Schwartzman, 1996). Aggression appears to be a general risk factor for diverse negative outcomes within the sample of participants from the Concordia project, and high levels of social withdrawal in childhood can modulate the developmental trajectory of aggression. In the Concordia study, *aggression* was defined as behaviors that attempt to harm either through verbal or physical means (Björkqvist & Niemëla, 1992; McCord, 1988; Moskowitz & Schwartzman, 1989; Moskowitz, Schwartzman, & Ledingham, 1985) based on peer nominations, whereas *social withdrawal* referred to behaviors that are socially isolating and can be associated with avoidance and fear (Moskowitz & Schwartzman, 1989). Aggression and social withdrawal can also be conceptualized by framing them in terms of underlying emotion-regulation processes, representing undercontrolled or overcontrolled emotional responses (Salovey & Sluyter, 1997) for aggression and social withdrawal, respectively.

In contrast with aggression, social withdrawal has been rarely studied as a predictor of outcomes within disadvantaged populations. It may predict the adoption of traditional life styles in women: specifically marriage, childbearing, and homemaking as a career (Caspi, Bem, & Elder, 1989). Although more might be known about the stability and consequences of aggression relative to social withdrawal, research suggests that both patterns of behavior can have negative sequelae throughout the life course depending on social, educational, and economic contexts (e.g., Huesmann et al., 1984). The combined pattern of aggression and withdrawal, which was identified and followed in the Concordia study, has generally shown extremely problematic outcomes during adolescence and early adulthood in most areas of functioning in both the women and men in the sample (e.g., school failure, substance abuse, internalizing problems) and an elevated pattern of gynecological and reproductive difficulties in the women. Aggression and social withdrawal additively reduce the likelihood of academic success (Bardone, Moffitt, Caspi, Dickson, & Silva, 1996; Caspi, Elder, & Bem, 1988; Schwartzman, Ledingham, & Serbin, 1985; Serbin et al., 1998). Through lowered educational attainment, they also indirectly increase the chances of financial disadvantage across the life course (Kokko, Sutherland, Lindstroem, Reynolds, & Mackenzie, 1998; Serbin et al., 1998). Both lower educational attainment and poverty are known to limit parents' access to social resources. Parental academic competence has also been shown to be linked with their offsprings' subsequent academic competence (Cairns, Cairns, Xie, Leung, & Hearne, 1998).

In the studies described in this chapter, extreme patterns of childhood aggression and the pattern of elevated aggression and withdrawal in combination were examined as predictors of a variety of later risks. A general hypothesis underlies our work: Aggression in girls, particularly aggression combined with withdrawn behavior, is related to ongoing problems in socioemotional functioning, impaired health, and difficulties in interpersonal relations across the life course. These problems are currently being examined from childhood into the formation of new families. At adolescence, childhood aggression was expected to be associated with lower academic ability, high school dropout, and elevated rates of risk taking (e.g., drugs and alcohol, early and unprotected sexual activity, smoking). In late adolescence and early adulthood, aggression was expected to influence timing and perinatal circumstances of becoming a parent and subsequent patterns of childbearing. Further, it was anticipated that girls with histories of childhood aggression would have difficulty becoming responsive and nurturing parents. When both aggression and withdrawal were high in childhood, social withdrawal was expected to add to the difficulties associated with childhood aggression.

In specifically considering the trajectories of women's lives, longitudinal studies must consider the importance of parenthood and parenting. Early parenthood, which is a major risk for girls from economically and socially disadvantaged backgrounds (Hechtman, 1989; Musick, 1993), has the potential to change young girls' lives in substantial and lasting ways. Teen parenthood is related to lower occupational status and a variety of psychosocial problems for women across their subsequent life course (Furstenberg, Brooks-Gunn, & Chase-Lansdale, 1989). Negative long-term outcomes for teen mothers are particularly likely if these young women are prevented from completing high school or continuing their education because of successive, closely spaced pregnancies and ensuing family responsibilities (Layzer, St. Pierre, & Bernstein, 1996). Problematic parenting is one important aspect of the life difficulties of aggressive girls as young adults.

The potential negative consequences of early parenthood are not restricted to young mothers, but include their offspring as well (Conger et al., 1994). Circumstances of birth play a major role in determining the child's future (Baldwin & Cain, 1980; Hardy et al., 1997; Hechtman, 1989; Layzer et al., 1996; Whitman, Borkowski, Schellenbach, & Nath, 1987). Mothers' health, physical and emotional maturity, education, and family support are all important predictors of their children's health and development. As the child confronts challenges throughout infancy and early childhood, the mother's resources and parenting ability have an ongoing impact on developmental outcomes for her offspring. In a longitudinal context of prediction from earlier events, birth circumstances, perinatal health of mother and infant, and parenting may be conceptualized as important points of transition and intergenerational transfer of risk, with implications for the future health and functioning of the entire family.

The present chapter examines the long-term outcomes of girls' aggression. It is organized temporally through childhood, adolescence, and young adulthood, extending to the early outcomes for the offspring of these aggressive girls. In the first section, we describe the sample that forms the Concordia Longitudinal Risk Project. In the next section, we describe the trajectories of highly aggressive girls in the Concordia sample in middle childhood, adolescence, and early adulthood. In the subsequent sections, we examine a number of outcomes predicted from aggression when the girls have become parents: (a) maternal health, parenting, and environment; and (b) developmental and health outcomes in the offspring. We then briefly summarize, posit some important conclusions and implications, and propose recommendations for intervention and policy based on our results to date.

THE CONCORDIA LONGITUDINAL RISK PROJECT

Overview of the Concordia Longitudinal Project: Design and Early Findings

The participants in the studies reviewed in this chapter come from a large, community-based research sample of disadvantaged families whose average income level and occupational status, for the most part, are significantly below the average levels for Canada and Quebec. This ongoing intergenerational study was begun by Jane Ledingham and Alex

Schwartzman (Ledingham, 1981; Schwartzman et al., 1985) in 1976–1978, when the parents of the current young participants were elementary school- age children.

Identification of the Original Sample

The Concordia project began in the school years 1976–1977 and 1977–1978 with the screening of 4,109 francophone school children attending regular Grade 1, 4, and 7 classes in French-language schools. These children lived in lower socioeconomic, inner-city neighborhoods of Montreal, Canada. Participation in the screening was voluntary, with over 95% of students consenting to participate; 1,770 children met the criteria for inclusion, including approximately equal numbers of boys ($n = 861$) and girls ($n = 909$) from each grade level.

The screening process involved the classification of children along the dimensions of aggression and withdrawal by means of a French translation of the Pupil Evaluation Inventory (PEI; Pekarik, Prinz, Liebert, Weintraub, & Neale, 1976), a peer nomination instrument. The PEI consists of 34 items that load onto three factors: *Aggression*, *Withdrawal*, and *Likeability*. Scale items assess not only the behavior of the child, but also peer's reactions toward the child. For the purpose of the Concordia project, children were screened only on the Aggression and Withdrawal factors. Approximately half of the original participants had elevated risk profiles due to extreme patterns of atypical behavior, whereas the other half of the sample was normative in terms of social behavior, but came from the same inner-city classrooms and disadvantaged neighborhoods.

Within each classroom, boys and girls were rated in separate administrations. Children were asked to nominate up to four boys and four girls in their class who best matched each item on the PEI. The number of nominations received by each child was summed for the Aggression and Withdrawal factors. These total scores were then subjected to a square root transformation to decrease skewness. Finally, transformed scores were converted to z scores for each sex, within each classroom to control for class size and gender differences in base rates of aggression and withdrawal. This procedure enabled appropriate comparisons of each child against the relevant norms for gender and age.

Percentile cutoffs were established to identify children who exhibited extreme scores on the Aggression and/or Withdrawal scales while enabling adequate sample sizes for statistical analysis. Children who scored above the 95th percentile on Aggression and below the 75th percentile on Withdrawal, relative to same-sex classmates, were selected for the aggressive group ($n = 101$ girls, 97 boys); the reverse criteria were used to select the withdrawn group ($n = 112$ girls, 108 boys). As a function of the low probability of achieving extreme scores on both dimensions, more liberal criteria were used to identify a sufficient number of children to form the aggressive– withdrawn group. Z scores equal to or above the 75th percentile on both Aggression and Withdrawal were criteria for membership in this group ($n = 129$ girls, 109 boys). Finally, age-matched children for whom z scores on Aggression and Withdrawal scales fell in the average range (i.e., between the 25th and 75th percentile) were selected for the contrast group ($n = 567$ girls; 547 boys). For a more extensive description of the original methodology, see Schwartzman and colleagues (1985; Ledingham, 1981; Ledingham & Schwartzman, 1981).

Unlike most longitudinal studies of childhood aggression or other childhood behavior problems, this is a community-based (rather than a clinical) sample. Using a community sample avoids the selection biases inherent in clinic-referred samples and is more representative of the Quebec population as a whole. However, unlike most other longitudinal studies of children from disadvantaged communities, specific atypical patterns of social behavior (i.e., aggression and withdrawal) were initially identified and could be followed as predictors within a population at high risk for psychosocial problems.

Another unique feature of the original design was the inclusion of an approximately equal number of girls and boys within each of the risk profiles based on comparisons to their same-sex peers. Consequently, the Concordia study is one of the few longitudinal studies worldwide that has followed a large sample of aggressive girls into adulthood. Due to the nature of the design, with some participants having patterns of atypical behavior and others with normative patterns of behavior, we are able to observe those factors that are predictive of positive adaptation—an important focus of recent research on risk and resiliency.

As the original participants reach their late 20s to early 30s, many have become parents. Although the study of offspring and the intergenerational transfer of risk was not originally planned, this opportunity now exists. Given the unique nature of the sample, the longitudinal data set, and the likelihood that parenting may be a particularly important outcome measure, intergenerational studies of the offspring of the Concordia sample were begun virtually as soon as children began to be born in the late 1980s (Serbin et al., 1991). The results to date strongly suggest that psychosocial risk may be transferred between generations via the behavior, functioning, environment, and socioeconomic circumstances of the participants as they become parents (Serbin et al., 1991, 1996, 1998, 2002).

Children growing up in disadvantaged conditions are likely to become the parents of another disadvantaged generation who, like their parents, are born with a high risk of serious psychosocial and health problems. However, longitudinal studies reveal that psychosocial risk is, as the term denotes, probabilistic. Many children from high-risk backgrounds grow up to have reasonably prosperous and productive lives despite their poor prospects at birth (Elder & Caspi, 1988; Furstenberg, Brooks-Gunn, & Morgan, 1987; Hardy et al., 1997; Rutter, 1987; Werner & Smith, 1992).

The general objective of our research is to identify risk and protective factors—those factors that predict maladaptive and adaptive adjustment—in a prospective longitudinal study of two generations. How girls' aggression is manifested across development, particularly the psychosocial, lifestyle, and health sequelae of girls' aggression, is underscored. The pathways through which aggression develops and the transfer across generations are also important foci.

TRAJECTORIES FOLLOWED BY HIGHLY AGGRESSIVE GIRLS IN THE CONCORDIA SAMPLE IN MIDDLE CHILDHOOD, ADOLESCENCE, AND EARLY ADULTHOOD

Beginning at the original point of identification of the Concordia sample in elementary school, the risk trajectory of aggression in girls has proved to be distinctive, although there are also many similarities between aggressive girls' and aggressive boys' experiences. Recall that the highly aggressive girls in the sample were defined according to gender-based norms: That is, they were more aggressive than the other girls in their class according to peer ratings. However, it was the highly aggressive boys who were described by peers in terms of a profile underlining public, disruptive behavior perceived as intrusive, uncontrolled, and immature (Schwartzman, Verlaan, Peters, & Serbin, 1995).

A second major consideration in projecting trajectories for aggressive girls is that at the time of identification the highly aggressive children of both sexes were likely to have lower IQs and lower standardized academic achievement test scores than either comparison or withdrawn group children (Ledingham, 1981; Schwartzman et al., 1985). In other words, aggression was associated with academic and cognitive difficulties in both sexes beginning as early as first grade. The joint constellation of aggression and withdrawal was particularly problematic, and this group of children had the lowest average IQ and school achievement scores in the sample.

In a first follow-up study of academic outcomes 3 years after identification, there were few gender differences in terms of the school progress of highly aggressive children: Both aggressive girls and boys were more likely to have repeated a grade or to have been placed in a special class for children with behavioral or learning problems. Approximately 41% of the highly aggressive children had repeated a grade within 3 years or had been placed in a special class, whereas 48% of the highly aggressive and withdrawn group repeated a grade (compared with 17% of the normative comparison children and 25% of the withdrawn group; Schwartzman et al., 1985). These failure rates continued into high school, with the original aggression scores predicting elevated rates of high school dropout for both sexes and the aggressive–withdrawn group failing at the highest rates. In other words, aggression was clearly a negative predictor of academic success within both short and long-term time frames especially if combined with other social and academic problems.

Aggression in elementary school-age girls was not solely problematic in terms of its association with lower cognitive or academic ability. Girls' aggression in elementary school continued to predict high school dropout even when academic ability scores were controlled statistically (Serbin et al., 1998). In other words, early aggression predicted later school dropout, even when children's cognitive and academic abilities were not impaired. Beginning in elementary school, the social and behavioral pathways to academic failure for girls and boys were somewhat different.

In an observational study of a sample of 174 fifth- and sixth-grade children on the playground (a younger group identified from among the same schools and using the same methods as the original Concordia project; Lyons, Serbin, & Marchessault, 1988; Serbin, Lyons, Marchessault, Schwartzman, & Ledingham, 1987; Serbin, Marchessault, McAffer, Peters, & Schwartzman, 1993), we found that peer-nominated aggressive girls and boys were more physically aggressive during play than nonaggressive children of either sex. In general, relatively few episodes of explicit or extreme aggression or violence were observed during this study of social interaction during recess periods. Most aggressive events were incorporated into episodes of rough-and-tumble play (e.g., tackling, pushing, hitting, or kicking during games or lining-up, etc.). The peer-identified aggressive girls spent much of their time playing with boys engaged in rough-and-tumble play behavior (an atypical behavior pattern for girls at this age), and most of their observed aggressive acts were directed at boys (rather than other girls).

Aggressive play is a much more normative pattern among boys in general than among girls (Serbin et al., 1993), and the peer-identified aggressive girls appeared to be integrating (or attempting to integrate) into primarily male play groups. Gender segregation is a well-documented social pattern among children of this age on the playground (see Maccoby, 1998; Serbin, Powlishta, & Gulko, 1993), and again the aggressive group of girls seemed to be violating a social norm with regard to their preferred play partners. Interestingly, although aggressive group boys were generally liked by their same-sex classmates, aggressive girls were disliked by other girls. Most disliked, among both sexes, however, were the aggressive–withdrawn children. These children, of both sexes, attracted more peer-initiated aggressive attacks on the playground than other children (Lyons, Serbin, & Marchessault, 1988; Serbin et al., 1987, 1993).

To summarize, girls' aggression in the later elementary school grades was associated with a preference for male playmates who were likely to reciprocate the rough play style, and this physical, rough-and-tumble style of play was disliked by other girls. This pattern of associating with boys, especially those with aggressive play styles, and being avoided by girls may be a core element in the subsequent development of aggressive girls. Girls who are drawn to peer groups that engage in aggression and other types of risk-taking behavior in elementary school may expand their repertoire of deviant behavior as they mature following the norms and values of their peer subgroup.

In early and mid-adolescence, girls' aggression was associated with elevated rates of self-reported smoking, alcohol, and illegal drug usage, suggesting that these girls continue to seek out behaviorally compatible peer groups probably comprised of boys and girls with similar aggressive or predelinquent behavioral styles if not actively engaging in delinquent behavior. In general, the aggressive girls report far less overt criminal or violent behavior than the aggressive boys during adolescence as reflected in their much lower arrest records (Schwartzman & Mohan, 1999). However, they do have a higher arrest rate in their late teens than other girls, and their self-reported risk-taking behavior such as smoking and drug use indicates a likelihood of continuing negative life trajectories.

As reported earlier, aggressive girls were more likely to drop out of high school than other girls, and this could not be attributed solely to their poorer academic or intellectual abilities. Rather the behavioral component in these equations seems to affect school success via patterns of peer relations, socioemotional problems, and risk-taking behavior as discussed previously. Once they have dropped out of high school, risk of early parenthood is greatly elevated (Serbin et al., 1998).

Another aspect of the risk-taking behavior and peer relations typical of the highly aggressive girls in the Concordia sample relates to their sexual behavior during adolescence. Examining the adolescent health care records of 853 women, childhood aggression predicted elevated frequencies of gynecological problems and acute infections between 11 and 17 years of age and of STDs and childbearing between the ages of 14 and 20 (Serbin et al., 1991). In other words, girls' childhood aggression seems to have predicted early, unprotected sexual activity during the teen years. This pattern continued into late adolescence and early adulthood, when teen parenthood, multiparity (defined as having more than one child by age 23), close spacing of successive births (less than 2 years apart), and obstetric and delivery complications were elevated risks for girls with childhood histories of aggression, especially those with a combined history of aggression and withdrawal (Serbin et al., 1998).

These fertility patterns are associated with problematic subsequent histories for both parents and children as opportunities for continuing education and higher occupational status are curtailed, along with a probability of lower income across the life course (Furstenberg et al., 1987, 1989). For offspring the risks extend to physical health and lack of socioeconomic support during the important prenatal period and continuing throughout childhood. As discussed next in the section describing outcomes for offspring, these concerns for the health of offspring of highly aggressive women, especially those born to teen mothers, were confirmed in an examination of their pediatric medical records.

Finally, mental health outcomes for highly aggressive girls were examined in late adolescence and early adulthood. Interestingly and consistent with the relatively low rates of criminal behavior in late adolescence and early adulthood by the women in the aggressive and aggressive–withdrawn groups, these peer-identified patterns were not associated with CD per se, but were predictive of elevated rates of depression and anxiety disorders (e.g., Schwartzman et al., 1995). In other words, aggression in girls appears to predict internalizing disorders in early adulthood, along with histories of adolescent risk-taking behavior (e.g., smoking, alcohol use, substance abuse, and unprotected sexual activity) as well as early school leaving and parenthood. We are currently studying the mental health status of the Concordia project participants as they complete the *vulnerability* period for major mental illness in early adulthood (i.e., mid-30s), and will have more information on rates of specific disorders within the next few years.

Some Implications for Continuing Adult Development and the Intergenerational Transfer of Risk

The stress associated with the lifestyle suggested by these histories is probably considerable: involving incremental social, economic, and educational disadvantage across adolescence, and the likelihood of early parenthood with inadequate social, emotional, and financial support. This cumulative and acute stress may, in part, account for the elevated rates of mental health problems in these women. Within other longitudinal samples, the lifetime probabilities of low occupational status, frequent job changes, welfare status, single parenthood, and marital instability are all likely to be elevated in women with histories of childhood aggression (Pulkkinen & Pitkanen, 1993). Because relationships and social support are an important part of this picture, it is also not surprising that girls with childhood histories of aggression are likely to form adult relationships with male partners having similar behavioral styles to their own (Peters, 1999). Undoubtedly these cumulative social, educational, emotional, occupational, and economic problems in early adulthood contribute to ongoing mental and physical health difficulties, along with many other problems of social-psychological adjustment. The long-term problems of aggressive girls cannot, however, be entirely attributed to their elevated risk for school dropout, early parenthood, and other stressful socioeconomic conditions. As we discuss later, childhood aggression seems to reflect a stable behavioral style that continues to influence social relations into adulthood, including marital interaction patterns and parent–child relationships.

PREDICTING MATERNAL HEALTH, PARENTING, AND ENVIRONMENT

It is clear from the preceding section that the aggressive girls in the Concordia sample demonstrate risk-taking behavior and aberrant peer relations across their development through to the end of adolescence and into young adulthood. Beyond the mothers' health records, one important route through which children are placed at risk is through the pre-, peri-, and postnatal care and environments provided to the developing child. These are considered to be important for healthy development (e.g., Casaer, deVries, & Marlow, 1991; Prechtl, 1968). The factors that surround the birth of the child can include numerous potentially important variables, ranging from nutritional status prior to conception and during pregnancy, substance ingestion during pregnancy, prematurity, birth weight, medical status at birth, birth trauma, delivery complications, length of hospitalization, multiparity, chronic illness, injuries, and the family and home environment after birth. These factors are all associated with important outcomes in terms of children's health and development. Thus, when a risk event occurs (prepregnancy, at conception, during prenatal development, during the perinatal period, or following birth), it is often interrelated with developmental outcomes (Kopp & Kaler, 1989).

Adverse conditions during early development are clearly important considerations that can affect children's long-term health and developmental outcomes. Pre-, peri-, and postbirth factors may be elevated or complicated by poverty and teenage pregnancy. For example, prepregnancy risks such as maternal chronic illness, history of drug use, and poor nutrition during childhood may cyclically occur in generations of people who are economically disadvantaged (Kopp & Kaler, 1989). Education is another means through which these factors may operate. Maternal education has been found to be correlated with parenting behavior and child outcome in numerous studies (e.g., Auerbach, Lerner, Barasch, & Palti, 1992; Serbin et al., 1998). Thus, there may be pathways of risk that include income, education, medical or health, status, emotional health, and home environment factors through which child outcome is affected (e.g., Berlin, 1997). As an endpoint in this cumulative process, the importance of the rearing environment cannot be overlooked because it has been shown to be a powerful determinant of subsequent outcome (e.g., Werner & Smith, 1992).

In the current phase of the Concordia project, we were interested in identifying specific characteristics of the family situation, parents, and/or child that promote adjustment in the face of psychosocial disadvantage. Previous studies have emphasized the role of parental education as a protective factor (Auerbach et al., 1992; Furstenberg et. al., 1987; Serbin et al., 1998). In this phase, we examined additional variables such as parental characteristics, family relationships, and the availability of social support because previous research (e.g., Cowen, Wyman, Work, & Parker, 1990; McLoyd, 1990) indicates that these variables may represent important buffers against negative outcomes. For purposes of the present chapter, we report on girls' childhood social behavior patterns—specifically aggression and aggression combined with social withdrawal—as predictors of maternal obstetric history and health, family risk variables, parenting, and home environment.

Predicting Maternal Health

Maternal health behaviors and symptoms in adults may vary as a function of childhood risk status, indicating that childhood social behavior may help predict future health outcomes and transmission of risk to the next generation. Girls who are seen as aggressive by their peers may develop different health habits and patterns of physical ailments, which may in turn affect the physical environments for their future children. Mothers who were aggressive in childhood were more likely to have smoked during their pregnancies (de Genna, 2001). Current maternal smoking in mothers of toddlers and preschoolers, which may have an impact on these mothers' and children's current and future health, was predicted by maternal childhood aggression. Moreover, maternal childhood aggression predicted maternal respiratory complaints including at least one experience of asthma, bronchitis, pneumonia, and sinusitis (in the mothers) 3 months prior to the time of our evaluation. Based on regression equations, the effects of childhood aggression on maternal health were above and beyond the effects of current maternal smoking. Finally, mothers high on both childhood aggression and withdrawal were more likely to currently suffer from hematological irregularities with lifestyle implications such as anemia, hypoglycemia, and diabetes.

Taken together, our findings suggest that the trajectories through which girls' aggression and the combination of aggression and withdrawal leads ultimately affect the health of the girls when they are becoming parents and that the process through which this is occurring is through their lifestyles. That is, risk-taking behavior (e.g., timing of sexual activity, early pregnancy) was shown to affect health problems in the young mothers. These health problems also affect their offsprings' developmental outcomes and health and contribute to the home environment. In essence, the offspring's long-term lifestyles are affected by mothers' health problems.

Predicting Parenting and Home Environment

Beyond health factors, the mother–child relationship and parenting are important contributors to the environment which the child grows and the child's socialization and development. As a result, in our search for important parenting and family variables that may place the offspring of the Concordia project participants at risk, one primary focus has been the mother–child relationship. The relationship between mother and child has been understood as one of the most important in the life of a child. It is within the context of early relationships that children develop skills and strategies that serve them for the rest of their lives (Bowlby, 1980). When this relationship is adaptive, children are likely to emerge well adjusted and free from major pathology. When this relationship is disrupted, however, be it through maternal psychosocial difficulty, maternal pathology, and/or family dysfunction, children are placed at risk for psychosocial disturbances (Beardslee, Bemporad, Keller, & Klerman, 1983; Caspi & Elder, 1988a, 1988b; Dumas, LaFreniere, & Serketich, 1995; Hammen et al., 1987; Patterson, 1982). During the first 3 years of life, important attachment processes and emotional organization take place (Emde, 1989; Fogel, 1993; Sameroff & Seifer, 1992). A parent's ability to be emotionally available, responsive, and attentive during these early years ultimately impacts the developmental outcome of his or her child (Biringen & Robinson, 1991; Egeland & Erickson, 1987). In considering whether mothers' childhood aggression might interfere with their abilities to effectively parent their young children, we explored unresponsive parenting toward infants, toddlers, and school-age offspring to see whether these would be apparent in mothers' interactions with their children.

In one study (Cooperman, 1996; Serbin et al., 1998), 84 women from the original sample together will their eldest children (5–12 years of age) participated in four videotaped laboratory tasks. The four laboratory tasks used in this study were selected so that a range of typical mother–child interaction scenarios might be observed. They included a free-play task, a teaching task, a negotiation task, and, finally, a conflict discussion task. The order of the tasks was designed to gradually move mother–child dyads from a relatively stress-free, optional interaction situation to a potentially anxiety-provoking, highly interactive, confrontational scenario in which a topic that provoked conflict between members of the dyad was selected for discussion. The sequence of the activities, save for the presence of the first task, was drawn from the work of Granger, Weisz, and Kanneckis (1994).

Using this paradigm, we examined whether maternal psychosocial difficulties in childhood would be predictive of reduced support, aggressivity, and unresponsiveness as indexes of maladaptive behaviors in interactions with their offspring. In general, both childhood aggression and maternal education proved to be independent predictors of maternal behavior. Aggression was predictive of unresponsive maternal behavior, whereas lower education predicted mothers' aggressive behavior toward offspring, lack of supportive behavior, and unresponsiveness.

We also examined whether mothers' psychosocial difficulties during childhood would predict maladaptive behavior patterns by offspring during the observed interactions. Children's behaviors of restlessness, aggressivity, and unresponsiveness toward their mothers were coded. Mothers' aggression in childhood was predictive of children's restlessness. In the prediction of aggressivity in children, a trend was observed for aggression. That is, the more aggressive a mother was as a child, the more aggressive her child was observed to be. Finally, there was a significant relationship between the mother's aggression in childhood and her child's current unresponsive behavior, such that the more aggressive the mother was in childhood, the more likely her child was to engage in unresponsive behavior during the observed interaction period.

Overall moderate support was obtained for the manifestation of problem behaviors in mothers with childhood histories of aggression and in their offspring. The amount of explained variance in both mother and child behavior attributed to the unique predictive abilities of maternal childhood aggression was small (approximately 6% of the variance). However, the fact that aggression variables provided any predictive validity is interesting given the 20-year time lag between the collection of the aggression and social withdrawal measures of the mothers' behavior when they were children and the current observations of mother and child behavior. Further analyses using path models with a larger sample from the Concordia project (Serbin et al., 1998) suggest that education is one pathway leading from aggression in childhood to child outcomes in the next generation. These results suggest the need to take into consideration not only the direct effects of mothers' behavioral tendencies, but their indirect effects as well.

In a further study of parents and offspring, we continued to study parenting and other processes through which intergenerational transfer of risk may occur by exploring the social and family environments within which children of this high-risk sample develop. Given that we knew that many offspring were having problems by the time they reached school age for the previous study, it was important to determine whether there were visible problems even earlier and what the nature of the early developing relationship between parent and child might be. Our aim was to identify patterns of parental history, family, and environmental risk that may be most detrimental for young children. This knowledge may in turn be used to develop appropriate interventions for implementation prior to these children entering school, when preventive strategies may be most effective.

At the time of this study, the parents were in their mid-20s and early 30s. Being more mature than those in previous investigations, we did not expect these parents to have faced the same challenges as the teenage mothers observed previously. The age span of the 175 children—12 to 72 months—was younger than we had previously studied and provided an opportunity to examine the interactions of mothers and their young children using naturalistic observations of mother–child play.

In one study of a subset of these families (Bentley, 1997; Bentley, Stack, & Serbin, 1998), we assessed the quality of the mother–child relationship during a 15-minute free-play session using the Emotional Availability Scales (Biringen, Robinson, & Emde, 1988). These scales consist of five relational measures of emotional availability capturing both maternal and child behaviors (i.e., maternal sensitivity, scaffolding, and hostility) and child responsiveness and involvement. It was hypothesized that maternal childhood risk status would disrupt levels of emotional availability toward the next generation. During these interactions, it was found that many mothers who had elevated levels of either childhood aggression or social withdrawal were able to demonstrate adequate levels of emotional availability in interacting with their children. However, our results reveal that mothers identified in their childhoods as both aggressive and socially withdrawn were likely to demonstrate hostile behaviors when interacting with their children. Given that analyses of these data were based on a small sample of families, it is premature to draw firm conclusions regarding the quality of the parent–child relationship and the intergenerational transfer of risk in this sample. Nevertheless, the observations to date indicate the presence of many parenting problems among these parents. Currently, we are expanding this study to a larger sample, and we are including a subsample of fathers from the Concordia sample and their spouses.

Other investigations have found similar patterns of mother–child interaction within risk samples (Crittenden, 1981; Dix, 1991; Egeland & Erickson, 1987). However, within the Concordia sample, primarily covert forms of hostility were statistically predicted, including sarcasm, boredom, and irritability. Although perhaps manifesting themselves in a slightly different form, these behaviors are consistent with those found in previous investigations within the Concordia study, in which aggressive and withdrawn mothers were more likely to be unresponsive and ignoring, which also transmit messages of social rejection to their children. Previous findings from the project have indicated that children with elevated levels of both aggression and withdrawal may be particularly at risk for maladaptive psychosocial functioning in adulthood (Moskowitz & Schwartzman, 1989). These documented problems in social functioning now appear to be reflected in mothers' interactions with their own children. This suggests both continuity of the aggressive and withdrawn behavior and a potential pathway for the intergenerational transfer of risk.

In other studies with the Concordia sample, we have examined specific forms of parenting, such as teaching styles, and also contextual variables that might be considered pathways or mechanisms for the transfer of risk. For example, in one study, we found that parents' childhood histories of aggression negatively predicted the provision of cognitive stimulation to their preschool-age offspring (Saltaris, 1999; Saltaris et al., 2001). Cognitive stimulation was observed in two contexts: (a) maternal scaffolding during a structured teaching task with puzzles, and (b) the quality of the home environment measured by the HOME scales (Caldwell & Bradley, 1984). These measures of cognitive stimulation were also demonstrated to be mediators of offsprings' cognitive competence. In another words, it appears that mothers' aggressive interpersonal style also affects their offsprings' cognitive development via an understimulating home environment and less than optimal interpersonal teaching styles.

PREDICTION OF OUTCOMES FOR OFFSPRING

We now turn to the health and functioning of the Concordia sample offspring. As anticipated, these children showed a variety of elevated risks from birth onward. However, it should be noted that in the offspring generation, like their parents, risk is by definition probabilistic. Although a greater number of Concordia project offspring may have a given problem than in the general population, many of the children—even those with multiple risk indicators in their histories and current situations—will not develop serious health, developmental, or behavioral problems.

Looking first at physical health outcomes, we examined the medical records of 94 children: the offspring born to women from the Concordia study as teenagers (Serbin et al., 1996). Between birth and age 4, these children's complete histories of emergency room hospital visits were obtained from the provincial records office. We found that mothers' childhood histories of aggression were predictive of annual rates of ER visits, specifically for treatment of injuries, acute infections, and asthma. Rates of emergency hospitalizations and emergency surgeries followed a similar pattern. In the most elevated risk group, the children of women with histories of both aggression and withdrawal, the average annual rate of ER visits for treatment between birth and age 4 was three, compared with a modal rate of zero in the children of the comparison group. Clearly the young offspring of the aggressive and aggressive–withdrawn women, at least those who had become teen mothers, were at elevated risk compared with the offspring of teen mothers who did not have aggression in their behavioral histories.

Although we do not know the direct reasons for these group differences, the health data have implications for behavior and environment. First, the injury patterns in the children of aggressive group mothers' raise the serious possibility of child abuse and neglect. We could not investigate this directly from the medical records available to us, which were intended to record service usage, but we are currently examining this possibility in an ongoing study. Similarly, the high rate of infections might suggest inadequate or unbalanced diets, weakened immune systems due to stress, or poor hygiene in home environments. It is fairly clear, however, that these results do not simply reflect family disorganization or inappropriate use of ER services (i.e., in lieu of regular medical care). Emergency hospitalization rates (with admission determined by medical staff) were consistent with patterns of walk-in ER visits (which may depend primarily on parental judgment and decision making; Serbin et al., 1996).

A related study involved home visits to 42 of these families: teen mothers from the Concordia sample with infant or preschool-age children (Serbin et al., 1991). We learned that some of the children were showing a variety of developmental delays that were predicted by mothers' behavioral histories of aggression, and that the home environments of these families tended to lack educational toys and other opportunities for cognitive stimulation and growth. Again mothers' history of aggression was the strongest predictor of the quality of the home environment and children's development, although a history of social withdrawal also predicted lower levels of cognitive stimulation in these families. These findings obviously parallel the reports of more stress and higher levels of depression and anxiety, which were found in the adolescent women with histories of childhood aggression and withdrawal. Maternal depression is a well-established risk factor for difficulties in parenting and home environment and may be a mediating factor in some of these families.

We next observed a group of the Concordia project's second-generation children about 5 years later, when many had reached school age (they ranged from 5–11). In this study, we included a group of 89 families in a half-day visit to our laboratories. These children had been born to adolescent or young adult mothers from the original four groups of the sample. Again we found problems in both children's and parents' functioning associated with mothers' history of aggression: Children's problems included behavioral and social difficulties, lower school achievement, and IQ performance. As described, we also observed patterns of coercive parenting and interaction styles (Patterson, 1982). Children's developmental and behavioral problems were predicted by a complex equation including mother's history of aggression and many intervening factors. However, we were encouraged that half of the children seemed to be functioning within the normal range on both behavioral and cognitive measures, and that this pattern of resilience was strongly predicted by mothers' level of educational attainment. In other words, in this subsample of children born to adolescent mothers, completion of high school and further education seemed to enable these mothers to provide a protective and stimulating environment for their children (Serbin et al., 1998).

Our most recent study of offspring, which is ongoing (e.g., Serbin, Stack, & Schwartzman, 2000), includes over 200 infant and preschool-age children born to parents in their late 20s or 30s. These families represent a broad range of backgrounds in terms of education, age at parenthood, and marital and occupational status. In this way, we are able to examine the effects of childhood variables such as aggression without confounding socioeconomic disadvantages (e.g., early parenthood), making it impossible to determine the specific effects of the early risk factors. In other words, because of the wide range of backgrounds represented in this subsample, we can now examine the effects of parental histories in more mature families (including families with two parents who are employed and living above the poverty line), in comparison with the context of early parenthood, lack of social support, and economic disadvantage.

In this sample of young children at preschool age, there was a wide range of outcomes in terms of children's health, development, social-behavioral skills, and cognitive functioning. Predictive factors also included a broad variety of historical and current characteristics, including specific aspects of parental behavioral and educational histories, home and environmental factors, and the child's individual temperament and behavioral characteristics. A brief description of the children's problems in the initial round of the study ($N = 175$) is given next:

Developmental, Behavioral, and Mental Health Problems
• Approximately 53% of the 175 young offspring were found to have current developmental and/or behavioral problems.
• Many of these children (36%) were *multiproblem*, exhibiting significant delays, family problems, and behavioral difficulties (overlap of about 40% between cognitive/language and behavioral problems).

- 23% of the 175 children received IQ scores below 85, indicating likelihood of ongoing developmental delays.
- Few of these problems had been detected or assessed by health service professionals prior to the study. Only 27% of the children having difficulties had received any developmental, psychoeducational, or speech/language services to date.
- The remaining 47% of the group appeared to be developing normally at the time of assessment, although an additional 11% of the total group (20 children) were experiencing serious family problems such as parental alcoholism or mental illness.
- Common physical health problems included: 30% reporting chronic and recurrent respiratory illness (asthma, bronchitis, upper respiratory infections, nasal allergies), 31% with frequent middle ear infections (otitis media), and 10% reporting severe illnesses (including cancer, epilepsy, heart problems, kidney problems, thyroid problems, lupus).

Main Predictors of Preschool Functioning
- Parental childhood characteristics and abilities: particularly mothers' childhood aggression, which negatively predicted outcomes for offspring (especially if combined with social withdrawal and/or low academic ability)
- Parental education: high school completion and years of postsecondary schooling
- Family economic status (including poverty level, welfare status)
- Maternal smoking
- Parenting behavior (including mothers' responsiveness, use of supportive teaching strategies, and emotional availability)
- Cognitive stimulation provided within the home environment
- Level of family and parenting stress
- Adequacy of social and emotional support for parents
- Gender of child: Among the offspring approximately twice as many boys as girls had developmental and/or behavioral problems. In the older group (ages 4–6), the overall prevalence of difficulties (including cognitive, language, and/or behavior problems) reached 73% for boys compared with 44% for girls.
- Boys also had histories of more physical health problems, including infant colic and middle ear infections.
- Physical health problems in children were predicted by a variety of historical and current factors, including perinatal problems, mother's smoking, and parenting stress, as well as mother's childhood history of aggression (which predicted mother's smoking, infant colic, and children's respiratory problems) and social withdrawal (which predicted frequency of both pre- and perinatal health problems).

The Influence of Poverty
- 44% of the families currently have incomes below the poverty line (Low Income Cut Off [LICO]; i.e., income level by family size by place of residence). 14.3% are currently receiving social assistance.

• Current poverty status of the family was predicted by parents' history of childhood aggression, in addition to other established risk factors such as high school dropout.

• Poverty intensified predictive relationships between risk factors and child outcomes: That is, risk factors (e.g., parental childhood aggression, education) were generally stronger predictors of child outcome within the poor sample than in the 56% who are not poor.

Protective Factors
• Financial security (income 10%+ above LICO)
• Parents' level of education (high school completion and number of years, postsecondary)
• Mothers' ability to stimulate their children's problem solving (scaffolding)
• Home environment with many opportunities for cognitive stimulation (e.g., provision of books and educational toys) .
• Parents' satisfaction with available socioemotional support

As seen in these results, the intergenerational transfer of risk is a complex process. Childhood aggression in girls places their offspring at risk for developmental and health problems, both through indirect or cumulative pathways such as lowered educational and occupational achievement and income over time, and also through more direct pathways including parenting styles, modeling of problematic interpersonal behavior, lack of effective cognitive stimulation, stress, and ongoing risk-taking behavior (e.g., smoking) within the home and parenting contexts.

From these results, it appears that male offspring may be more vulnerable to the health, cognitive, and behavioral effects of family risk profiles than female offspring. However, the girls also showed a variety of problems, although at a lower overall rate than the boys, and parental history was predictive of problems in offspring of both sexes. Further, as with the general literature on aggression and other childhood problems such as developmental delay, the gender ratio of prevalence does not mean that girls' difficulties can be ignored. Aggressive girls, with their different, milder, or less obvious problems than boys, are still likely to grow up to have negative life trajectories involving themselves and their families as demonstrated by the results of the Concordia project to date.

Summary of Intergenerational Risk

A variety of current indexes of family functioning were related to children's development. Most of these findings replicate the broad literature indicating that parenting stress, parenting skills, quality of the home environment, parental smoking, and parents' mental health predict children's health, development, and behavior. What is new here, first, is the examination of how parents' childhood behavioral histories predict resources and family functioning in adulthood. Second, the results demonstrate a cumulative risk pattern, indicating an additive and multiplicative relation between these historical factors and specific aspects of current family functioning as predictors within a high-risk population of children.

It is important to note that protective factors that predict positive child outcomes were also found—namely, financial security, parents' level of education, mothers' ability to stimulate their children's problem solving, home environment with many opportunities for cognitive stimulation (e.g., provision of books and educational toys), and availability of socio-emotional support. Education appeared to enhance family functioning and parenting abilities directly, as well as making possible a higher level of income that impacted the well-being of family members in many important ways, including pre- and perinatal health and the subsequent quality of the child's home environment.

Parents' childhood histories of aggression and withdrawal predicted many of the most powerful family influences on children's development. Specifically, childhood aggression predicted parenting stress, parental smoking, mothers' mental health, quality of the home environment, and mothers' ability to provide cognitive stimulation to their preschoolers' (scaffolding). Childhood withdrawal predicted child outcomes because of its relation to mothers' educational attainments, subsequent family income, and an unexpected relation to perinatal health, subsequent childhood illness, and parenting stress.

Within this lower SES, inner-city sample of parents and their children, parents' childhood aggression predicted future family poverty, both directly and indirectly, via lower levels of educational attainment. In other words, continuity of a problematic behavioral style from childhood into adulthood may be implicated in lowered adult occupational attainments and, in some cases, eventual welfare dependency.

In terms of current functioning, it is clear that the correlated triad of distress measures, including mother's mental health problems, child behavior problems, and parenting stress, present a formidable challenge to families in this population. Addressing the factors that may prevent or alleviate this combined pattern of distress might include improving socioeconomic levels of support, as well as providing educational opportunities for parents.

CONCLUSIONS AND RECOMMENDATIONS

The problematic life course of aggressive girls is the focus of an increasing number of longitudinal studies currently being carried out across a diverse range of countries and regions, including ongoing projects in Canada, the United States, Britain, Scandinavia, Germany, and New Zealand. It is now acknowledged that this behavior pattern is likely to be indicative of serious social and academic difficulties for the child him or herself, as well as having important negative consequences (such as victimization and bullying) for peers and others living in the child's social environment. The long-term impact of girlhood aggression is just beginning to be understood in terms of life trajectories for aggressive girls, as well as impact on current and future family members, society at large, and, most recently, impact on the next generation: children born to girls with histories of aggressive behavior. The impact of aggression across the life course from childhood to adulthood in a given individual is clearly modulated by contextual factors, including environmental conditions, experiences, and events. Cultural, social, family, educational, and economic conditions are likely to either exacerbate or buffer outcomes for high-risk children with a pattern of aggressive behavior.

In this chapter, we focused on a longitudinal sample growing up in inner-city Montreal, which has been followed from elementary school age into young adulthood. The women in the sample followed a wide variety of life trajectories according to the profiles of risk and protective events and conditions they experienced. Early aggression appears to have had negative consequences via at least two distinct routes. First, the aggressive behavioral patterns visible to peers in the children's elementary school classes seem to reflect a distinct interpersonal style, which is fairly stable across age. This style is reflected in successive social relationships, including those with peers, partners and spouses, and, eventually, offspring. The negative impact of this pattern in girls may be most obvious in continuing violent, neglectful, or coercive interpersonal relations in successive stages of the life course (e.g., bullying and coercive peer relations; dating and spousal violence; child neglect and abuse; elder abuse). It is also seen in terms of associated health risks (e.g., smoking, substance abuse, early and unprotected sexual activity) and violations of legal and social conventions (e.g., traffic infractions and other nonviolent crime, school dropout, early parenthood, unemployment, welfare dependence). Such activities are also related to modeling and support from the peer group with which aggressive girls associate. These subsequent difficulties doubtlessly continue the negative trajectory of highly aggressive girls. Indirect effects of early aggression via poor educational achievement, poverty, social and physical environments, and ill health are also visible in this sample. Again these indirect pathways were found for both the parent and offspring generations.

On the more positive side, however, buffering factors (notably academic ability and educational achievement) were also identified within the Concordia sample. Income (closely related to educational attainment) is also a powerful predictor and contextual modulator of the long-term outcomes of girlhood aggression. Many of the women (and their offspring) are now doing relatively well despite their poor prospects in childhood or early adolescence. The challenge for researchers in this field is to pinpoint the processes whereby risk and buffering factors operate, as well as the amount of risk for specific negative outcomes that may be quantitatively attributed to specific predictors, and to identify these in the contexts of research, social, educational, and health policy.

With regard to specific implications for future research directions, the following issues are underscored:

1. The need to continue to follow aggressive girls across their life course, looking at outcomes such as mental and physical health, social and occupational functioning, and family relations as important domains in middle adulthood and beyond.
2. The need to understand the direct and indirect processes whereby these children and their families remain at risk over time.
3. The need to better understand social, environmental, cultural, economic, and other contextual factors as modulators of the risk process.
4. A better understanding of the biological and health factors involved in aggressive behavioral styles in girls, both in terms of the origins and maintenance of aggressive behavior and its consequences for women over the life course.
5. Parallel studies of aggressive boys should be carried out within these research contexts: Family, health, and occupational outcomes have also been understudied for aggressive boys: Most of the research on aggression and CD in boys has focused on risk for delinquency, crime, substance abuse, and so on.

Some implications of these findings for social and health policy from these studies can also be summarized:

- Aggression in girls is a predictor of long-term social, academic, and health problems that can be identified as early as Grade 1. Accordingly, a main implication of these findings is the need to identify high-risk children early and provide appropriate and comprehensive intervention to families. A need for educational, economic, mental health, medical services, and social support from birth onward is implicated in these results as essential for the healthy development of children from high-risk backgrounds.
- By the time children reach elementary school with patterns of aggression, social withdrawal, and poor cognitive and language skills, it may be too late to prevent academic and social problems. In elementary school-age populations, intensive and continuing programs to identify children with these problems and intervene appropriately are necessary.

- The need for academic, social, and health support for high risk high-school-age girls—to help them complete high school and prevent early parenthood—is strongly supported by these results.
- Finally, the need for education, social, and economic support to high-risk families with young children, including those of women with a history of aggressive social behavior, is strongly supported by these results.

There has been a great deal of progress in recent years in our knowledge and understanding of the complex ways in which aggressive behavior places children at risk for ongoing problems across the life course. With regard to aggression in girls, this pattern is now acknowledged as a stable indicator of risk for continuing social, emotional, occupational, and health difficulties for both the girls and their families. The relation between girlhood aggression and intergenerational risk is also being clarified. Girls and boys do not live on separate planets even if we sometimes refer to the *two worlds* of childhood to describe their separate playgroups and stereotyped roles (Maccoby, 1998). Their developmental trajectories obviously intersect, particularly in adolescence and parenthood. If we are to understand the origins and sequelae of aggression in general, we need to include both females and males within our conceptual and empirical frameworks.

ACKNOWLEDGMENTS

This research was partially supported by grants from the Seagram Fund for Innovative Research (Concordia University), the Strategic Fund for Children's Mental Health (Health Canada), and the National Institute of Mental Health. The Concordia Longitudinal Risk Research Program was originated in 1976 under the direction of Jane Ledingham and Alex Schwartzman. We thank Claude Senneville, Xiaoming Tang, and Katayoun Saleh for their assistance in data analysis. We also thank Vivianne Bentley, Jessica Cooperman, Natacha de Genna, Jennifer Karp, Pascale Lehoux, Christina Saltaris, Valerie McAffter, Patricia Peters, Keith Marchessault, and Judith Lyons for contributing to various stages of the Concordia Intergenerational Project. We are particularly grateful to the Regie d'Assurance-Maladie du Québec for their assistance in the analysis of medical records. Finally, we are most indebted to the participants in the study.

REFERENCES

Auerbach, J., Lerner, Y., Barasch, M., & Palti, H. (1992). Maternal and environmental characteristics as predictors of child behavior problems and cognitive competence. *American Journal of Orthopsychiatry, 62*(3), 409–420.

Baldwin, W., & Cain, V. S. (1980). The children of teenage parents. *Family Planning Perspectives, 12*, 34–43.

Bardone, A. M., Moffitt, T. E., Caspi, A., Dickson, N., & Silva, P. A. (1996). Adult mental health and social outcomes of adolescent girls with depression and conduct disorder. *Development and Psychopathology, 8*, 811–829.

Beardslee, W. R., Bemporad, J., Keller, M. B., & Klerman, G. L. (1983). Children of parents with major affective disorder: A review. *American Journal of Psychiatry, 140*(7), 825–832.

Bentley, V. M. (1997). *Maternal childhood risk status as a predictor of emotional availability and physical contact in mother–child interactions: An inter-generational study.* Unpublished master's thesis, Department of Psychology, Concordia University.

Bentley, V. M., Stack, D. M., & Serbin, L. A. (1998, April). *Maternal childhood risk status as a predictor of emotional availability in mother–child interactors: An inter-generational study.* Paper presented at the 10th Biennial International Conference on Infant Studies, Atlanta, GA.

Berlin, L. (1997). *Poverty, early development and early intervention.* Symposium sur la pauvreté et le rendement scolaire, Université de Montréal, Montréal, Québec.

Biringen, Z., & Robinson, J. (1991). Emotional availability in mother–child interactions: A reconceptualization for research. *American Journal of Orthopsychiatry, 61*(2), 258–271.

Biringen, Z., Robinson, J. L., & Emde, R. N. (1988). *The emotional availability scales: Infancy to early childhood version.* Unpublished manuscript, University of Colorado, Health Sciences Center, Denver.

Björkqvist, K. (1994). Sex differences in physical, verbal, and indirect aggression: A review of recent research. *Sex Roles, 30*(3/4), 177–188.

Björkqvist, K., & Niemëla, P. (1992). New trends in the study of female aggression. In K. Björkqvist & P. Niemëla (Eds.), *Of mice and women: Aspects of female aggression* (pp. 3–16). San Diego, CA: Academic Press.

Bowlby, J. (1980). *Attachment and loss: Vol. 1. Loss, sadness and depression.* New York: Basic Books.

Cairns, R. B., & Cairns, B. D. (1994). *Lifetime and risks: Pathways of youth in our time.* New York: Cambridge University Press.

Cairns, R. B., Cairns, B. D., Neckerman, H. J., Ferguson, L. L., & Gariepy, J. L. (1989). Growth and aggression: I. Childhood to early adolescence. *Developmental Psychology, 25*, 320–330.

Cairns, R. B., Cairns, B. D., Xie, H., Leung, M. C., & Hearne, S. (1998). Paths across generations: Academic competence and aggressive behaviors in young mothers and their children. *Developmental Psychology, 34*(6), 1162–1174.

Caldwell, B., & Bradley, R. (1984). *Home observation for measurement of the environment.* Homewood: Dorsey.

Capaldi, D. M., Crosby, L., & Stoolmiller, M. (1996). Predicting the timing of first sexual intercourse for at-risk adolescent males. *Child Development, 67*(2), 344–359.

Capaldi, E. J. (1992). The organization of behavior. *Journal of Applied Behavior Analysis, 25*(3), 575–577.

Casaer, P., deVries, L., & Marlow, N. (1991). Prenatal and perinatal risk factors for psychosocial development. In M. Rutter (Ed.), *Biological risk factors for psychosocial disorders* (pp. 139–174). New York: Cambridge University Press.

Caspi, A., Bem, D. J., & Elder, G. H. (1989). Continuities and consequences of interactional styles across the life course. *Journal of Personality, 157*, 375–406.

Caspi, A., & Elder, G. H., Jr. (1988a). Childhood precursors of life course: Early personality and life disorganization. In E. M. Hetherington, R. M. Lerner, & M. Perlmutter

(Eds.), *Child development in life-span perspective* (pp. 115–142). Hillsdale, NJ: Lawrence Erlbaum Associates.

Caspi, A., & Elder, G. H., Jr. (1988b). Emergent family patterns: The inter-generational construction of problem behavior and relationships. In R. Hinde & J. Stevenson-Hinde (Eds.), *Relationships within families: Mutual influences* (pp. 218–240). Oxford: Oxford University Press.

Caspi, A., Elder, G. H., & Bem, D. J. (1988). Moving against the world: Life course patterns of explosive children. *Developmental Psychology, 23*, 308–311.

Conger, R. D., Elder, G. H., Jr., Lorenz, F. O., Simons, R. L., & Whitbeck, L.-B. (1994). Families in troubled times: Adapting to change in rural America. *Social Institutions and Social Change*. Hawthorne, NY: Aldine de Gruyter.

Cooperman, J. (1996). *Maternal aggression and withdrawal in childhood: Continuity and inter-generational risk transmission*. Unpublished master's thesis, Department of Psychology, Concordia University.

Cowen, E. L., Wyman, P. A., Work, W. C., & Parker, G. R. (1990). The Rochester Child Resilience Project: Overview and summary of first year findings. *Development and Psychopathology, 2*(2), 193–212.

Crick, N. R., & Grotpeter, J. K. (1995). Relational aggression, gender and social psychological adjustment. *Child Development, 66*, 710–722.

Crittenden, P. M. (1981). Abusing, neglecting, problematic, and adequate dyads: Differentiating by patterns of interaction. *Merill Palmer Quarterly, 27*(3), 201–218.

de Genna, N. (2001). *An investigation of physical health in high-risk mothers and their preschoolers: An inter-generational study*. Unpublished master's thesis, Department of Psychology, Concordia University.

Dix, T. (1991). The affective organization of parenting: Adaptive and maladaptive processes. *Psychological Bulletin, 110*(1), 3–25.

Dumas, J. E., LaFreniere, P. J., & Serketich, W. J. (1995). Balance of power: A transactional analysis of control in mother–child dyads involving socially competent, aggressive, and anxious children. *Journal of Abnormal Psychology, 104*(1), 104–113.

Egeland, B., & Erickson, M. F. (1987). Psychologically unavailable caregiving. In M. R. Brassard, R. Germain, & S. M. Hart (Eds.), *Psychological maltreatment of children and youth* (pp. 110–120). New York: Pergamon.

Elder, G. H., Jr., & Caspi, A. (1988). Human development and social change: An emerging perspective on the life course. In N. Bolger, A. Caspi, G. Downey, & M. Moorehouse (Eds.), *Persons in context: Developmental processes* (pp. 77–113). New York: Cambridge University Press.

Elder, G. H., Caspi, A., & Downey, G. (1986). Problem behavior and family relationships: Life-course and inter-generational themes. In A. B. Sorensen, F. E. Weiner, & L. R. Sherrod (Eds.), *Human development and the life course: Multi-disciplinary perspectives* (pp. 293–340). Hillsdale, NJ: Lawrence Erlbaum Associates.

Emde, R. N. (1989). The infant's relationship experience: Developmental and affective aspects. In A. J. Sameroff & R. N. Emde (Eds.), *Relationship disturbances in early childhood* (pp. 33–51). New York: HarperCollins.

Farrington, D. P. (1991). Psychological contributions to the explanation of offending. *Issues in Criminological and Legal Psychology, 1*(17), 7–19.

Farrington, D. P. (1994). Early developmental prevention of juvenile delinquency. *Criminal Behavior and Mental Health, 4*(3), 209–227.

Fogel, A. (1993). Developing through relationships: *The origins of communication, self, and culture*. New York: Harvester Wheatsheaf.

Fry, D. P., & Gabriel, A. H. (1994). The cultural construction of gender and aggression. *Sex Roles, 30*(3/4), 165–167.

Furstenberg, F. F., Brooks-Gunn, J., & Chase-Lansdale, L. (1989). Teenaged pregnancy and childbearing. *American Psychologist, 44*, 313–320.

Furstenberg, F. F., Jr., Brooks-Gunn, J., & Morgan, S. P. (1987). *Adolescent mothers in later life.* New York: Cambridge University Press.

Granger, D. A., Weisz, J. R., & Kanneckis, D. (1994). Neuroendocrine reactivity, internalizing problems and control-related cognition in clinic referred children and adolescents. *Journal of Abnormal Psychology, 103*(2), 259–266.

Hammen, C., Gordon, D., Burge, D., Adrian, C., Jaenicke, C., & Hiroto, D. (1987). Maternal affective disorders, illness, and stress: Risk for children's psychopathology. *American Journal of Psychiatry, 144*, 736–741.

Hardy, J. B., Shapiro, S., Melitis, E. D., Skinner, E. A., Astone, N. M., Ensminger, M. E., Laveist, T., Baumgarner, R. A., & Starfield, B. H. (1997). Self-sufficiency at ages 27 to 33 years: Factors present between birth and 18 years that predict educational attainment among children born to inner-city families. *Pediatrics, 99*, 80–87.

Hechtman, L. (1989). Teenage mothers and their children: Risks and problems. A review. *Canadian Journal of Psychiatry, 34*, 569–575.

Huesmann, L. R., Eron, L. D., Lefkowitz, M. M., & Walder, L. D. (1984). The stability of aggression over time and generations. *Developmental Psychology, 20*, 1120–1134.

Kokko, H., Sutherland, W. J., Lindstroem, J., Reynolds, J. D., & Mackenzie, A. (1998). Individual mating success, lek stability, and the neglected limitations of statistical power. *Animal Behavior, 56* (3), 755–762.

Kopp, C. B., & Kaler, S. R. (1989). Risk in infancy: Origins and implications. *American Psychologist, 44*, 224–230.

Layzer, J., St. Pierre, R., & Bernstein, L. (1996). *Early life trajectories of teenage mothers vs. older mothers.* Paper presented at the annual meeting of the Society for Research on Adolescence, Boston, MA.

Ledingham, J. E. (1981). Developmental patterns of aggressive and withdrawn behavior in childhood: A possible method for identifying preschizophrenics. *Journal of Abnormal Child Psychology, 9*(1), 1–22.

Ledingham, J. E., & Schwartzman, A. E. (1981). L'identification de nouvelles populations a risque élevé: Le risque du chercheur. In G. Lauzon (Ed.), *Actes du Colloque sur la Recherche Sociale.* Québec: Ministere des Affaires Sociales.

Lyons, J., Serbin, L. A., & Marchessault, K. (1988). The social behavior of peer-identified aggressive, withdrawn, and aggressive/withdrawn children. *Journal of Abnormal Child Psychology, 16*(5), 539–552.

Maccoby, E. E. (1998). *The two sexes: Growing up apart, coming together.* Cambridge, MA: Harvard University Press.

Magnusson, D. (1988). Individual development from an interactional perspective. In D. Magnusson (Ed.), *Paths through life*, Vol. 1. Hillsdale, NJ: Lawrence Erlbaum Associates.

McCord, J. (1988). Parental behavior in the cycle of aggression. *Psychiatry: Interpersonal and Biological Processes, 51*(1), 14–23.

McLoyd, V. C. (1990). The impact of economic hardship on Black families and children: Psychological distress, parenting, and socioemotional development. *Child Development, 61*(2), 311–346.

Moskowitz, D. S., & Schwartzman, A. E. (1989). Painting group portraits: Studying life outcomes for aggressive and withdrawn children. *Journal of Personality, 57*(4), 723–746.

Moskowitz, D. S., Schwartzman, A. E., & Ledingham, J. E. (1985). Stability and change in aggression and withdrawal in middle childhood and early adolescence. *Journal of Abnormal Psychology, 94*(1), 30–41.

Musick, J. S. (1993). *Young, poor, and pregnant: The psychology of teenage motherhood.* New Haven, CT: Yale University Press.

Olweus, D. (1984). Development of stable aggressive reaction patterns in males. Advances in aggression research. In D. Blanchard & C. Blanchard (Eds.), *Aggressive behavior* (pp. 104–137). New York: Academic Press.

Patterson, G. R. (1982). *A social learning approach to family intervention: Volume 3. Coercive family processes.* Eugene, OR: Castalia.

Pekarik, E. G., Prinz, R. J., Liebert, D. E., Weintraub, S., & Neale, J. M. (1976). The Pupil Evaluation Inventory: A sociometric technique for assessing children's social behavior. *Journal of Abnormal Psychology, 4*(1), 83–97.

Peters, P. L. (1999). *Assortative mating among men and women with histories of aggressive, withdrawn, and aggressive–withdrawn behavior.* Unpublished doctoral dissertation, Concordia University, Montreal, Quebec.

Prechtl, H. (1968). Neurological findings in newborn infants after pre- and perinatal complications. In J. Jonix, H. Visser, & J. Troelstra (Eds.), *Aspects of prematurity and dysmaturity* (pp. 303–312). Leiden, The Netherlands: Stenfert Kroese.

Pulkkinen, L., & Pitkanen T. (1993). Continuities in aggressive behavior from childhood to adulthood. *Aggressive Behavior, 19,* 249–263.

Robins, L. N. (1986). The consequences of conduct disorders in girls. In D. Olweus, J. Block, & M. Radke-Yarrow (Eds.), *Development of antisocial and prosocial behavior* (pp. 385–414). New York: Academic Press.

Rutter, M. (1987). Psychosocial resilience and protective mechanisms. *American Journal of Orthopsychiatry, 57*(3), 316–331.

Salovey, P., & Sluyter, D. J. (1997). Emotional development and emotional intelligence: Educational implications. New York: Basic Books.

Saltaris, C. (1999). *The influence of intellectual stimulation on the cognitive functioning of high-risk preschoolers: Implications for the transmission of risk across generations.* Unpublished master's thesis, Department of Psychology, Concordia University.

Saltaris, C., Serbin, L. A., Stack, D. M., Karp, J. A., Schwartzman, A. E., & Ledingham, J. E. (under review). *Nurturing cognitive competence in preschoolers: A longitudinal study of inter-generational continuity and risk.* Manuscript under review.

Sameroff, A. J., & Seifer, R. (1992). Early contributors to developmental risk. In J. Rolf, A. S. Masten, D. Cichetti, K. H. Nuechterlein, & S. Weintraub (Eds.), *Risk and protective factors in the development of psychopathology* (pp. 52–66). New York: Cambridge University Press.

Scaramella, L. V., Conger, R. D., Simons, R. L., & Whitbeck, L. B. (1998). Predicting risk for pregnancy by late adolescence: A social contextual perspective. *Developmental Psychology, 34*(6), 1233–1245.

Schwartzman, A. E., Ledingham, J., & Serbin, L. A. (1985). Identification of children at risk for adult schizophrenia: A longitudinal study. *International Review of Applied Psychology, 34*(3), 363–380.

Schwartzman, A. E., & Mohan, R. (1999, June). *Gender differences in the adult criminal behavior patterns of aggressive and withdrawn children.* Paper presented at the 9th Scientific Meeting of the International Society for Research in Child and Adolescent Psychopathology, Barcelona, Spain.

Schwartzman, A. E., Verlaan, P., Peters, P., & Serbin, L. (1995). Sex roles as coercion. In J. McCord (Ed.), *Coercion and punishment in long-term perspectives* (pp. 362–375). New York: Cambridge University Press.

Serbin, L. A., Cooperman, J. M., Peters, P. L., Lehoux, P. M., Stack, D. M., & Schwartzman, A. E. (1998). Inter-generational transfer of phsychosocial risk in women with childhood histories of aggression, withdrawal or aggression and withdrawal. *Developmental Psychology, 34*, 1246–1262.

Serbin, L. A., Lyons, J., Marchessault, K., Schwartzman, A. E., & Ledingham, J. (1987). Observational validation of a peer nomination technique for identifying aggressive, withdrawn and aggressive–withdrawn children. *Journal of Consulting and Clinical Psychology, 55*(1), 109–110.

Serbin, L. A., Marchessault, K., McAffer, V., Peters, P., & Schwartzman, A. E. (1993). Patterns of social behavior on the playground in 9- to 11-year-old girls and boys: Relation to teacher perceptions and to peer ratings of aggression, withdrawal and likeability. In C. Hart (Ed.), *Children on playgrounds: Research perspectives and applications*, (pp. 162–183). Albany: SUNY Press.

Serbin, L. A., Moskowitz, D. S., Schwartzman, A. E., & Ledingham, J. E. (1991). Aggressive, withdrawn, and aggressive/withdrawn children in adolescence: Into the next generation. In D. Pepler & K. A. Rubin (Eds.), *The development and treatment of childhood aggression* (pp. 55–70). New York: Guilford.

Serbin, L. A., Peters, P. L., McAffer, V. J., & Schwartzman, A. E. (1991). Childhood aggression and withdrawal as predictors of adolescent pregnancy, early parenthood, and environmental risk for the next generation. *Canadian Journal of Behavioral Science, 23*(3), 318–331.

Serbin, L. A., Peters, P. L., & Schwartzman, A. E. (1996). Longitudinal study of early childhood injuries and acute illnesses in the offspring of adolescent mothers who were aggressive, withdrawn, or aggressive–withdrawn in childhood. *Journal of Abnormal Psychology, 105*(4), 500–507.

Serbin, L. A., Powlishta, K., & Gulko, J., (1993). Sex roles, status, and the need for social change. *Monographs of the Society for Research in Child Development, 58*(2), 93–95.

Serbin, L. A., & Stack, D. M. (1998). Introduction to the special section: Studying inter-generational continuity and the transfer of risk. *Developmental Psychology, 34*, 1159–1161.

Serbin, L. A., Stack, D. M., & Schwartzman, A. E. (2000). *Identification and prediction of risk and resiliency in high-risk preschoolers: An intergenerational study.* Final Report (#6070–10–5/9515); Child, Youth and Family Health Unit, Child and Youth Division, Health Canada.

Serbin, L. A., Stack, D. M., Schwartzman, A. E., Cooperman, J. M., Bentley, V., Saltaris, C., & Ledingham, J. (2002). A longitudinal study of aggressive and withdrawn children into adulthood: Patterns of parenting and risk to offspring. In R. Peters & R. McMahon (Eds.), *Children of disordered parents* (pp. 43–70). New York: Kluwer Academic/Plenum.

Werner, E., & Smith, R. (1992). *Overcoming the odds: High-risk children from birth to adulthood.* Ithaca, NY: Cornell University Press.

Whitman, T. L., Borkowski, J. G., Schellenbach, C. J., & Nath, P. S. (1987). Predicting and understanding development delay of children of adolescent mothers: A multidimensional approach. *American Journal of Mental Deficiency, 92*(1), 40–56.

Zoccolillo, M., Pickles, A., Quinton, D., & Rutter, M. (1992). The outcome of childhood conduct disorder: Implications for defining adult personality disorder and conduct disorder. *Psychological Medicine, 22*(4), 971–986.

Commentary: Aggression Among Females

Joan McCord
Temple University

Childhood aggression predicts problems in girls as it does in boys. Yet until recently aggressive girls have been largely overlooked both as purveyors of problems for others and as deserving of attention in their own right. Therefore, articles in this book will help shape how research about female aggression is addressed, and I particularly welcome the opportunity to examine how the issues have been framed.

The chapter by Stack, Serbin, Schwartzman, and Ledingham (chap. 10) contains three themes that deserve emphasis. The first is that aggressive girls are at heightened risk for encountering difficulties along the route toward adulthood and, subsequently, are likely to become poor parents. A second theme is that the aftermath of female aggression during childhood seems different from that found for males. A third theme is that, despite the heightened risk, a majority of aggressive girls seem to have matured to lead normal and healthy lives.

Because of the careful grounding of their study in a longitudinal design, the evidence Stack et al. presented is not subject to retrospective biases. Nevertheless, it is limited by the fact that the women studied were still too young for their children to have reached adolescence. Indeed most of the analyses depended on only those who had become teenage parents.

Stack et al. showed that aggression tends to be constant throughout the life span. Therefore, it seems reasonable to expand their consideration of how aggressive women behave in their families by considering other data that focus on family interactions with adolescents. For this purpose, I turned to data from the Cambridge-Somerville Youth Study. The study involved

232 mothers observed in their homes over approximately 5.5 years when their sons were between the ages of 10 and 16. The women were selected because they were living in impoverished areas of Cambridge or Somerville Massachusetts, and they had sons under the age of 10 who could be matched to another boy on a variety of variables predictive of delinquency (see McCord, 1979, for additional details). Social workers reported their observations of the families to which they were assigned between 1939 and 1945. Their case records were coded in the late 1950s, with a minimum agreement of 84% for two raters reading the same records for variables used in analyses reported here. Sons in the study were retraced (with 98% success) more than 30 years after the study ended.

Coded behavior indicated that in 175 of the families neither parent was unusually aggressive, in 34 families only the father was particularly aggressive, in 20 families only the mother was aggressive, and in 3 families both parents were highly aggressive. Therefore, the data fail to indicate that aggressive women selected aggressive men as spouses as suggested by Zoccolillo, Paquette, and Tremblay (chap. 9). Nor in this sample were the aggressive women more likely than others to have been teenagers when the sons in this study were born. A slight difference, albeit one not statistically significant, differentiated the education of the three groups of women: Whereas 14% of the mothers in nonaggressive families had finished high school, only 10% of the wives of aggressive men and 5% of the aggressive mothers had done so.

For purposes of additional analyses, the 3 families with both parents aggressive were included with the 20 in which only the mother was considered aggressive. The aggressive mothers were more likely than either the wives of aggressive men or the nonaggressive wives of nonaggressive men to be promiscuous (26% vs. 9% for each of the other two groups; $p < .033$), and they were more likely to be alcoholics (22% vs. 9% of the wives of aggressive men and 6% of the wives of nonaggressive men; $p < .025$). Their husbands were also more likely to be alcoholics as were the aggressive husbands of nonaggressive women: 43% of the husbands of aggressive women, 59% of the aggressive husbands, and 25% of the nonaggressive men married to nonaggressive women were alcoholics.

Clearly, as suspected by Stack et al., the aggressive women tended to be poor parents. They were less likely to be affectionate, less likely to be consistent and nonpunitive in their discipline, and less likely to exhibit the self-confidence required to deal with problems arising in the course of daily life. Their children were less likely to be supervised, and the parents were more likely to be in open conflict (see Table 10.1).

In 1936 and 1937, teachers rated the boys in the study. Their ratings indicate that 22% of the nonaggressive parents had boys described by their

TABLE 10.1

PARENTAL BEHAVIOR

| | Which Parent was Aggressive | | | |
| | Neither Parent | Father | Mother | 2 df |
Behavior	(N = 175)	(N = 34)	(N = 23)	p <
Mother affectionate	52%	35%	30%	.046
Mother consistent and nonpunitive	35%	21%	4%	.004
Mother self-confident	35%	9%	9%	.001
Son supervised	62%	35%	48%	.009
Parents in open conflict	24%	62%	52%	.001

teachers as fighters, and 24% of the sons of aggressive men were so described. In comparison, 48% of the sons of aggressive mothers had been described as fighters by their teachers ($p < .023$).

Criminal records were checked when the boys were men in their 40s. Those who had been reared either by an aggressive father or mother were more likely than their peers to have been convicted for a crime on the FBI Index. Whereas 26% of those with no aggressive parent had been convicted, 53% of those with an aggressive father and 61% of those with an aggressive mother had been convicted for at least one Index crime ($p < .001$). In summary, the evidence supports the suggestion made by Stack et al. that aggressive women contribute to a cycle of violence through poor parenting practices.

The second theme of Stack et al. is that aggressive girls follow a trajectory different from those of either aggressive boys or nonaggressive girls. Their evidence, from a francophone sample in Canada, is confirmed through a longitudinal study of a cohort of African Americans first studied in Chicago. In that study, we found that aggression among the girls, measured during their first grade in school at age 6, predicted depression ($p < .004$) as well as violence ($p < .002$) by age 32 years. Among the boys, however, early aggression predicted violence ($p < .006$), but not depression (McCord & Ensminger, 1997).

The third theme we consider—the successes of those whose early years foretold adult difficulties—is one that should be taken seriously. Researchers have had a tendency to settle for predictors as if they determined actions. In fact, chapter 10 might be faulted for leaning in this direction.

Mark Zoccolillo et al. focused on the transmission of CD from mothers to their offspring. They suggested that, to reduce CD, girls should be taught to avoid selecting sexual partners who also have CD. In this suggestion and elsewhere in their chapter, the authors appear to accept behavioral genetics—an approach that relies on phenotypes (i.e., properties produced by the individual's genetic constitution, the environment, and their interaction), not genes. Causal inferences made by behavioral geneticists are specific to the population under study at the time they are studied. Furthermore, behavioral genetics overlooks the fundamental interaction between biology and environment.

It is a mistake to apportion influences between the genetic and environmental. Biological processes always operate in environmental contexts, and environmental conditions influence biological processes. Although biological processes may increase risk for transmitting aggression, CD, or social success, these risks become behaviors in combination with training and opportunities. A focus on the biosocial processes that influence behavior would be an important contribution to understanding antisocial behavior.

Using the Cambridge-Somerville Youth Study data, I have shown that, after controlling for biological risk of criminality, childrearing makes a large difference in whether sons of criminals become criminal (McCord, 1991). It may be wiser to teach mothers how to care for their infants and help them rear well-behaved children than attempt to manipulate genetic material about which so little is understood.

The science of horticulture demonstrates how plants depend on environment for their development. Espaliers[1] are one example of careful training, making clear that even trees need not develop in a particular form. Intentional shaping of human choices might not be more difficult.

REFERENCES

McCord, J. (1979). Some childrearing antecedents of criminal behavior in adult men. *Journal of Personality and Social Psychology, 37*(9), 1477–1486.
McCord, J. (1991). The cycle of crime and socialization practices. *Journal of Criminal Law and Criminology, 82*(1), 211–228.
McCord, J., & Ensminger, M. E. (1997). Multiple risks and comorbidity in an African-American population. *Criminal Behaviour and Mental Health, 7*, 339–354.

---

[1]Espalier is a tree or shrub trained to grow in a flat plane against a wall, often in a symmetrical pattern.

Author Index

A

Aber, J. L., 4, *24*
Abramovitch, R., 15, 16, *23*, *26*
Achenbach, T. M., 56, 57, *71*, 114, 115, *131*, 171, *188*
Acoca, L., 91, *92*
Adams, R. G., 196, *211*
Adler, P. A., 122, 123, 126, *131*
Adler. P., 122, 123, 126, *131*
Adrian, C., 267, *281*
Ageton, S. S., 81, *93*, 193, 198, *210*, *212*
Aguilar, D., 128, *131*
Ahlbom, A., 106, 110, 118, *133*
Alder, C., 149, 150, 154, *158*, 164, *165*
Al-Issa, I., 55, *71*
Allen, L., 56, 59, *73*
Allen, V., 127, *134*
Allman, C., 228, *249*
American Psychiatric Association, 30, *44*, 192, *210*, 232, *248*
Amos, D., 5, *27*
Anderson, D. R., 56, *71*, 157, *158*
Andrews, B., 197, *211*
Andrews, D. W., 105, *132*, 193, *212*
Angold, A., 30, *44*
Anthony, B. A., 22, *26,* 191, 192, 197, *213*
Aos, S., 210, *211*
Appel, M., 98, *101*
Appelgate, B., 30, 32, 34, *45*
Armsden, G. C., 193, 205, *211*
Artz, S., xvi, xvii, xviii, xix, 124, *138*, 139, 140, 141, 142, 143, 145, 146, 156, *158*, 161

B

Ary, D., 194, 209, *213*, *214*
Asplund-Peltola, R. L., 13, 14, *26*
Assiter, S., 231, 235, *251*
Astone, N. M., 258, 261, *281*
Atlas, R., 18, *26*
Attar, B. K., 79, *92*
Auerbach, J., 266, *278*
Augimeri, L. K., 140, *158*, 187, *189*
Auslander, W. F., 208, *213*

B. C. Police Services Branch, 141, *158*
Bachrach, C. A., 80, *92*
Bacon-Shone, J., 56, 58, *73*
Baillargeon, R. H., xvi, xvii, xx, 97
Baines, M., 149, 154, *158*, 164, *165*
Balach, L., 228, *249*
Balch, P., xv, *xxiii*
Baldwin, W., 258, *279*
Bandura, A., 111, *131*, 176, *188*
Bank, L., 76, *94*
Barasch, M., 266, *278*
Bardige, B., 153, *159*
Bardone, A. M., 191, *211,* 229, 237, *248*, 257, *279*
Barkley, R. A., 32, *44*
Barnoski, R., 210, *211*
Barnsley, 138
Barrett, D. E., 18, *23*
Barrett, K. C., 33, *46*
Bartlett, N., 162, *165*
Bates, J. E., 7, 11, 19, *23*, *24*, 56, *71*, 79, *92*, 173, *188*

Battin-Pearson, S., 183, *188*
Baugher, M., 228, *249*
Baumgarner, R. A., 258, 261, *281*
Bax, M., 56, *72*
Bayles, K., 7, 19, *23*, 173, *188*
Beaman, J., 176, *190*
Bear, G. G., 118, *135*
Beardsall, L., 15, *24*
Beardslee, W. R., 197, *213*, 267, *279*
Belcher, L., 208, 209, *211*
Beller, E. K., 56, *71*
Bem, D. J., 4, *24*, 256, 257, *279*, *280*
Bemporad, J., 267, *279*
Bennett, D. S., 7, 19, *23*, 173, *188*
Bentley, V. M., 260, 269, *279*, *283*
Berger, R., 140, 141, *158*
Bergman, L. R., 19, 20, *28*, 105, 125, *134*
Bergsman, I. R., 76, *92*, 202, *211*
Berlin, L., 266, *279*
Bernard, T. J., 33, *45*
Berndt, T. J., 113, *131*
Bernstein, L., 258, *281*
Bernstein, V. J., 229, 246, *249*
Berry, C. A., 174, *188*
Besag, V. E., 184, *188*
Besnier, N., 124, *131*
Biafora, F. A., 79, *95*
Biederman, J., 32, *44*, *46*
Biglan, A., 194, *213*
Bingham, C. R., 195, *212*
Bird, H. R., 30, 32, 34, *44*, *45*, 100, *101*
Biringen, Z., 267, 269, *279*
Bishop, S. J., 80, *93*
Björkqvist, K., xv, *xxii*, 5, 6, *23*, *25*, 76, 91,
         93, *94*, 106, 109, 110, 111, 112,
         114, 115, 117, 118, 119, 124,
         131, *133*, *134*, 141, *158*, 185,
         188, *189*, 192, *211*, 254, 255,
         256, *279*
Blais, M., 139, 145, 146, 156, *158*
Bleske, A., 229, 232, *250*
Block, J., 97, *101*, 197, *215*
Bloom, M., 198, *211*
Blum, D., 140, *158*
Blyth, D. A., 113, *131*
Boivin, M., 70, 71, *74*, 110, *136*
Bond, L. A., 56, 57, *72*
Borkowski, J. G., 258, *283*
Botvin, G. J., 195, *212*
Boulerice, B., 9, *25*, *28*, 56, *73*
Boulton, M., 4, 16, *28*

Boundy, B. E., 56, *72*
Bourne, P., 141, *158*
Bowlby, J., 267, *279*
Boyle, M. C., 3, 5, 6, 7, 20, *26*, *28*, 198, *214*
Boyle, M. H., 169, *171*, *189*, 229, 248
Bradley, R., 270, *279*
Breaux, A. M., 56, *72*
Breen, M. J., 32, *44*
Brennan, P. A., 241, *249*
Brent, D. A., 228, *249*
Brestan, E. V., 169, *188*
Bromet, E., 56, *72*
Brooks, J., 11, *23*, 34, *44*,
Brooks-Gunn, J., xx, *xxii*, 35, *45*, 80, *93*,
         196, *212*, 257, 261, 264, 266, *281*
Brown, C. H., 196, *211*
Brown, G. W., 197, *211*
Brown, J. D., 115, *131*, *135*
Brown, L. M., 4, *24*, 141, 153, *158*
Brown, M. M., 7, 19, *23*, 173, *188*
Brunham, R., 195, *214*
Bukowski, W. M., 16, *27*, 246, *251*
Burchinal, M. R., 226, *250*
Burge, D., 267, *281*
Burkam, D. T., 42, *45*
Burns, B. J., 30, *44*
Burts, D. C., 16, 17, *25*
Buss, A. H., 43, *44*
Butts, J. A., 75, *94*
Bybee, J., 33, *44*

C

Cadenhead, C., 78, 79, *92*
Cadoret, R. J., 225, 227, 231, *249*, *250*
Cain, V. S., 258, *279*
Cairns, B. D., xv, xvi, xvii, xxi, xviii, xx,
         xxi, *xxii*, 4, 5, 6, 18, *24*, 35, *44*,
         79, 82, *95*, 99, *101*, 105, 106,
         107, 109, 110, 111, 112, 115,
         116, 117, 118, 119, 120, 121,
         125, 126, 128, 130, *132*, *136*,
         161, *165*, 169, 186, *188*, 192,
         193, *211*, 255, 257, *279*
Cairns, R. B., xv, xvi, xvii, xxi, xviii, xx,
         xxi, *xxii*, 4, 5, 6, 18, 20, *24*, 27,
         35, *44*, 79, 82, *95*, 99, *101*, 105,
         106, 107, 109, 110, 111, 112,
         114, 115, 116, 117, 118, 119,
         120, 121, 125, 126, 128, 129,
         130, 131, *131*, *132*, *136*, 161,

165, 169, 183, 186, *188*, *190*, 192, 193, 198, *211*, *214*, 255, 257, *279*

Caldwell, S. B., 196, *213*, 270, *279*,

Calhoun, G., 200, *211*

Campbell, S. B., 5, *24*, 56, 69, *72*

Canino, G., 30, 32, 34, *45*

Cantwell, D. P., 228, *249*

Capaldi, D. M., 76, 90, *94*, 193, 194, 195, 196, *211*, 225, *249*, 255, *279*

Capaldi, E. J., 255, *279*

Caplan, M., 194, *215*

Cardarelli, A. P., 15, *25*

Carlson, C. L., 33, *44*

Carlson, E., 128, *131*

Carver, K., 80, *92*

Casaer, P., 265, *279*

Casas, J. F., 89, 91, *92*, 115, 118, *132*, 192, *212*

Caspi, A., xv, xvi, xxi, *xxiii*, 4, 9, *24*, 31, 32, *44*, 169, *188*, 191, *211*, 218, *221*, 225, 229, 232, 237, *248*, *249*, 255, 256, 257, 261, 267, *279*, *280*

Cassidy, B., 225, 229, 231, 235, 246, *249*

Catalano, R. F., 229, *249*

Cederblad, M., 56, *72*

Cernkovich, S. A., 105, 130, *133*, 193, 198, *212*, 219, *221*

Chalmers, J. B., 198, *211*

Chamberlain, P., xvi, xviii, xix, 199, *211*, *212*, 218

Chase-Lansdale, L., 80, *93*,196, *212*, 257, 264, *281*

Chen, F., 200, *211*

Chesney-Lind, M., 139, 140, 141, 150, 156, *159*, 182, *188*, 198, *212*

Chess, S., 43, *46*

Chopak, J. S., 195, *212*

Cicchetti, D., 4, *24*

Clark, S., 194, *211*

Clogg, C. C., 80, *92*

Cobham-Portorreal, C. S., 22, *26*

Cobham-Portorreal, N. K., 191, 192, 197, *213*

Cohen, D., 33, *44*

Cohen, J., 34, *44*

Cohen, P., 34, *44*,100, *101*

Coie, J. D., xvi, xvii, 17, *24*, 76, 77, 78, 79, 80, 81, 82, 83, 89, *92*, *93*, *94*, 95, 97, 196, *215*,

Cole, P. M., 31, 33, *44*, *46*

Compas, B. E., 35, *45*

Conger, R. D., 176, *190*, 194, *215*, 255, 258, *280*, *282*

Connell, D., 197, *213*

Connolly, J., 9, 18, *24*

Cooperman, J. M., 23, *27*, 225, 226, 246, *251*, 257, 260, 262, 263, 264, 266, 267, 268, 272, *280*, *283*

Corbett, J., 56, *73*

Cornely, P., 56, *72*

Corter, C., 15, 16, *23*, *26*

Costello, E. J., 30, *44*

Cowen, E. L., 266, *280*

Craig, W. M., xviii, xix, xx, 6, 9, 16, 17, 18, *24*, *26*, *27*, 48, 116, 118, 130, *135*, 180, *189*

Creasey, L., 197, *211*

Creighton, G., 145, 146, *159*

Crick, N. R., 5, 16, *24*, 31, *44*, 89, 91, *92*, 106, 109, 114, 115, 118, *132*, 185, *188*, 192, *212*, 254, 255, *280*

Crittenden, P. M., 269, *280*

Crockett, L. J., 195, *212*

Crosby, L., 105, *132*, 193, 195, *211*, *212*, 225, *249*, 255, *279*

Crowther, J. H., 56, 57, *72*

Cullen, K. J., 56, *72*

Cunningham, W. A., 99, *101*

D

Daly, M., 22, *24*

Davies, M., 100, *101*

Dawe, H., 98, *101*

De Coster, S., 10, *25*

de Genna, N., 266, *280*

Deater-Deckard, K., 79, *92*

DeBaryshe, B. D., 19, 20, *26*

Debus, R., 115, *134*

DeKlyen, M., 11, *25*

Dennis, K. D., *45*

Derogatis, L. R., 202, *212*

Derzon, J., 140, *159*

Desrosiers, H., 237, *249*

deVries, L., 265, *279*

DeWolf, D. M., 16, 17, *25*

Diaz, T., 195, *212*

Dickson, N., 229, 237, *248*, 257, *279*

DiClemente, C. C., 208, *213*

Dishion, T. J., 4, 16, 17, *24*, *26*, 105, *132*, 176, *189*, 192, 193, *212*

Dix, T., 269, *280*

Dobkin, P. L., 230, *249*
Dodge, K. A., 10, 11, *24*, 43, *44*, 76, 77, 79, 82, 83, 89, *92*
Dollard, J., 111, *132*
Doob, L. W., 111, *132*
Doreleijers, T., 169, *189*
Dorer, D. J., 197, *213*
Dowler, S., 13, *24*
Downey, G., 255, *280*
Dubow, E. F., 187, *188*
Dulcan, M. K., 30, 32, 34, *45*
Dumas, J. E., 267, *280*
Duncan, T., 209, *214*
Dunn, J., 15, *24*
Dunne, J. E., 169, *190*
DuRant, R. H., 78, 79, *92*
Dutton, K. A., 115, *131*

E

Eagly, A. H., 5, *24*
Earls, F., 56, 57, *72*, 200, 212
Eaton, W. O., 71, *72*
Eddy, J. M., 199, *212*
Edelbrock, C. S., 56, 57, *71*
Eder, D., 111, 112, 113, 124, *132*, *133*
Edwards, C. P., 55, *74*
Egeland, B., 128, *131*, 267, 269, *280*
Eilertsen, D. E., 231, *249*
Elder, G. H., 4, *24*, 255, 256, 257, 258, 261, 267, *279*, *280*
Eley, T. C., 225, 231, *249*
Elliott, D. S., 35, *44*, 77, 81, *92*, *93*, 193, 198, 210, *210*, *212*
Ellis, 138
Elsenheart, M., 154, *159*
Elze, D., 208, *213*
Emde, R. N., 267, 269, *279*, *280*
Eme, R. F., 55, *72*
Emshoff, J., 208, 209, *211*
English, D., 169, *190*
Enke, J. L., 124, *132*
Enns, L. R., 71, *72*
Ensminger, M. E., 105, *133*, 258, 261, *281*, 287, *288*
Epstein, S., 115, *133*
Ericksen, K. P., 195, *212*
Erickson, M. F., 267, 269, *280*
Erkanli, A., 30, *44*
Eron, L. D., xvi, *xxiii*, 11, 22, *24*, *25*, 77, 82, 87, *93*, 137, *159*, 255, 256, *281*

Eronen, M., 36, *44*
Evans, C. C., 112, *132*
Ewing, L. J., 5, *24*
Ey, E., 35, *45*
Eyberg, S. M., 169, *188*

F

Fagot, B. I., 10, *24*, *25*, 35, *44*, 70, 72, 225, *249*
Faraone, S. V., 32, *44*, *46*
Farmer, T. W., 105, 128, 130, *133*, *135*
Farr, F., 145, 146, *159*
Farrington, D. P., 77, *93*, 105, 106, 125, *133*, 255, *280*
Fehr, B., 221, *221*
Feldman, J. F., 5, *27*
Ferguson, L. L., 5, 6, 18, *24*, 106, 107, 111, 117, 119, *132*, 161, *165*, 192, *211*, 255, *279*
Fergusson, D. M., 193, 194, 195, *215*, 230, 231, 235, 241, 246, *249*, *251*
Feshbach, N. D., 106, 107, 116, 117, *133*
Fienberg, S. E., 61, *72*
Finch, S., 11, *23*
Fine, G. A., 124, *133*
Finkelhor, D., 15, *25*
Fitzpatrick, K. M., 78, *93*
Fleming, J. E., 229, *248*
Flowers, R., 140, *159*
Fogel, A., 267, *280*
Forehand, R., 194, *213*
Forester-Clark, F. S., 113, *131*
Fraczek, A., 76, 91, *94*
Frankel, K. A., 56, *71*
Frick, P. J., 30, 32, 34, *45*, *46*, 90, *94*, 130, *135*, 228, *250*
Friedman, A., 183, *188*
Friend, A., 228, *249*
Fry, D. P., 255, *281*
Fullilove, R., 195, *214*
Furstenberg, F. F., 80, *93*, 196, *212*, 257, 261, 264, 266, *281*
Fuss, D., 143, *159*

G

Gabriel, A. H., 255, *281*
Gabrielli, W. F., Jr., 197, *213*
Galen, B. R., 5, *25*, 77, *95*, 106, 107, 113, *133*, 185, *188*

Garber, J., 43, *44*
Gariepy, J.-L., 5, 6, 18, *24*, 105, 106, 107,
    111, 117, 119, 121, 130, *132*,
    161, *165*, 192, *211*, 255, *279*
Garmezy, N., 4, *25*, 43, *45*
Garrison, C. Z., 80, *95*
Gaub, M., 33, *44*
Gerrard, M., 71, *73*
Gest, S. D., 105, 126, 130, *132*
Gibbs, J. T., 77, *93*
Gil, A., 79, *95*
Giller, H., 100, *101*
Gilligan, C., 4, *24*, *25*, 141, 153, *158*, *159*
Giordano, P. C., 105, 130, *133*, 193, 198,
    212, 219, *221*
Gjone, J., 231, *249*
Gomes-Schwartz, B., 15, *25*
Goodenough, F., 98, *101*
Goodman, L. A., 246, *249*
Goodman, S. H., 34, *45*, 100, *101*
Goodwin, M. H., 121, 123, 124, *133*
Goodwin, M. P., 15, *25*
Gordon, D., 267, *281*
Gordon, R. A., 56, *73*, 228, 235, 241, *251*
Gorman-Smith, D., 76, *93*
Gottfried, A. W., 31, *45*
Gottman, J. M., 51, *52*, 124, *133*
Gould, M. S., 32, *44*
Gove, W. R., 55, *72*
Graber, J. A., xx, *xxii*
Graham, P. J., 56, 59, *73*
Graham, S., 76, *93*,
Granger, D. A., 268, *281*
Grant, K. E., 35, *45*
Graziano, J. H., 241, *251*
Green, J. A., 114, *132*
Green, S. M., 32, *45*, 191, *213*, 228, 235,
    241, *251*
Greenberg, M. T., 11, *25*, 193, 205, *211*
Greenwald, A. G., 115, *133*
Grekin, E. R., 241, *249*
Griffin, K. W., 195, *212*
Grimes, C. L., 51, *52*
Grotpeter, J. K., 5, 16, *24*, 89, 91, *92*, 106,
    109, 115, 118, *132*, 185, *188*,
    192, *212*, 254, 255, *280*
Grunebaum, H. U., 197, *213*
Gualtieri, I., 70, *72*
Guerin, D. W., 31, *45*
Guerra, N. G., 17, *25*, 77, 79, *92*, *93*
Gulko, J., 262, *283*

Gunderson, J. G., 198, *215*

H

Hagan, R., 10, *24*, 70, *72*
Hagell, A., 100, *101*
Hagenaars, J. A., 247, *249*
Hakola, P., 36, *44*
Hallinan, M. T., 113, *132*
Hammen, C., 267, *281*
Hanmer, T., 153, *159*
Hans, S. L., 225, 229, 235, 246, *249*
Harden, P. W., 56, *73*
Hardy, J. B., 258, 261, *281*
Hare, E. H., 197, *212*
Hare-Mustin, R., 157, 158, *159*
Haren, P. W., 4, *28*
Harper, G. W., 81, *93*
Hart, C. H., 16, 17, *25*, 116, 117, 118, *134*
Hart, E. L., 30, 32, 34, *45*
Hart, H., 56, *72*
Hartdagen, S., 228, *250*
Hartman, C., 169, *189*
Hartmark, C., 34, *44*
Hartung, C., 30, 31, *45*
Harwood, R. L., 194, *215*
Hawkins, D. F., 76, 77, *93*
Hawkins, J. D., 183, *188*, 229, *249*
Hay, D., 76, *93*
Hearne, S., 257, *279*
Hechtman, L., 257, 258, *281*
Heimer, D., 10, *25*
Heinen, T., 247, *249*
Henry, B., 31, 32, *44*, 200, *212*
Henry, D. B., 76, *93*
Henson, L. G., 229, 246, *249*
Herb, T., 55, *72*
Herjanic, B. L., 226, 228, *250*
Hicks, R., 70, *72*
Hill, J., 193, *214*
Hill, K., 183, *188*
Hiroto, D., 267, *281*
Hirschi, T., 43, *45*
Hitchcock, P., 195, *214*
Hodges, K., 83, *93*
Hofferth, S. L., 196, *213*
Holland, D., 154, *159*
Holmes, J., 141, *159*
Honzik, M. P., 56, 59, *73*
Hops, H., 12, 13, *25*, 178, *189*
Horn, M., xv, *xxii*

Horowitz, J. M., 15, *25*
Hort, B., 10, *25*
Horwood, L. J., 230, 246, *249*
Hoven, C., 100, *101*
Howell, C. T., 56, 57, *71*, 114, 115, *131*
Howell, K., 183, *188*
Hoyenga, K. B., 112, *133*
Hoyenga, K. T., 112, *133*
Hoyt, D. R., 194, *215*
Hoza, B., 8, *26*
Hudley, C., 76, *93*
Hudson, A., 150, *159*
Huesmann, L. R., xvi, *xxiii*, 17, 22, *25*, 76, 77, 82, 87, 91, *93*, *94*, 255, 256, *281*
Hughes, S., 225, 229, 231, 235, 246, *249*
Huizinga, D., 81, *93*, 193, *212*
Humphreys, A. P., 16, *25*
Hutchings, B., 197, *213*
Huttunen, A., 130, *135*
Hwu, H. G., 226, 232, 237, *252*
Hyde, J. S., 5, *25*
Hyman, C., 17, *24*, 80, 81, 82, 83, 89, *92*, *94*

I

Illich, I., 124, *133*
Inhelder, N., 112, *133*
Ippolito, M. F., 187, *188*

J

Jacklin, C. N., 5, *26*, 55, *73*
Jacobs, M. R., 78, 79, *92*
Jacobson, 138
Jaenicke, C., 267, *281*
Jaffe, P., 176, *188*
Japel, C., 9, *25*, 70, 71, *74*, 110, *136*
Jenkins, J., 15, *25*
Jenkins, S., 56, *72*
Jensen, P. S., 30, 32, 34, *45*, 100, *101*, 228, *249*
Jersild, A., 98, 99, *101*
Jette, M., 237, *249*
Ji, T., 226, 232, 237, *252*
Jiwani, Y., 141, *159*
Johnson, C., 176, *190*
Johnson, J., 34, *44*
Johnson, P., 176, *189*
Jones, J., 32, *46*

Jurgens, J., 200, *211*

K

Kaler, S. R., 265, *281*
Kalichman, S., 208, 209, *211*
Kanneckis, D., 268, *281*
Karp, J. A., 270, *282*
Kasen, S., 34, *44*
Kaukiainen, A., 5, 6, *23*, 76, 91, *94*, 106, 110, 112, 118, *131*, *133*, 185, *188*, 192, *211*
Kavanagh, K. H., 12, 13, *25*, 178, *189*
Kazdin, A., 181, *189*
Keating, D. P., 112, *134*
Keenan, K., xvi, xvii, xx, 5, 7, *25*, *26*, 32, 33, 34, 36, *44*, *45*, 48, 56, 69, 72, 173, *189*, 191, 192, *213*
Kellam, S. G., 196, *211*
Keller, M. B., 197, *213*, 267, *279*
Keltikangas,-Jarvinen, L., 13, 14, *26*
Kendall-Tackett, K. A., 15, *25*
Kenny , D. A., 115, *134*
Kenrick, D. T., 115, *134*
Kerr, M., 246, *251*
Kersten, J., 150, *159*
Kindermann, T., 121, *132*
King, L. J., 228, *250*
Kinney, D. A., 112, *133*
Kinnunen, U., 100, *101*, 127, *135*
Kit-fong Au, T., 206, 208, *213*
Klein, N., 22, *26*
Klerman, G. L., 267, *279*
Klerman, G. R., 197, *213*
Koch, H., 98, *101*
Koegl, C. J., 140, *158*, 187, *189*
Kohlstadt, V., 195, *214*
Kokko, H., 257, *281*
Kokko, K., 100, *101*
Koot, H. S., 56, 58, 60, 70, *72*
Kopp, C. B., 265, *281*
Kotchick, B. A., 194, *213*
Kovacs, M., 196, *213*, 231, 235, *250*
Kramer, S., 183, *188*
Kreisher, C., 183, *188*
Krol, R. S. M., 196, *213*, 231, 235, *250*
Krueger, R., 229, 232, *250*
Ku, H., 192, *212*
Kupersmidt, J. B., 51, *52*, 80, 83, *93*, *95*, 196, *215*
Kutash, K., 199, *213*, *214*

L

Ladewski, B., 42, *45*
LaFreniere, P. J., 267, *280*
Lagerspetz, K. M. J., 6, *25*, 76, 91, *93*, *94*,
    106, 109, 110, 111, 112, 114,
    115, 117, 118, 119, 124, 130,
    131, *133*, *134*, *135*, 185, *188*,
    189, 192, *211*
Lahey, B. B., 30, 32, 34, *45*, 56, *73*, 228,
    235, 241, *250*, *251*
Lam, E., *138*, 141, 143, 156, *158*
Langbehn, D. R., 225, 227, 231, *250*
Larson, C. P., 56, 58, *73*
Laub, J. H., 76, 77, *93*
Lauori, P. W., 197, *213*
Lauritsen, J. L., 76, 77, *93*
Laveist, T., 258, 261, *281*
Layzer, J., 258, *281*
Le Blanc, M., 35, *46*
Leadbeater, B. J., 80, *93*
Ledingham, J. E., xviii, xix, xxi, 23, *28*, 35,
    46, 169, *190*, 255, 256, 257, 259,
    260, 261, 262, 263, *281*, *282*,
    283, 285
Lee, V. E., 42, *45*
Lees, 141
Lefkowitz, E. S., 82, 87, *93*, 206, 208, *213*
Lefkowitz, M. M., xvi, *xxiii*, 22, *25*, 255,
    256, *281*
Lehoux, P. M., 23, *27*, 225, 226, 246, *251*,
    257, 260, 262, 263, 264, 266,
    267, 268, 272, *283*
Leib, R., 210, *211*
Leinbach, M. D., 10, *24*, *25*
Lenox, K., 82, *92*
Lenssen, V., 169, *189*
Lerner, Y., 266, *278*
Leung, M. C., 115, 126, *132*, *134*, 257, *279*
Leung, P. W. L., 56, 58, *73*
Leve, C. S., 225, *249*
Leve, L. D., xvi, xviii, xix, *218*
Levene, K. S., xvii, xix, xx, 140, *158*, 181,
    187, *189*, *218*
Leventhal, B. L., 228, 235, 241, *251*
Lewin, K., 129, *134*
Lewis, D. O., 22, *26*, 191, 192, 197, *213*
Lichtenstein, P., 225, 231, *249*
Liddle, C., 233, *250*
Liebert, D. E., 259, *282*
Lieh-Mak, F., 56, 58, *73*

Lightfoot, M., 209, *213*
Linder, C. W., 79, *92*
Lindstroem, J., 257, *281*
Links, P. S., 229, *248*
Lipsey, M., 140, *159*
Little, R. A., 232, *250*
Little, T. D., 99, *101*
Liu, X., 241, *251*
Lochman, J. E., 17, *24*, 80, 81, 82, 83, 89,
    92, *94*
Loeber, R., xvi, xvii, xx, 7, 11, *26*, 30, 32,
    34, 35, 36, *45*, 48, 76, 77, 82,
    93, 130, *134*, 173, *189*, 191,
    213, 228, 235, 241, *251*
Loney, J., 35, *45*
Long, A., 56, *73*
Lorenz, F. O., 255, 258, *280*
Ludolph, P., 197, *215*
Luk, S. L., 56, 58, *73*
Luthar, S., 105, 130, *134*
Lynam, D. R., 9, *24*, 169, *188*, 228, *250*
Lynch, M., 181, *189*
Lynskey, M. T., 246, *249*
Lyons, J., 262, 263, *281*, *283*
Lyons, N., 153, *159*
Lyons-Ruth, K., 197, *213*
Lytton, H., 11, *26*

M

Maccoby, E. E., 4, 5, 11, 16, 18, *26*, 47,
    48, *52*, 55, *73*, 113, 129, *134*,
    219, *221*, 262, 278, *281*
Machessault, K., 262, 263, *281*, *283*
MacIntyre, I., *138*, 141, 143, 156, *158*
Mackenzie, A., 257, *281*
Maczewski, M., *138*, 141, 143, 156, *158*
Madsen, K. C., xvii, xix, xx, 185, *189*, 218
Magnusson, D., 9, 19, 20, *28*, 105, 106,
    125, 127, *134*, *135*, 255, *281*
Mahoney, J. L., 114, 115, 118, *136*
Maier-Katkin, D., 33, *45*
Mandel, R., 98, *101*
March, C. L., 5, *24*
Marchessault, K., 6, 17, 18, *27*, 184, *190*
Mareck, J., 157, 158, *159*
Marinos, V., 140, *160*
Markey, F., 98, 99, *101*
Markon, K., 89, *92*, 115, *132*
Marlow, N., 265, *279*
Marsh, H. W., 115, *134*

Martin, D., 228, *249*
Martin, S. L., 226, *250*
Maslin, C. A., 56, *71*
Masse, B., 35, *46*
Masse, L. C., 230, 246, *249*, *251*
Maughan, B., 11, 19, *26*, *27*, 169, 183, *190*
Maumary-Gremaud, A., 80, 81, 89, *94*
McAffer, V. J., 6, 17, 18, *27*, 106, *135*, 184,
        190, 229, 231, 235, *251*, 255,
        262, 263, *283*
McBurnett, K., 30, 32, 34, *45*, 228, *250*
McConaughy, S. H., 114, 115, *131*
McCord, J., 16, *24*, 256, *281*, 286, 287,
        288, *288*
McCoy, L., 141, *158*
McCracken, G. D., 172, *189*
McDuff, P., 4, *28*, 56, 70, 71, *73*, *74*, 110,
        136
McEvoy, L., 235, *250*
Mcfarlane, J. W., 56, 59, *73*
McGee, R. O., 31, 32, *44*, 56, *73*
McKeown, R. E., 80, *95*
McKnight, K., 51, *52*
McLoyd, V. C., 78, *94*, 266, *281*
McMahon, T., 105, 130, *134*
McMillen, J. C., 208, *213*
McNeilly-Choque, M. K., 116, 117, 118, *134*
Mednick, S. A., 197, *213*, 241, *249*
Melitis, E. D., 258, 261, *281*
Menard, S., 81, *93*
Mennin, D., 32, *46*
Merikangas, K. R., 197, *213*
Merten, D. E., 113, 121, *134*, 152, 153, *159*
Mettetal, G., 51, *52*, 124, *133*
Metzler, C. W., 194, *213*
Meyers, J., 231, 235, *251*
Michel, M. M., 182, 183, *189*
Miettinen, O., 56, 58, *73*
Miller, J. Y., 229, *249*
Miller, K. S., 194, *213*
Miller, L., 17, *25*
Miller, N. E., 111, *132*,
Miller, N. L., 195, *212*,
Miller, T. L., 34, *45*, 56, *73*,
Miller, W. R., 208, *213*,
Miller-Johnson, S., xvi, xvii, 80, 81, 89, *94*,
        97
Mills, A., 191, 195, 206, *214*
Misle, B., 197, *215*
Moffitt, T. A., xv, xvi, xxi, *xxiii*, 7, 9, 20,
        24, *26*, 31, 32, 34, *44*, *45*, 76, 82,

        94, 130, *134*, 169, *188*, 191,
        200, *211*, *212*, 218, *221*, 225,
        228, 229, 232, 237, *248*, *249*,
        250, 257, *279*
Mohan, R., 263, *282*
Montplaisir, J., 70, 71, *74*, 110, *136*
Moore, B. L., xvi, xvii, 97
Moore, K. A., 196, *21*
Moore, T., 11, 16, *27*
Moreland, S., 199, *211*
Morgan, S. P., 80, *93*, 261, 264, 266, *281*
Moritz, G., 228, *249*
Mosher, M., 118, *132*
Moskowitz, D. S., 255, 256, 270, *281*,
        282, *283*
Moskowitz, K. S., 22, *28*, 169, *190*
Mowrer, O. H., 111, *132*
Murphy, G. E., 228, *250*
Musick, J. S., 257, *282*
Must, M., 98, *101*

N

Nagin, D., 225, *250*
Nath, P. S., 258, *283*
Neale, J. M., 259, *282*
Neckerman, H. J., 5, 6, 18, *24*, 105, 106,
        107, 111, 117, 119, 130, *132*, 161,
        165, 192, 193, *211*, 255, *279*
Nelson, C., 209, *214*
Nelson, D. A., 89, 91, *92*, 115, *132*
Nelson, L. J., 116, 117, 118, *134*
Neubauer, P. B., 56, *71*
Newman, D. L., 225, *249*
Newth, S. J., 56, *73*
Nicholson, D., 139, 145, 146, 156, *158*
Niemëla, P., xv, *xxii*, 1 41, *158*, 255, 256,
        279
NIMH Multisite HIV Prevention Trial
        Group, 206, *214*
Noell, J., 194, 209, *213*, *214*
Norris, F., 208, 209, *211*
Nurss, J., 208, 209, *211*

O

O'Brien, K. M., 89, 91, *92*, 115, *132*
O'Connell, P., 18, *26*
O'Connor, T., 225, 227, *251*
O'Leary, D., 176, *189*
O'Leary, K. D., 196, *214*

Oberklaid, F., 5, 27, 31, 46, 56, 59, 73
Office of Juvenile Justice and Delinquency
    Prevention, 75, 91, 94
Offord, D. R., 3, 5, 6, 7, 20, 26, 28, 169,
    171, 189, 198, 214, 229, 248
Ogbu, J. U., 76, 76, 94
Ogle, R. S., 33, 45
Okamoto, 150
Olafsdottir, P. M., 156, 159
Olsen, S. F., 116, 117, 118, 134
Olson, S. L., 8, 26
Olweus, D., 82, 89, 94, 105, 130, 134, 184,
    189, 255, 282
Ontario Association of Children's Mental
    Health Centres, 171, 189
Orenstein, P., 154, 159
Osterman, K., 5, 6, 23, 76, 91, 94, 106, 110,
    112, 118, 124, 131, 133
Owen, L., 194, 211

P

Pacifici, C., 209, 214
Padian, N., 195, 214
Pagani-Kurtz, L., 246, 251
Paine, R., 124, 135
Pajer, K. A., 191, 214, 229, 250
Pakaslahti, L., 13, 14, 26
Palti, H., 266, 278
Paquette, D., xvi, xx, xxi
Paquette, J. A., 50, 52, 77, 95, 110, 135, 286
Parker, G. R., 266, 280
Parker, J. G., 16, 27
Parker, S., 112, 132
Partridge, F., 56, 73
Paternite, C. E., 35, 45
Patterson, G. R., 4, 10, 15, 17, 19, 20, 26,
    43, 45, 76, 90, 94, 176, 179, 189,
    196, 211, 228, 250, 267, 272, 282
Pawlby, S. J., 191, 195, 206, 214
Pear, R., 105, 130, 135
Pears, K. C., 225, 249
Pekarik, E. G., 259, 282
Peltonen, T., 6, 25, 106, 109, 115, 117, 118,
    119, 134, 185, 189
Pendergrast, R. A., 78, 79, 92
Pepler, D. J., xvii, xviii, xix, xx, 6, 7, 9, 11,
    15, 16, 17, 18, 19, 20, 21, 23, 24,
    26, 27, 48, 116, 118, 130, 135,
    179, 180, 184, 187, 189, 192,
    214, 218, 221

Perper, J. A., 228, 249
Perrin, J. E., 121, 132
Perron, D., 35, 46
Perry, D. G., 10, 17, 27
Perry, L. C., 10, 17, 27
Pérusse, D., 4, 28, 56, 70, 71, 73, 74, 110,
    136
Peters, M. F., 50, 52
Peters, P. L., 23, 27, 106, 135, 225, 226,
    229, 231, 235, 246, 251, 255,
    256, 257, 260, 261, 262, 263,
    264, 265, 266, 267, 268, 270,
    271, 272, 282, 283
Peters, P., 6, 17, 18, 27, 184, 190
Peters, R., 16, 24
Petersen, A. C., 35, 45
Pettit, G. S., 11, 24, 79, 92
Phipps, P., 210, 211
Piaget, J., 112, 133
Pickles, A., 11, 19, 26, 27, 30, 35, 46, 169,
    183, 190, 193, 197, 215, 226,
    228, 231, 232, 234, 237, 246,
    251, 256, 283
Pierce, E. W., 5, 24
Pihl, R. O., 4, 28, 56, 73, 246, 251
Pine, D. S., 241, 251
Pitkänen, L., 98, 99, 101
Pitkänen, T., 77, 87, 94, 255, 256, 264, 282
Pless, I. B., 56, 58, 73
Plomin, R., 43, 44, 227, 250
Poe-Yamagata, E., 75, 94
Poulin, F., 16, 24
Powlishta, K., 262, 283
Prechtl, H., 265, 282
Price, R. K., 191, 192, 197, 214, 226, 231,
    232, 235, 237, 250, 252
Prinz, R. J., 259, 282
Prior, M., 5, 27, 31, 46, 56, 59, 73
Pugh, M. D., 105, 130, 133, 193, 212, 219,
    221
Pulkinnen, L., xv, xxiii, 5, 6, 20, 27, 77,
    87, 89, 94, 99, 100, 101, 105,
    126, 127, 135, 169, 183, 190,
    255, 256, 264, 282
Putallaz, M., 51, 52

Q

QSR NUD*IST 4, 172, 190
Quay, H. C., 30, 32, 34, 45

Quinton, D., 11, 19, *26*, *27*, 30, 35, *46*, 169, 183, *190*, 191, 193, 195, 196, 197, 206, *214*, *215*, 226, 228, 231, 232, 234, 237, 246, *250*, *251*, 256, *283*

R

Racine, Y., A. 3, 5, 6, 7, 20, *26*, 169, 171, *189*, 198, *214*, 229, *248*
Ramsey, E., 19, 20, *26*
Rankin, R. J., 115, *135*
Rathouz, P. J., 34, *45*
Ray, J., 169, *190*
Regier, D. A., 232, 232, 237, *250*
Reid, J. B., 4, 17, *26*, 176, *189*, 199, *212*, 228, *250\
Reid, K., 199, *211*
Reitsma-Street, M., 141, 142, *159*
Reynolds, J. D., 257, *281*
Rhule, D., 51, *52*
Richman, N., 56, 59, *73*
Ridge, B., 7, 19, *23*, 173, *188*
Riecken, T., *138*, 141, 143, 156, *158*
Riley, A. W., 56, *73*
Rivera, V. R., 199, *213*, *214*
Roberts, M. A., 33, 35, *45*
Roberts, W. L., 6, *27*, 116, 118, *135*
Roberts, W. R., 16, 17, *27*
Robins, L. N., xxi, *xxiii*, 19, 21, 22, *27*, 34, 35, 36, *46*, 169, 183, *190*, 191, 192, 197, 200, *212*, *214*, 226, 228, 231, 232, 235, 237, *250*, 255, *282*
Robinson, C. C., 116, 117, 118, *134*
Robinson, J., 267, 269, *279*
Robinson, W. L., 81, *93*
Rodkin, P. C., 105, 130, *133*, *135*
Rogers, K., 195, *215*, 229, 230, 231, 232, 235, *252*
Rojas, M., 34, *44*
Rolf, J. E., 56, 57, *72*
Romney, D. M., 11, *26*
Rönkä, A., 100, *101*, 127, *135*
Roscoe, B., 15, *25*
Rose, S. A., 5, *27*
Rose, S. L., 5, *27*
Rosenbaum, A., 196, *214*
Rosenbaum, J. L., 187, *190*, 196, 202, *214*
Rosenberg, F. R., 113, *135*
Roth, C., 228, *249*

Rothberg, S., 106, 110, 118, *133*
Rozak, B., 157, *160*
Rozak, T., 157, *160*
Rubin, D. R., 233, *250*
Rubin, K. H., 16, *27*, 218, *221*
Ruffins, S., 197, *215*
Rutter, M., xv, xvi, xxi, *xxiii*, 4, 19, 23, *25*, *27*, 30, 35, 43, *46*, 55, *73*, 100, *101*, 169, 170, 183, *190*, 193, 196, 197, *214*, *215*, 218, *221*, 225, 226, 227, 228, 231, 232, 234, 237, 246, 248, *250*, *251*, 256, 261, *282*, *283*
Rychtarik, R. G., 208, *213*
Rys, G. S., 118, *135*

S

Salmivalli , C., 106, 110, 118, 130, *133*, *135*
Salovey, P., 256, *282*
Saltaris, C., 260, 270, *282*, *283*
Sameroff, A. J., 267, *282*
Samuelson, H., 197, *213*
Sanford, S., 111, 124, *133*
Sanson, A., 5, *27*, 31, *46*, 56, 59, *73*
Sauzier, M., 15, *25*
Scaramella, L. V., 255, *282*
Scheier, L. M., 195, *212*
Schellenbach, C. J., 258, *283*
Schlossman, S., 20, *27*, 169, 183, *190*, 198, *214*
Schneider, B. H., 118, *136*
Schwab-Stone, M., 34, *45*
Schwartzman, A. E., xviii, xix, xxi, 6, 17, 18, 22, 23, *27*, *28*, 35, *46*, 106, *135*, 169, 184, *190*, 225, 226, 229, 231, 235, 246, *251*, 255, 256, 257, 259, 260, 261, 262, 263, 264, 266, 267, 268, 270, 271, 272, *281*, *282*, *283*, 285
Schweers, J., 228, *249*
Sears, R. R., 111, *132*
Sedighdeilami, F., 7, 17, 19, 20, 21, *27*, 179, 184, *189*
Sedikides, C., 115, *135*
Seidman, L. J., 32, *46*
Seifer, R., 267, *282*
Serbin, L. A., xviii, xix, xxi, 6, 17, 18, 22, 23, *27*, *28*, 106, *135*, 169, 184, *190*, 225, 226, 229, 231, 235,

246, *251*, 255, 256, 257, 259,
    260, 261, 262, 263, 264, 266,
    267, 268, 269, 270, 271, 272,
    279, *281*, *282*, *283*, 285
Serketich, W. J., 267, *280*
Shaffer, D., 30, 32, 34, *45*
Shahar, G., 99, *101*
Shapiro, S., 258, 261, *281*
Sharpe, D., 98, *101*
Shaw, D. S., 5, *25*, 32, 33, 34, *45*, 56, 69,
    72, 192, *213*
Shaw, G. K., 197, *212*
Shaywitz, B. A., 174, *188*
Shaywitz, S. E., 174, *188*
Sheldon, R., 139, 140, 141, *159*
Showalter, B. A., 191, 192, 197, *213*
Showater, C., 22, *26*
Sickmund, M., 75, *95*
Sigman, M., 206, 208, *213*
Silberg, J., 225, 227, *251*
Silva, P. A., xv, xvi, xxi, *xxiii*, 9, *24*, 31, 32,
    44, 56, *73*, 169, *188*, 200, *212*,
    218, *221*, 225, 229, 232, *248*,
    249, *250*, 257, *279*
Silverman, E., 141, *159*
Silverthorn, P., 34, *46*, 90, *94*, 130, *135*
Simonoff, E., 225, 227, *251*
Simons, R. G., 113, *135*
Simons, R. L., 176, *190*, 255, 258, *280*, *282*
Singer, J. D., 87, *94*
Skaalvik, E. M., 115, *135*
Skinner, E. A., 258, 261, *281*
Slavens, G., 79, *92*
Slomkowski, C., 15, *24*
Slusarcick, A. L., 105, *133*
Sluyter, D. J., 256, *282*
Smart, D., 5, *27*, 31, *46*, 56, 59, *73*
Smetana, J. G., 70, *73*
Smith, D., 141, *158*
Smith, P. K., 16, *25*, *28*, 130, *135*, 184, *190*
Smith, R., 261, 266, *283*
Smith, S., 208, 209, *211*
Smolkowski, K., 194, *213*
Snyder, H. N., 75, *95*
Snyder, J., 79, *95*
Sones, G., 106, 107, 116, *133*
Spaulding, J., xv, *xxiii*
Speltz, M. L., 11, *25*
Spiker, D. G., 197, *213*
Spoof, I., 13, 14, *26*
Sroufe, L. A., 7, *28*, 128, *131*

St. Lawrence, J. S., 206, *214*
St. Pierre, R., 258, *281*
Stack, D. M., xviii, xix, xxi, 23, *27*, 225,
    226, 246, *251*, 257, 260, 262,
    263, 264, 266, 267, 268, 269,
    272, *279*, *282*, *283*, 285
Staghezza, B., 32, *44*
Stallard, P., 56, *73*
Stangl, D. K., 30, *44*
Stanhope, L., 15, *23*
Stanton, W., 229, *248*
Starfield, B. H., 258, 261, *281*
Statistics Canada, 3, *28*,
Stattin, H., 9, *28*, 106, 127, *134*, *135*
Steffen, V. J., 5, *24*
Steinberg, L., 71, *73*
Steiner, H., 169, *190*
Stemmler, M., 35, *45*
Stevenson, J. E., 56, 59, *73*, 225, 231, *249*
Stewart, M. A., 225, 227, 231, *249*, *250*
Stiffman, A. R., 208, *213*
Stoolmiller, M., 194, 195, 209, *211*, *214*,
    255, *279*
Stouthamer-Loeber, M., xvi, xvii, xx, 11, *26*,
    35, *45*, 48, 76, 77, *93*, 130, *134*
Strayer, J., 33, *44*
Streuning, E. L., 34, *44*
Stringfield, D. O., 115, *134*
Stroul, B., 199, *215*
Strube, M. J., 115, *135*
Sundet, J. M., 231, *249*
Sutherland, W. J., 257, *281*
Sutton, J., 130, *135*
Swift, D. J., 117, 119, 120, *136*
Szatmari, P., 7, *28*, 229, *248*

T

Tamm, L., 33, *44*
Taradash, A., 9, 18, *24*
Taylor, D. I., 79, *95*
Taylor, J., 153, *159*
Taylor, S. E., 115, *135*
Terry, R., 17, *24*, 80, 81, 82, 83, 89, *92*,
    94, 95
Thibault, J., 237, *249*
Thissen, D., 71, *73*
Thomas, A., 43, *46*
Thomas, C. W., 31, *45*
Thomas, P., 34, *46*
Thompson, R., 208, *213*

Thorne, B., 18, *28*
Tieger, T., 55, 69, 71, *73*
Tiet, Q. Q., 100, *101*
Tiihonen, J., 36, *44*
Tolan, P. H., 34, *46*, 76, 77, 79, *92*, *93*
Tomada, G., 118, *136*
Topping, M., 208, 209, *211*
Townsend, M. A. R., 198, *211*
Travillion, K., 79, *95*
Trembaly, R. E., xvi, xvii, xx, xxi, *xxiii*, 4,
    9, *25*, *28*, 29, 30, 35, *46*, 47, *52*,
    56, 70, 71, *73*, *74*, 97, 99, *101*,
    110, *136*, 225, 230, 237, 246,
    249, *250*, *251*, 286
Trocki, K. F., 195, *212*
Trocme, N., 182, *190*
Troughton, E. P., 225, 227, 231, *249*, *250*
Tsuang, M. T., 32, *44*
Tweed, D. L., 30, *44*

U

Underwood, M. K., xvi, xvii, 5, *25*, 50, *52*,
    77, 80, *95*, 97, 106, 107, 110,
    113, *133*, *135*, 185, *188*, 192,
    195, 196, 206, *215*

V

Valois, R. F., 80, *95*
Van Acker, R., 77, *93*, 105, 130, *135*
Van Der Ende, J., 35, *46*
Van Dijk, M., 169, *189*
Varma, K., 140, *160*
Velez, C. N., 34, *44*
Verhulst, F. C., 35, *46*, 56, 58, 60, 70, *72*
Verlaan, P., 261, 264, *283*
Vermunt, J. K., 63, *74*, 247, *251*
Vicary, J. R., 195, *212*
Vincent, M. L., 80, *95*
Vitaro, F., 9, *25*, 29, 30, *46*, 230, 246, *249*,
    251
Voti, L., 196, *213*, 231, 235, *250*

W

Waite, L. J., 196, *213*
Wakschlag, L. S., 225, 228, 235, 241, 246,
    251
Walder, L. D., xvi, *xxiii*, 22, *25*, 82, 87, *93*,
    255, 256, *281*

Waldman, I. D., 30, 32, 34, *45*
Walker, R., 115, *134*
Walsh, M. M., 187, *189*
Wangby, M., 19, 20, *28*
Ward, J. V., 79, *95*, 153, *159*
Warheit, G., 79, *95*
Wasserman, G. A., 241, *251*
Way, N., 80, *93*, 164, *165*
Weber, W., 32, *46*
Webster, C. D., 140, *158*, 187, *189*
Webster-Stratton, C., 34, *46*, 90, *95*
Weintraub, S., 259, *282*
Weiss, R. J., 10, 17, *27*
Weissberg, R. P., 194, *215*
Weisz, J. R., 268, *281*
Wente, M., 150, *160*
Werner, E., 261, 266, *283*,
Werner, N. E., 89, 91, *92*, 115, *132*
West, P. A., 226, 228, *250*
Westen, D., 197, *215*
Whitbeck, L.-B., 194, *215*, 255, 258, *280*,
    282
Whiteman, M., 11, *23*
Whithecomb, J., 140, *160*
Whithing, B., 55, *74*
Whitman, T. L., 258, *283*
Whitney, I., 184, *190*
Widaman, K. F., 99, *101*
Widiger, T., 30, 31, *45*
Willet, J. B., 87, *94*
Williams, L. M., 15, *25*
Williams, S., 56, *73*
Willms, J. D., xvi, xvii, xx, 97
Wilson, M., 22, *24*
Wilson, S. K., 176, *188*
Winn, D., 80, 89, *94*
Wolfe, D., 176, 182, *188*, *190*
Woodruff, R. A. J., 228, *250*
Woodward, L. J., 193, 194, 195, *215*, 231,
    235, *251*
Woodworth, G., 225, 226, *249*
Work, W. C., 266, *280*
Worthman, C. M., 30, *44*
Wozniak, 16, 17
Wyman, P. A., 266, *280*

X

Xie, H., xvi, xvii, xviii, xx, xxi, 5, 79, 82,
    95, 105, 106, 107, 112, 114,
    115, 116, 117, 118, 119, 120,

121, 125, 128, *136*, 161, 186,
257, *279*

Y

Yates, W. R., 225, 227, 231, *249*, *250*
Yeager, C. A., 22, *26*, 191, 192, 197, *213*
Yoder, K. A., 194, *215*

Z

Zahn-Waxler, C., xx, *xxiii*, 31, 33, *44*, *46*
Zak, L., 176, *188*
Zanarini, M. C., 198, *215*

Zelli, A., 17, *25*
Zillman, D., 111, *136*
Zimiles, H., 42, *45*
Zoccolillo, M., xvi, xx, xxi, *xxiii*, 4, 21,
    28, 29, 30, 34, 35, 36, *46*, 56,
    70, 71, *73*, *74*, 90, *95*, 110, *136*,
    183, *190*, 191, 193, 195, 197,
    215, 225, 226, 227, 228, 229,
    230, 231, 232, 234, 235, 237,
    246, *249*, *251*, *252*, 256, *283*,
    286
Zoll, D., 197, *213*
Zweben, A., 208, *213*

Subject Index

A

Academic performance, *see* School performance
Attention-Deficit Hyperactivity Disorder (ADHD), 7–9, 32, 33, 48, 173, 228
  see also Hyperactivity
Attention-Deficit Disorder (ADD), 7–9, 173–174
  see also Inattention
Adolescence, 14, 18, 21, 110–112, 127, 193, 263
Adolescent mothers, 231, 241, 243–244, 257, 271, 272, 285
  see also pregnancy, early
Adoption studies, 227, 231, 241–242
Adult adjustment, 193
Age differences, 4, 5, 36, 65, 69, 98, 99, 107, 110, 111, 112, 115, 124, 129, 130
Age of onset, 34, 90, 130
Aggression, *see also* Violence
  covert, 43
  indirect, 5, 107, 108, 109, 192
  outcomes of, 89, 169, 191, 202, 231, 234, 235, 265, 272, 287
  physical, xvii, xviii, 5, 6, 16, 18, 20, 55–71, 75–91, 97–98, 105–131, 137, 139, 145, 150, 151, 155, 162, 185, 253–256, 262
  proactive, 70–71, 99
  reactive, 70–71, 98, 99, 120, 123
  relational, 5, 31, 109, 116, 192, 254
  social, xviii, 5–6, 16, 31, 50, 51, 91, 106–131, 161–163, 184–185, 192, 200, 255
  verbal, 5, 16, 98, 113, 120, 128, 185, 253–256
  and withdrawal, 256–257, 259–261, 263, 269–270, 271
  with parents, 12–15
  witnessing of, 78
Alcohol and drug use, 36, 81, 142, 175, 192, 193, 204, 235, 241, 263, 286
Antisocial behavior, *see* Aggression and Violence
Antisocial personality disorder, 22, 30, 35, 36, 232, 233, 237
Anxiety, *see* Internalizing problems
Arrest, 39–40, 42, 82, 84, 87, 90, 125, 192, 196, 200, 202–203, 263
Assessment of aggression
  in fathers, 232–234
  in mothers, 230–232, 237–243
  peer ratings/report/nominations, 17, 80, 83, 97–98, 109, 114, 115, 116, 117–118, 125, 196, 256, 259, 262
  parent ratings/report/narratives, 7, 12, 17, 19, 21, 31, 37, 38, 61, 81, 90, 170, 171, 172, 174, 175, 176, 177, 178, 180, 182–183, 185, 186, 237, 241
  teacher ratings/report, 33, 35, 81, 114, 117–118, 126, 286–287
  self/child ratings/report/narratives, 6, 7, 12, 13, 17, 19, 21, 50,

81–82, 83–84, 90, 115,
117–118, 121, 172, 178, 179,
184–185, 193, 199, 202, 205,
237, 238–239, 244, 247
Attachment, 10–11, 218, 267–268

B

Battered women, 15
Behavioral genetics, 288
Body image, 143–145
Boundaries, 177–178
Bullying, 18, 153, 184, 276

C

Child abuse/neglect, 271
Childbearing
early, 20, 80, 89
see also Pregnancy
Coercive behaviour
among siblings, 15, 179
parent-child, 176–177, 194, 241, 242,
246, 272
relationships, 276
Comorbidity, 21, 32, 33, 35, 36, 43, 191,
228–229, 255
Comparison groups, 236
Computer-assisted technology, 209
Conduct disorder/problems, xvii, xx, xxi, 5,
7, 8, 19, 20, 21, 22, 29–43,
47–52, 174, 191, 192, 195, 197,
277, 288
maternal, 197, 225–248
paternal, 197, 229, 232, 241, 245
Continuity of aggression, *see* stability of
aggression
Crime, xviii, 75–76, 81, 126, 127, 130, 139,
141, 199, 200, 233, 255, 263,
264, 287, 288
Culture, 91
Custody workers, 149

D

Delinquency, 81–82
Depression, *see* internalizing problems
Desistance, 130
Developmental delays, 271, 273
Developmental model, 170
Developmental trajectories, xv, xvi, xvii,
xviii, xx, 4–6, 14, 19, 20, 22, 23,

33, 34, 36–37, 42, 43, 48, 49,
51, 90, 100, 125, 126, 127, 128,
130, 169–170, 173, 182, 217,
221, 253–278, 285, 287
see also outcomes of aggression
Divorce, 196
see also Parents' marital conflict
DSM III R/DSM III, 30, 232, 243
DSM IV, 30, 34, 35, 231, 232, 237

E

Emergency visits, 271
Empathy, xxi, 33
Employment, 256
Environmental risk, 37, 40, 78, 186,
227–228, 232, 234, 235
Epidemiology, 6, 56–59, 69, 75, 141, 191,
229
Ethnicity, 50, 75–91, 106, 287
Externalizing problems, 15, 81, 83, 85–86,
89, 90, 171

F

Family
context, xx, 10–11, 219
dysfunction, 176, 200
interaction, 14
Father, 179, 181, 183, 269
absent, xx, 178, 232, 233, 241
aggression, 178, *see also* Conduct
Disorder, Paternal
Friendships, xiii, 113, 123, 142, 148, 151,
152, 164, 184, 193, 205, 219
same sex, 206

G

Gangs, 78, 81
Gender
differences, xv, xvi, xvii, xviii, 5, 6, 7,
10, 11, 15, 16, 17, 18, 22,
30, 31, 32, 33, 34, 35, 36,
41, 42, 55–71, 75, 76,
79–80, 81–82, 83, 84–85,
86–87, 90, 100, 106, 107,
112, 113, 116, 117–118,
121, 124, 126, 130, 141,
142, 146, 149, 157, 169,
173, 174, 180, 185, 192,

193, 198, 200, 201, 202, 219,
221, 254, 255, 261, 263, 273,
274, 277
stereotypes/role norms, 10, 17, 21, 30,
31, 70, 82, 112, 114, 143,
146, 147, 148, 150, 151, 153,
154, 157, 162, 163, 164, 192,
198, 262
Genetic influences, 226–228, 232, 248, 288
Gossip, xvii, 51, 106, 109, 110, 113, 115,
116, 119, 124, 185
Grade repetition, 261–262
Guilt, 33

H

Health problems, 257, 270–271, 273, 276
High risk environment, *see* environmental
risk
Home environment, 270, 271
Homicide, 22, 36, 254
Hostile attributions, 10, 17
see also Social-cognitive factors
Horizontal violence, 155
Hyperactivity, 7–9, 100, 174

I

Impulsivity, 32
Inattention, 7–9, 20, 174
Incarceration, 198, 199, 202
Ineffective parenting, 11, 196, 197, 218,
257, 286, 287
Infancy, 173
Intergenerational transmission of risk, xx,
22, 169, 175, 196, 197, 219,
225–248, 253–278, 288
Intelligence/IQ, 261, 272, 273
Internalizing problems, 15, 21, 22, 33, 36,
43, 81, 83, 86–87, 90, 192, 228,
235, 255, 264, 271
Intervention, xix, xxi, xxii, 91, 100, 128,
129, 155, 156, 157, 163, 164,
180, 194, 197–200, 206–210,
217, 219–221, 229, 230, 245,
277–278, 288
by teachers, 120, 129
foster care, 199–200
mother-daughter discussion, 206–207
outcome of, 199, 202, 220
parent training, 181

J

Juvenile justice system, 149, 150,
191–210, 219

L

Latent class analysis, 231, 246–247
Learning disabilities, 173
Logit models, 61, 63–65, 67
Longitudinal studies, xviii, 19, 21, 22, 35,
37, 43, 51, 60–61, 77, 79, 81,
82–83, 90, 99, 106, 110, 111, 120,
125–128, 130, 183, 193, 194, 196,
197, 226, 235, 236–244, 247,
253–278, 285, 286

M

Marital conflict, 22
Maternal
aggression, 265–278, 286, *see also*
Conduct Disorder, maternal
education, 40, 241, 265–266, 268
health, 266–267
hostility, 269
responsiveness, 267, 269
rejection, 270
warmth, 241
Media, 254
Mental health services, 198, 273
Missing data, 233
Motivation, 50
Motor activity, 71

O

Observation studies, 6, 12, 13, 15, 18, 98,
115–116, 262, 267–268, 270
Obstetrical factors, 264
Oppositional Defiant Disorder, 32–34

P

Parents'
affection, 178
aggression, 139, 275
discipline/practices, 11, 14, 70, 78, 79,
176, 177, 270
education, 275
family dysfunction, 175

hostility, 14
marital conflict, xvii, xx, 15, 40, 41, 42,
        48, 286–287
monitoring, 194–195
psychopathology, 40, 42, 228, 229
stress, 78
see also Father, Ineffective Parenting,
        Maternal, Relationships
Physical abuse, 181, 197
Paternity, 233–234
Peer, *see also* friendships
    conflict, xviii, 99, 116, 119, 123
    context, 16–19, 162, 183
    deviant, 9, 81, 82, 192, 193, 194, 205,
            219, 230, 246, 263
    isolation, 17, 79, 82, 106, 123, 162, 184,
            185
    mentoring, 208–209
    popularity, 18, 112, 113, 153
    prosocial, 194, 205, 219
    rejection, 17, 81–83, 123, 184, 185, 262,
            263
    status, 112, 113, 121, 122, 196
    younger, 185
Perpetrator, identity of, 109, 110, 116, 118, 119
Policy, 277
Poverty, 78, 187, 241, 257, 264, 273–274, 275
    see also socioeconomic status
Pregnancy, 39–40, 89, 151, 203, 233
    early, 42, 192, 195–196, 235, 255, 263
    risk of, 183, 193
Prevention, xxi, 52, 91, 100, 128, 129, 138,
        156, 164, 174, 220, 230,
        245–247, 277, 278
Problem solving
    aggressive, 15
    skills, 14
Professional education, 174
Program evaluation, 138
Prosocial behaviour, 116, 142, 208
Protective factors, xix, 274, 275, 276
Puberty, 112, 124
    early, 9, 48

Q

Qualitative study, 139–158, 170–187, 234

R

Racial identity, 79

Racism, 78
Relationships, 220
    abusive, 196
    concern with, 153
    context, 47–48
    mother-child, 267
    mother-daughter, xx, 13–14, 48, 142,
            174, 175, 176, 177, 180, 218
    parent-child, 174
    romantic, xviii, 9, 18, 112, 127, 129,
            152, 195, 209, 219
    student-teacher, 182
Resilience, 261, 272, 277
Risk factors, 14, 42, 43, 70, 80, 89, 122,
        125, 139, 140, 171, 172, 173,
        174, 200, 201, 218, 219, 229,
        240, 241, 245, 258, 264–266,
        273
    cumulative, 3–4, 8, 9, 20, 228, 234,
            275
Role reversal, 178
Rough and tumble play, 262, 263
Rumours, *see* Gossip
Runaway, 199

S

School
    dropout, 9, 20, 183, 257, 262, 263
    performance/attainment, 9, 19–21, 32,
            79, 126, 182, 183, 196, 229,
            257, 258, 261–262, 272, 276
    suspension, 39, 42, 183
    system, xxi, 183
Self-concept, 80
Sex differences, *see* gender differences
Sexual abuse/assault, 15, 142, 145, 150,
        151, 152, 181–182, 186, 197
Sexual activity, 193, 257
    early, 20, 80
    health, 91, 205–210, 263
    risky, 9, 81, 194, 195, 197, 203–210,
            255, 263
Sexual harassment, 144–145, 146, 149, 151
Sexually transmitted diseases (STDs),
        195, 203–210, 263
Siblings, 37, 41, 48, 70, 139, 179
    conflict, 180
    interactions/relationships, 8, 15–16
    see also Coercive behaviour among
            siblings

Single parent, 176
Social
    cognitive factors, 10, 14, 17, 111–112
    context, 50
    learning theory, 111
    networks, 50, 79–80, 110, 112, 120,
        121, 122, 123, 127, 128, 130,
        162, 186
    services, 198
    skills, 8, 9, 18, 33, 51, 110, 194
    status, 78, 115, 124, 129, 144, 152, 153,
        154–155, 162, 163
    withdrawal, 256, 259, 262, 271, 275
Socioeconomic status (SES), 40, 42, 77,
    78, 79, 83, 91, 235, 259–260
Smoking, 229–230, 243–244, 257, 263,
    264, 266
    prenatal, 228, 230, 235, 241, 243–245
Special education, 20–21, 261–262
Spouse
    deviant, 194, 197, 232, 265, 286
    prosocial, 23, 48, 194
Stability of aggression, 22, 35, 77, 82,
    84–87, 89, 91, 99, 130, 225, 255,
    276
Substance use, *see* alcohol and drug use
Suicide, 192, 254

Survival analyses, 87

T

Temperament, 31–32, 176
Treatment of aggression, *see* Intervention
Truancy, 20, 237
Twin studies, 227, 231

U

Unemployment, 183

V

Verbal abuse, 181
Victimization, 22, 78, 123, 148, 152, 163,
    184, 276
Violence, 6, 13, 35, 81
Violent relationships, 22

Y

Young offenders, 13
Youth workers, 144, 156, 164